# A Tapestry of
# African Histories

# A Tapestry of African Histories

## With Longer Times and Wider Geopolitics

Edited by
Nicholas K. Githuku

LEXINGTON BOOKS
*Lanham • Boulder • New York • London*

Published by Lexington Books
An imprint of The Rowman & Littlefield Publishing Group, Inc.
4501 Forbes Boulevard, Suite 200, Lanham, Maryland 20706
www.rowman.com

86-90 Paul Street, London EC2A 4NE

British Library Cataloguing in Publication Information Available

**Library of Congress Cataloging-in-Publication Data**

Names: Githuku, Nicholas K. (Nicholas Kariuki), editor, author.
Title: A tapestry of African histories : with longer times and wider geopolitics / edited by Nicholas K. Githuku.
Description: Lanham : Lexington Books, [2021] | Includes index. | Summary: "This book studies African history through a geopolitically transcendent lens that brings African countries into conversation with other relevant histories both within and outside of the continent. The collection analyzes historical figures, struggles for independence and stability, social and economic development, and legal and human rights issues"— Provided by publisher.
Identifiers: LCCN 2021039579 | ISBN 9781793623935 (hardback) | ISBN 9781793623942 (ebook)
Subjects: LCSH: Africa, Eastern—History. | Africa, Eastern—Historiography.
Classification: LCC DT365.5 | DDC 967.6—dc23
LC record available at https://lccn.loc.gov/2021039579

# Contents

Foreword            vii
*Daniel Branch*

Introduction: The Future of History: Transtemporal,
Transnational across Geographical Borders     xiii
*Nicholas K. Githuku*

**1**   On Writing Kenya's History        1
     *John M. Lonsdale*

**2**   From the Upper Delaware River to the Banks of
     the Monongahela via Lake Victoria     21
     *Robert M. Maxon*

**3**   Myth and Reality in the Forging of a Kenyan
     National History: Oginga Odinga's Heroism    43
     *Robert M. Maxon*

**4**   Daniel arap Moi: A Challenge for Historians    63
     *Robert M. Maxon*

**5**   Ainsworth after Dark: The Pied Piper of African
     Development in Colonial Kenya, 1895–1920?    87
     *Okia Opolot*

**6**   Challenge to African Democracy: The Activism
     and Assassination of Pio Gama Pinto     113
     *Godriver Wanga-Odhiambo*

**7**   Eastlands, Nairobi: Memory, History, and Recovery            135
       *Betty Wambui*

**8**   Plagues and Pestilences in Late Nineteenth-Century
       Samburuland                                                  161
       *George L. Simpson, Jr., and Peter Waweru*

**9**   The Evolution of Imperial Social Development Policy
       and Practice in British Sudan: A Comparative Case Study
       of the Gezira and Zande Schemes                              179
       *Joseph M. Snyder*

**10**  Illusions about a Boom in Cotton Production in
       Southern Nyanza during the Depression, 1929–1939             203
       *Peter Odhiambo Ndege*

**11**  Community Development in Post-Independence Malawi:
       Deciphering Some Local Voices                                223
       *Gift Wasambo Kayira*

**12**  Regime Policing and the Stifling of the Human Rights
       Agenda: Late Colonial and Postcolonial Malawi, 1948–Present  245
       *Paul Chiudza Banda*

**13**  The Constitution and Change-the-Constitution Debate
       in Independent Kenya, 1963–2002                              269
       *Anne Kisaka Nangulu*

**14**  The Building Bridges Initiative Déjà Vu: "A Whitewash
       Process Taking Us Forward by Taking Us Backwards"            293
       *Nicholas K. Githuku and Robert M. Maxon*

**15**  House of *Mlungula*—"Norms in the Margins and
       Margins of the Norm": Of Computer "Glitches,"
       Moving Human Fingers and Illicit Financial Flows             317
       *Nicholas K. Githuku*

Index                                                              345

About the Contributors                                            355

# Foreword

## Daniel Branch

This book is a touching and necessary effort to mark a career spent well. It is an excellent volume in its own right, full of verve and original thought. Running through its pages, however, is a highly successful effort by its editor and contributors to repay intellectual debts to Professor Robert Maxon. Taking his own scholarship in isolation—not least his contributions here—Maxon is a fine historian and one worthy of the praise contained within the various chapters here. But this book is also a tribute to Maxon the collaborator, the mentor, and the editor. In these various roles, Maxon has made key contributions to the history of Kenya and the wider region. The gratitude expressed to Maxon by the authors and editor is made on behalf of a much larger community of scholars.

Although three of the contributors address topics beyond the borders of Kenya (and all the papers have important arguments to make to generalist readers), the primary focus of the book is rightly on Kenya. It is there where Maxon has left the greatest impression; all of the country's historians are indebted to Maxon, not just the readers of his work, those he mentored, or his collaborators. Put simply, the historical profession in Kenya would look very different were it not for Maxon. There are few academics about which such a claim would be justified.

The most obvious of Maxon's influences on the historiography and academic practice of history is through his own scholarship. Maxon has made several key interventions to the study of the history of Kenya and the wider region. His autobiographical chapter in this book describes his intellectual and personal engagement with Kenya in typically modest terms. Yet as a historian of agriculture, social and economic change, the establishment of the colonial state, and, most recently, the country's constitutional history, Maxon has helped extend our understanding of complex but critically important themes in Kenya's history. He has done so in various ways, perhaps most notably his study of the colonial state-building of John Ainsworth.[1] However, given this volume, it is his contributions to edited collections, both as editor and author, that deserve greatest attention.

As a tribute to Maxon's scholarship, this collaborative volume could not be more fitting. His co-authored chapter here with Nick Githuku and the wider book are wholly in keeping with the way Maxon has worked as a historian. Maxon is a key member of a golden generation of scholars of Kenya. His entry into this group was marked by his 1973 contribution to the *Kenya Historical Review*, the journal of the Historical Association of Kenya.[2] Through that journal and the efforts of other publishing ventures, most notably perhaps the history list of the East African Publishing House, during the 1960s and 1970s historians from Kenya and overseas professionalised the study of the country's past. However, for all the great monographs and journal articles of this era, one of the most striking aspects of the work of this group of historians was their collaborative effort to jointly produce several landmark texts in the historiography of the country. Following a tradition established by Bethwell Ogot's *Hadith* series from the late 1960s and 1970s, key edited collections in the 1980s and 1990s sustained Kenyan history writing through the darkest days of the rule of Daniel arap Moi.

As his biographical chapter in this volume explains, Maxon was a key part of these joint efforts. His survey chapter on the history of agriculture, for instance, is an invaluable contribution to William Ochieng's 1990 *Themes on Kenyan History*, which also includes key contributions by William Ochieng' and Tabitha Kanogo.[3] Alongside Kanogo, Ochieng', and Bethwell Ogot, Maxon contributed two chapters—one on the colonial conquest and the other on post-colonial economic and social development—to Ochieng's excellent 2002 collection on the history of Western Kenya, itself a tribute to Gideon Were.[4] With Ochieng', Maxon edited one of the precious few efforts to produce an economic history of Kenya, writing four of the chapters himself and co-authoring a fifth with Kanogo.[5]

The highlight of Maxon's collaborative work is undoubtedly his contributions to Ochieng' and Ogot's pathbreaking collection, *Decolonization and Independence in Kenya, 1940-93*. More than twenty-five years from its publication, the book remains one of the key texts on the history of decolonizing and post-colonial Kenya. Its contributors—Ogot, Ochieng', E.S. Atieno Odhiambo, Wunyabari Maloba, and Ndege—are still counted by their peers as being among the most influential scholars in the Kenyan historical profession, some sadly posthumously. Maxon was a fitting member of the writing group for this landmark volume. With an outstanding chapter of his own on social and cultural change in Kenya between independence and the death of Jomo Kenyatta, Maxon also co-authored a second with Ndege, who completed his PhD at West Virginia University under Maxon's guidance.[6] The piece with Ndege on the impact of structural adjustment on the Kenyan economy and politics typifies the very best of Maxon's work. Empirically sharp and judicious in its analysis, it is an outstanding example of Maxon's determination to historicise contemporary debate.

Given their previous work together, the inclusion in this volume of Peter Ndege's chapter on the Nyanza cotton boom of the late 1930s is particularly noteworthy. Ndege's inclusion was given further poignancy by his passing in July 2021. His chapter here is an illustration of the fragility of our connection to the pioneering generation of historians who created the field of Kenyan history. Maxon himself remains one such connection, as does John Lonsdale, another contributor here. In his chapter, Lonsdale reminds us of the challenges that Kenya's historians are facing and reflects on the relative comfort enjoyed by those of us who write about the country's past from the comfort of positions overseas. At times in Kenya's past, the writing of history by Kenyans has been considered by the state to be subversive. Individual historians and academic departments were under pressure as a result. Some historians fled into exile, others remained at home but were silenced.

Through good times and bad, Maxon has worked hard to support his Kenyan colleagues and their scholarship. The importance of Maxon's work with the Moi University, the University of Nairobi, Maseno University, the Masinde Muliro University of Science and Technology, and the Catholic University of Eastern Africa cannot be overstated. His development of collaborative PhD programmes with those universities, and others since, has helped forge a generation of historians who have shaped our understanding of Kenya's past. The work of some of this cohort is wonderfully showcased here. Not least because of Maxon's efforts (and as the contributions to this book demonstrate), and despite continuing challenges, Kenya's own historians are thriving, both at home and overseas.

That point is reiterated repeatedly through this book by its Kenyan contributors, all colleagues or former students of Maxon who exhibit his imprint in one way or another. From community development in Malawi to financial crime in Kenya, the range of the book is impressive. Thoroughly researched and provocatively argued, this volume provides a rich seam of historical research that exhibits many of the same characteristics which define Maxon's own work. Anne Nangulu's chapter, for instance, engages directly with Maxon's efforts to situate the political debates around constitutional reform within the country's wider political context. Nangulu's chapter is evidence of the continuing strength of one aspect of Kenyan historiography: direct engagement by historians with the political debates of the present. Githuku and Maxon's chapter on the Building Bridges Initiative is another such example. But the chapters speak to a wide range of themes and approaches.

George Simpson and Peter Waweru's study of the environmental and medical history of late nineteenth-century Samburuland has an added potency
given the conditions of global lockdown in which this book was produced.
Betty Wambui's chapter on Nairobi's Eastlands is very different in evidential
basis and theoretical focus, but is no less rooted in place than Simpson and
Waweru's chapter.

Maxon's use of biography to explore the wider themes of histories of politics and state-building, as best represented by his study of John Ainsworth, is
well represented in this volume. Opolot Okia returns to Ainsworth himself,
while in a much-needed chapter Godriver Odhiambo examines the life and
death of Pio Gama Pinto, the first victim of a series of high-profile assassinations in the post-colonial period. Joseph Snyder, Gift Wasambo Kayira,
and Paul Chiudza Banda's contributions remind us that Maxon's influence
is measurable outside the borders of Kenya and the United States. Joseph
Snyder, developing Maxon's ideas about colonial rule in practice, shows us
how development policy shaped the nature of late-colonial rule in Sudan.
Kayira, another former student of Maxon at West Virginia, examines a theme
of critical importance to many a post-colonial African state: community
development and the question of local agency. Paul Chiudza Banda straddles
the boundary between the colonial and the post-colonial period to examine
the role of the Malawian Police Force in terms of human rights.

The contributors of this volume are to be congratulated for their efforts
to bring this wide-ranging but coherent set of papers together. It is a further
example of the value of collective academic labour that maintains the fine
tradition of such works within the historiography. Such editorial labour often
goes unrewarded within a discipline whose practitioners often attribute the
most significance to works of individual scholarship. In truth, however, the
contribution of historians to the historiography of Kenya and the wider region
should not be restricted solely to the sole authoring of particular works. At
least as much emphasis should be given to the work they commissioned,
edited, advised, and championed. By these measures, Maxon has few equals.

Non-African historians of the region are now (rightly) being challenged
about the privileges we enjoy and the distorting effect on the production of
knowledge we cause by our overwhelming dominance of the book series of
university presses and academic journals. There are a handful of legitimate
responses to this challenge. One, as Jean Allman argues, is to "step aside."[7]
Another would be to follow Maxon's path and embrace scholarship as a
collective venture to be done in partnership with African-based colleagues.
Without adopting the language of developmentalism, Maxon has invested
his time and energy in the careers of many other historians, not just his own.
He has helped nurture a wide array of dissertations to completion, helping
young historians establish themselves as professional academics along the

way. He has supported the growth of entire academic departments in Kenya. That he has done while maintaining his own research is testament to a sharp mind and a generous spirit. The fruits of these collective labours are vividly demonstrated here.

## NOTES

1. Robert Maxon, *John Ainsworth and the Making of Kenya* (University Press of America: Lanham MD, 1980).

2. Robert Maxon, "John Ainsworth and Agricultural Innovation in Kenya," *Kenya Historical Review*, 1, 2 (1973), 151-62.

3. Robert Maxon, "Agriculture," in William Ochieng' (ed.), *Themes in Kenyan History* (East African Educational Publishers, Nairobi: 1990), 29-35.

4. Robert Maxon, "Colonial Conquest and Administration," in William Ochieng', *Historical Studies and Social Change in Western Kenya* (East African Educational Publishers, Nairobi: 2002), 93-109; Robert Maxon, "Economic and Social Change Since 1963," in Ochieng', *Historical Studies*, 293-68.

5. William Ochieng' & Robert Maxon (eds), *An Economic History of Kenya* (East African Educational Publishers, Nairobi: 1992).

6. Robert Maxon, "Social and Cultural Changes," in Bethwell Ogot & William Ochieng' (eds), *Decolonization and Independence in Kenya, 1940-93* (East African Educational Publishers, Nairobi: 1995), 110-50; Robert Maxon & Peter Ndege, "The Economics of Structural Adjustment," in Ogot & Ochieng' (eds), *Decolonization and Independence*, 151-86.

7. Jean Allman, "Academic Reparation and Stepping Aside," *Africa's a Country* website [https://africasacountry.com/2020/11/academic-reparation-and-stepping-a side – accessed 23 July 2021].

# Introduction

## The Future of History: Transtemporal, Transnational across Geographical Borders

### Nicholas K. Githuku

The future of history as an academic pursuit, and discipline, will be characterized by the study of multiple themes with intersecting timeliness, and will simultaneously be transnational across geographical borders. Indeed, this revitalized and broadened transformation is already with us. The contoured landscape of various approaches to the study of history as a discipline—its subject matter, its pull, its role or uses, and its reach—has changed considerably in the twentieth and twenty-first centuries. Let it suffice to say that history, indeed, is the *study of the future*.[1] Not just a dry and boring study of the distant past. Historians are no longer comfortable or content with studying continental or global geopolitical, social, and economic events across the superficial divide of time as if they were disparate or disconnected. The evolution of the career of history as a specialized area or field of knowledge, therefore, is far removed from its humble origins of storytelling and memorization of facts and dates of events or as a form of literature, evolving to history as a philosophy connecting results with causes[2] and to a critical human science of reckon alongside the social sciences of sociology, anthropology, and political science. Of great import, too, has been the critical cross-pollinating series of turns in the historical profession, namely social, cultural, gendered, imperial, postcolonial, global, and transnational perspectives hitched to a transtemporal close examination of both micro- and macro-historical phenomena.[3]

As it always has, the discipline of history continues to be robust and agile, and has preserved its definitive twentieth-century signature of an unfolding subject in full blossom, undergoing "an unprecedented expansion," even as "it . . . emerges intact from the confrontation with its sister sciences owing to the soundness of its tried and true methods, its chronological moorings, and its reality."[4] And, like in the last century, history continues making itself anew in various ways including, but not limited to, first incorporating new approaches while tackling new problems. Moreover, the new historian is no longer preoccupied with the danger of being invaded by other neighboring sciences or disciplines that may have once "threatened" to engulf or dissolve it,[5] but, rather, the *longue durée* as a trend in historical writing and thinking—"in terms of time, movement, human agency (or the lack of it), and human interaction with the physical environment and the structural cycles of economics and politics."[6] As an approach to thinking about various historical subjects, this method at once proffers the discipline "as a guide to action in the present, using the resources of the past, to imagine alternative possibilities in the future," while spanning a wide range of disciplines.[7] This contribution of the Annales School to economic history, historical demography, history of material culture, the history of mentalities and social history, and so on[8] enables us, as students of both the micro-past and macro-past, to understand "the stakes and implications of changes that range from institutional forces shaped over the last decade to climatic forces shaped over the millennia of evolution."[9] While ambitious, Braudelian *longue durée*, which rejects "the primacy of the written and the tyranny of the event," drawing history "toward the slow, almost static realm," it has also reinforced "history's tendency to dig down to the level of the quotidian, the ordinary, the 'little people.'" History has also made itself new "by the new conception of contemporary history, which is still trying to define itself in terms of such notions as 'immediate history' or 'history of the present,' refusing to reduce the present to an inchoate past and thus challenging the well-established definition of history as the science of the past."[10]

In addition, as a discipline, new history has been made "by deepening and adding to certain traditional areas of history without challenging their basic assumptions." This includes economic history to which one could add or combine to include the political, psychological, and cultural, to study whole systems. To this, demographic history has brought complexity through its various models thus adding "information about mentalities and cultural systems."[11] All said, the entire collective combining under one banner "religious history, literary history, the history of science, political history, and the history of art," has moved the discipline toward "total history by focusing on such globalizing concepts as the sacred, texts, codes, power, and monuments."[12]

Furthermore, according to Goff and Nora, history has made itself new "by incorporating new objects that previously lay beyond its reach and outside its territory" like climate, the body, myths, and festivals, "the unconscious of psychoanalysis, language as studied by modern linguistics, cinematographic images, public opinions polls—all these things are connected with new human sciences," and have now been "confiscated" by historians. Even cooking, "once considered too unimportant for historians to notice," has attracted interest demonstrating "the growing importance of two new realms of history, the history of material civilization and that of techniques."[13] Besides analytical or thematic categories, some of which are noted above, such as the history of daily life, the Italian *microstoria* and the history of women and/or gender, there have been some changes in orientation, for instance, numerous critical, cross-pollinating historiographical "turns" including social turn; the cultural turn of the 1970s; the linguistic turn; the imperial turn—thus bursting the presumed territorial, cultural, and political boundaries between European nations and their colonial holdings; the postcolonial turn, which prompted the subsequent growth and development of global history; and the transnational turn.[14] As a result of such "critical transnational and transtemporal perspectives," nowadays "historians can be guardians against parochial perspectives and endemic short-termism."[15] The main objectives of this new rise of the discipline of history, and the uses of history across the disciplines, are to examine and critically analyze key drivers of social change; and to see "how the past develops over centuries and millennia," and how, then, "thinking about the past," can be utilized "to see the future"; and to grasp and grapple with perennial questions of power, authority and legitimacy, land ownership and distribution, climate change, poverty and equality, capitalism and exploitation, and governance.[16] In so doing, historians have been able to transcend beyond the confines of "periodization" or "periods" whenever necessary to study intersecting timelines, and to focus on broader transnational geopolitics and topics. As such, it is a critical human science tasked with the mission of enlightening, reform, and change.[17] Indeed, this discipline may yet be a social leveler.

In this compilation of a tapestry of African histories, readers will find chapters that aspire to history's classical mission. In chapter 1, "On Writing Kenya's History," John Lonsdale rises to the occasion by presenting a brilliant analysis of the need to reconceptualize Kenya's history both in terms of the time periods and historical context. Lonsdale correctly observes that the "three-part periodization: precolonial, colonial, and post-colonial" of African history is problematic, and proffers an alternative chronology, one that, as he suggests, allows historians and those for whom they write, to find and appreciate "greater insight into how Kenyans themselves drove history." Lonsdale proposes a novel periodization of history that invites us to "look at the changing relations between pastoralism and agriculture; by enquiring into the social inequalities within agriculture alone, over the *longue durée*, the long term." This, he points out, presents us with a dynamic view of an unfolding and changing African past as opposed to the prevalent or predominant one that views the "precolonial" as a "flat start-line that was waiting for real history, colonial history." Furthermore, it is an approach to Kenyan, East African, and African history that is geopolitically transcendent since it helps to bring the vast continental coastline into other pertinent hinterland histories, and not only that of other far-flung places such as the Islamic Middle East, India, or even China. Ultimately, Lonsdale presents readers with a unique view of history. One in which the often dismembered or dis-aggregated rupture between precolonial, colonial, and postcolonial times or histories is not only softened but also more geographically inclusive. Lastly, he makes an excellent point about not needing to be a member of the community being studied to understand their history—and/or their spatial experiences across time.

The significance of this observation lies in nudging African specialists of African history in the continent and in the Diaspora, to appreciate contributions, in some instances spanning entire lifetimes, made by practitioners such as himself, Bruce Berman, Jan Vansina, Robert July, Joseph E. Harris, David Northrup, Thomas Spear, Richard Waller, David Anderson, Lotte Hughes, Fredrick Cooper, Patrick Manning, and many other important historians among them, Robert Maxon. In this volume, Maxon provides an illumining autobiographical account of how his life (and career) got caught up and intertwined with that of the colony of Kenya in the throes of becoming an independent nation in the early 1960s. Indeed, this chapter links Maxon to the making of Kenya's history, to which he has made considerable contribution including the important historical classic, *Struggle for Kenya: The Loss and Reassertion of Imperial Initiative, 1912-1923*, which demonstrates how Kenya nearly became a white man's country after the First World War.

In chapter 2, "From the Upper Delaware River to the Banks of the Monongahela via Lake Victoria," Maxon covers a lot of ground with clarity and modesty, as is his signature style. But one of the fascinating things about the vast and impressive knowledge of the interesting story of Kenya that rather imperiously intruded, and got intertwined with his own life's story, is how Maxon relates it. Having worked closely under his able and generous tutelage at the department of history at West Virginia University (WVU), Morgantown, West Virginia, the beauty of learning and writing about Kenya's economic and political history with him was that the subject became *alive*. Never dry nor distant but close-up and personal, complete with firsthand anecdotes such as, "Oh, I remember watching *this* or *that* on television in the late 1950s," or, "At the end of *that* film, *Mzee* Jomo Kenyatta drives away from the camera and the crowd toward the glowing orange orb of the setting sun." This is the kind of personal touch that the reader will find and enjoy in this interesting firsthand rendition of a story that started in the upper reaches of the Delaware River, and onto the banks of the Monongahela ending up, between 1962 and 1963, by the shores of Lake Nam Lolwe in Western Kenya, far away from the enormous excitement for Africans, at times interspersed and tempered with colonial anxieties in Nairobi, and intense European anxieties across the land.

Indeed, the reader is invited to peer into and vicariously enter the inner sanctum of the mind and experiences of a historian as she or he trudges the times and highlights the moments of the day today that become written history. This, in and of itself, carries incandescent value to aspiring students of history, and to, or for the subject, a glowing effervescence that attracts an even wider audience beyond the delimitations of the academy. One such little but fascinating detail is the author's account of the heydays of, and persistent, if stubborn, ethnic rivalries of early independent Kenyan soccer. An avid sports fan, a young Maxon, with his towering frame, in Chavakali, lent his goalkeeping skills, wearing the number one jersey for "the famous North Nyanza team as well as for Kakamega Black Stars in the Kenya National Football League and Harambee Maseno in the Kenya FA Cup." Indeed, because of his soccer playing days, Maxon met his wife who hails from western Kenya, a region that has preoccupied his scholarly work.

Maxon follows this autobiographical work on his dalliance with the country's culture and history, with two biographical entries on two important political figures who have, most definitely, left their footprints in the sands of time. In chapter 3, "Myth and Reality in the Forging of a Kenyan History," he focuses on an area of national history that both politicians and historians, and Kenyans at large, have flirted with but shied away from and shunned. That is, "heroism" as a topic of study. Although since the 1960s leading scholars such as Ali Mazrui have observed the significance "of remembering past heroes in 'building up national consciousness,'" and "'to give the idea of the Nation warmth,'" in 2007, a national task force led by one of my academic mentors at the University of Nairobi, V.G. Simiyu, was rather hard-pressed to identify and recognize for veneration, the nation's heroines and heroes.[18] While the Simiyu national heroines and heroes task force submitted its report to the then Minister of State for National Heritage, no further action has since been taken by the government to honor exemplary figures of national importance who have made significant contributions in various ways. This is one of the reasons why choosing to examine the heroism of Oginga Odinga in "Kenya's anti-colonial struggle with a specific focus on some of his actions in 1959 and 1960," as Maxon does in this chapter, is crucial.

Maxon's contribution to the literature commemorating and celebrating the contributions and sacrifices made by the country's preeminent daughters and sons include his caution to scholars to ensure that this body of work "provides an accurate and definitive account." This is what he does regarding what are, according to him, two specific signature moments in which Odinga the Elder demonstrated characteristics of heroism such as courage, frankness, self-sacrifice, and persistence. These events, early in his long career spanning the colonial and postcolonial era, were Odinga's emphatic refusal of the chance to become Kenya's first chief minister; and a little-known instance, "at a critical moment in the independence struggle and specifically the movement for constitutional change away from the constitutional philosophy of multi-racialism favored by Lennox-Boyd and Sir Evelyn Baring," he confronted the former in April 1959.

Maxon's last biographical entry in this volume, chapter 4, "Daniel arap Moi: A Challenge for Historians," was written in response to the demise, on Tuesday, February 4, 2020, of Kenya's "all-seeing political giraffe," Daniel Toroitich arap Moi, whose public career, like Odinga's, straddles colonial and postcolonial history. While presenting this dexterous and talented leader as a little-understood and scarcely studied challenge to historians, Maxon ably demonstrates that his emergence, preeminence, and ultimate dominance in the political arena was not inexorable. The author carefully traces the evolution of Moi's significant political career back to his entry into the arena of public affairs characterized by anti-colonialism, in 1955, when he joined the colony's Legislative Council (LegCo). From thereon, Maxon provides a close blow-by-blow account of how Moi gradually climbed the rungs of political influence within the small but steadily growing group of African colonial elites. This Moi did by dint of relentless acumen, sheer dedication to hard work, a knack for building social relationships beyond his Kalenjin ethnic base, and "forthrightness and willingness to take risks." The author identifies the end of the second Lancaster House constitutional conference, at the end of 1963, as a critical defining moment of "Moi's emerging leadership skills and his future in Kenyan politics." What is remarkable about this chapter is not just the impressive and minute details that emerge in this reflection of Moi's career and place in the nation's political history, but also the fondness and familiarity with which Maxon relates this account. In addition, the mastery with which he deploys copious archival evidence that peppers this account, indeed, ought to be an indictment to those who study the East African nation. The amount of archival material cited in this chapter serves as a gentle nudge, especially to historians, that this important political figure should no longer remain a challenge for a book-length study.

Two other biographical contributions in this volume are Okia Opolot and Godriver Odhiambo's chapters 5 and 6 on John Dawson Ainsworth and Pio Gama Pinto, respectively. Okia's chapter 5, "Ainsworth After Dark: The Pied Piper of African Development in Colonial Kenya, 1895–1920?," is well-written, thoroughly researched, and readable. Okia opens the chapter with an introduction of this colonial administrator who served in various capacities during the early period of Kenya's history. In this well-balanced examination of the development legacy left behind by Ainsworth, it is quite clear that, whatever his detractors or admirers had to say about his work, Ainsworth was an exemplary forebear of a distinct class of agrarian and scientific policy, and development, experts who would emerge and wield great influence and power in the late colonial era, and in the postindependence period in leading international development agencies such as the United Nations, the International Monetary Fund, and the World Bank.[19] Benevolent and well-meaning on the surface, the impact of such international "experts" of African development, whether colonial or postcolonial, as Okia demonstrates in the case of Ainsworth, is not always advantageous. This was the case with some of the policies pursued by Ainsworth. If anything stands out in this chapter, it is that Ainsworth's legacy could, very well, be the embodiment of an early British colonial administrator "Coping with . . . Contradictions," standing, as he did, right in the thick of things early in the development of the colonial state in Kenya.[20]

In chapter 6, "Challenge to African Democracy: The Activism and Assassination of Pio Gama Pinto," Odhiambo succeeds in illuminating this Goan Indian, Pinto, who "stood up against colonialism, neo-colonialism, capitalism and," imperialism clad in whatever garb, and for this, he would, in the end, pay the ultimate price. All this played out against the background of the heated Cold War circumstances. In laying out the background to a searching study and discussion of a man cut down in 1965 in the prime of his youth, Odhiambo aptly captures a micro- and macro-story that is evidence of the unique tapestry of African histories that are, at once, intertwined with expanding European international mercantilism and globalization, the continent's subsequent "discovery" of Europe, and the intrusion of Europeans into centuries-old relations between the Indian subcontinent, China, and the East African coast. It is this outward expansion of Europe that had brought the Portuguese to East African trading city-states and the opposite end of the Indian Ocean, along the southwestern coast of the Indian subcontinent where Goa is situated. In introducing her subject, Odhiambo tells us of Pinto's multiracial ancestry, like many Goans, both now and then, who bear both Indian and Portuguese blood. Odhiambo intersperses this biography of a kind, indeed, the first on Pinto, with other important Goan personalities who made political, professional, and commercial contributions in colonial and postcolonial Kenya including Fitzval R.S. de Souza, John Maximian Nazareth, and Joseph Zuzarte Murumbi (who was partially of Goan extraction via his father). Like in the Maxon brief biography of Moi, Odhiambo sheds light on an important freedom fighter that Kenyans cannot afford to forget. This work is to be lauded for pioneering in a subject that, no doubt, merits a book-length examination and analysis.

In chapter 7, "Eastlands, Nairobi: Memory, History, and Recovery," Betty Wambui offers a comprehensive and deeply felt treatment of a very specific and unique layered, multiethnic, and dynamic neighborhood of the city of Nairobi, her beloved "Eastlands," where she was born and bred. This work is unique because it is a close analysis of a mostly suburban residential area that is, for the most part, only depicted in popular culture, and specifically music videos by talented young people of the neighborhood. Wambui decries the historical and sociopolitical neglect of the area that started out as the "first urban home for Africans in colonial Kenya," that is nowadays dominated by lower- and middle-class denizens. The author ensconces this study against the broader and wider spatial and human character of Nairobi. Importantly, she also dedicates a section of the chapter to a discussion of how the topography and settlement patterns, following the ubiquitous east-west lay and planning of major cities in Africa and elsewhere including the city of London, are a crucial factor "in creating and reproducing conditions of structural inequality and deprivation." The sole focus on scarcely studied residential places, such as Embakassi, Makadara, Bahati, Jericho, Buru Buru Phases I to V, Dandora among other adjacent areas of Eastlands, is a significant contribution to the study of urban cities. Furthermore, this work makes bold recommendations, one of which is to single out the area as a crucial urban locale that has made a unique contribution to "the country's memory as the home of Independence," and the forging of a national identity.[21] Wambui claims that if this work remains undone, "the resulting aperture" will feed "into a pattern of marginalization and alienation for communities such as those associated with Eastlands." It shall be interesting to see the kind of impact that this chapter is going to have in the long term. After all, it raises some serious questions that merit, and that should evoke, more scrutiny.

Chapter 8, "Plagues and Pestilences in Late Nineteenth-Century Samburuland," by George L. Simpson, Jr., and Peter Waweru, stands in stark contrast to Wambui's chapter 7 on urbanity. In this chapter, the reader is transported to the northern reaches of the East African Rift of the Great Rift Valley, an old prehistoric place. Once there, at a different and perilous time, c.1865–c.1879, plagued by pestilence, one finds the Samburu, largely a resilient pastoral Nilotic-speaking ethnic group. Ensconced and tucked away generally northwest of the towering heights of Mt. Kenya, the Samburu of this dynamic and upbeat time in the eve of European colonialism, were fierce warriors, the *Tarigirik laji*, who despite their temporal and spatial remoteness made sporadic contacts with aMeru and aEmbu ivory hunters, "who trekked long distances from the Somali coast at Kismaayo as well as Swahili and Zanzibari merchants," and the occasional wandering aKamba trader.

But Simpson and Waweru inform the reader that, unbeknownst to them, the "bovicentric Samburu," at a time before European science had touched this part of Africa, in interacting with these hunting and trading "outsiders," they were contracting microorganisms that had a catastrophic effect on humans as well as their herds. These authors then proceed to narrate the decimation of the Samburu at the onslaught of the dreadful cholera epidemic that had struck their Maasai neighbors in 1869. Yet, this was only the first of the contagions that they would suffer. Contemporaneous reports cited by these authors attributed the origination of the disease to the Indian Ocean and, specifically, Zanzibar Island, which David Livingstone described as a "stinkbar," on account of the rife stench hanging in the air there. This epidemic would be followed by hunger and cattle plagues including rinderpest; and then drought and smallpox, which were the final calamitous act of Nature that curtain-raised for the *main event* that would follow in the 1890s, the imposition of British colonial rule. This small chapter is intense and packed with crucial lessons to learn from when read through the lens of the catastrophic opening of the twenty-first century scarred as it is by the global coronavirus-19 pandemic, the most disastrous public-health crisis in over a century.

Chapters 9–11 touch on community or social development, and/or colonial agrarian experiments in western Kenya, former British Sudan, and postindependence Malawi. Chapter 9, "The Evolution of Imperial Social Development Policy and Practice in British Sudan: A Comparative Case Study of the Gezira and Zande Schemes," by Joseph M. Snyder is a case study of the Gezira and Zande agrarian experiments, that were not unlike some of Ainsworth's agrarian ideas for African social development, and the training of a small class of farmers who could make the best use of permanently established irrigation schemes. Indeed, one finds similar colonial contradictions that bedeviled well-intentioned agrarian projects in British Sudan as in colonial Kenya, and elsewhere in Africa. In the case of Sudan, Snyder identifies a few obstacles that belied the onset of "a pilot scheme for social development embedded within the Gezira Irrigation Scheme," namely the demands of wartime, which made several planning aspects of the work impractical; lack of "machinery to implement many of the initiatives under the agricultural policy, chief among these" being "the inability of the Department of Agriculture to provide trained Sudanese as field inspectors"; and pecuniary hurdles related to the war.

Turning the Zande Scheme, Snyder demonstrates the depth of the schism that finally tore Sudan into two within the first few years of the twenty-first century. Snyder notes that the British in 1930, if not a lot earlier, "acknowledged the South's separate identity with the promulgation of its Southern Policy" with "the ostensible purpose . . . to safeguard the Southern Black African provinces." The ultimate result was the conception of the "so-called Zande Scheme," the main objective of which was self-sufficiency so as to ensure, "the orderly emergence of the inhabitants of central Africa as 'happy, prosperous, literate communities based on agriculture and participating in the benefits of civilization.'" The envisioned vehicle to this end was then propitiously identified as "an irrigation scheme anchored by the cultivation of cotton but sustained by various cash crops."[22] Ominously, "in a marked departure from standard practice," the main architect of the scheme "discarded the use of experimental or pilot research projects to extrapolate the likelihood of success or failure of the larger endeavor . . . . The Zande Scheme was to be an all-or-nothing undertaking." Suffice it to say, as Snyder observes, even before the scheme was implemented, an ad hoc committee appointed to oversee it abandoned its self-sufficiency element. Gutting the scheme to the core, other composite elements were discarded, and by 1947, "the Zande Scheme was no longer recognizable as a bold experiment in social emergence" and change, according to the author.

Chapter 10, "Illusions about a Boom in Cotton Production in Southern Nyanza during the Depression, 1929–1939," by Peter Odhiambo Ndege addresses the short-lived cotton boom among the Luo of southern Nyanza in Western Kenya between 1934 and 1939, attributes this to the challenge posed by the Great Depression, and the subsequent dramatic fall of prices in the United States and Europe. This far-removed economic downturn caused by the Wall Street stock market crash of 1929 triggering economic turmoil in the industrialized world, according to Ndege, accentuated apparent internal undertones of the same financial stress and strain in the nascent colonial economy in East Africa and elsewhere on the continent. This new constraint was exacerbated by the heavy reliance of the colonial economy on agricultural exports, "the internal domination of settler over African agriculture," which is one of the obvious internal contradictions of the political economy, "and . . . the over-reliance of settler agriculture on the financial support and supply of labour by the state." In southern Nyanza, and the rest of the colony, "the depression led to a period of extreme reproduction squeeze" characterized by famine, suppressed commodity prices made worse by the upward adjustment of taxes and lack of economic opportunities. In the end, as Ndege observes, this hodgepodge of "crises and contradictions beset the cotton growing industry." Added to this economic tragedy of Luo peasant cotton farmers in southern Nyanza were long periods of heavy rainfall, "drought and locust invasions, which led to bad and almost no harvests" between 1929 and 1934. The development of the *Mumboist* millennial protests against the British colonial administration also served to weaken agricultural policies as a result of the detention and deportation of these political dissidents. Overall, the author adequately explains why this cotton boom was short-lived and why this setback was never successfully resolved within the period of scrutiny. But importantly, this work demonstrates the interplay and interaction of far-removed geopolitical factors with local ones closer home and, thus, underscoring the necessity for scholars to work with transpatial and transtemporal frameworks that are wider and longer, respectively.

Chapter 11, "Community Development in Postindependence Malawi: Deciphering Some Local Voices," by Gift Wasambo Kayira examines ways in which local self-driven African development initiatives were started, developed, and sustained. This is a fresh and radical departure from the preoccupation with the study of top-bottom imposed, so-called "expert-driven rural development," imperial agrarian programs that, more often than not, were resisted by African societies, and not unusually, ended up in failure as chapters 9 and 10 attest. Kayira studies the Wovwe rice irrigation scheme in northern Malawi, which "was established in the 1960s and operated under" local African expertise "until the early 2000s when the Malawian government devolved its management to local farmers." This government intervention was soon contested "when the new management of the scheme proved ineffective."

The thin veil of community trustee management did not, of necessity, render opaque the government's overreach to continue operating it as an expert-driven top-down agrarian development project. No sooner had this apparent community trustee management model effected than Wovwe was bedeviled by management shortfall, financial hardships, and water shortages. Invested participating local farmers immediately took advantage of these organizational challenges, "contested the authority" of its government-imposed hirelings on whom "expert" trusteeship now rested. These farmers proceeded to protest and disobey constitutional rules, withheld their labor toward the maintenance of scheme facilities, "and appealed to" hidden and underlying informal African traditional mores and channels of authority as opposed to the more formal leadership ones. This is a brilliant study that sheds light not only on the little-understood local dynamic of why some imperial agrarian projects failed but also reveals a deeper history of the latent potential in, or of, community-led development initiatives in Africa. Furthermore, this study demonstrates that ordinary people, who usually lie in the margins of formal power, can and do negotiate their involvement in the development process and often triumph. This important observation by Kayira begs the question of whether the preemptory *Triumph of the Expert* did not come a little too soon.[23]

Chapters 12–14 of the volume touch on constitutional, legal, and human rights issues tinged with the usual politics in more recent times, of course, all tied to the early and deep colonial history. In chapter 12, "Regime Policing and the Stifling of the Human Rights Agenda: Late Colonial and Postcolonial Malawi, 1948–Present," Paul Chiudza Banda looks at how the Malawi Police Force (MPF) has violated human rights in the country from the late 1940s to the present. Banda posits that the history of the struggle for human rights in Malawi cannot be fully understood outside the dual framework of decolonization and the Cold War era. He contends that both have had significant influences on the operations of the late colonial and postcolonial states. Various efforts undertaken by the government, with bilateral donor countries and agencies of the West looking over the shoulders of Malawian officials, have fallen short of curbing human rights violations. The author opens the chapter with the examination of how the British Colonial Office's (CO) "initial tilt towards the extension of Bill of Rights," as enshrined in the Universal Declaration of Human Rights (UDHR), was lulled as it was feared that enactment and implementation there, and elsewhere in the colonies, would accelerate and fuel "widespread demands for independence" and self-determination "by nationalist leaders." The meager accruing benefit in as far as the extension of the Bill of Human Rights was concerned in colonial Malawi was the provision of "some form of African representation in the Legislative Council," which "began in the mid-1950s." The reluctance and delay of the implementation of the Bill of Rights in British Central Africa (now Zambia, Zimbabwe, and Malawi) was mainly to protect long-entrenched imperial economic interests in the region. The British government also feared the threat "posed by the global spread of communism." And of course, as already mentioned, they "were unwilling to hand over political power to Africans."

The irony, however, is that even when independence was won in the Central African country, and the reigns of state and political power were handed over to nationalists, the human rights track record did not significantly improve, according to the author. Banda observes that, like most other African states, the postcolonial Malawian state proved to be an "imported state," betraying continued colonial practices, structures, and ideologies, which were, ironically, now emulated by erstwhile nationalists. Yet, on paper, the new postcolonial leadership of the president, Dr. H.K. Banda, "adopted the Bill of Rights introduced in the 1963 Constitutional Order-in-Council." Soon, caught up in a "cabinet crisis" barely two months after independence, President Banda fell out with a few members of his cabinet over domestic policies and foreign relations—specifically, Malawi's relations with China. The West-leaning new president of Malawi opposed opening diplomatic relations with Communist China, while some members of his government favored it. Subsequently, challenged by his own cabinet and seeking to consolidate political power, President Banda, formerly a champion of the Bill of Rights, did not hesitate to remove it from the constitution by July 1966. This marked an era of flagrant violation of human rights in the country only comparable to, and reminiscent of, the colonial era with the MPF as the chief perpetrator.

Chapter 13, "The Constitution and Change-the-Constitution Debate in Independent Kenya, 1963–2002," by Anne Nangulu deals with constitution-writing, and the evolution of the Kenyan constitution from 1963 to 2002. She observes that during this period, the constitution was so considerably amended that its essential spirit and character was transformed. Not unlike the removal of the Bill of Rights in Malawi, in President Jomo Kenyatta's Kenya, early postcolonial constitutional amendments were engineered by him and his political allies in government and sought to consolidate the power of the executive vis-à-vis other arms of government, as well as perceived or real political rivals, and disgruntled dissidents. During the era of President Daniel arap Moi, Nangulu further notes, amendments, especially those made in the 1990s, were largely government responses to the political demands of parliamentarians, members of the civil society, and citizens for reforms to return the country back to multipartyism and democracy. By this time, there was widespread, and a groundswell of, opposition to the one-party *de jure* system under Moi's feared ironclad dictatorship.

Indeed, Moi and Kenyatta's constitutional amendments had so morphed and empowered the executive arm of government such that, the subsequent evolution led to the emergence of postcolonial Kenya as a "bureaucratic-executive state."[24] One in which popular anti-colonial forces and voices of political dissent were muted; individual freedoms and rights withered; and the democratic political space increasingly circumscribed. This, then, as Nangulu argues, is what created a groundswell of pressure for a reorientation of the constitution to restructure the alignment of power. This pressure, according to the author, was also inspired by deteriorating living standards exacerbated by the skyrocketing cost of living, and runaway inflation; crumbling infrastructure and lack of access to decent healthcare and education services not to mention other social welfare issues; and general government maladministration. It was also recognized, especially by a coterie of young brilliant legal minds, politicians, and businessmen, that Kenya's independence constitution, discounting the postcolonial construction of an imperial executive by both Kenyatta and Moi, was far from ideal. As such, as the country entered the twenty-first century, Nangulu concludes, it faced the looming and pressing challenge of having to overhaul the constitution by carrying out a far-reaching and extensive comprehensive review that would create and usher in a new constitutional order. This long-delayed dream and objective was ultimately realized with the promulgation of the 2010 constitution.

But, alas, the new constitutional order that was ushered in by President Mwai Kibaki's second administration, less than a decade after its promulgation, in some quarters of the Kenya body politic, is wanting. Yet, as written, and as the 2010 constitution stands, it is arguably one of the world's finest constitutions, if ever there was one. While the quest and long-standing struggle for the extensive review and overhaul of the old independence constitution was a push from below, renewed post-2010 calls for constitutional amendments are elite-driven, and therefore, of a highly suspicious nature. This suspect top-down political push for the redrawing of the 2010 constitution is the subject of chapter 14, "The Building Bridges Initiative Déjà vu: 'A Whitewash Process Taking Us Forward by Taking Us Backwards,'" by Nicholas Kariuki Githuku and Robert Maxon. This proposal to amend the 2010 constitution was the lovechild of erstwhile nemeses from rival historical and political dynasties, Uhuru Muigai Kenyatta, the president of Kenya between 2013 and 2022, and Kenya's only prime minister (since Jomo Kenyatta between June 1, 1963, and December 12, 1964) under Kibaki's second administration, Raila Amollo Odinga, between 2008 and 2013.

This political rapprochement sealed with a symbolic "handshake" in March 2018, followed an extremely bitter, fiery, and fierce presidential contest between the two political behemoths in 2017, which brought the country to the precipice of an all-out civil war, reminiscent of the bloody post-2007 presidential elections. The concomitant electoral tensions and political temperatures were heated in the buildup to the 2017 elections, and only got worse following accusations between the two, Kenyatta the Younger and Odinga the Younger, and their respective followers, of electoral malpractice and rigging. This, eventually, led to the annulment of presidential election results by the Supreme Court of Kenya. Subsequently, the presidential elections were repeated under dubious circumstances with Odinga refusing to participate in the rerun elections. The unfolding political drama ended with the swearing-in of Kenyatta as the (un)duly elected president, and the unprecedented installation of Odinga as Kenya's second "people's president" at Uhuru Park in the country's capital. Matters came to a head. The country now had two presidents. If the political tensions were high in the two presidential elections of August 8 and October 31, 2017, they soared to a high octane leading to at least 30 violent deaths. These unbearable palpable political ethnic tensions only eased when the two politicians proffered a mutual olive branch.

Secret private talks between the two kicked up the Building Bridges Initiative (BBI) national consultation process that concluded with the writing of two reports in successive sequence in 2019 and 2020.[25] This cycle of events, Githuku and Maxon postulate, is emblematic of the rough-and-tumble of the country's tumultuous political history since the troublesome 1950s. One of the authors' aims in the chapter is to put this latest political milestone in historical context and perspective while assessing the significance of the BBI reports going forward. In this regard, this chapter argues that the BBI reports, like other momentous constitution-writing moments, government reports, and policy papers, are a whitecap in the undulating political evolution of the state and, as such, counsel Kenyans to, perhaps, curb their cyclic enthusiasm and euphoria. Kenyans have been here many times before; and, after all, the nation-state is still coming to birth. Indeed, the chapter suggests that this bridge-building process is but a building block in a continuous state-building project and should not be expected to be the end-all and be-all silver bullet that will solve the country's various problems (and especially not the two twin tyrannies of ethnic expectation and institutionalized corruption that feed off each other and are inextricably connected).[26] Another object of this entry is to assess the pros and cons of the BBI while evaluating its value, especially vis-à-vis the 2010 constitution. In this respect, Githuku and Maxon argue that the BBI report ("the report" heretofore)[27] accentuates the 2010 constitution.

Indeed, they make the argument that as a process calculated to stave off bloodshed and political disaster, the BBI process was, by and large, an elite initiative as opposed to being people-led and -driven as the protracted constitution-writing process of the 2000s was and, therefore, not as radical and revolutionary. It is little wonder then that sections of society have characterized the report as an "apology" of the elites' failure to live up to, and to fully implement, the 2010 constitution. As part of assessing the pros and cons of the BBI process, the authors also engage with the troubling question that continues to be a constant obstacle to the implementation of the constitution—namely what is the price of democracy, and can Kenyans afford it? It is argued that the question of affordability harks back to the first ambitious *majimbo* or independence constitution written in Lancaster, England, which Kenyatta the Elder quickly scuttled at independence, hence the authors' view that the country has been here before.

"House of *Mlungula*—'Norms in the Margins and Margins of the Norm: Of Computer 'Glitches,' Moving Human Fingers and Illicit Financial Flows" is the last chapter in this volume. In this chapter, I argue that Kenya is patently a house of *mlungula*—that is, a kleptocracy where both the government and society are imbued by corruption and runaway greed. I assert that corruption so permeates society like an unavoidable hydra that it scarcely leaves anyone untouched or unaffected. For evidence to support this assertion, I simply turn to an old African adage of long-standing used to justify varying and different acts of corruption and malfeasance. That is, the unwritten code expressed in the African proverb, "the goat eats where it's tethered." Elaborating further, I point to the fact that it is not surprising to find corruption and the "trading of favors," *bakshish*, among lawmakers; among revenue collection officials; among parents, teachers, and students in schools and universities; among doctors, nurses, and staff in hospitals; in corridors of justice among judges and magistrates; and even in the so-called "disciplined armed forces," including the police. However, this chapter goes further to examine what I comprehend as the zenith of the complete or gross disregard of African norms of kinship, mutuality, and reciprocity because of wanton greed and corruption. Seldom is there any human progress and technological advancement, I evaluate, that does not alter society. Whether one talks about printing in the sixteenth century, which rocked Europe with the spread of Protestantism; or various machines behind the Industrial Revolution; or Lonsdale's *ng'ombe na mkuki* (cow and spear) and the *njembe na kalamu* (hoe and pen) revolutions in Africa—in this volume—technological advancement has always transformed and/or forged societies.

Although this is not a phenomenon confined to Kenya and Africa, my chapter is a reflection of how the combination of "itchy" human fingers and the rapid development of digital technologies—such as mobile banking, electronic money transfer, cryptocurrencies such as Bitcoin, and online banking and gambling services, all of which are quite popular in Kenya— have facilitated or contributed to illicit financial flows ranging from corruption, illegally earned, or transfer, of money and cybercrime (read: fraud) among others, such as tax evasion and tax avoidance, organized crime, human trafficking, and "many other forms of crime . . . associated with these illegal activities." The proliferation and establishment of digital technologies in the twenty-first century as an acceptable way for transacting business and money transfer, I argue, has encouraged financial chicanery ensuring that universal ethical norms such as accountability and responsibility have not only been pushed to the outer margins, but has also meant that the margins of the norms have been pushed to the limit and, often, been ruptured with impunity.

On behalf of all the contributing authors featured in this collection of chapters that form an unusual but congealing tapestry of African histories with longer times and wider geopolitics, I hope that disparate audiences of the general reading public; constitutional specialists and human rights outfits; Africanist historians, and scholars in other neighboring fields and specialties; development agency and policymakers, and agricultural specialists and field officers; government leaders in Africa and around the world, and civil servants; journalists and public intellectuals; practitioners of different professions including but not limited to bankers, lawyers, and local, national and international accountants and financial specialists; authors interested in life-writing and the auto/biographical form of writing; and seekers of wisdom and knowledge, in general, shall all find this volume useful and enjoyable.

## NOTES

1. *Study of the future*, not in the sense of a discipline that takes on, as the subject of study, the future. Rather, "study of the future," in the sense of a discipline on the rise, and a discipline to which many are turning for answers to address new and old problems such as questions about power, authority and legitimacy, land ownership and distribution, climate change, poverty and equality, and capitalism and exploitation, among others. Indeed, history as the study of the future, has, over the years, established itself as a critical human science of reckon.

2. John Lukacs, *The Future of History* (New Haven: Yale University Press, 2011), 6–7.

3. Jo Guldi and David Armitage, *The History Manifesto* (Cambridge: Cambridge University Press, 2014), 120–125.

4. Jacques Le Goff and Pierre Nora, *Constructing the Past* (trans. By Arthur Goldhammer), "New Objects and New Methods," in (eds.) Jacques Revel and Lynn Hunt, *Histories: French Constructions of the Past—Postwar French Thought*, Volume I (New York: The New Press, 1995), 326.

5. Goff and Nora, *Histories*, 324 and 325.

6. Guldi and David Armitage, *The History Manifesto*, 10.

7. Ibid., 10 and 121.

8. Fernando Sánchez Marcos, "Historiography of the 20th and 21s Centuries," in http://culturahistorica.org/historiography/historiography-of-the-19th-and-20th-centuries/, Accessed on March 4, 2021.

9. Guldi and Armitage, *The History Manifesto*, 123.

10. Goff and Nora, *Histories*, 325.

11. Ibid.

12. Ibid.

13. Ibid., 326.

14. Marcos, "Historiography of the 20th and 21s Centuries."

15. Guldi and Armitage, *The History Manifesto*, 125.

16. Ibid., 9, 19, 34–37, 81, and 84.

17. Ibid., 30, 123 and 124.

18. See the Executive Summary of "Report of the taskforce for country-wide data collection on criteria and modalities of honouring national heroes and heroines," submitted to the then Minister of State for National Heritage Suleiman Shakombo, by Taskforce chair V.G. Simiyu, August 2007; and Lotte Hughes, "'Truth be Told': Some Problems with Historical Revisionism in Kenya," *African Studies* 70 (August 2011): 182–201.

19. Joseph M. Hodge, *The Triumph of the Expert: Agrarian Doctrines of Development and the Legacies of British Colonialism* (Athens: Ohio University Press, 2007).

20. Bruce Berman and John Lonsdale, "Coping with the Contradictions: The Development of the Colonial State in Kenya, 1895-1914," *The Journal of African History*, 20 (1979): 487–505.

21. Here, it is important to point out that the doyen of national politics, Oginga Odinga, discussed above, early in his political career lived in Jericho, in Eastlands.

22. This cash-crop element involving the planting of coffee, sugar, and oil palms would later be jettisoned.

23. See Hodge, *The Triumph of the Expert: Agrarian Doctrines of Development and the Legacies of British Colonialism*.

24. "Bureaucratic-executive state" in the sense used by Daniel Branch and Nicholas Cheeseman in, "The Politics of Control in Kenya: Understanding the Bureaucratic-Executive State, 1952–78," *Review of African Political Economy* 33 (2006): 13–22.

25. The first BBI report was launched at the Bomas of Kenya, Nairobi with much pomp and aplomb on Thursday, November 7, 2019, and the second one was unveiled with even greater jubilation on Wednesday, October 21, 2020.

26. See Nicholas Githuku's separate chapter contribution in this volume.

27. The reference "the report," applies to the second October 21, 2020, BBI report.

# BIBLIOGRAPHY

Berman, Bruce, and John Lonsdale, "Coping with the Contradictions: The Development of the Colonial State in Kenya, 1895-1914," *The Journal of African History* 20 (1979): 487–505.

Branch, Daniel, and Nicholas Cheeseman "The Politics of Control in Kenya: Understanding the Bureaucratic-Executive State, 1952–1978," *Review of African Political Economy* 33 (2006): 11–31.

Goff, Le Jacques, and Pierre Nora, *Constructing the Past* (trans. By Arthur Goldhammer), "New Objects and New Methods," in (eds.) Jacques Revel and Lynn Hunt, *Histories: French Constructions of the Past—Postwar French Thought*, Volume I (New York: The New Press, 1995).

Guldi, Jo and David Armitage, *The History Manifesto* (Cambridge: Cambridge University Press, 2014).

Hodge Joseph M., *The Triumph of the Expert: Agrarian Doctrines of Development and the Legacies of British Colonialism* (Athens: Ohio University Press, 2007).

Lukacs, John, *The Future of History* (New Haven: Yale University Press, 2011).

*Chapter 1*

# On Writing Kenya's History

## John M. Lonsdale

E. H. Carr, once upon a time a fellow of my Cambridge University college, gave a series of lectures in 1960 on *What Is History?* The book of the lectures is still widely read, although our views on why history matters have changed since then.[1] History is never the past in all its complications; it is that very little of the past that happens to be recorded. National archives save only around 5 percent of government papers—when there was paper. Not many children keep their parents' private papers. Carr nonetheless believed that the surviving snippets of preselected evidence had a practical value. While he did not believe the past repeated itself, he did think the patterns of causation that historians unpicked could nonetheless help to clarify present-day problems. This confidence in history's quasi-prophetic role has now virtually disappeared; it too nearly suggests that what we think is important for us today chooses what was of importance to people in the past. As the Italian historian Benedetto Croce once admitted, "all history is contemporary history." To avoid that trap, most historians now suggest that history has a more oracular quality: As its shrine-keepers, we do not predict; rather, we present a range of past experiences that may help our readers to think for themselves. We offer our readers food for thought, neither lessons nor predictions. And they should remember Eric Hobsbawm's warning that historians are "poppy growers" to the "heroin addicts" among their readers. True, he was thinking especially of nationalists, political activists for whom any nation without a history is "a contradiction in terms." Precisely. This is why any Kenyan with an interest in her country's history should read me with some skepticism. For Carr issued a parallel warning: That our imaginations can feed only on those stories that a particular historian chooses to tell, and in ways that support his or her own convictions. "Study the historian," he advised, "before you begin to study the facts."[2]

1

This warning applies to all historians everywhere, but especially to anybody who reads this chapter. I am a son of the British Empire. How can I dare to suggest what may be important to think about in the history of Kenya, a former colony? My grandfather was a resident commissioner in Nigeria between the two world wars. My father was an officer in the Royal Navy before he became a priest in the Anglican church; he ministered to the British community in Eldoret and Kisumu in the 1950s and 1960s. True, there were always more Africans than Europeans in his church services; he also volunteered to go into the forests to live with the Mau Mau *itungati* as a hostage for British good intentions during one of the surrender negotiations. I myself did my military service in the King's African Rifles in the late 1950s. But, again, I knew that my sergeant-major, Maingi, and my "platoon warrant officer," Odera, were better soldiers than me, that corporal Kimutai told better jokes, and my batman Lesimoi Lakalale was smarter. Even so, how can I, a superannuated imperialist, think I can offer ideas on their history that Kenyans might find useful to think with?

I call to my defense Kenya's senior historian, my *mwalimu* or *jabilo*, Professor Bethwell Ogot. He denies that a historian's ethnicity, nationality, class, or gender gives him or her any privileged insight. Ogot trusts, instead, in historical method—which means no more than a humane sympathy and a skeptical mastery of evidence that, together, help us to critically understand people other than ourselves, with different beliefs, acting in other contexts, facing unfamiliar problems and likely to leave self-serving evidence behind them. Ogot denied that their identity could give anyone a superior understanding of people seemingly like themselves in the past. To believe otherwise presupposed a double impossibility: That there are timeless, changeless, human categories, whether woman, African, African American, Jew, or English, and so on, and that therefore *only* women, Africans, African Americans, Jews, or English people could understand their respective histories.[3]

When in 1960 I was a student, the most influential historian of Tudor England was Sir Geoffrey Elton. He had been born Gottfried Ehrenberg, coming to Britain as a German Jewish refugee from the Nazis. His interpretations have since been overturned—but that's the common fate of all historians. Because, as Kathryn Tidrick, a Scottish biographer of Mahatma Gandhi, has pointed out, historians argue with each other. They test their colleagues' hypotheses; they question their use of evidence. This constant peer review matters more than a historian's identity. Any scholar who subjects her- or himself to their fellow scholars' scrutiny has the right to speak on any topic of their choice.[4]

While one's identity neither guarantees nor prevents one from being a valid historian, intellectual freedom is vital if we are to write what we believe the evidence tells us. Who is free to write what they think to be a critically honest assessment, reached within what they acknowledge to be their political or theoretical perspective, is vital, not least in the recent history of Kenya. In remembering that in the recent past, my Kenyan colleagues have lacked that freedom, I hope to answer three questions: Why does Kenya need a history and of what sort? How should it be periodized? And how can one contrive to meet real people in the past?

## WHY DOES KENYA NEED A HISTORY?

When asked such questions by British students, I used to answer: "So that you will know how much your freedoms owe to the struggles of your ancestors and, therefore, why they are worth defending." Also, remembering Ogot's insistence that history is a discipline of contexts, I would add that these struggles must be understood within their particular context, whether in Britain or beyond its shores. Moreover, things have changed in the past, often for the better. They can change again. To know that is another reason to study history.

How might one apply these insights to Kenya's history? Jomo Kenyatta, the first president, asserted that all had fought for freedom: Yes, but within how long a time frame, and in what contexts, local and global? And, to return to my earlier question: who is free to write this sort of history? I find it troubling that a retired imperialist has been more able to study and publish on Kenya's history than the Kenyan friends and colleagues of my generation.

Thirty years ago the novelist Ngugi wa Thiong'o set out the problem. In his Foreword to Maina wa Kinyatti's edition of the Mau Mau Field Marshal Dedan Kimathi's papers, he asked: "Why is history subversive?" His reply was like mine: Because history was about "human struggle," first with the forces of nature and then with other people over how to reward the labor that produced nature's riches. But stories of struggle obviously terrify tyrants, who therefore "*rewrite* history, make up official *history*; if they can put cotton wool in their ears and in those of the population, maybe *they* and *the people* will not hear the *real* call of history, will not hear the *real* lessons of history."[5] Rulers can also hide the evidence of their misdeeds, as we British tried to do with respect to abuses committed in the Mau Mau detention camps. But it was also British historians who brought the hidden files of shameful evidence to light, an example of how historians can reveal the subversive truths of their country's past, if free to do so.[6]

But the issue is more complex than Ngugi realized. One hundred and forty years ago, the French historian Ernest Renan also thought national histories should be forgotten or told in comfortable lies—and he was a democrat, not a tyrant. He knew all nation-states had violent pasts—built on civil wars, on religious or ethnic cleansing, on imposing a national language, and so on. Renan wanted his fellow citizens to trust each other enough to engage in open political debate—and thought that that would be impossible if historians kept on reminding them that their ancestors had fought each other in the past.[7]

Ogot rejects Renan's advocacy of a democracy protected by historians' deceit. Like Ngugi he also refuses the comfortable cotton wool of official history.[8] But it takes courage to tell the subversive history of struggle we find in our evidence. Many Kenyan scholars were detained and tortured, my friend Atieno Odhiambo among them, for telling subversive truths in the last three decades of the twentieth century, that time of political paranoia under both Kenyatta and Moi. As a non-Kenyan, I have only suffered the minor inconvenience of having my research notes stolen by the police special branch. Unlike too many of my Kenyan friends, I have been left free to write. Academic freedom is a serious matter, especially for historians. Only more recently has a Kenyan like Nick Githuku felt free to produce work critical not only of British colonials but also of powerful Kenyans.[9] If Kenyans are to learn from the sort of history Ngugi and Ogot think they need, then the freedom of their historians must always be our collegial concern.

But now, if we want to give Kenyans a history of ancestral struggles for freedom and respect, what stories can we tell, and with what periodization, what chronology of change? And which contexts will best help us to appreciate the lives of individual men and women?

## PERIODIZATION

All historians face the problem of periodization. History, as Ngugi also said, is about change—but which changes are the most important? When did they occur and how long did they take? What other stories do they displace? In African history, there has long been a conventional answer to those questions. No historian likes it, but it is hard to get away from a three-part periodization: precolonial, colonial, and postcolonial. It suffers from at least three problems.

First, the precolonial period can be thousands of years long and, if humanity chooses to survive, postcolonial time will get ever longer. For most of Africa, the colonial years will always remain shorter than a lifetime. And yet, because the colonial rule is the best documented of our three periods, historians will always be tempted to think it the most important.

Second, this periodization looks to rest on a series of ruptures, when historical continuities can be at least as important. The initial rupture of imperial conquest divides precolonial from colonial time and, because we know more about the latter than the centuries that preceded it, it is all too easy to imply that African history began only around 1890, as white colonists believed at the time. If we then think of the colonial rule as a single period, we may not notice its changes of character, some of them due to the tensions between metropolitan imperialism and local colonialism. Bob Maxon's *Struggle for Kenya*, for instance, shows how Kenya nearly became a White Man's Country after the First World War. Imperial London had to fight to recover the power it had lost to the white-settler, colonial, Nairobi during the war—an example of how the wider context can shape a local conflict.[10]

And then, at the other end of colonial rule, if independence came after a bloody struggle, a costly rupture bought with people's lives, any continuity of economic policy thereafter may look to be a betrayal, as, indeed, many Kenyans believe of their independent years. It is an issue that tortures the national memory, and for which a different periodization may produce a more openly discussable if still difficult answer, as I will suggest.

But before I propose my alternative chronology, a final objection to our conventional historiography is that it seems to hand all culturally creative capacity to the colonialists.[11] If we know little of the precolonial history and believe, as my first boss Terence Ranger used to believe, before he revised his opinion, that colonial officials invented the tradition that Africans naturally lived in distinctive tribes.[12] As Adrian Hastings complained, that suggests Africans lacked their own imagination of community and so had no political will of their own.[13] It is in search of greater insight into how Kenyans themselves drove history, if under circumstances not of their choosing, that I offer my different periodization. It originates in Ngugi's observation that humanity's first struggle is with nature.

Local struggles with nature have been varied, complex, and have changed. Kenya possesses diverse environments, with arid plains, almost deserts in the north; higher, seasonally dry, savannah plateaux in and beside the Rift Valley; and, higher still, well-watered uplands. Each environmental niche demanded its own expert struggle with nature if its inhabitants were to achieve socially responsible livelihoods, using skills learned and disciplined within their ecologically knowledgeable cultures.

Africanist historians increasingly argue that how people learned to manage these struggles was the basis of their ethnic culture, their ethnic morality, what I call their "moral ethnicity."[14] By this I mean not "tribal" kinship but the social conventions, initially argued between immigrant strangers, that govern both the self-conduct that aspires to self-mastery and the social relations that set collective and reputational limits to this ambition. "Ecological ethnicities" not only developed different relations of production to exploit their varied environments but also produced different goods, pastoral, agricultural, or animal. These complementary economies encouraged market exchange, so that Kenya's past is a history not only of building civic trust *within* different communities but also of commercial trust-building *between* them—interspersed with the periodic conflicts of their young. It's a history worth thinking about.

Tom Spear and Richard Waller's collection, *Being Maasai*, is the best place to read up on this argument.[15] They emphasize that ethnic groups were communities of plural origin that had learned a productive skill—herding, hoeing, or hunting—rather than corporate bloodlines of primordial descent. They exchanged people as well as goods when, especially during famines, their poorer members sought refuge with patrons in another more fortunate group, in return for loyal service or cut-price marriage. Myths of ethnic origin used to acknowledge these different migrant streams. Spear and Waller also confirm that ethnic groups borrowed and adapted philosophies and practices of social responsibility, especially the age and generation sets that gave many Kenyan peoples a shared social culture. Wealthy householders who had best mastered their particular environment were everywhere respected, provided they repaid their social debts. They had to acknowledge, with loans of land or livestock, the cooperation they received from kin and clients. Failure to meet these expectations of reciprocal civic virtue was to deny opportunity to others and so risk a fiery death, sanctioned by popular anger. Such fears of sorcery could also attach to any solitary, perhaps envious, poor. Resting on the premise that no household, however large, could safely prosper on its own, the rules of civilized behavior were argued out over centuries. They are good to think with today.

But how does this analysis of precolonial society, its skills, its norms, its exchanges, its interdependence, its fluidity, inform a new periodization of history? By inviting us to look at the changing relations between pastoralism and agriculture; by enquiring into the social inequalities within agriculture alone, over the *longue durée*, the long term. For simplicity's sake I leave Kenya's small hunting groups out of the picture, often despised by other, later, immigrants as uncivilized, too idle to struggle with nature.

The first advantage of this proposed periodization is that it invites us to look at the changes within precolonial time. This must no longer be seen as a flat start-line that was waiting for real history, colonial history, to begin. It also helps to bring the Indian Ocean coast into Kenya's history, always a difficulty, since before the late nineteenth century the more significant context for coastal history was the Islamic Middle East, not the East African interior.

To sum up the importance of this distant past, I turn to my colleague Mary Mwiandi, lately chair of the University of Nairobi's history department. We met in 2009, at a conference that discussed how historians might deter Kenyans from killing each other in pursuit of electoral advantage. Mary proposed the most concise of historical peace formulae: "We're all immigrants, and we're all here."

While historical linguists go back two thousand years, for my argument it's enough to go back only as far as 1800, when much of central Kenya began to suffer prolonged drought. Lake Baringo may have dried out completely by 1830, when more reliable rains then returned. Famished remnants of people had to rebuild their social orders; no age-set sequence seems to begin before this date. If later famines are any guide, these working communities will have been helped to recover by refugee strangers from the worst-hit areas: Survival was a ladder of social as much as ethnic differentiation. Some learned new, resilient, ways of cultivating and herding. It is in this context of recovery that one can best introduce the Indian Ocean coast to "upcountry" history, as coastal traders in search of ivory (more often than slaves) entered the intensive regional market exchanges that helped neighboring groups to recover from killer famine.[16]

This history softens the rupture between the precolonial and colonial times. Before the 1890s, Kenya's ecological ethnicities seem to have interacted more or less as equals. No cultivating community aimed to colonize a pastoralist's environment or vice versa, since that would demand different skills from those they had already learned—something else to remember when I end with today's politics of ethnicity.

In the later nineteenth century, in this my first period of agrarian history, each ecological ethnicity seems to have become increasingly specialized, some more purely pastoralist, others more heavily dependent on the hoe and both, therefore, more reliant on exchange with the other. But calamity struck again as the century ended, not only with drought and famine but also rinderpest, a new cattle plague for which there was no known remedy. Maasai suffered the worst.[17]

In the same years not only did the British annex the East African Protectorate—later Kenya Colony—but the first Christian missionaries also settled upcountry. Specialized recovery from famine, cattle plague, and mission literacy is, in my periodization, at least as significant as colonial conquest.

Rinderpest and school mark the start of my second period, an agri-educational revolution. I'd like to give this process a more melodious KiSwahili name, the *njembe-na-kalamu* revolution: A revolution of hoe and pen, the victors over cow and spear, *ngombe na mkuki*.

This long revolution, which went through successive phases, underlies all else in Kenya's modern history. In all the fields of economy, culture, and politics it raised the value of agricultural and horticultural land and produce, and of tree crops like coffee and tea, to the disadvantage of pastoralism. Moreover, the incomes of African farmers financed the growth of Western schooling essential for modern political power, all at the expense of the pastoralists. This was and is a more fundamental and enduring process than one can derive from our conventional chronology. In its later stages, the revolution also fostered the social inequalities inherent in rural capitalism—a process essential to understanding Mau Mau.

But let me give another illustration of what my new periodization suggests, leaving Mau Mau to my next theme, that of context. In the usual three-part periodization of Kenya's history, independence and the end of white settler-dom is, to repeat, generally portrayed as a rupture whose radical possibilities were betrayed into neocolonial dependence by a comprador elite subservient to British culture and interests. My periodization sees not betrayal but conti-nuity. That is because, for me, white-settler farmers played a vital, if unwit-ting, role in the *njembe-na-kalamu* revolution. As with most revolutions, this originated in an event whose full significance was not apparent at the time, when the British expropriated most of the best pastoral land in Maasai and Kalenjin country and handed it on easy terms to white farmers. Rich settlers like Lord Delamere spent a fortune in discovering what could be grown. And, in a later phase, it was largely to protect the settlers from African land hunger that the government, as Joseph Hodge has shown,[18] took steps to raise African smallholder incomes—in a second colonial occupation that, after 1945, gave nationalism much of its funds and nationalists, therefore, an interest to defend.

So continuity was bound to follow independence. Smallholder farming, especially in its tea and coffee zones, had larger markets than for the pas-toralists' beef. This was the dynamo behind independent Kenya's relative economic success. Independence, therefore, saw no economic betrayal but, in combination with the settlement schemes on the former "white highlands," an intensification of the revolution of hoe and pen. Sponsored by a state ruled by the educated sons of peasants rather than pastoralists, cultivators expanded into the pastoral regions that the colonial government had previously sold to white settlers. After regional devolution, *majimbo*, failed to protect the los-ers, much of the oppression and violence of Kenya's recent history can now be seen as counterrevolution, in which leaders of what were once pastoral peoples have tried to match the power and prosperity of the children of hoe and pen.

But in what contexts do real individuals and their personal struggles for respectability, reputation, and satisfaction appear? I take the agrarian revolu-tion as my first context, with the Empire and religion to follow—global con-texts that have helped to shape the lively plurality of today's Kenya.

## PEOPLE AND CONTEXTS

If my revised periodization is to enrich history with humanity, then the *njembe-na-kalamu* revolution must be the first context in which to place our actors. And if, with Mary Mwiandi, we admit that all Kenyans are immigrants, our actors will be not only black but also brown and pink.

In the precolonial centuries, we cannot know who helped to initiate the revolution by introducing, say, maize to central Kenya or who discovered how best to avoid tick fever in cattle. However, Jean Hay's researches in the Luo and Luyia borderlands give us a clue: She found that it was the *women* who bartered seeds and plants with each other across the linguistic frontier, to improve their food security with a responsible householder's experimental care.[19] Historians are often accused of underplaying the role of women; they are essential to this particular story.

But colonial conquest then imposed a state. Its officials were all men—John Ainsworth one of the earliest among them; Maxon's biography of Ainsworth was correctly subtitled "and the making of Kenya."[20] Following the women of western Kenya, Ainsworth was an experimentalist and revolutionary. Before 1914, he tried to protect Nyanza's smallholders—largely the women, left in charge by migrant-worker husbands and sons—from strangulation by white-settler interests. Because he was then duty-bound to coerce African labor in and after the First World War his reputation has suffered but one cannot understand the *njembe-na-kalamu* revolution without him. Or without men like John-Paul Olola, one of the first agricultural assistants, a marvelous example of an official animator, and in 1963 one of my liveliest informants as I researched for my PhD. Between the wars, impatient with their ignorance, Olola harried Luo chiefs into planting new crops; kept his eye on colonial politics by filing in a tin trunk his cuttings from the white settlers' *East African Standard*; and, much later, advised Oginga Odinga on how to enter capitalist commerce.[21] In Central Province, my favorite agrarian revolutionary was the complete opposite of Olola: Koinange wa Mbiyu, an illiterate, polygynous, patron of mission education, the first Kikuyu to own a plough, and to pump water up from a stream to save his wives the labor of water-collection, but also a propertied patron who, more than most, permitted his clients' continued access to some of the many acres that he bought—a senior chief who, unlike many, never lost his people's confidence.

This brings me to Mau Mau—but not to the first person one might name. For I begin with Wanjiru wa Kinyua, who in 1929 wrote to the Kikuyu newspaper, *Muigwithania*, from Ngata Farm. She was nervous, a woman daring to enter the men's political domain.[22] But she illustrates both elements of the *njembe-na-kalamu* revolution: Wanjiru was a squatter, tenant farmer of a white landlord, a hoe-wielding colonist on what had been Maasai ranchland; she was also literate. And there is a third point to notice: Her home address. Twenty years later, Ngata Farm witnessed some of the first Mau Mau initiations conducted in the Rift Valley.

That was because, like other revolutions, the revolution of hoe and pen began to consume its own. In its first phase, until 1940, commercial agriculture exploited extensive methods of cultivation. This was because labor was scarce and land abundant in both the African reserves and in the "European" lands seized from pastoralists. Only about 2 percent of the so-called "white highlands," if also its most fertile area, was taken from the cultivating Kikuyu. At first, the settlers demanded that the government provide them with forced labor. This was never a sustainable solution. White farmers had to learn to act as African patrons. They attracted scarce workers by letting out surplus acres to labor-tenant families, their squatters. Most of these were Kikuyu. African patrons like Koinange also let dependents produce for the market. The interests of white landlords, black patrons, and black workers did not in this first phase conflict. Squatters sweated to cultivate Maasai pasture; they made it their own by right of *kuna*, first clearance. This enabled them to look to a future when they or their children would join heirs with their white landlords. Precolonial clients had had the same hopes as their patrons.

But the context changed: The Empire went to war again. The Second World War created new markets for Kenya; farming became profitable. In this next phase of revolution, it paid to work the land more intensively. Population was growing. Labor was no longer scarce; land was becoming more so. White settlers and African patrons, especially those closest to Nairobi's markets, became rural capitalists. Their dependents lost rights to land-usage. Many squatters and, in the reserves, juniors or tenants lost their hopes of *ithaka na wiathi*, the propertied self-mastery that made one a fully adult householder. Mau Mau members, like the machine-breaking farmworkers of early nineteenth-century England, revolted against this onset of rural capitalism, white and black. The revolution of hoe and pen had started to consume itself. That Mau Mau became more than this, a small imperial war, owes more to two other contexts of Kenya's modern history: the Empire and world religions.

The British Empire was a mosaic of diverse interests and anxieties; Kenya's colonialists, white settlers, had only their own self-interest to consider. The Empire, however, recognized Kenya's Indians as imperial citizens as well as the settlers; it also relied, globally, on the Indian army. For half Kenya's colonial history, the white settlers' chief opposition came not from African nationalism but, indirectly, from what the Empire feared more: The interest that India's own nationalists took in their kinsmen overseas. After 1947 Nehru's India, the first non-white successor to the Empire, was the only strong external supporter of the Kenya African Union.

Nor can one explain the early growth of African exports, years before settlers exported much, without Allidina Visram and Alibhai Jeevanjee. These Indian Muslim traders were even more revolutionary than Ainsworth and Olola. Still less can one explain the startling career of Harry Thuku, that pioneer revolutionary of hoe and pen and leading rural capitalist. His animation of African protest in the early 1920s learned from the struggle between Indians and settlers over Kenya's future.[23] Indians told Thuku that the Empire, unlike Kenya Colony, was a realm of free speech and equal citizenship: London would listen to him as much as to Delamere or Jeevanjee. London did not do so, of course, but this myth of a liberating empire led Johnstone Kenyatta to make his pilgrimage to the Empire's heart in 1929, seeking a share in English freedoms.

The imperial context also explains why Mau Mau became more than a protest against rural capitalism. For the then colonial secretary, Oliver Lyttelton, and Dedan Kimathi shared the same understanding of geopolitics. Lyttelton was struggling to retain Britain's sway over Africa in the Cold War era. Kimathi knew this: He called not only for the release of Seretse Khama and Kabaka Mutesa of Buganda from imperial exile but also compared Mau Mau with the North Koreans and the Vietminh guerillas in what was still called Indo-China.[24] Britain was therefore determined to defeat Mau Mau. Only then could Kenya be decolonized within the western camp. The Mau Mau war was not only a Kikuyu civil war to save self-mastery from the clutches of rural capitalism, nor merely a fight to recover squatter rights of first clearance, nor only a forest conflict between Kimathi's arrogant Parliament and Mathenge's *riigi* vision of independent householders. It was all these things: Kenya's history, to follow Ogot rather than Renan, needs these complications. But it was the imperial need to make decolonization safe that both made the violence of the Mau Mau war so disproportionate and why independent Kenya got the ruling class it did, the so-called Loyalists, often led by rural capitalists busily investing in their children's higher education.[25] Furthermore, Kenyatta's student experience of Moscow in 1930 had made him detest communism as the enemy of self-mastery.

But the Empire, with its Indian and Cold War dimensions, was not Kenya's only external context. The American context, too, appeared first in the mission societies that concentrated on Kenya's pastoral societies. The more spectacular U.S. bid for Kenya's future, seen in Tom Mboya's airlift, accentuated Kenya's ideological divide. But I want to end with the British missionary context. This added the masculine power of the pen to the economic resilience of the women's hoe. More than half Kenyatta's ministers at independence were graduates of the Alliance High School, founded by Protestant mission churches. Indeed, one could chart the lives of many modern Kenyans with a periodization based on the mission-supplied pen alone. My first Kenyan research student, Ben Kipkorir, one of the first literates among his own Marakwet people, alerted us to how many leading Kenyans of the "independence elite" were the children of men and women who were the first either to run away to school, or who as patrons had sponsored the first missionaries in their area.[26]

It is an extraordinary story. It starts with the nineteenth-century *kitoro*, runaway, coastal Christianity. Youths defiant of their parents followed upcountry, the same youths who matured into ethnic patriots between the wars.[27] Independence encouraged the *KiBenzi* or *utajiri*, middle-class, "mainstream" Christianity of today. Few Kenyans know of their first Christian martyr, David Koi, a Church Missionary Society teacher from Giriama, whom Arab slave-owners decapitated in 1882 for daring to run a school for runaway slaves.[28] Why is he not celebrated like the Ganda Christians martyred two years afterward? British missionaries were among the settlers' most vocal critics in the years before Africans raised their voices. My favorites are the Owens of Maseno: Walter Owen, tutor to the first literate Luo politicians— the settlers called him the "archdemon of Kavirondo"—and Olive his wife, once known as *mikayi*, the grandmother who educates a family.[29] Anyone can read the Bible as a revolutionary manifesto, translated by missionaries into many vernaculars. Karari Njama strengthened the morale of his Mau Mau *itungati* by reminding them that they were not the first freedom fighters to suffer: the Israelites had done so centuries earlier.[30]

To mention Henry Okullu, Timothy Njoya, and David Gitari is to remember how much the churches tried to protect citizens against tyranny in the years of Kenya's paranoia, from 1969 to 2002—reliant on a faith and Biblical precedent that had become wholly Kenyan.[31] Mission Christianity did not so much "colonize" African minds, as is sometimes said, as redefine households as the moral core of honor. Can the same be said of charismatic Pentecostalism? I discussed this with my taxi driver, as one does, when last in Nairobi. My cabby, Joseph, was a Catholic from Murang'a. I asked him what he thought of the Prosperity Gospel. He was loud in his disapproval: "God only helps you *when you sweat!*" I wondered how many Kikuyu pioneers had thought the same as they cleared their forests centuries ago—and would they have invoked the Bantu God Murungu, or the Gikuyu Mwene-nyaga, or the Maasai Ngai? And are these Gods the same as the Luo Nyasaye, Islam's Allah, or the Trinity?

This brings me to my conclusion: In which I will try to tie together the need for deep history, the revolution of hoe and pen, and the global context of Kenya's story. I hope this thematic knot will make the past helpful for Kenyans to think with. Two issues seem ripe for reflection, the foundational hybridity of ethnicity and the changing sources and legitimacy of powerful wealth.

First then, what strikes me most about the precolonial past is Mary Mwiandi's truth: The variety of immigrant ancestors for every ethnic group. A century ago, African informants openly admitted this to the first colonial officials. How many young Kenyans have the knowledge or courage to admit to that now? So I make a serious if impractical suggestion: that the Ministry of Education award an annual prize, perhaps to be called the *Karibuni*, "You are all welcome," prize, to the high school student who best illustrates the multiple origins of her or his ethnic group in the style of Daniel Defoe, who wrote the *True-Born Englishman* in 1701, when Britain had a Dutch king, sandwiched between previous French, Welsh, and Scottish dynasties and our present German line:

Thus from a mixture of all kinds began
That het'rogeneous thing, an Englishman:
In eager rapes and furious lust begot
Betwixt a painted Briton and a Scot . . .
In whose hot veins new mixtures quickly ran,
Infus'd betwixt a Saxon and a Dane . . .
Fate jumbled them together, God knows how;
Whate'er they *were* they're true-born English *now* . . .
A true-born Englishman's a contradiction,
In speech an irony, in fact a fiction . . .
Since scarce one family is left alive
Which does not from some *foreigner* derive.

Second, Kenyans might think about how the revolution of hoe and pen transformed the civic virtue of private patronage into the political corruption of public office. Wealthy households used to produce "men of morale and courage," as Jomo Kenyatta put it in *Facing Mount Kenya*—people whose peaceably productive domestic management recommended them as civic leaders in local struggles against nature. How did this civic virtue within scattered moral ethnicities become today's cynical manipulation of competitive political tribalism? How might this consequence be challenged? There are two issues here, arenas of competition and sources of power.

I have suggested that in precolonial times ecological ethnicities had no desire to colonize other people's different environments. Competition for reputation and authority was local; winners proved themselves by their household's mastery of nature, thanks in part to mutually productive relations with clients. Today's competition is unified, focused on access to central state power, little modified by the new constitution. Not to compete is to be ignored. And local power is now derived from political leverage in Nairobi, an influence not easily scrutinized from below.

The history of change in these arenas of competition for reputation and power is the history of Kenya's state-building. It began early; the British needed African allies. As outsiders they had to win what legitimacy they could by appropriating it from such local authority as already existed. But for state power to co-opt indigenous authority was also to corrupt it.[32] For the authority acquired a monopoly of coercive force—provided by police, courts, and prison—unknown to the stateless past. The British also rewarded their allies with opportunities intended to help them manage their old, inter-dependent, social order. But since this help usually entailed exemption from a colonial imposition or access to an official opportunity, factional intrigue flourished. In precolonial times, power had offered fewer prizes. This moral mutation intensified when chiefs and others became rural capitalists, no longer patrons but landlords. Nineteenth-century European state-building had seen struggles to separate public office from social hierarchy. Colonial state-building did the reverse, looking for hierarchy to support public office. Colonial rulers, conscious of their strangeness, needed officials with the social roots of responsible patronage. This conjuncture of contradictory roles contaminated both African wealth and colonial rule.[33]

Here, then, is a history that offers food for thought. If that was how a tradition of social accountability became corrupted, how might its virtue be restored? The alliance of wealth and office is common throughout the world; it would not be easy to disentangle. But Kenyans who know their history are well equipped to consider the problem, in a language of moral and politi-cal responsibility that, I have suggested, is very much their own: It can still embarrass the insolence of wealth in the ballot box.[34] I have argued that, in the "ecological ethnicities" of the past, survival and well-being depended on unequal reciprocities, in which gender, age, wealthy patronage, and dependent clientage, all had a negotiated place. This dialogue between self-mastery, the adult freedom to manage a household, and the unequal ties of community that protected liberty from domination used to be the discursive core of moral ethnicity. Emma Hunter has shown how the inherited argu-ment that social constraint promotes personal freedom has animated political debate in Tanzania.[35] Why not also in Kenya?

I cannot end without asking how the cultures of Kenya's wider contexts influence the different respectabilities and standards of self-conduct or inti-macy, in a Kenyan plurality of being. How, for instance, does one become *muungwana*, a freeborn Muslim, in an era that can barely remember its opposite, slavery? How can one achieve the independent adulthood of being *msomaji, muthomi,* or *jasomo*, a literate, nominally Christian, with a computer-ized pen, if unable to afford the property on which to construct a hoe-wielding household? For the household remains the heart of Kenyan honor, perhaps especially the honor of women. A freeborn Muslim woman at the coast once lived in seclusion, behind doors or, if outside, within an enveloping *buibui*. Upcountry, the mothers of freedom who bared their buttocks to President Moi's police were morally entitled to shock householder honor when this is abused by the men who are expected to protect them.[36] How then are both women equally Kenyan?

I don't know the answers. The history I have sketched may help Kenyans understand some of the origins and the value of this plurality: It is the essence of Kenya today, as of its past—as is true of all other nations. I hope that some Kenyans may see my suggested history as one that helps them reflect on how to live up to the struggles of their past and so work to change the future, to enlarge the political liberties that protect personal freedom.

## NOTES

1. I am grateful for the comments I have received from David Anderson, Nicholas Githuku, Muoki Mbunga, Ian Parker, and Richard Waller, but all responsibility is mine.

2. E. H. Carr, *What is History?* (Harmondsworth: Penguin, 1964), 23. See also a former fellow East Africanist, John Tosh, *Why History Matters* (London: Red Globe Press, 2nd edition, 2019); Eric Hobsbawm, "Ethnicity and Nationalism in Europe Today," *Anthropology Today* 8 (1992), 3–8.

3. Bethwell Allan Ogot, *Who, if Anyone, Owns the Past? Reflections on the Meaning of "Public History"* (Kisumu: Anyange Press, 2010), 20–21.

4. Kathryn Tidrick, "Who Gets to Write History? The Question of 'Legitimacy'" (New Delhi: India International Centre, Occasional Paper 52, 2013); my thanks to Warris Vianni for bringing this to my attention.

5. Ngugi wa Thiong'o, "Foreword," in *Kenya's Freedom Struggle: The Dedan Kimathi Papers*, ed. Maina wa Kinyatti (London: Zed, 1987), xiii.

6. David M. Anderson, "Guilty Secrets: Deceit, Denial, and the Discovery of Kenya's 'Migrated Archive,'" *History Workshop Journal* 80 (2015), 142–60.

7. Ernest Renan, *Quest-ce q'une nation?* (Paris: Sorbonne, 1882).

8. Ogot, *Who, if Anyone?*, 22–29.

9. Nicholas K. Githuku, *Mau Mau Crucible of War: Statehood, National Identity, and Politics of Postcolonial Kenya* (Lanham, MD: Lexington Books, 2016).

10. Robert M. Maxon, *Struggle for Kenya: The Loss and Reassertion of Imperial Initiative, 1912-1923* (Cranbury, NJ: Associated University Presses, 1993).

11. Richard Reid, "Past and Presentism: The 'Precolonial' and the Foreshortening of African History," *Journal of African History* 52 (2011), 135–55.

12. Terence Ranger, "The Invention of Tradition in Colonial Africa," in *The Invention of Tradition*, edited by Eric Hobsbawm and Terence Ranger (Cambridge: Cambridge University Press, 1983), 211–62; for his second thoughts see his chapter in Paris Yeros, *Ethnicity and Nationalism in Africa: Constructivist Reflections and Contemporary Politics* (Basingstoke: Macmillan, 1999), 113–44.

13. Adrian Hastings, *The Construction of Nationhood: Ethnicity, Religion, and Nationalism* (Cambridge: Cambridge University Press, 1997), 149. See also Richard Waller, "Ethnicity and Identity," in *The Oxford Handbook of Modern African History*, edited by John Parker and Richard Reid (Oxford: Oxford University Press, 2013), 94–113.

14. John Lonsdale, "The Moral Economy of Mau Mau," in *Unhappy Valley: Conflict in Kenya and Africa*, by Bruce Berman and John Lonsdale (London: James Currey, 1992), 265–504.

15. Thomas Spear and Richard Waller, eds., *Being Maasai: Ethnicity and Identity in East Africa* (London: James Currey, 1993).

16. David M. Anderson and Michael Bollig, eds., *Resilience and Collapse in African Savannahs* (Abingdon: Routledge, 2017).

17. Richard Waller, "Emutai: Crisis and Response in Maasailand 1883-1902," in *The Ecology of Survival: Case Studies from Northeast African History*, edited by Douglas Johnson and David Anderson (London: Lester Crook, 1988), 73–112.

18. Joseph M. Hodge, *Triumph of the Expert: Agrarian Doctrines and the Legacies of British Colonialism* (Athens, OH: Ohio University Press, 2007).

19. Margaret Jean Hay, "Economic Change in Luoland: Kowe 1890-1945" (PhD diss., University of Wisconsin, 1972).

20. Robert M. Maxon, *John Ainsworth and the Making of Kenya* (Lanham, MD: University Press of America, 1980).

21. Oginga Odinga, *Not Yet Uhuru* (London: Heinemann, 1967), 79.

22. Lonsdale, "Moral Economy of Mau Mau," 320–21.

23. Sana Aiyar, *Indians in Kenya: The Politics of Diaspora* (Cambridge, MA: Harvard University Press, 2015).

24. Julie MacArthur, ed., *Dedan Kimathi on Trial: Colonial Justice and Popular Memory in Kenya's Mau Mau Rebellion* (Athens, OH: Ohio University Press, 2017), 200.

25. David M. Anderson, "Making the Loyalist Bargain: Surrender, Amnesty, and Impunity in Kenya's Decolonization, 1952-63," *International History Review* 39 (2017), 48–70.

26. B. E. Kipkorir, "The Inheritors and the Successors," *Kenya Historical Review* 5 (1977), 143–61.

27. Derek Peterson, *Ethnic Patriotism and the East African Revival: A History of Dissent, c. 1935-1972* (Cambridge: Cambridge University Press, 2012).

28. W. B. Anderson, *The Church in East Africa, 1840-1974* (Nairobi: Uzima Press, 1977), 15–17.

29. Emily Onyango, "Women Leaders Rising Up: A Case Study of the Anglican Church of Kenya 1844-1945," *Mission Theology in the Anglican Communion*: www.missiontheologyanglican.org/article/women-leaders-rising-up-a-case-study-of-the-anglican-church-1844-1945/ accessed April 5, 2019.

30. Donald L. Barnett and Karari Njama, *Mau Mau from Within* (London: MacGibbon & Kee, 1966), 184–85.

31. Henry Okullu, *Church and State in Nation Building and Human Development* (Nairobi: Uzima, 1984); Timothy Njoya, *Out of Silence* (Nairobi: Beyond Magazine, 1987); David Gitari, *In Season and Out of Season: Sermons to a Nation* (Carlisle: Regnum, 1996); Gideon Githiga, *The Church as the Bulwark Against Authoritarianism* (Oxford: Regnum, 2001).

32. John Lonsdale, "The Conquest State of Kenya, 1895-1905," in *Unhappy Valley: Conflict in Kenya and Africa*, by Bruce Berman and John Lonsdale (London: James Currey, 1992), 37–39.

33. Patrick Chabal and Jean-Pascal Daloz, *Africa Works: Disorder as Political Instrument* (Oxford: James Currey 1999), 3–16.

34. Peter Lockwood, "The Buffalo and the Squirrel: Moral Authority and the Limits of Patronage in Kiambu County's 2017 Gubernatorial Race," *Journal of Eastern African Studies* 10 (2019), 1–18.

35. Emma Hunter, *Political Thought and the Public Sphere in Tanzania: Freedom, Democracy, and Citizenship in the Era of Decolonization* (Cambridge: Cambridge University Press, 2015), 11–14.

36. Margaret Strobel, *Muslim Women in Mombasa, 1890-1975* (New Haven: Yale University Press, 1979).

## BIBLIOGRAPHY

Aiyar, Sana. *Indians in Kenya: The Politics of Diaspora*. Cambridge MA: Harvard University Press, 2015.

Anderson, David M. "Guilty Secrets: Deceit, denial, and the Discovery of Kenya's 'Migrated Archive.'" *History Workshop Journal* 80 (2015): 142–60.

———. "Making the Loyalist Bargain: Surrender, Amnesty, and Impunity in Kenya's Decolonization, 1952-63." *International History Review* 39 (2017): 48–70.

——— and Michael Bollig, eds. *Resilience and Collapse in African Savannahs*. Abingdon: Routledge, 2017.

Anderson, W. B. *The Church in East Africa, 1840-1974*. Nairobi: Uzima Press, 1977.

Barnett, Donald L., and Karari Njama. *Mau Mau from Within*. London: MacGibbon & Kee, 1966.

Berman, Bruce, and John Lonsdale. *Unhappy Valley: Conflict in Kenya & Africa*. London: James Currey, 1992.

Chabal, Patrick, and Jean-Pascal Daloz. *Africa Works: Disorder as Political Instrument*. Oxford: James Currey, 1999.

Gitari, David. *In Season and Out of Season: Sermons to a Nation*. Carlisle: Regnum, 1996.

Githiga, Gideon. *The Church as the Bulwark Against Authoritarianism*. Oxford: Regnum, 2001.

Githuku, Nicholas K. *Mau Mau Crucible of War: Statehood, National Identity, and Politics of Postcolonial Kenya*. Lanham, MD: Lexington Books, 2016.

Hastings, Adrian. *The Construction of Nationhood: Ethnicity, Religion, and Nationalism*. Cambridge: Cambridge University Press, 1997.

Hay, Margaret Jean. "Economic change in Luoland: Kowe 1890-1945." PhD diss., University of Wisconsin, 1972.

Hodge, Joseph M. *Triumph of the Expert: Agrarian Doctrines and the Legacies of British Colonialism*. Athens, OH: Ohio University Press, 2007.

Hunter, Emma. *Political Thought and the Public Sphere in Tanzania: Freedom, Democracy and Citizenship in the Era of Decolonization*. Cambridge: Cambridge University Press, 2015.

Kipkorir, B. E. "The Inheritors and the Successors." *Kenya Historical Review* 5 (1977): 143–61.

Lockwood, Peter. "The Buffalo and the Squirrel: Moral Authority and the Limits of Patronage in Kiambu County's 2017 Gubernatorial Race." *Journal of Eastern African Studies* 10 (2019): 1–18.

Lonsdale, John. "The Moral Economy of Mau Mau." In *Unhappy Valley: Conflict in Kenya and Africa*, by Bruce Berman and John Lonsdale (1992): 265–504.

MacArthur, Julie, ed. *Dedan Kimathi on Trial: Colonial Justice and Popular Memory in Kenya's Mau Mau Rebellion*. Athens, OH: Ohio University Press, 2017.

Maxon, Robert M. *John Ainsworth and the Making of Kenya*. Lanham, MD: University Press of America, 1980.

———. *Struggle for Kenya: The Loss and Reassertion of Imperial Initiative, 1912-1923*. Cranbury, NJ: Associated University Presses, 1993.

Njoya, Timothy. *Out of Silence*. Nairobi: Beyond Magazine, 1987.

Odinga, Oginga. *Not Yet Uhuru*. London: Heinemann, 1967.

Ogot, Bethwell. *Who, if Anyone, Owns the Past? Reflections on the Meaning of "Public History."* Kisumu: Anyange Press, 2010.

Okullu, Henry. *Church and State in Nation Building and Human Development*. Nairobi: Uzima, 1984.

Onyango, Emily. "Women Leaders Rising Up: A Case Study of the Anglican Church of Kenya, 1844-1945." *Mission Theology in the Anglican Communion*: www.m issiontheologyanglican.org/article/women-leaders-rising-up-a-case-study-of-the-a nglican-church-1844-1945/ (Accessed 5 April 2019).

Peterson, Derek. *Ethnic Patriotism and the East African Revival: A History of Dissent, c. 1935-1972*. Cambridge: Cambridge University Press, 2012.

Ranger, Terence. "The Invention of Tradition in Colonial Africa." In *The Invention of Tradition*, edited by Eric Hobsbawm and Terence Ranger. Cambridge: Cambridge University Press, 1983: 211–62.

———. "Concluding Comments." In *Ethnicity and Nationalism in Africa: Constructivist Reflections and Contemporary Politics*, edited by Paris Yeros. Basingstoke: Macmillan, 1999: 113–44.

Reid, Richard. "Past and Presentism: The 'Precolonial' and the Foreshortening of African History." *Journal of African History* 52 (2011): 135–55.

Renan, Ernest. *Quest-ce q'une nation?* Paris: Sorbonne, 1982.

Spear, Thomas, and Richard Waller, eds. *Being Maasai: Ethnicity and Identity in East Africa*. London: James Currey, 1993.

Strobel, Margaret. *Muslim Women in Mombasa, 1890-1975*. New Haven: Yale University Press, 1979.

Tidrick, Kathryn. "Who Gets to Write History? The Question of 'Legitimacy'." New Delhi: India International Centre, Occasional Paper 52 (2013).

Wa Kinyatti, Maina, ed. *Kenya's Freedom Struggle: The Dedan Kimathi Papers*. London: Zed, 1987.

Wa Thiong'o, Ngugi. "Foreword." In *Kenya's Freedom Struggle: The Dedan Kimathi Papers*, edited by Maina Wa Kinyatti. London: Zed, 1987.

Waller, Richard. "Emutai: Crisis and Response in Maasailand, 1883-1902." In *The Ecology of Survival: Case Studies from Northeast African History*, edited by Douglas Johnson and David Anderson. London: Lester Crook, 1988: 73–112.

———. "Ethnicity and Identity." In *The Oxford Handbook of Modern African History*, edited by John Parker and Richard Reid. Oxford: Oxford University Press, 2013: 94–113.

*Chapter 2*

# From the Upper Delaware River to the Banks of the Monongahela via Lake Victoria

Robert M. Maxon

This brief account of a career in higher education links two continents in a journey of personal and intellectual enlightenment and fulfillment. It is the story of an individual growing up in upstate New York, then taking an unusual academic and career path that led to the Lake Victoria basin on the eve of Kenya's independence, back to New York in the mid-1960s, to western Kenya for dissertation research, and finally to the banks of the Monongahela River in Morgantown, West Virginia. This is written at the end of 50 years as a member of the History faculty at West Virginia University.

## FOUNDATIONAL EXPERIENCES

The beginning point of this journey is listed in official records as Oneonta, New York, which sits on the banks of the Susquehanna, not the Delaware, and reflects my parents' choice of hospital for their firstborn. At that time, my parents were living in Andes, New York, a few miles away from the east branch of the Delaware. My father was a physical education teacher at Andes Central School. Interestingly, Andes was his mother's (also a teacher) hometown, while my father grew up a few miles to the east, and across some substantial hills, in the village of Bloomville on the West branch of the Delaware.

Bloomville is where I spent my formative years. This farming village opened its first high school during the Great Depression. There, in 1932, my mother Isabelle Mead, a Syracuse University graduate, began her career as a history and civics teacher and girls basketball coach. My father, a graduate of Ithaca College, taught part-time at the Bloomville High School but moved to Andes in 1936 to take a full-time position as a physical education

21

teacher and coach. My parents married in 1937; I arrived on the scene two years later.

Over the next few years, we moved around as my father changed teaching assignments. When we returned to my father's hometown in 1948, I entered grade four in the then Bloomville elementary school in the South Kortright Central School district, completing high school at age 17 in 1957. My great passion during these growing years was not academics; however, it was sports, particularly baseball.

My mother's interest in, and knowledge of, history was also an important influence on this sports enthusiast. She kept several of the books she used in her university courses, and these formed a part of my reading fare growing up. The books dealt with American and European history with little or no reference to Africa. I had few opportunities to learn about that continent's history.

By the end of my high school years, I was fixed on history as my favorite subject and the focus of further study in college. My parents had always made it clear that I was expected to go to a research university, which was not the norm for most of my fellow students in our rural area. The emphasis on history as a subject and a career as a teacher led to a desire to combine teaching history/social studies with coaching sports such as basketball, baseball, and soccer. The high school I attended offered soccer as a fall sport, rather than American football.

The mention of soccer as well as basketball and baseball, at this point, is important for its impact on my life and career. At the start of my third year in high school, however, our soccer coach (who was also the basketball coach) told me that I must join the soccer team if I wanted to play varsity basketball. He stressed that it would provide needed fitness. I got to play as a starter on the team, though not as a goalkeeper as I wanted.

The experience did lead to my joining the varsity team in basketball, though not as a starter. The team did well despite changes in coaches during the school year. Fortunately for me, the new coach took it upon himself to encourage and work with me to improve my basketball skills. This led the way to my senior year in high school. For me, it was the proverbial story of the one-year-wonder. I was fortunate to set school records in scoring, both for the season and for a single game. This wonder was recruited by some small colleges and two major universities, Duke and Syracuse. For most, the coaches had a connection with my father from his days as a coach and referee. He was much sold on Duke after a visit in early1957. I visited in April and was guaranteed a place on the Freshman basketball team as a "walk on." Syracuse was interested in me to do the same thing, but my father believed that the coaches at Duke, both of whom had roots in upstate New York, were better teachers and role models. As things turned out, both Duke and Syracuse had critical roles to play in my academic development.

My journey to Durham, North Carolina, in September 1957 opened a new chapter in my education and career preparation. It was at first a tough transition, far away from where I grew up. I played sparingly on the Freshman basketball team and did not even try out for the soccer team. That Freshman year was my only participation in sports at Duke. Academically, I was determined to major in History, and the highlight of my first year was my History course. It was Western civilization taught by Dr. Frederic Hollyday. This quickly became a not-to-be-missed class. Doc Hollyday was a brilliant lecturer who combined a gift for narrative with critical insights. He held the attention of his class by delving into what some might term historical trivia. Later, I patterned my approach to class lectures after Doc Hollyday. When it came time to take upper-division courses in my third year at Duke, I was most happy to be able to take his two-semester history of nineteenth-century Europe. During both semesters, there was not an empty seat in the classroom.

It was at the end of my Freshman year that I received an initial suggestion that Africa might be a possible field of study. It came in the form of a speech at the 1958 South Kortright graduation ceremonies. The featured speaker was our then member of the House of Representatives, Katherine St. George. She told those in attendance what she experienced in attending Ghana's independence celebrations the previous year. She was struck by the enthusiasm among Ghanaians who were now free of colonial rule, and urged that Africa would become increasingly important in world affairs in the second half of the century. Thus Americans needed to know more about the continent. I have always remembered this speech as I made Africa the focus of my life's work, though it did not lead me to immediately change my interest in European history.

My third year at Duke was my most successful academically as I took mostly history and political science courses. In addition to the two nineteenth-century Europe courses, I took the two-semester Russia survey with my faculty advisor, Professor John S. Curtiss. The two courses were fully enrolled, not surprising for the 1959–1960 academic year, with the Cold War raging. Professor Curtiss always had his lectures well planned and his exams challenging but fair. Perhaps it was my performance in the two classes, but Professor Curtiss saw some potential in me for further study, more than I did myself, at the end of that year. His advice to me then, and in the following year, was to undertake graduate study in History. It took a bit of time for that to sink in and for me to believe that his confidence in me was justified.

However, I was intent on high school teaching and coaching and planned to take education classes and practice teaching in my final year as an undergraduate. Spring semester 1961 practice teaching experience took me to New Hanover High School in Wilmington, NC, a site distant from the Duke campus in several respects. The segregated high school and city were in the midst of growing protests related to the civil rights movement in the American south. For me, it was interesting in several ways, not least of which is teaching social studies classes that focused on state and local government while assisting the baseball coaches and supervising some PE classes and after-school activities in the gym. I had been brought up to believe in human equality in every respect, and while those beliefs were challenged at Duke, practice teaching introduced new elements in the form of racial discrimination almost daily.

While in Wilmington, moreover, my future was shaped in a significant way as I was offered the chance to join the initial group of Americans to serve as a high school teacher in then British East Africa through the Teachers for East Africa (TEA) program. This life-changing experience resulted from concern over what I should do after graduation. By the start of practice teaching, I had concluded that the best way to obtain a permanent teaching certification was to obtain a master's degree in education before going into the job market. Thus I began 1961 by applying to Teachers College, Columbia University, and to Syracuse for financial aid and admission. Shortly after the start of the semester, I noticed a call for applications to TEA, a new initiative of the U.S. government to be administered by Teachers College. I gave the matter some thought and applied. It seemed like an opportunity to do something constructive by working in Africa.

To be truthful, I knew little about the continent and even less about East Africa (which according to the program information included Kenya, Tanganyika, Uganda, and Zanzibar). At Duke, the scramble for Africa was touched upon in my European history classes, but mainly from the perspective of the motives and actions of European nations involved. Only in my junior year, did I take a political science class in international relations that focused on more than a cursory study of Africa. The professor who taught the class was not a trained Africanist but one of many scholars who recognized the potential importance of Africa in world affairs and the need for college-educated Americans to know more about the continent. It was through this experience that I first was introduced to detailed information on Kenya, notably from the pages of John Hatch's *Africa Today and Tomorrow*. This class experience was a factor in my application to TEA, but certainly not the major reason.

Nevertheless, the application for acceptance into TEA soon assumed greater significance. It was not long after I started my practice teaching at the end of March that I received first a rejection letter from Syracuse with regard to financial aid and admission. This was soon followed by a letter from Teacher's College stating they were unable to offer any form of support for graduate work. These rejections seemed to leave me with only the TEA possibility or seeking a teaching job. I was not optimistic about being accepted given these rejections. There was plenty to keep me busy in my first teaching experience, and I had less time to consider what seemed to have been failed initiatives. Then came an April 14, 1961, telegram from the TEA administrator which reached me in Wilmington via Durham. I was to report for an oral interview in Chapel Hill on the campus of the University of North Carolina in two days (a Saturday). In the pre-interstate era, this meant a difficult trip.

I could not make a bus connection but was able to borrow a car and made the trip in time for the Saturday afternoon interview. From my perspective, the interview went poorly as I had little time to prepare. Thus upon my return to student teaching, I mentally wrote off the option of teaching in East Africa as another closed opportunity. I was more than a little surprised to receive news, a month later, that I had been accepted for the TEA program. I quickly returned my acceptance as the chance to travel and work abroad now seemed the best option for the next two years. As things worked out, this proved a momentous decision so far as my life and career were concerned. Following graduation, I returned to Bloomville to prepare for the start of teaching in East Africa.

## FIRST EXPERIENCES IN EAST AFRICA

The latter did not actually begin until January 1962 as I spent the summer months at Columbia followed by a month at the University of London Institute of Education and October to December at then Makerere College in Kampala, Uganda. I was included in Group C of the inaugural TEA volunteers; this was for those who had completed teacher training in the United States but had yet to hold a teaching job. We arrived at Kampala, near the north shore of Lake Victoria, and undertook further preparation for teaching with a specific focus on East Africa.

I had yet to learn what my teaching assignment would be or where I would be teaching. This first experience in Africa came via taking classes and living in a college dormitory. We also were able to experience Kampala life as Uganda moved toward independence. The critical 1961 pre-independence constitutional conference was taking place in London as my group arrived. We were able to witness the return of the Kabaka of Buganda from the conference to great adulation from the populace of the city.

As I attended classes, I decided to focus on history and physical education as the courses I would prepare to teach. I attended classes geared toward those disciplines, and I also gained my first exposure to East African history in Professor Kenneth Ingham's class which focused on the scramble for East Africa and the British and German takeover. The class certainly heightened my interest. Professor Ingham, then head of the Makerere History department, was most impressive as he presented his lectures with no notes whatsoever, something I had never experienced in any university history class.

This initial experience in East Africa was quite significant in many ways. There was a culture shock, as we had been warned might be the case during our orientation in New York. This included greetings and personal interactions as well as bargaining in stores. We were treated to a much different diet in the residence halls (I stayed in University Hall) than that of most mid-century Americans. Most of the students at Makerere were friendly and receptive, and we were made welcome on campus. This was particularly the case with several students from Kenya whom I got to know and connected with later through my posting to that country. I was able to play basketball regularly and was chosen as a member of the Makerere basketball team for the university games held in Nairobi in December.

By the start of November, we received our school assignments. Mine was a school in western Kenya. I had not expressed any preference as to country or school, unlike most of my colleagues who wished to teach in Uganda or Tanganyika. This set me on a course that led to an interest in Kenya that became the focus of my career. As a matter of fact, only a few of the first TEA contingent were posted to teach in Kenya. My first visit to Kenya followed the appointment as fellow TEA volunteer Dale Otto and myself traveled to Kisumu by lake steamer for a weekend visit. We got to know the school and more specifics on our assignments as well as the then western Kenya roads swamped by the extraordinary rains in the second rainy season of that year. My second visit was by train from Kampala as part of the Makerere contingent for the annual university games with the then Royal College. I saw a bit of Nairobi as a result, but I had little opportunity to meet many ordinary Kenyans as the capital seemed to me to be very colonial in terms of continuing segregated facilities.

These experiences opened the way to three years in Kenya, an influential sojourn in many ways. I spent two years as an Education Officer (high school teacher) at Chavakali High School and a third year at Kakamega Secondary School. Chavakali, 20 miles from Nyanza Gulf of Lake Victoria and at 5,000 feet above sea level, was a day secondary, *harambee* (self-help) school in then North Nyanza district (Vihiga County today) while Kakamega (at 5,100 feet), the regional headquarters for Western Region when I was there, was an established boarding school with a fifth form (science and math) on the British model. I taught History at both schools as well as English language and literature, biology, geography, and Swahili (Form 1 at Kakamega). I served as games master at both schools.

At those two schools, I learned a lot about Kenya and western Kenya in particular. At Chavakali, for example, teachers lived in close proximity to the local population, and this enabled much cross-cultural learning. I became increasingly proficient in the Swahili language while there, and it was also there that I had my first teaching success through the good performance of the students who undertook the Cambridge Overseas History exam in 1963. My move to Kakamega in 1964 allowed me to have experience at a boarding school and also to continue my interest in sports. There, as in Chavakali, I played soccer as a member of the famous North Nyanza team as well as for Kakamega Black Stars in the Kenya National Football League and Harambee Maseno in the Kenya FA Cup. Most significant also during these three years, I met my wife as a result of soccer playing and thus established a permanent link with this part of western Kenya.

My Kenyan soccer career led to other significant experiences that involved cross-cultural education and growth as a person. Understanding other cultures and improving my knowledge of Swahili helped to develop skills and interests that furthered my academic career. Communicating with teammates on the field and in pre-game sessions was significant as I quickly concluded that since a majority of my teammates did not speak fluent English, I would have to adapt rather than ask for a translator. As can be guessed from the teams listed above, I was the first European to play for these sides, thus participating at the end of segregation in sport that had marked Kenya's previous history. This came with numerous challenges, but only a couple will be mentioned here. One of the first newspaper reports of my matches in Swahili newspapers referred to me by name and then the descriptive phrase *"ambaye ni mzungu"* (who is a European/white person). I raised this description to a reporter who was based in Kakamega, and told him that I was an American, not a European as I did not want to be identified as a colonialist or colonial official. To my satisfaction, his next match report included *"ambaye ni mwamerika,"* but for fans of all ages I was, and remained, *mzungu* on the soccer pitch.

A second example of language experience also emerged from reports in the Swahili newspapers (*Taifa Leo* and *Baraza*) which involved learning respect for cultural nuances. My goalkeeping style was such as to cause more than one sports reporter to describe me as *nyani tupu* or just *nyani*. The dictionary I consulted gave the English meaning as ape or baboon (*nyani tupu* can be understood as a raw or wild baboon or naked ape). I was a bit concerned since I had gone to college in the American south and understood that such words were part of racist language directed against Black people and African-American athletes, in particular. I wondered if I was being characterized in a similar fashion and was concerned that I was perceived by some as a baboon. After a team practice, I, therefore, confronted a local journalist who had used the words. He responded that I should not be upset as that description was not meant to be negative in any way. To play like a *nyani* when describing a goalkeeper was a great compliment! I was not convinced at first, but several of my teammates told me the same thing. Our team captain took me aside to explain that was fine if our opponents thought that I was a good enough player to deserve such a nickname. Needless to say, I afterward put my reservations aside and would only add that over many years my wife still refers to me as *nyani tupu*.

1964 proved a particularly busy and productive year as time flew by and not just through playing soccer on three teams as I taught an additional Swahili class and served as a sponsor for the school's historical society. By the second half of the year, I had decided to pursue graduate work in history rather than in education. College teaching was now my career goal. I narrowed my graduate school choices to UCLA and Wisconsin for African history, and had in mind possible topics for research in grad school. These were influenced by the three years I had spent in western Kenya, but not completely so. I was interested in the history of the Luyia people as well as that of the region encompassed by then Nyanza Province. My time in Kakamega produced an interest in the gold rush of the 1930s as there were still visible links to that era 30 years later. In terms of specifics, I was thinking along the lines of political and administrative history.

## GRADUATE SCHOOL

I returned to the United States in time to spend Christmas with my family, but 1965 brought choices to be made. The American intervention in Vietnam was broadening and military service was an option for someone of my age. I also wished to finalize a choice of graduate school so as to start in the Fall Semester. I decided not to undertake the military option, and enrolled at SUNY Oneonta (25 miles from my family home) as a full-time graduate student. During that semester, I received admission to both Wisconsin and UCLA, though without financial aid in either case.

Wisconsin was my first choice, due to the presence of Philip Curtin and Jan Vansina, two pioneers in the emerging field of African History. I was accepted there to study South Asian history. I was disappointed but felt I could still focus my studies on South Asians and East Africa. On a visit to Madison, I met neither Professor Curtin nor Vansina and learned that I would need to focus strictly on South Asian history. Thus I returned to Bloomville now planning to attend UCLA. The African history faculty there made it clear that I should be able to pass one of the required African language exams in my first year. I thought that I could, but to make doubly sure I decided to enroll in the Swahili course offered by the Program of Eastern African Studies (PEAS) at Syracuse during the first summer session. That decision moved me in a new direction.

Upon starting the class at Syracuse, I was able to demonstrate competency, and PEAS offered me a graduate teaching assistantship for the coming academic year. The Peace Corps had awarded the university contracts to organize and carry out training programs for Tanzania and other African counties. Individuals able to teach Swahili were in demand. I had to make a hasty decision that turned out to be a great one for me. This meant applying to the History department at Syracuse and getting accepted in record time while assisting with a Peace Corps trainee group. With the PEAS leadership pressing for my admission, I was fortunate also that Dr. Curtiss was a colleague of then chair of the Syracuse History department, Professor Warren Walsh. I was able to enroll for the start of the Fall Semester. Besides an assistantship, my decision to attend Syracuse was a result of family health concerns. It did not seem a good idea to travel across the country for further study in light of those.

Nevertheless, my first year at Syracuse was influenced by the fact that the department had no African historian. I thus took the nineteenth- and twentieth-century European history courses as well as a seminar in East African politics. Africa and modern Europe became two graduate fields; later, I decided on a field in modern British history as a supplement to my interest in colonial Kenya. Despite the fact that I was unable to take African history courses, I undertook research papers for the politics and European imperialism seminars based on several primary sources. Without doubt, my most significant experience during the first year was coming under the guidance of Professor Fred Burke, head of PEAS. A political scientist, Professor Burke was an early specialist in Eastern Africa, who was an excellent role model and mentor. He promised that a historian specializing in East Africa would be hired for the 1966–1967 academic year, and this was the case. I also owe a huge debt to Professor Burke for his professional and personal advice during my time at Syracuse.

The arrival of Professor Robert Gregory in September 1966 provided me with a valued mentor and role model. Dr. Gregory had studied British imperial history at UCLA, but, like others of his generation, he transitioned to African history since his first book focused on imperial policy toward the East African region. A few months prior to his arrival, the Syracuse library had obtained microfilms of a substantial portion of the Kenya National Archives (KNA). These two events propelled me on the way to a career in research on Kenya. For example, I used the archival material to write a seminar paper on the Kakamega gold rush during my second year. Even more significant, Dr. Gregory received a National Science Foundation grant to publish a guide to the KNA microfilms, and I worked as a research assistant during my third year in graduate school.

In addition, I spent increasing time during my second and third years considering an appropriate dissertation topic as well as career and life choices. The first of these was the result of the fact that I had been allowed to skip the master's thesis and go directly to complete a PhD via course work and a dissertation. Professor Walsh offered me this chance, and I took it. He also urged me to give up African History as an unimportant field that was only a passing fad and focus on European history. I am thankful I declined to do that.

As for life choices, by the end of 1967, I became engaged to a young woman I had met while teaching in Kenya, Felicia Ayiro. She was then studying nursing in England, and we planned to live and work in Kenya following marriage. I hoped to be able to obtain a teaching post at the University of Nairobi and my fields of study as well as research interests reflected that plan.

With regard to the dissertation, I considered several research topics which, as in other fields within African History, would make a young scholar first in line for research and the creation of new knowledge. Among the topics I was drawn to were the conquest and establishment of colonial rule in Kenya, the origins of European settlement, the conquest and establishment of colonial rule in western Kenya, particularly among the Luyia subtribes, and the political history of what became Western Province at independence. The political emphasis reflected a relative lack of interest in economic and social history.

By 1968, all those potential research topics had been closed as a result of research and publication by other scholars. For example, Dr. Gideon Were, one of the first Kenyans to earn a PhD in history, included the start of colonial rule in his history of the Luyia, and the colonial era political history of the Nyanza region was researched by Dr. John Lonsdale. I was also aware that any proposal to conduct historical research in Kenya would have to be approved by Professor B. A. Ogot, head of the Nairobi University History department. He wished scholars to choose topics and regions that had not been the focus of scholarly research. I had to move quickly to choose an area and a topic that fit the realities of the situation.

My choice was the colonial history of the Gusii (known as the Kisii in colonial times) people of southwestern Kenya. I felt that there were several good reasons for this, despite the fact that I had visited Kisii District (today roughly the area encompassed by Kisii and Nyamira counties) a grand total of one time during my three years as a teacher. First, the late conquest of the Gusii, meant that colonial rule started in 1907, later than other parts of Nyanza, and all the relevant archival records were in Kenya and Britain. Second, I had become familiar with those archival records as a result of research for a guide to the KNA microfilms. Third, Gusiiland or the Gusii highlands region had been the focus of study by two western anthropologists whose publications provided a good grounding for the study of the people's history. Finally, I was encouraged by two Syracuse graduate students from Gusiiland. One, Dr. Zachery Onyonka, was most helpful to me in gaining research clearance and assisting me with research in the field. I was fortunate to pass the oral qualifying exams for doctoral candidacy and to receive support for my research project, which I had titled British rule in Gusiiland, in the form of a Fulbright award and a Shell International Fellowship.

## BACK TO KENYA

Having received research clearance, I arrived in Kenya on Kenyatta day 1968 together with my wife and infant daughter. I had done some research at the Public Record Office (PRO), London, particularly investigating records of the Gusii resistance to colonial control in 1905, 1908, and 1914. We decided to make Nairobi our home base as Felicia quickly got a job as one of the few African-registered nurses at Nairobi Hospital. It was not long after I began archival research that I realized that I had set a very ambitious goal in seeking to cover the whole of the experience of the Gusii under colonial rule in my dissertation research. There was a much more extensive archival record than I had anticipated, to say nothing about field research in the form of oral interviews.

Researching the colonial experience of the Gusii (1907–1963) was to be a challenge, and indeed this research would take up a substantial portion of my career. Perhaps the best example was/is Gusii economic history. The archival documents were numerous and detailed as Gusiiland was the site of the initial government-approved coffee cultivation by Africans, and the region also became an important producer of maize, bananas, pyrethrum, and tea. I thus was forced to give more attention and study to economic history. A particularly valuable source were the records of the Nyanza Province agricultural department. Titled Agriculture Kisumu in the archives, I was one of the first scholars to utilize these records, and I am pleased that they have been an important research resource for myself and several of the graduate students I supervised at West Virginia and Moi universities.

The struggle to get as much archival and field research completed by the end of my grant support (July 1969) meant that I did not really get a start on writing the dissertation, though it had been my intention to complete and defend it by that time. The end result was to have been a job in Kenya starting in August or September. Suffice it to say that these plans did not work out. I could not get a teaching job at Nairobi University since I had only a bachelor's degree. Then, rather unexpectedly, came the job offer at a research university in the United States. I have Dr. Gregory to thank for this since it was he who met the then acting provost of West Virginia University (WVU), Dr. Robert Munn, in Nairobi. I was at first pleasantly surprised to receive a letter from the WVU History department asking me to submit an application for a teaching position. I did so with little expectation that I would receive an offer of a job, given my degree status. Thus, I was surprised when I received the offer of a tenure-track position. The letter arrived a day or two before I was to go to the field for two weeks, and Felicia and I had not made a decision. Upon my return to Nairobi, I found a telegram requesting an immediate response to the job offer. I sent back a telegram accepting the post. There remained much to be done for research in western Kenya as well as in the Nairobi archives.

With my appointment in mind, I began work on a paper that might be published as an article; the subject was the start of coffee growing in the Gusii highlands. I also sought to broaden my understanding of the evidence I had collected. I was most fortunate to have the counsel of Professor Ogot who helped to point me in the right direction with regard to interpretation as well as suggestions for further investigation. It was he who put me in touch with two other scholars whose influence on my career proved to be substantial: William Ochieng' and E. S. Atieno Odhiambo, both then doctoral students at the University of Nairobi. Ochieng' was particularly helpful as his dissertation research focused on Gusii traditional history. Our meeting marked the beginning of a scholarly collaboration and a lasting friendship. Both were a source of inspiration and advice during my career. It is sad to note that both have passed away, though their legacy lives on through their many publications on Kenyan history. Professor Ogot remains a most esteemed mentor. It was one of the proudest moments in my career to have received from him, as chancellor of Moi University, an honorary degree in December 2010.

## TO THE BANKS OF THE MONONGAHELA

July 1969 came all too soon, and it was off to WVU with detours to carry out further field research in the Lake Victoria region and at the PRO. Prior to leaving Kenya, I told my father-in-law that we would stay in the United States for three years and then return to work and live in Kenya. We arrived at the banks of the Monongahela after the start of Fall Semester classes as WVU, unlike Syracuse, began classes in August.

My teaching assignment was two sections of the Western civilization survey (to 1600) and an upper-division course, English history to 1660. The latter had 100 students enrolled, but the department took mercy on me by splitting the class in half. This first academic year in Morgantown proved challenging in several ways. The class preparations were time-consuming and I also had to create new courses in African history and get those approved. I worked hard on weekends and nights to get the first draft of my dissertation completed. I also completed a paper for submission to the 1969 East African social science conference. At Professor Ogot's suggestion, the subject was the 1908 Gusii resistance to colonial rule and its brutal suppression. I was not able to attend the conference, but the paper led to a request from the then editor of the *Transafrican Journal of History* to revise and submit it as an article.

My second year at WVU brought new opportunities and challenges. I continued to teach the Western civilization survey, with a two-semester survey of African history as my upper-division courses. The latter were not only open to undergraduates, but graduate students also enrolled. This helped to expand enrollment to acceptable levels and gave me the chance to work with graduate students, something I had never anticipated when I started graduate school. As we moved forward, four students completed the master's degrees with a field in African history, and three followed up by a field in African history for the doctorate. It was my privilege to supervise the dissertations of all three. Two of these, completed by Duke Talbot and Jake Seitz, were on Kenyan topics. Both were of interest to me, and Duke's study of 1930s African agriculture in Kenya helped to push me in that direction and toward Kenyan economic history more broadly. The third, Carl Hunt, completed a dissertation on an African diaspora topic. Dr. Hunt was the first of many African-American and African students to complete the program at WVU. 1971 also proved significant for me as I was finally able to defend my dissertation, though I did not officially graduate until the following year.

I was thus fortunate to be able to continue to teach and work with graduate students. My superiors at WVU were more than patient, perhaps because I was able to publish the coffee article and coauthor a guide to the KNA. In fact, the department put me up for early promotion in both 1972 and 1973, though this was vetoed by college and/or university administrators. Promotion to associate professor with tenure finally came in 1974. This was certainly welcome, and by that time I had added another research interest to that of the Gusii experience under colonial rule. I was still convinced that I did not have enough material to turn the dissertation into a book, and some colleagues told me that a book on Gusii history would not sell in the existing market for academic books.

## RESEARCH AND PUBLICATION AND ADVANCE IN ACADEMIA

This new research interest was the career of John Ainsworth, an influential early British administrator in Kenya. I began in earnest during a family trip to Kenya in the summer of 1972 (as per the commitment to my in-laws). I used the time for further archival investigation on Gusii colonial history as well. The question for me was which would lead most rapidly to the publication of a book that would bring about a promotion to professor, and I eventually concluded that a book on Ainsworth was more feasible. Following summer trips to Britain and research at Rhodes House in Oxford and the PRO, I had completed a manuscript by the time of my first sabbatical during Spring Semester 1979. I was fortunate to receive a fellowship from the U.S. Office of Education that allowed me and my family to stay in Kenya until July. The research topic the sabbatical and the grant supported was imperial policy toward Kenya before, during, and after the First World War. I envisioned it leading to a book that would end with the Devonshire Declaration of 1923.

However, I did not spend all my time researching that subject. Far from it, I revised my draft of the Ainsworth book. Having talked to one of the staff at the Kenya Literature Bureau (who was Gusii), I now felt more optimistic that my dissertation could become a book, and devoted some of my time to that end. I expended more effort, however, in writing a draft of a history of East Africa from earliest times to the end of the 1970s. I and a Kenyan colleague in the United States had agreed on a plan to publish a textbook for use in our classes and elsewhere detailing the histories of East and Central Africa. I completed a draft of the East African segment of the book by the time I returned to the United States. We submitted our manuscript for our two-volume history to several publishers, but it was turned down on the basis of cost and probable lack of demand.

As a result, I put it and the potential Gusii colonial history book on the back burner, and moved forward with the book on Ainsworth's career. After some canvassing, the University Press of America agreed to publish it in 1980. This book, together with a coauthored article from the Ainsworth research and two drawn from my Gusii research earned a promotion to full professor in 1982. That opened the door to a much more productive period of my scholarly career than before.

## NEW PUBLISHING INITIATIVES

One reason for this was my focus on finally moving my dissertation to publication as a book and as a textbook on East Africa. The latter came about first as my patron, Dr. Munn, agreed, as head of WVU Press, to publish the book as long as it was no more than 300 pages. It was published in 1986 after Dr. Munn's unfortunate death, but it has since then gone through two further editions (1994 and 2009), East African (1989 and 1994), and Chinese (2010) editions. The Gusii history was published by Fairleigh Dickinson University Press in 1989. The decade also witnessed the publication of two articles from my Gusii research and three from research on imperial relations. A final aspect of my 1980s scholarship emerged as a result of now Professor Ochieng's interest and concern that university undergraduate and graduate students in Kenya and elsewhere did not have sufficient and up-to-date books and articles to support advanced study. This led him to conceive and edit several books beginning in 1989. He asked me to contribute chapters on a variety of issues; some reflected my previous interests and expertise, but others forced me to expand my knowledge. The first of these was a chapter in *A Modern History of Kenya*. It detailed Kenya's history in the 1920s for which I was able to use research done on imperial relations.

In addition to this, the 1980s brought additional challenges and opportunities my way. I supervised two doctoral students during the decade, and both (Tom Ofcansky and Amos Beyan) came to WVU with well-defined dissertation topics. By the time Amos completed his degree requirements, I was serving as a department chair (1983–1989). While chair, circumstances propelled me to increase my efforts to bring out publications. As noted earlier, I had already done a good deal of work in drafting possible articles and books, and it now proved valuable in terms of the publications above. Three of my 1980s publications came from the research on imperial relations; two were published in the *Journal of Imperial and Commonwealth History (JICH)* and one in the *Transafrican Journal of History* during the 1980s. The last of these, appearing in 1989, coincided with the start of a major change in my scholarly trajectory.

## FIRST MOI UNIVERSITY INTERLUDE

This came about as a result of a sabbatical spent (1989–1990) at Moi University outside Eldoret, Kenya. I had long wished such a long sabbatical in Kenya. Fortunately for me, Professor Ochieng' had moved to the new university as head of the History department there. He arranged for me to join the new department. Neil Bucklew, then WVU president, was also very supportive of this as a means of building international connections. I thus arrived at the Moi campus, then still under construction, in August 1989.

My one year there proved productive in many ways. In addition to teaching undergraduates, I helped start the graduate program for the History department. Another result was to begin an increased enrollment of doctoral students studying under my supervision at WVU. I had supervised five doctorates prior to 1990; afterward, I was privileged to supervise 23. One of those five was an African; after that time the majority of those supervised were from Kenya and other African countries. This was the result of a link between WVU and Moi University that later expanded to include Maseno University, the University of Nairobi, the Catholic University of Eastern Africa, and Masinde Muliro University of Science and Technology. The linkage provided for faculty at those institutions to come to WVU to complete a doctoral degree in History with the institutions jointly providing financial support. A key element in this linkage was the need to rapidly expand teaching and research capacity at Kenyan universities in light of the rapid growth of the number of such institutions and student enrollment in the 1980s and 1990s. The Kenya universities provided the participating faculty with study leave which included support for travel expenses and keeping the individuals on salary during their time in the United States, while WVU provided graduate teaching assistantships and travel support for research and attendance at professional conferences. Later we were able to recruit promising Kenyan scholars who were not employed by one of their universities to come to WVU with the support of teaching assistantships here.

Finally, the research results of the sabbatical enabled me to complete the book that became *Struggle for Kenya* as well as to contribute to several influential research initiatives. Among these was the publication of an influential economic history of Kenya and *Decolonization and Independence in Kenya, 1940–1993*. Professor Ochieng' had already assigned me several chapters for the first book, and I had completed drafts. After arrival at the university, he tasked me to write further chapters on economic history. Because of his heavy responsibilities as dean in charge of graduate studies, I assumed much of the editing work for the volume in preparing the book for the publisher. This was a valuable experience, and I was gratified that Bill decided to include me on the title page as coeditor. My initial contribution to the decolonization and independence book, on the other hand, was a chapter on social and cultural change during the Kenyatta years (1963–1978) and later a coauthored chapter on Kenya's economy during the initial years of the Moi presidency. I wrote the former at Moi University and the latter at WVU after my return from sabbatical. Social history was relatively new to me, but I followed the dictates of the editor in terms of the topics to be covered. However, it was my decision to rely quite heavily on quantitative data just as I had done for my chapters in *An Economic History of Kenya*.

## ECONOMIC HISTORY EMPHASIS

Both these books, published in the 1990s, have been influential if one counts the number of citations for the chapters I wrote. The social and cultural chapter is also noteworthy for having been plagiarized by none other than Kenya's second president, Daniel arap Moi, as part of a December 1999 speech. Earlier, in 1993, I published *Struggle for Kenya* after my return to WVU. I was pleased that Fairleigh Dickinson (and Associated University Presses) were willing to publish it. This reassessment of imperial policy and its motivation, culminating in the Devonshire Declaration of 1923 is, according to some colleagues, among my best contributions.

By the time it was finished, I had transitioned to colonial economic history in the Lake Victoria basin. I believed that this was important in light of Kenya's economic situation in the 1990s and later, and my investigations in the KNA revealed huge, unused sources, some of which had only recently been added to the archives. I decided to focus my work on the Gusii highlands as there was still much for historians and policy-makers to understand, and to undertake the study of a region I knew a bit about, but had never researched or written about, the present-day Vihiga County. I thus began archival research on both Gusiiland and Vihiga in 1990 and followed up on that during the summer of 1994 as a visiting professor at Moi University. By the time of my 1998 sabbatical, the research had borne fruit in the publication of one of my favorite articles on tobacco growing in western Kenya and another revisiting and reinterpreting the start of coffee growing in Gusiiland. While the main geographical focus of the first was neither Gusiiland nor Vihiga, the methodological approach reflected in the title was one I tried to utilize in several other studies on agrarian issues during that and the next decade, bringing in all stakeholders involved in agricultural development: peasants, entrepreneurs, and the state. The second 1994 article represented a rather different approach than had my 1972 article.

The 1998 sabbatical allowed for further field and archival work so as to complete the basis for the book that became *Going Their Separate Ways*. I had drafted several chapters prior to my arrival. By this time, moreover, the link between WVU and Moi and Maseno universities that had been forged in 1990 had developed quite nicely. Starting in 1990 and continuing in the new century, several faculty and former students at Moi and Maseno came to WVU to pursue a PhD in history under my supervision. The majority carried out research on economic and/or agriculture-based historical studies. Several of these contributed to my work while others built upon it in their articles, chapters, and books. These include Peter O. Ndege, Priscilla Shilaro, Anne Nangulu, Nicholas Makana, Martin Shanguhyia, Kennedy Moindi, John Mwaruvie, and Godriver Odhiambo. The publication of *Going Their Separate Ways,* toward the end of my second stint as department chair in (1998–2004), was a climax of sorts to my research on agriculture in colonial western Kenya. The narrative and conclusions reached as a result of the comparative study of Vihiga with Gusiiland between 1930 and 1950 benefited greatly from the research and publications of several of those former students listed above.

My final sabbatical spent at Moi University in 2006, on the other hand, found me working in new areas of research interest as well as old. The latter was reflected in my joining with Professor John Akama and other Gusii scholars to produce a volume that focused on Gusii culture and culture change. I had met and worked with some of the contributors on earlier visits to the university and the sabbatical enabled us to put the finishing touches on the edited book. I also completed a draft of what I conceived to be a book on Kenya's constitutional history during the period from roughly 1950 to independence in 1963. This new thrust in research emerged around the turn of the century.

## LATE COLONIAL CONSTITUTIONAL HISTORY

My original intent had been to follow my study of agrarian history with a focus on the late colonial and early independence periods of Kenya's history through a study of one of the "founding fathers" of the new nation. My choice was a study of Masinde Muliro, whom I regard as a principled politician. As I began to consult potential records in the former PRO, now the British National Archives, however, I discovered many files and a massive amount of documents relating to constitutional negotiations and conferences in the 1950s and 1960s. None of these had featured in any published scholarly work. I thus turned my attention to this rich documentary record, aiming to write a definitive history of constitution-making. I used several trips to Kenya to get started and stopped in London to collect archival material as well. I also used Spring Semester and Thanksgiving breaks to spend more time in Britain at the archives and the Rhodes House Library.

I carried a suitcase full of notes to Moi University for my Spring Semester 2006 sabbatical. These were useful as I completed research in the KNA and moved to begin writing. The draft was quite lengthy, though I had not really finished, by the time my wife and I left Kenya in July 2006. Two more research trips to Britain in late 2006 and summer 2008 ensued before I felt prepared to attack the subject adequately. Upon completion, the manuscript stood at almost 900 typed pages. I submitted a proposal to Fairleigh Dickinson University Press, but the editors politely told me that the word count was too large to make a saleable book on that topic. I then decided to write two volumes on constitutional negotiations and conferences. One was to describe the evolution of the self-government and independence constitutions, which came into effect during 1963, along with the associated politics, and the other to describe the emergence of Kenya's constitutions during the 1950s, particularly the Lyttleton and the Lennox-Boyd constitutions, and concluding with the 1960 Lancaster House constitutional conference. Both books were published in 2010. I planned to publish a separate book on federalism or *majimbo* in late colonial Kenya, but illness and surgery delayed the completion of that project until 2017. Then, I published a volume that dealt with federalism in the 1940s and 1950s. The final stage of the *majimbo* saga (1961–1963) is still to be written.

## THEMES AND THEORIES

In this final segment of the chapter, I wish to touch on some of the themes and theories that have marked my scholarship. At the time I started my dissertation research, issues relating to African resistance to, and collaboration with, colonial rule were coming to the forefront in terms of a theoretical perspective. This paradigm came to impact my research and publication on the Gusii experience of colonial rule, and is reflected in the "conflict and accommodation" title noted earlier. Since my dissertation and book took the Gusii experience of colonial rule to Kenya's independence in 1963, I also grappled with the issue of the rise of nationalism. I was much influenced by John Lonsdale's 1968 article. I sought to look at the roots of the late impact of mass nationalism in the Gusii highlands through the reaction of various groups, all of whom were conditioned by continued Gusii resistance and a relatively conservative accommodation to colonial rule through, for example, western education. This led to the interpretation of the Gusii involvement in mass nationalism set out in the book and articles.

While still grappling with these issues, I, like many others, had to confront the inadequacy of modernization theory and some of its offshoots, such as the standard interpretation of Kenya's economic history prior to 1960: that the colonial economy emerged solely as a result of external initiatives in the form of European settlers and the agricultural development they fostered. The new dependency theory craze of the 1970s and 1980s added to this narrative other external forces, seemingly more critical than the settlers, such as international capital in its varied forms and influences. In view of my research interest in the first decades of my career, I was forced to assess these paradigms and found difficulties in applying them to my research findings. A huge difficulty was the absence of African agency in dependency analysis. The majority of Kenya's population were not actors or innovators but merely acted upon.

A few examples will hopefully suffice to illustrate this concern. My research of John Ainsworth's career clearly indicated that the "we built a country" narrative long propagated by Kenya Europeans and their literary champions was not accurate. I found plenty of archival evidence, for example, that settlers had not come to Kenya and begun farming the so-called empty or uninhabited land. Virtually all the European farms near Nairobi were inaugurated after the removal of African inhabitants. Just as significant, the major exports of the East Africa Protectorate down to 1914 came from African households, not settler farms. As I moved to study imperial relations and began to concentrate on economic history, other alleged Kenyan experiences expounded by dependency theorists appeared to be at odds with historical records. In this regard, I mention such propositions as that an African peasantry ceased to exist in Kenya prior to 1940 since the penetration of capitalism in the colony had turned all peasants into proletarians. The latter proposition, first dismantled by Bruce Berman and John Lonsdale in 1979, did not hold water as I researched the economies of Gusiiland and Vihiga during the period 1930–1950. In both cases, proletarianization followed, and coexisted with, peasantization. Put another way, areas such as those experienced both the export of commodities and the migrant labor rather than the first activity being supplanted by the second.

While immersed in economic history, I reckoned with other themes and theoretical frameworks. An interesting example was Goran Hyden's uncaptured peasantry theory. I found his explanation of an exit option quite applicable to the data that I uncovered, but I saw little evidence of an uncaptured peasantry in Vihiga or Gusiiland, especially not in recent decades. My research findings aligned me more with the analyses and theoretical perspectives of Henry Bernstein and Jonathon Barker. Like Barker, I came to view the role of the state as a significant influence in rural colonial Africa. These views have been borne out by the research findings of several of the doctoral students I supervised.

As in the case of economic history and my scholarship on Kenya's late constitutional history, my research has been based firmly on primary sources, most notably the records in the Kenya and British national archives. This has also come to characterize what can be termed the WVU approach to Africa's history as that is reflected in the research and publication of most of our History department graduates. Most hold academic positions in the United States and Kenya. Those graduates, I am certain, will continue this emphasis moving into the future.

I will close with a word of gratitude to all the graduate students I have been fortunate to work with toward expanding historical knowledge. They made my work as a teacher and a researcher, both challenging and most rewarding. As noted earlier, the group (four now deceased) includes 3 who completed dissertations on diaspora topics, 2 on West African history, and 22 on East African topics (all but two primarily on Kenya). The diversity of subjects studied parallels the individuals: among that group of scholars have been 12 Kenyans, 4 from other African countries, and 11 U.S. citizens, including four African Americans. As suggested earlier in this narrative, I owe much to my mentors and colleagues: none more than Professor Ochieng'. Finally, I wish to thank Nicholas Githuku and Bekeh Utiatiang for their work in making the conference a reality and to Nicholas for bringing this book to publication.

## FURTHER READING

Akama, John and Robert M. Maxon. eds. *Ethnography of the Gusii of Western Kenya: A Vanishing Cultural Heritage.* Lewiston, NY: Edwin Mellen Press, 2006.

Barker, Jonathon. *Rural Communities Under Stress: Peasant Farmers and the State in Africa*, Cambridge: Cambridge University Press, 1989.

Bernstein, Henry. "African Peasantries: A Theoretical Framework." *Journal of Peasant Studies* 6 (1979): 421–43.

Gregory, Robert G., Leon Spencer and Robert M. Maxon. *A Guide to the Kenya National Archives*. Syracuse: PEAS, 1969.

Hatch, John C. *Africa Today and Tomorrow*. New York: Praeger, 1960.

Hyden, Goran. *Beyond Ujamaa in Tanzania: Underdevelopment and an Uncaptured Peasantry*. Berkeley and Los Angeles: University of California Press, 1980.

Lonsdale, John. "Some Origins of Nationalism in East Africa." *Journal of African History* 9 (1968): 119–46.

Robert M. Maxon. "The Absence of Political Associations Among the Gusii Prior to 1940." *Transafrican Journal of History* 10 (1981): 113–24.

———. "African Production and Support of European Settlement in Kenya: the Uasin Gishu-Mumias Railway Scheme, 1911-1914." *Journal of Imperial and Commonwealth History* 14 (1985): 52–64.

———. *Britain and Kenya's Constitutions, 1950-1960*. Amherst, NY: Cambria Press, 2011.

———. *Conflict and Accommodation in Western Kenya: the Gusii and the British, 1907-1963*. Rutherford, NJ: Fairleigh Dickinson University Press, 1989.

———. "The Early Days of the Gusii Coffee Industry in Kenya, 1933-45." *Journal of Developing Areas* VI (1972): 365–82.

———. *East Africa: An Introductory History*. Morgantown: WVU Press, 1986.

———. *Going Their Separate Ways: Agrarian Transformation in Kenya, 1930-1950*. Madison, NJ: Fairleigh Dickinson University, 2003.

———. *John Ainsworth and the Making of Kenya*. Washington: University Press of America, 1980.

———. "Judgement on a Colonial Governor: Sir Percy Girouard in Kenya." *Transafrican Journal of History* 18 (1989): 90–100.

———. "A Kenya Petite Bourgeoisie Enters Local Politics: the Kisii Union, 1945-1949." *International Journal of African Historical Studies* 19 (1986): 451–62.

———. *Kenya's Independence Constitution: Constitution-Making and End of Empire*. Lanham, MD: Fairleigh Dickinson University Press, 2011.

———. *Majimbo in Kenya's Past: Federalism in the 1940s and 1950s*. Amherst, NY: Cambria Press, 2017.

———. "Social and Cultural Change." In *Decolonization and Independence in Kenya, 1940-1993*, edited by W. R. Ochieng' and B. A. Ogot, 110–47. London: James Currey, 1995.

———. "Stifling Capitalism in Rural Africa: the Gusii Coffee Industry, 1932-1939." *Journal of Third World Studies* 11 (1994): 317–50.

———. *Struggle for Kenya: The Loss and Reassertion of Imperial Initiative, 1912-1923*. Rutherford, NJ: Fairleigh Dickinson University Press, 1993.

———. "Up in Smoke: Peasants, Capital and the Colonial State in the Tobacco Industry in Western Kenya, 1930-1939." *African Economic History* 22 (1994): 111–39.

————. "Where Did the Trees Go? The Wattle Bark Industry in Western Kenya, 1932-1950." *International Journal of African Historical Studies* 34 (2001): 565–85.

Ochieng', W. R. and R. M. Maxon, eds. *An Economic History of Kenya*. Nairobi: East African Educational Publishers, 1992.

Saeteurn, Muey Ching. "'A Beacon of Hope for the Community': The Role of Chavakali Secondary School in Late Colonial and Early Independent Kenya." *Journal of African History* 58 (2017): 311–29.

## Chapter 3

# Myth and Reality in the Forging of a Kenyan National History

## Oginga Odinga's Heroism

### Robert M. Maxon

Following the publication of the report of a presidential task force in October 2019, varied topics and themes arising from what is popularly known as the Building Bridges Initiative (BBI) became part of Kenya's national discourse. Discussion of the BBI report again took center stage following the October 2020 release of the report of the Steering Committee on implementation. Thus the BBI recommendations seem certain to have an impact on several aspects of Kenyan life in the run-up to the 2022 national elections. These are likely to include politics and governance as well as social and educational changes as Kenyans seek to build a more inclusive society. The focus of this chapter is one of the issues identified by the BBI reports: the lack of a national ethos and the need for a national history. Specifically, the role of heroes in the forging of a national history will be examined by reference to two episodes from the lengthy career of one of Kenya's leading nationalists and national heroes, Oginga Odinga.[1]

Chapter 2 of the BBI task-force report identified the lack of a national ethos as a cause of disunity and exclusion and thus a major problem for Kenya. The report called for developing a national ethos that will recognize diversity while promoting inclusion.[2] This is to be done by major consultations that will produce a vision of Kenya as a united nation. That vision must be accompanied by "an official and inclusive history."[3] The officially commissioned history, according to the report, should "go back 1000 years and provide an accurate and definitive account" of critical themes in Kenyan history; in terms of this chapter, "anti-colonial struggles" are recommended as a key area for such a national history.[4]

In many parts of the world, such a theme begins and ends with the story of heroes. For example, one of several guiding principles for the Steering Committee report is "recognition for heroic acts, and personal and group sacrifices in service of our nation."[5] Kenyan president Uhuru Kenyatta stated in his *Mashujaa* Day speech of October 2020 that "there is no history without heroes."[6] Particularly mentioned were individuals who, in a variety of ways, struggled against colonial control and sought to bring it to an end. Not surprisingly, Oginga Odinga was mentioned in the president's speech.

Such heroism is hardly a new topic for study. Almost 60 years ago, Ali Mazrui noted, with regard to Kenya, the importance of remembering past heroes in "building up national consciousness." He went on: "To give the idea of the Nation warmth, it is often necessary either to personify it metaphorically or, more effectively, to give some human form in national heroes."[7] More recently, the biographer of a prominent Kenya politician wrote that the political history of a country, to a large extent, "is the summation of stories of individuals who have been involved in the moulding of its political path."[8] Concentration on individual heroes can easily turn into the "great man" theory of history which makes such a person unique as a prime mover of events which might otherwise not have happened. Many historians also give attention to the material conditions existing at the time the individual lived and the varying factors that produced his/her actions at a given time.

Such accounts of heroes can provide critical elements of national histories as their lives may illustrate important values and motivations that inspire current and future generations to embrace a national ethos reflecting, for example, courage, self-sacrifice, determination, and patriotism. However, focus on heroes has often led to exaggeration with regard to the individual's activities and achievements or, more seriously, fabrication in terms of events or distortion by selectively describing what actually happened.[9] Thus such stories of national heroes often mix myth with facts, some to such a degree that myths and legends become accepted as truthful historical narratives. Guarding against the latter is important, and a key is to ensure the history produced provides an accurate and definitive account as suggested above. As this chapter will demonstrate, accuracy has often been difficult to ascertain in the face of distortions and fabrications. A common reason for inaccuracy is failure to consult all available sources, particularly archival.[10]

## MYTH: HEROISM IN REFUSING
## GOVERNOR RENISON, 1960

On the other hand, the main thrust of this chapter is the heroism of Oginga Odinga in Kenya's anti-colonial struggle with a specific focus on some of his actions in 1959 and 1960. The 1960 episode will be discussed first because of its contemporary significance. The story of Odinga turning down an offer from Kenya's then governor, Sir Patrick Renison, has often been referred to since the so-called handshake agreement of March 2018 between Odinga's son and political heir Raila and Uhuru Kenyatta, son of Kenya's first prime minister (1963–1964) and president (1964–1978), Jomo Kenyatta. A key significance of the story revolves around Oginga Odinga rejecting the chance to become Kenya's first chief minister as he believed such a position must go to a man that Africans in Kenya regarded as their leader, the then detained Jomo Kenyatta. That being the case, Kenyans should expect Uhuru to facilitate Raila's taking the presidency when his term comes to an end in 2022.[11] As the "debt" owed by the Kenyatta family to the Odingas is critical, it is clearly important to examine and analyze the story of Odinga's rejection of high office. As will be seen, such an examination shows that the story is myth rather than reality.

It made its first appearance in print more than three decades after the events are alleged to have taken place. The story that follows formed part of an introduction to Professor H. Odera Oruka's book describing and analyzing Oginga Odinga's philosophy. Relatively brief, the account includes no footnotes or references of any kind. Later in the book, the reader meets an account, similar in several respects, in the form of a question and answer session between Jaramogi Odinga and Professor Oruka. The first begins following the heading "a showdown with the governor." Oruka wrote:

Once the settlers had realized the magnitude of the pressure to have Kenyatta as the first prime minister, they planned to head it off by offering incentives to Odinga. The governor, Sir Patrick Renison, invited Odinga to State House, Nairobi, in 1960. He sent a driver to pick Odinga up from his modest house in Nairobi's African estate of Jerusalem. Once inside the state house, the governor's offer was simple and direct. We wish to hand over power to the African nationalists. If you agree, we propose you head such a government. He said this standing up and looking straight into Odinga's eyes.

Equally simple and direct was Odinga's response: "If I accept your offer, I will be seen as a traitor to my people. The British cannot elect me a leader to my people. That is the stage of the appointment of chiefs, a stage which we have now surpassed. Kenyatta is around, just here at Lodwar. Release him and allow him to lead us, he is already our choice."

With a sweating brow, the governor wasted no more time. "Good-bye Mr. Odinga!" And he called the driver to return the "primitive" man back to his African quarters.[12]

The second account offers additional details and highlighted Odinga's rejection. There the governor concluded with the words: "You know Odinga, we

British are determined to keep Kenyatta away. You are lucky we are offering you leadership of Kenya."[13] Asked for his reaction, Odinga responded, in heroic fashion, by a first person account. "I answered, 'thank you Sir, but I cannot accept this. Thank you very much for thinking of me, but I cannot accept the offer. If I did and tomorrow Kenyans heard that I had done so, they would treat me as a traitor. They would believe rightly that I had betrayed them.'"[14]

More than two decades later, these accounts received new publicity through an August 2013 lecture at the University of Nairobi by Professor Ali Mazrui and a written version later posted online. In his reflection on the Africanization of the executive branch in Kenya, the distinguished political scientist claimed that the process started "when Oginga Odinga struck a blow for democracy in the last days of colonial rule" or more specifically against "external selection of African leaders." In Mazrui's account, obviously influenced by Odinga's recollection presented in Oruka's book:

Odinga was invited to the Residence of the British Governor of Kenya, Sir Patrick Renison, and offered the leadership of the first African government in Colonial Kenya. The event occurred in Government House (now called State House) in Nairobi in 1960. The British Governor and the Kenyan nationalist were both standing when the offer was made. It seemed to be the chance of a lifetime. It turned out to be Oginga Odinga's last opportunity to become Premier of Kenya. Oginga Odinga is reported to have responded as follows to the Governor: "If I accept your offer, I will be seen as a traitor to my people. The British cannot elect me leader to my people . . . Kenyatta is around, just here at Lodwar. Release him and allow him to lead us; he is already our choice."

Sir Patrick was temporarily stumped. He then summoned the driver to take Oginga Odinga back to his native quarters in Nairobi.[15]

Beyond this description, Professor Mazrui's interpretation added an important element to the story. He emphasized Odinga's sacrifice in "what turned out to be his last opportunity to lead Kenya. His incumbency could have transformed the ethnic configurations of post-colonial Kenya." If Odinga had accepted the offer, Kenya history would have been dramatically different since he "could have presided over the release of Jomo Kenyatta, and Kenyatta might have become Odinga's Vice President instead of the other way around."[16] This interpretation provided a foundation for self-sacrifice in Odinga's support for democracy "at enormous cost to his future presidential aspirations."[17]

It was not long before this account and interpretation were propagated widely in the Kenya press and among the public. Directly referencing Professor Mazrui's paper, an interestingly titled *Daily Nation* article took the position that Odinga's words to Renison "changed the course of Kenya political history forever." Furthermore, Odinga "threw away an opportunity to lead Kenya, a chance he craved to his death."[18]

These accounts form the basis of Odinga's heroism in relatively clear terms. He was offered the chance to be Kenya's first chief minister/prime minister, but as a true nationalist he put his country before self in turning it down. Quite apart from this episode, this was an image that Odinga had long cultivated and demonstrated on several occasions. It is easy to spot in reading Professor Oruka's account of his discussions with Jaramogi—for example, the emphasis on three qualities of courage, frankness, and persistence that, in the book, marked Odinga's political life. In the examples described above, Odinga exemplified those characteristics, even if his frankness and stubborn persistence could be said to have harmed his political fortunes.[19] For his actions in turning down the governor as with his later split with Jomo Kenyatta, Odinga proclaimed that he regretted nothing; he did "what was right at the time. Had I done otherwise, I would have done what was wrong."[20]

Looking at the heroic account itself, and in a broader context, an assessment of the accuracy of the narrative is now called for. What is fact and what is a myth? To begin, it must be acknowledged that this was Odinga's account, and his alone, as no published account of the 1960 offer exists. Nor do press accounts or archival sources so far discovered dating from that time. As a result, none of the published scholarly works that have made extensive use of British and Kenyan archives refer to such an offer. These include Charles Hornsby's detailed history of independent Kenya[21] and Professor W. O Maloba's impressively document two-volume biography of Jomo Kenyatta.[22] Even more critical, no mention is made of Renison's alleged offer in *Not Yet Uhuru*, Odinga's memoir published in the 1960s.[23]

Yet there are some facts that serve to confirm that Odinga's described behavior was not out of character, and that he was a recognized leader among the African members of Legislative Council (LegCo) elected in March 1957 who as a group successfully campaigned to overthrow the Lyttleton Constitution (1954–1958) and the Lennox-Boyd constitution (1958–1960). Even before the election, Odinga had a deserved reputation as a principled and courageous individual. In a pre-election forecast appearing in the right-wing European settler-owned weekly magazine, *New Comment*, an African contributor described Odinga as an able administrator and a nationalist who "is not a man to accept a ministerial post simply because of *posho*. He never compromises in matters of principle."[24] Moreover, Odinga held a top leadership position within the African Elected Members Organization (AEMO) as chairman during the organization's campaign to end the Lennox-Boyd constitution. He provided key leadership, for example, in the November 1958 walkout by AEMO members during an address by then Governor Sir Evelyn

Baring.[25] As will be seen later in the chapter, Odinga led an African and Asian delegation to London to meet with SofS Alan Lennox-Boyd in April 1959.

However, the question of myth or factual account with regard to Odinga's heroism in 1960 requires closer study. As noted earlier, no archival record of this meeting exists. More critically, there is archival evidence, both direct and confirmatory, that an offer of the chief minister position to Odinga did not happen. First, there is the issue of the position of chief minister or prime minister. It was normal practice in British African colonies during the era of decolonization to appoint a chief minister from elected members of a LegCo. In 1960, Julius Nyerere held that position in neighboring Tanganyika. Such a member would be expected to command the support of a majority of elected members and be responsible for the choice of other ministers and the port-folios they would hold. At the inauguration of internal self-government, the final stage of British colonial constitutional development, the chief minister position was replaced by that of prime minister. Interestingly, Kenya never had a chief minister in the move to internal self-government (June 1, 1963) and independence (on December 12, 1963).

The call for the appointment of a chief minister was one of several key demands of the AEMO, particularly during 1959–1960, but the British gov-ernment refused to accede. Prior to the first Lancaster House constitutional conference (LH1) in London (January 18 to February 22, 1960), Odinga, speaking on behalf of the African members of LegCo on November 30, 1959, included "an African as Chief Minister" as one of their aims for the coming conference.[26] The demand for a rapid move to self-rule, governed by a party with a majority in the LegCo "irrespective of race or origin," was put forward by Ronald Ngala, leader of the African delegation at the 1960 conference, when the African members met SofS Iain Macleod in Nairobi on December 16.[27] It is significant to note that the records of the meeting indicate that Macleod offered no comment on the specifics of the African demands.

At LHI, moreover, Macleod and his CO advisors were unreceptive to the idea of a chief minister for Kenya as part of constitutional changes and, as it turned out, any time in 1960. Struggling to promote agreement at the con-ference, Macleod told his cabinet colleague R. A. Butler on February 1 that African delegates wanted a chief minister system with all ministers appointed on his advice, but the British government could not accept this even if it meant a breakdown of the conference.[28] On February 11, Macleod made it clear to the leaders of the African delegation, Ngala and Tom Mboya, that he was not planning to introduce a chief minister position at this stage of Kenya's consti-tutional development; such a step, he concluded, lay in the future.[29] When the African delegation met Macleod the following day to give him their response to the constitutional plans he had presented to the conference participants,

Ngala informed him that the African elected members "reluctantly accepted" the SofS's view that it was not yet possible to appoint a chief minister.[30] Even at the end of the year, the CO was not prepared to change the LH1 constitution to provide for a chief minister.[31]

This archival evidence is hard to square with Odinga's account. Did he forget over the years or deliberately fabricate the story? Accepting the Odinga account seems also to require that Sir Patrick Renison deliberately went against the policy of the SofS and was approved by the British cabinet in offering the post of chief minister to Odinga during 1960. This is most unlikely. One way to approach the issue is to examine other major concerns of Renison and Macleod before, during, and after LH1. A key factor was the British resolve not to make any substantial change to the LH1 constitution prior to its implementation. Such a constitutional change as the appointment of a chief minister might open the door "to a flood of other demands in coming months," Macleod told Renison in mid-March.[32] Changes would only be possible after the elections under a common roll system that would result in the new legislature and council of ministers. It took most of the rest of 1960 to prepare for the elections which eventually were carried out in the first two months of 1961. Another powerful reason for Macleod, in particular, was strong opposition from many members of his Conservative Party. They were adamant that the SofS was moving too fast toward African majority rule in Kenya.[33] Similarly, Macleod and his advisors were cognizant of the criticism that the African members of Kenya's LegCo had broken the Lyttleton and Lennox-Boyd constitutions and forced their replacement well before the date the British government had planned for that to occur.

A particular concern in this regard was the CO and Renison's view that African elected members must take positions on the council of ministers. This had been a goal since the first African elections in March 1957, and it was a priority for SofS Lennox-Boyd when he announced the new constitution that came to bear his name in November of that year. A key element in the AEMO campaign against that constitution was the refusal to take up a ministerial appointment. For the CO, the goal of elected African LegCo members as ministers grew in importance as LH1 drew near. At the December 1959 meeting with Macleod mentioned earlier, Renison told the nationalists that "real progress" toward their goal of self-government could come about when they "crossed over from being the Opposition to being the Government."[34] The CO's draft of the LH1 final report expressed the governor and SofS's hope to bring some further African ministers into the council of ministers at once rather than waiting until the new constitution was in force. The SofS and Renison informed the African delegation of this at a February 22 meeting, and it was agreed that further discussions would take place in Nairobi following the governor's return from the conference.[35]

Renison wasted little time in moving to bring this about. On his February 25 arrival, he told reporters that he understood the AEM "were considering favourably the idea of a number of them going into the present government."[36] This attempt to put pressure on the AEM did not lead to any immediate move from them as it took a month to make the governor's hope a reality. One reason, among many, for the long delay was Odinga's attitude and activities. This was partly because, as the leadership of the colonial state viewed the issue, Odinga was not considered for a ministerial post, leave alone that of chief minister. On March 7, for example, Renison met with Ngala, Mboya, and Masinde Muliro, whom he recognized as the AEM most influential at the LH1 talks as well as among the most qualified to hold a portfolio. Renison told them that he wished to appoint three AEM to the council of ministers and that they were his choices. Bringing Mboya into the council and associating him with government policy rather than remaining outside was a particular priority.[37] When news of the meeting on the 7th reached Odinga, he immediately opposed the idea of any AEM taking a portfolio and issued a public statement to that effect. He cleverly based his stand on the fact that by joining the council of ministers, his AEM colleagues would be serving under the Lennox-Boyd constitution, something all of them had long refused to do.[38]

Thus began a long process which concluded at the end of March with the appointment of three AEM ministers, though not Mboya or Muliro. Personality, ethnic factors, as well as disagreement over the specific portfolios caused the delay in addition to Odinga's maneuvers to influence the appointments.[39] The process was marked by almost daily correspondence between Renison and the CO, as was the case with ministerial appointments in 1961. It is inconceivable that such would not have been the case with Odinga's appointment as chief minister. Renison would not have initiated such a process without keeping Macleod informed every step of the way.

Moreover, Odinga's activities upon his return from LH1 were quite well documented in reports of the Kenya Special Branch. No mention of appointing Odinga as chief minister exists in these documents. These indicate that in addition to the African ministerial appointments, Odinga's time was much occupied in March, April, and May with the prime role he played in trying to establish a colony-wide African political party. This movement actually began over the second half of 1959 with the emergence of the Kenya National Party (KNP) and the Kenya Independence Movement (KIM). The opposing groups among the AEM reflected personal and ethnic differences as well as contrasting visions of Kenya's constitutional future. These produced a split in the AEMO and the breakup of the Constituency Elected Members Organization (CEMO) which Odinga headed early in 1959. Ironically, displeasure with Odinga's leadership was a factor in the split that led to the formation of the KNP after June.[40] By the end of August, the AEM were split.

Odinga lost his post as AEMO leader but was chosen as president of KIM.[41] While the AEM came together by the end of the year to unite as a single delegation behind the leadership of Ngala (KNP) and Mboya (KIM), Odinga was left out of leadership at LH1.

Following the conference, it was the KIM leadership and vision for Kenya's future that held sway, and Odinga, in particular, moved to create a new, colony-wide, nationalist political party that could appeal to a broad spectrum of Kenya's African population and pressure Britain to grant early independence. In fact, political maneuvering consumed much of Odinga's time during March, April, and May 1960 and left him little to consider becoming chief minister. The Special Branch reports of the period provide detail of the process that led to the formation of the Kenya African National Union (KANU), and, significantly, Odinga's failure to exclude Mboya from leadership and to create a single-party political system. Mboya became secretary of KANU and the Kenya African Democratic Union (KADU) was formed in June.

Odinga's failure to achieve those goals in 1960 throws significant doubt on the accounts provided by Professor Mazrui and in Professor Oruka's book. If Odinga could not exclude his rival Mboya nor achieve his goal of a single-party system, what success could be expected from his appointment as chief minister? He had embraced an inclusive policy as leader of the CEMO delegation, but within months set out on a path that ended with exclusion. Odinga later explained these outcomes as being the result of machinations by Kenya's European settlers and the British colonialists who used all sorts of tricks to deny and delay independence.[42] Although such an interpretation is not wrong, it should not divert us from examining his agency as a leading Kenyan nationalist. It is significant also that the council of ministers that Odinga (or Kenyatta) would lead in 1960 was one in which Africans were a minority. European settlers, colonial civil servants, and Asian ministers outnumbered them.

One other relevant matter in considering the 1960 chief minister appointment is the way Renison and other leaders of the colonial state had come to view Odinga's activities after LH1. As is now well known, the British rulers of Kenya believed that from that time forward to independence, Odinga was regularly in receipt of funds from the Soviet Bloc, including China.[43] In August, he visited China, and when he returned from a trip to Europe in October, his passport was temporarily seized.[44] One has only to understand that one of Britain's consistent aims for Kenya's decolonization was to keep the colony out of the Soviet Bloc to seriously question any offer a British governor allegedly made to Odinga to become chief minister in 1960.

The analysis so far has focused on the governor's alleged offer to Odinga. That the accounts provided by Oruka and Mazrui are myth rather than factual has been demonstrated. There is no verification in archival sources and much evidence that puts the offer in doubt. But this should not diminish Oginga Odinga's status as a hero in Kenya's national history. There is no need to invent examples of heroism since there exist documented instances that demonstrate Odinga's courage in the fight for freedom and the building of a new nation. The chapter now turns to one such example of heroism, only briefly touched upon in Odinga's memoirs and largely unmentioned in other historical accounts of this period. This was the April 1959 confrontation at the CO that found Odinga directly at odds with then SofS Lennox-Boyd.[45]

## HEROISM: CONFRONTING LENNOX-BOYD, APRIL 1959

This incident came at a critical moment in the independence struggle and specifically the movement for constitutional change away from the philosophy of multiracialism favored by Lennox-Boyd and Sir Evelyn Baring. The AEM walkout in November 1958 was part of this, as were the calls for constitutional change from Asian-elected members in the LegCo. From early 1959, both African- and Asian-elected members boycotted the LegCo sittings in support of their demand for constitutional change toward expanded voting rights leading to universal suffrage on a common roll. Specific demands included the holding of a roundtable constitutional conference on Kenya's future and the appointment of a constitutional expert to advise the Kenya and British governments as well as Kenya politicians on the constitutional way forward.[46]

As public support for this approach grew stronger, the AEM came together with other LegCo members to form a national delegation, representing the main racial groups. This was the Constituency Elected Members Organization (CEMO). As chair of the AEMO, Odinga was much involved in this significant initiative. He was chosen to lead an inclusive CEMO delegation to London to place the group's demands before the SofS. Odinga wrote to Lennox-Boyd on March 13 to announce that the "African, Indian and Arab Elected Members and Mr. S. V. Cooke" had decided to travel to London on April 12 and asked to meet the SofS on the following day. Their motive, Odinga wrote, was "to seek a speedy and peaceful solution of the constitutional situation in Kenya," to ensure for a move toward "genuine democracy" and thus pave the way to "peace, prosperity and stability throughout the country."[47] Lennox-Boyd was not enthusiastic for a meeting with such a delegation at that time but realized he would have to meet with them. Nevertheless, he told Baring that he had no intention of offering concessions as far as the fundamentals of the constitution bearing his name were concerned.[48]

What Odinga and his colleagues did not know at the time the delegation's visit was contemplated was that the CO and Baring were considering a statement of policy for Kenya that would include the holding of a conference on the constitutional future. What should be included in this policy statement and when it was to be made influenced the timing of the Odinga delegation's visit.[49] The CO eventually decided that Lennox-Boyd should make his statement in the House of Commons before he met the delegation. As a result of this and the SofS's other commitments, the CEMO meeting with Lennox-Boyd was pushed back to April 27.[50] Lennox-Boyd made his statement on April 23, but there would still be plenty for Odinga's delegation to discuss.

Civil servants in the EAD had learned more details of the CEMO delegation's concerns following Lord Perth's two meetings with members of the delegation in Nairobi on April 6 and 10.[51] The EAD thus prepared for the April 27 meeting with that in mind, identifying issues the delegation would likely raise and suggesting possible responses the SofS might make. Most important in terms of general strategy was not to allow the delegation to go away with anything they could represent to public opinion in Kenya "as a victory forced from a reluctant Colonial Secretary." The EAD staff were certain that the state of emergency and certain specific regulations, such as control over political meetings and associations and detention without trial, would come up for discussion as Kiano, in particular, had raised these in the Nairobi meetings with Lord Perth and at a discussion with the latter at the CO on April 23.[52] Thus they suggested Lennox-Boyd should push back by pointing out that both political parties in Great Britain had long agreed that "some of those who were worst infested with Mau Mau must continue to be detained, possibly for a long time." The brief also urged the SofS to express concerns over "inflammatory speeches" at AEM public meetings. Without mentioning Odinga by name, the brief went on to suggest that the SofS "could particularly mention the speeches made inside and outside Kenya which represented Jomo Kenyatta in an innocent light and commended him to the admiration of the people." The EAD staffers reminded that Kenyatta "was fairly convicted by the courts" and that conviction had recently been "in effect confirmed by the Macharia verdicts."[53]

These were points of view that Lennox-Boyd shared, and that Odinga was the specific target of this advice became clear at the April 27 meeting with the CEMO delegation. The latter totaled eight (four African, three Asian, one Arab) as Cooke did not travel to London.[54] The delegation answered the SofS's welcome through Dr. Kiano seeking clarification on several matters included in his speech to the House of Commons. Kiano and the others were pleased when he responded to a question as to limits that might be placed on matters to be discussed at the conference as he did not envision any constitutional subject would be barred from consideration. The delegation also received an encouraging response in that Lennox-Boyd was open to seeking advice from constitutional experts before and during the coming conference. It was on the issue of emergency regulations that disagreement arose. The SofS expressed his view that Kenya was not to be an "Africa for the Africans" nation, but one with equal citizenship for all racial groups. Taking his cue from the EAD brief, he expressed his concern about "the remarks glorifying Kenyatta the convicted organizer of Mau Mau and the Kenya African Union; these, he was sure, could only enhance the risks to order of colony-wide associations."[55]

To this challenge, Odinga refused to be put in his place. He responded bravely and forthrightly. He intervened to express his conviction "and that of the Africans" that Kenyatta was their leader and should be released. He went on to assert that the colonial state and the Europeans in Kenya "were just as much to be blamed for what had happened as Kenyatta," and that the emergency had occurred because "legitimate grievances of the Africans had not been satisfied." Kenyatta had to return "to live at peace" for Africans to live peacefully. According to the official report, Odinga concluded his emotional interjection by stating that he himself resented "the injustice done to Kenyatta." An irate SofS sought the last word on this matter by stating that while he respected "Mr. Odinga's sincerity," he did not share his views on Kenyatta.[56] Those present agreed to meet for further discussions on April 30.

Lennox-Boyd was clearly shaken by Odinga's courageous defense of Kenyatta, but in his telegram to Baring the following day he went into several other matters arising from the meeting, such as the conference and its timing, the work of constitutional experts (or expert), and the loosening of emergency regulations, particularly relating to public meetings and political associations. The latter topic led him to Odinga's stand as he reported that he warned the delegation "that the spread of the Kenyatta Cult" could only delay the easing of emergency regulations. The SofS continued: "Odinga immediately launched into an impassioned defence of, and plea for, Kenyatta" and release of detainees, and "disappointingly none of the others took him up, though they seemed rather embarrassed. This is just the sort of extreme attitude we had hoped to overcome by our flexible approach and I found it depressing."[57]

Odinga's heroic stance deserves recognition, but while the SofS was shocked by his defense of Kenyatta, it is also surprising that Odinga made no mention of the confrontation in his memoirs. In his discussions of the April 1959 delegation to the CO, he emphasized the promise of a constitutional conference, though as noted above, it was conceded before the April 27 meeting. He did recall that the delegation "raised the question of the Emergency, pressing that it should be ended." Later in the same paragraph, he "stressed that if the Emergency were not lifted by the time the new constitutional conference opened, the Africans of Kenya would feel there was no prospect of cooperation."[58] As to why Odinga did not go into detail regarding his "impassioned" defense of Kenyatta, one can only speculate. Perhaps he did not wish to do so at the time of the book's publication since he did not want to remind readers of past praise when he and Kenyatta were then political enemies.

Nevertheless, the story of Odinga's heroism on this occasion did not end with the April 27 meeting. Not only did he demonstrate leadership through confronting the SofS at the CO, but he also followed up by astute action so as to make significant gains for the African case against the Lennox-Boyd constitution and in favor of democratization in Kenya. This occurred even as irritation at the CO followed the outburst on April 27. Lord Perth, second in command there, demonstrated this when he wrote a note to the SofS the next day to express the need to not "let Odinga get away with it as it were regarding Kenyatta." Perth felt that should not mean getting "into a hot argument," but the SofS should "firmly state that there is another side to the case," particularly for the effect it would have on the rest of the delegation.[59] In his response to the CO report of the meeting, Baring urged a hard line be taken "on emergency relaxation" as "the Kenyatta cult is still strong." He maintained: "any Kikuyu hearing the words of someone advocating this cult regards them as a call to renew violence."[60]

However, Odinga and the delegation did not stand pat in preparing for the second meeting on April 30. The CEMO leaders, after consultation with their colleagues in Kenya, decided to end their LegCo boycott. Thus, the April 30 meeting began not with a chastisement of Odinga, but with Lennox-Boyd saying how glad he was to hear the delegates had decided "to resume their normal constitutional role." Odinga answered Lennox-Boyd that they too should "contribute to the better atmosphere and the spirit of co-operation which had made its appearance." When the issue of emergency regulations was raised later in the discussion, the SofS stressed that neither he nor Baring was prepared to consider "the possibility of relaxing or terminating Jomo Kenyatta's restriction order." Even so, Kiano and Muliro made telling points with regard to the discriminatory way the emergency regulations disadvantaged African politicians in terms of meetings and political organizations. It was at that juncture that Odinga said that if the state of emergency was not removed before the coming conference, Africans would feel there was no real cooperation.[61]

The following day, the delegation held a press conference in London. According to the CO report, Odinga did most of the talking. In a statesman-like manner, he took a moderate stance in stating that the SofS had given them a good audience and listened to the issues delegates raised. The delegation even went out of its way to appeal to European settlers in Kenya through promises that an African ruled Kenya would respect individual rights and not adopt discriminatory policies.[62] A major advance had occurred on the path to the constitutional change that emerged from LH1. Only a few months before there had been hostility and stalemate as AEM not only boycotted the LegCo, but also the royal visit Kenya by the Queen Mother.[63] Much of the credit for the gains made by the CEMO and the better understanding with the CO should go to Odinga.

Lennox-Boyd's assessment of the meetings with the delegation and Kenya's constitutional future was different. He gave voice to these in a long personal letter to Kenya's governor two weeks after the second meeting. He felt that treating the delegation cordially and listening to their views was well received in Britain, even among Labor MPs. The SofS was most impressed by Kiano's "ability and flexibility" while he felt "Odinga himself was clearly fully committed emotionally on the Kenyatta issue." However, Lennox-Boyd convinced himself that after Odinga's outburst on the 27th, the latter "obviously received a warning by the others to restrain himself at later meetings."[64] As was his practice, Baring took more than two weeks to respond to the SofS's observations and questions. He told Lord Perth that the results of the CO handling of what the governor termed "the Kiano delegation in London" was "admirable." He reported that he had recently had a long talk with Odinga and Ngala and found them "in a reasonable frame of mind."[65] The momentum created by Odinga's delegation and his leadership in its aftermath was critical as he continued to forcefully advocate for an independent and inclusive Kenya.

It is difficult to dispute Dr. Badejo's inclusion of Jaramogi Odinga among the individuals who made significant marks on Kenyan political history.[66] In his long career in politics, he demonstrated several characteristics of heroism, such as courage, frankness, self-sacrifice, and persistence.[67] The mythical 1960 episode highlighted these traits, but surely it is more appropriate to recognize his heroism in terms of actual actions taken. The second example in this chapter also illustrates these virtues in Odinga's purposeful action as a campaigner for national freedom. He was forthright in stating his views, avoiding the trap the CO had set for him even as other members of the delegation remained quiet. This incident of heroism has the virtue, unlike the accounts of Odinga's declining the post of chief minister, of being an accurate and verifiable episode drawn from archival sources during the final stages of Kenya's saga of national independence. An accurate account, though perhaps less dramatic than the fictional rejection of the Kenya governor's offer of leadership, presents contemporary Kenyans with an example of heroism in attacking injustice, exclusion, and an absence of basic human rights that remains, as in 1959, key elements in establishing a national ethos. As noted on *Mashujaa* Day 2020, "the more we ponder our history in its truest form, the more liberated we become."[68]

## NOTES

1. Dr. B.A. Badejo recognized Odinga as one of five Kenyans who "provided the foundation for the political history of Kenya." Babafemi A. Badejo, *Raila Odinga An Enigma in Kenyan Politics* (Lagos: Yintab Books, 2006), xii.

2. Republic of Kenya, *Building Bridges to a United Kenya: from a nation of blood ties to a nation of ideals* (Nairobi: Presidential Taskforce on Building Bridges to Unity Advisory, 2019), 30. Republic of Kenya, *Report of the Steering Committee on the Implementation of the Building Bridges to a United Kenya Taskforce Report* (Nairobi: Government Printer, 2020), Annex A, 27–28; 32–33.

3. *Building Bridges to a United Kenya*, 31.

4. Ibid., 32.

5. *Report of the Steering Committee,* Annex A, 33.

6. "Uhuru's full *Mashujaa* Day speech," *Nation*, October 20, 2020.

7. Ali Mazrui, "On Heroes and Uhuru-Worship," *Transition* No. 11 (1963): 24.

8. Badejo, *Raila Odinga*, xi.

9. As Professor Mazrui noted. Mazrui, "On Heroes," 23.

10. A twenty-third-century Kenyan example is "Warrior Otenyo," a Gusii young man elevated to heroism as an anti-imperialist fighter for his actions in 1908. The resulting legend exposes the crass brutality and inhumanity of the British rulers of Kenya. Versions appearing in the press over the past decade as well as on the internet have one thing in common: they make no use of archival material currently located in the Kenya National Archives that present differing evidence. See "Elders Demand Apology," *Daily Nation*, June 12, 2013; "Return Gusii freedom fighter Otenyo Nyamaterere's skull group tells Britain," *Daily Nation,* September 22, 2015. "Warrior Otenyo," *Wiipedia*,en.wikipedia.org/warrior_otenyo, accessed May 27, 2020.

11. For example, Kwendo Opanga, "Why Raila will be the man to beat in 2022 elections," *Sunday Nation*, May 3, 2020. The respected commentator noted that one reason Raila was the man to beat was his dad "refused to be made premier by the colonialists, insisting there would be no independence without jailed Kenyatta."

12. Prof. H. Odera Oruka, *Oginga Odinga: His Philosophy and Beliefs* (Nairobi: Initiatives Publishers, 1992), 6.

13. Ibid., 79.

14. Ibid.

15. Ali A. Mazrui, "Half a Century of the Post-Colonial Judiciary and State Formation: The African Experience," *Kenya Law*, October 11, 2013, http:/kenyalaw.org/kenyalawblog/post-colonial-judiciary-and-state-formation-the-african-experience, accessed November 7, 2019.

16. Ibid.

17. Ibid.

18. "If only Jaramogi became Kenya's first primier [*sic*] as the governor had wanted . . ." *Daily Nation,* November 16, 2013.

19. Ourka, *Oginga Odinga*, 27–28.

20. Ibid., 81.

21. Charles Hornsby, *Kenya: A History Since Independence* (London: I.B. Tauris, 2012).

22. W.O. Maloba, *Kenyatta and Britain: An Account of Political Transformation, 1925-1963* (New York: Palgrave Macmillan, 2018) and W.O. Maloba, *The Anatomy of Neo-Colonialism in Kenya: British Imperialism and Kenyatta, 1963-1978* (New York: Palgrave Macmillan, 2017).

23. Only one mention is made of Renison in the book. There Odinga recalled a meeting after Lancaster House I in 1960. The subject was the release of Kenyatta from restriction. Oginga Odinga, *Not Yet Uhuru* (Nairobi: Heinemann, 1967), 182.

24. Dick Gachui, "African Forecast African Elections," *New Comment,* February 22.1957/ The comments were also directed at Odinga's opponent, B.A. Ohanga, the first African to accept a ministerial portfolio in colonial Kenya.

25. The British and colonial state response to AEMO demands was addressed to him. Baring to Odinga, November 27, 1958, British National Archives (BNA): CO 822/1342.

26. "Changes Proposed Next Year," *Times,* December 1, 1959.

27. Confidential Record of Meeting Held at Government House Nairobi on December 16, 1959; The Stand of the African Elected Members of Kenya LegCo, handed to the SofS at Government House on December 16, 1959, BNA: CO 822/2100.

28. Minute by Macleod to Home Secretary, February 1, 1960, BNA: CO 927/354.

29. Note of a Meeting Between the SofS, Mr. Ngala and Mr. Mboya on February 11, 1960, BNA: CO 822/2359.

30. Record of a Meeting between the SofS and the African Constituency Elected Members on Friday, February 12 at 2:45 p.m., BNA: CO 822/2359. Renison was present at this meeting, and there was no mention made of a post-conference change in the British government's position. In his summary telegram to the acting governor, Walter Coutts, Renison made no reference to the appointment of a chief minister in 1960. SofS to Officer Administering Government, Kenya, telegram, immediate, secret, and personal, for Coutts from Renison, February 15, 1960, BNA: CO 822/2354.

31. Minute by F.D. Webber to W.B.L. Monson, December 29, 1960, BNA: CO 822/1910. Webber was head of the East African Department (EAD) at the CO.

32. Macleod to Renison, telegram, emergency, secret, and personal, March 16, 1960, BNA: CO 822/2754.

33. Macleod to prime minister, May 31, 1960, BNA CO 967/354. In the minute, Macleod proposed to publicly refute criticism "that we are going too fast."

34. Record of Meeting held at Government House on December 16, 1959, BNA: CO 822/2100.

35. Secret Note of Meeting with African Constituency Elected Members on February 22, 1960, BNA: CO 822/2754; Draft of Final Conference Report, February 1960, BNA: CO 822/2365.

36. "Constitution a Step to Independence," *EAS,* February 26, 1960.

37. Governor's Deputy to SofS, telegram, immediate and secret, March 7, 1960, BNA: CO 822/2754.

38. Governor's Deputy to SofS, telegram, immediate, and secret, March 8, 1960, BNA: CO 822/2754.

39. Ngala, Dr. J. G. Kiano, and James Nzau Muimi took portfolios which were formally announced on March 31. Renison to SofS, telegram, emergency, and secret, March 31, 1960, BNA: CO 822/2754. For further detail see Kenya Special Branch Headquarters Intelligence Summary No. 3/60 for the period March 1 to 31, 1960, BNA: CO 822/2058.

40. Extract from Kenya Special Branch Headquarters Intelligence Summary #6/59 for the period June 1 to June 30, 1959, BNA: CO 822/1427. Particularly upset with Odinga's leadership were Muliro, Daniel arap Moi, and Kiano.

41. "Kenya Africans at Loggerheads," *Times*, August 24, 1959. Baring to SofS, telegram, immediate and secret, August 24, 1959, for Webber from Griffith-Jones, BNA: CO 822/1343.

42. Oruka, *Oginga Odinga*, 49.

43. For an excellent treatment, see Maloba, *The Anatomy*, 34–38.

44. "Productive Work Drive," *Times*, August 15, 1960; "Mr. Odinga's Passport Confiscated," *Times*, October 27, 1960.

45. Odinga, *Not Yet Uhuru*, 163–64.

46. Ibid., 163. Robert M. Maxon, *Britain and Kenya's Constitutions, 1950-1960* (Amherst, NY: Cambria Press, 2011), 217–18.

47. Odinga to Lennox-Boyd, March 13, 1959, BNA: CO 822/1342. The other AEM members of the delegation were Kiano, Moi, and Muliro.

48. SofS to Baring, telegram, secret, and personal, March 16, 1959, BNA: CO 822/1342. He referred to the delegation as "a visit to London by Kiano and others." The CO's low regard for Odinga was well illustrated here, but events made Odinga the key figure no matter what the CO thought. Baring, however, urged the SofS to be "careful not to go very far with this group." In his view, the CEMO "was a stunt arranged by Mboya in an effort to show a united anti-European front." Baring to Lennox-Boyd, telegram, priority, secret, and personal, March 20, 1959, BNA: CO 822/1342.

49. For details of the process by which the British and Kenya governments worked out the statement between February and April see Maxon, *Britain and Kenya's Constitutions*, 228–35.

50. Lennox-Boyd to Baring, telegram, immediate, secret, and personal, April 5, 1959, BNA: CO 822/1342. By that time Odinga had made clear to Lord Perth, Minister of State for the CO, that any statement must include "the ultimate goal for the territory." Baring to SofS, telegram, immediate, secret and personal, April 10, 1959, BNA: CO 822/1342.

51. Record of a Meeting Held at Government House on April 6 between Lord Perth and Members of LegCo and Record of a Meeting Held at Government House on April 10 between Lord Perth and elected members of LegCo, BNA: CO 822/1342. All four African members of the CEMO delegation attended both meetings as did Cooke

and the Asian lawyer J.C.M. Nazareth. Zafrud Dean, A.J. Pandya, Dr. S.G. Hassan, and Sheikh Mahfood Mackawi attended one of the sessions.

52. Ibid. Kiano and Muliro came to London several days before the rest of the delegation. They met Lord Perth after the SofS had stated his agreement in parliament to a constitutional conference and expert constitutional adviser. Both the AEM were pleased with that part of the SofS's statement. SofS to Baring, telegram, immediate, secret, and personal, April 23, 1959, from Lord Perth, BNA: CO 822/1342.

53. Brief for meeting with the Constituency Elected Members led by Mr. Odinga on Monday, April 27, 1959, BNA: CO 822/1343.

54. A photo of the delegation appeared in the April 28 issue of *The Times*.

55. Record of Meeting Held on April 27 in the CO between the SofS and CEMO delegation, BNA: CO 822/1343.

56. This was not the final word on the subject as future president Moi intervened to express the hope that Kenyatta's place of restriction be exchanged for somewhere "more healthy." Ibid.

57. Lennox-Boyd to Baring, telegram, emergency, secret, and personal, April 28, 1959, BNA: Co 822/1343.

58. Odinga, *Not Yet Uhuru*, 163–64. As will be seen, Odinga made the latter statement at the meeting on April 30.

59. Note from Lord Perth to SofS, April 28, 1959, BNA: CO 822/1343.

60. Baring to SofS, telegram, emergency, secret, and personal, April 30, 1959, BNA: CO 822/1343. Baring made little direct reference to Odinga, however; he viewed Mboya as the main promoter of the "Kenyatta cult" and a potential threat to security.

61. Confidential Record of Meeting on April 30, 1959. Between the SofS and CEMO, BNA: CO 822/1343.

62. Lennox-Boyd to Baring, telegram, immediate, and confidential, May 1, 1959, BNA: CO 822/1343. "Delegates Pleased by Kenya Talks," *Times*, May 2, 1959.

63. "Africans Boycott of Royal Visit," *Times*, January 18, 1959.

64. Lennox-Boyd to Baring, secret, and personal, May 13, 1959, BNA: CO 822/1343. There was a bit of wishful thinking in the SofS's comment. Given the lack of information available from the recollections of Odinga or other members of the delegation, it is hard to know for certain. Nazareth recalled, more than 20 years later, that other members of the delegation had misgivings as to the wisdom of raising Kenyatta's restriction. J.M. Nazareth, *Brown Man, Black Country* (New Delhi: Tidings Publications, 1981), 345.

65. Baring to Perth, secret, and personal, May 29, 1959, BNA: CO 822/1343. Baring's opinion of Kiano was not without qualification, however. In his April 30 telegram, the governor reminded Lennox-Boyd that Mboya had the effect on Kiano "that a weasel has on a rabbit." Baring to SofS, telegram, emergency, secret, and personal, April 30, 1959, BNA: CO 822/1343.

66. Badejo, *Raila Odinga*, xii.

67. Oruka, *Oginga Odinga*, 27, 52.

68. "Uhuru's full *Mashujaa* Day speech, *Nation*, October 20, 2020.

# BIBLIOGRAPHY

## Primary Sources

British National Archives, London

## Colonial Office Records

CO 822/1342-1343, 1427, 1910, 2058, 2100, 2354, 2359, 2365, 2754
CO 927/354

## Secondary Sources

"Africans Boycott Royal Visit." *Times,* January 18, 1959.

Badejo, Babafemi A. *Raila Odinga An Enigma in Kenyan Politics.* Lagos: Yintab Books, 2006.

"Changes Proposed Next Year." *Times,* December 1, 1959.

"Constitution a Step to Independence." EAS, February 26, 1960.

"Delegates Pleased by Kenya Talks." *Times,* May 2, 1959.

"Elders Demand British Apology." *Daily Nation,* June 12, 2013.

Gachui, Dick. "African Forecast African Elections." *New Comment,* February 22, 1957.

Hornsby, Charles. *Kenya: A History Since Independence.* London: I.B. Tauris, 2012.

"If only Jaramogi became Kenya's first primier [*sic*] as the governor had wanted . . ." *Daily Nation,* November 16, 2013. New York: Palgrave Macmillan, 2017.

"Kenya Africans at Loggerheads." *Times,* August 24, 1959.

Maloba, W.O. *The Anatomy of Neo-Colonialism in Kenya: British Imperialism and Kenyatta, 1963-1978.* New York? Palgrave Macmillan, 2017.

———. *Kenyatta and Britain: An Account of Political Transformation, 1929-1963,* New York: Palgrave Macmillan, 2018.

Maxon, Robert M. *Britain and Kenya's Constitutions, 1950-1960.* Amherst, NY: Cambria Press, 2011.

Mazrui, Ali A. "Half a Century of the Post-Colonial Judiciary and State Formation: The African Experience." *Kenya Law.* October 11, 2013, http://kenyalaw.org/k enyalawblog/post-colonial-judiciary-and-state-formation-the-african-experience.

———. "On Heroes and Uhuru-Worship." *Transition* No. 11 (1963): 23–28.

"Mr. Odinga's Passport Confiscated." *Times,* October 27, 1960.

Odinga, Oginga. *Not Yet Uhuru.* Nairobi: Heinemann, 1967.

Opanga, Kwendo. "Why Raila will be the man to beat in 2022 elections." *Sunday Nation,* May 3, 2020.

Oruka, Prof. H. Odera. *Oginga Odinga: His Philosophy and Beliefs.* Nairobi: Initiatives Publishers, 1992.

"Productive Work Drive." *Times,* August 15, 1960.

Republic of Kenya. *Building Bridges to a United Kenya: from a nation of blood ties to a nation of ideals.* Nairobi: Presidential Task Force on Building Bridges to Unity Advisory, 2019.

————. *Report of the Steering Committee on the implementation of the Building Bridges to a United Kenya Taskforce Report.* Nairobi: Government Printer, 2020.

"Return Gusii Freedom Fighter Otenyo Nyamaterere's skull group tells Britain." *Daily Nation*, September 22, 2015.

"Uhuru's full *Mashujaa* Day speech." *Nation*, October 20, 2020.

"Warrior Otenyo." *Wikipedia*, en.wikipedia.org/warrior_oenyo.

*Chapter 4*

# Daniel arap Moi

## *A Challenge for Historians*

### Robert M. Maxon

This chapter was written following the death of Daniel arap Moi, Kenya's second president, on February 4, 2020. Moi's long career in politics has yet to be subjected to detailed historical treatment marked by the extensive use of primary sources and rigid analysis. The sole biography, officially commissioned by Moi, is disappointing from several perspectives.[1] The varied favorable and unfavorable critiques of his career that appeared in the Kenyan and international press following his death raised as many questions as they answered. The great majority, as in earlier years, was marked by factual inaccuracies. These are some of the challenges facing historians in any assessment of President Moi's political career and its impact. Confronting these will require careful attention to context and to detail in searching out and utilizing primary sources. In this chapter, two periods of the late president's political career will be used to illustrate problems and avenues of research that may suggest potential answers. The two periods of focus are the start of the political career and the critical turning point in that career that marked September and October of 1963.

### POLITICAL BAPTISM

Moi's entry into Kenyan politics began, as is well known, in October 1955 when he joined the colony's Legislative Council (LegCo) upon the resignation of the then African representative member for the Rift Valley, John ole Tameno. He was not elected to this position, as often stated after his death, but was selected by the colonial establishment as a sober and hard-working man who had shown himself a responsible individual through his work as a teacher and headmaster. He was well thought of by European missionaries and colonial administrators, and Moi rapidly won support from the Kalenjin and Maasai elite in the Rift Valley, in contrast to his predecessor. Tameno, a Maasai, had been nominated to the LegCo following the constitutional changes announced in 1951 that provided six nominated seats in that body for Africans.

Moi was able to successfully entrench himself in the evolving political system in the mid-1950s by a combination of hard work, social relationships, economic drive and acumen, and good luck. At the time of his LegCo entry, the Mau Mau war was still ongoing, and this proved a factor in Moi's success. By the end of 1955, Governor Sir Evelyn Baring and Secretary of State for the Colonies (SofS) Alan Lennox-Boyd were anxious that those ethnic communities which were supporting the colonial state through service in the army and police should have representation in the LegCo and civil service. Moi, a Kalenjin, was one such individual to benefit from this.[2] As Dr. Lynch has described, he also used personal contacts and seniority together with now available opportunities to begin to accumulate wealth through the process of straddling in business and agricultural endeavors that left him well placed to succeed in electoral politics.[3] As a member of LegCo, he was well positioned to take advantage of the economic and social opportunities created by the now reformist colonial state through the Swynnerton Plan and educational expansion. He supported and took advantage of the capitalist transformation experienced in Kenya starting in the late 1950s, but, as will be seen later, changes in land ownership would raise critical issues for Moi and other African elected members (AEM).

Moi was hardly unique in taking advantage of these opportunities resulting from colonial development and anti-Mau Mau policies, but he was more successful than many of his peers. This was illustrated by his success in the first African elections of March 1957. Moi faced two opponents for the Rift Valley constituency made up primarily of Kalenjin and Maasai voters. He defeated the former member Tameno (who lost his deposit) and future political ally Justus ole Tipis in the rural constituency with the smallest number of voters in the election.[4] It is generally agreed that Moi's success in this initial electoral contest of his career owed little to ethnicity and most to the personal contacts he had made as a teacher and member of LegCo, his attention to his constituents interests, his "elder" status in contrast to his rivals, and his increasing wealth that he used to foster support.[5] From Baring's perspective, Moi and Ngala represented "personally moderate men" who would not push for rapid political change toward democracy and decolonization, unlike such newly elected members as Tom Mboya and Oginga Odinga.[6]

Even before the election, the question of his future political stand, as a moderate or radical, loomed large in Moi's thinking. It became even more so after March 1957. Upon his entry into LegCo, Moi had not sought to "rock the boat" by articulating an overtly nationalist stance, but the election result presented challenges to this posture. Was Moi to accept the colonial political situation as it was in 1955, working only to achieve material improvement while pushing any demand for self-government to a distant future seen by most Europeans in Kenya to lie many decades away? Or was he to hitch his wagon to the so-called multiracialism reflected in the Lyttleton Constitution of 1954 which sought the racial sharing of political power with Kenya's European settlers playing the leadership roles and Africans advancing gradually to take responsible political and administrative positions in a multiracial Kenya? In contrast to the latter, how should he respond to the demands of colleagues such as Mboya, Odinga, and Muliro for "undiluted democracy" and rapid decolonization with Africans, the majority of the colony's population, playing the leading role? Moi worked out answers to these questions over the next five years. They were a significant part of his political baptism and deserve much closer study than has been given in accounts of his political career.

While he stayed out of the spotlight initially, Moi disappointed Baring and other colonial officials as his moderate views did not cause him to break ranks with the rest of the newly elected AEM. He joined them in the African Elected Members Organization (AEMO) whose aim from the first was to destroy the Lyttleton Constitution and to replace it with a new governing document that provided greater representation and authority for Africans with majority rule as their ultimate goal. In a matter of months, the solidarity of the AEMO combined with growing support among Kenya Africans to achieve the ending of the Lyttleton Constitution in November of 1957. Moi played no leadership role in this campaign, but he loyally backed his peers in their non-cooperation while fully participating in the discussions that led to the ending of the Lyttleton plan and the announcement of the Lennox-Boyd Constitution by the SofS.[7] A feature of this campaign that appears to have had an influence on Moi was the solidarity of the AEM in refusing to budge from their demands and turning down minimal concessions from the SofS and governor. Unity was clearly important, but the months ahead witnessed difficulty in maintaining a united stand from the AEMO.

This fact emerged as the now 14 AEM carried on united opposition to the Lennox-Boyd Constitution in 1958–1959. For Moi and his colleagues, now including a second Kalenjin member of LegCo, the question of accepting reformist colonialism and not moving to independence was answered in the negative. What remained at issue were questions of speed and form of transition. Moi loyally supported the AEMO refusal to participate in the Lennox-Boyd plan (e.g., by refusing to accept a ministerial position). He was willing to do so if his colleagues decided to follow that path as he was confident of overwhelming support from his constituents.[8] Later in 1958, he demonstrated a moderate position in joining the majority of AEM in criticizing Odinga for his LegCo statement that Jomo Kenyatta was recognized as a leader by the African community. According to the Special Branch, Moi and the others argued that the AEM was "the true leaders" of the African people of Kenya; only if Kenyatta was released from restriction and subsequently elected to the LegCo might he be acceptable as their leader.[9]

Moi joined his fellow elected members in demanding that the British government convene a conference to plan a new constitutional path leading to majority rule. The British government made public a promise to do just that in April 1959, and by that time Moi, despite the prohibition of colony-wide African political parties, had joined some AEM in seeking to bring together a multiracial group of LegCo members to push for such a conference and involving an inclusive approach to constitutional change, rather than one that was solely focused on African members. This provided Moi with the opportunity to be part of a multiracial delegation representing the Constituency Elected Members Organization that traveled to London to meet the SofS in April, after the latter had announced his plan to hold a constitutional conference.

The delegation leader was Odinga, and he and colleagues Muliro and Dr. J.G. Kiano dominated the meetings with Lennox-Boyd. At the first meeting on April 27, Odinga and the others raised the issue of the continuing state of emergency and how it worked to the disadvantage of African LegCo members in their attempts to hold public meetings with their constituents. In response, the SofS criticized what he termed remarks in Kenya "glorifying Kenyatta" whom Lennox-Boyd identified as "the convicted organizer of Mau Mau." Odinga responded with an emotional defense of Kenyatta. While other African and Asian delegates sat quietly, saying nothing, Moi followed Lennox-Boyd's rejection of Odinga's comments, according to the record of the meeting, by expressing a hope that Kenyatta's place of restriction might be exchanged for "somewhere more healthy."[10] This episode clearly impacted Moi as he never mentioned it in public, though it must have remained in his memory for a long time.

The differing Odinga and Moi reactions to the criticism of Kenyatta and by extension African nationalism was part of a split that divided AEM over the rest of 1959 as Kenya's politicians prepared for what became the first Lancaster House constitutional conference. Moi opted to cast his lot with those favoring gradualism and the building of an inclusive political vehicle to push for constitutional change leading to independence. One may see in this Moi's moderate and even conservative approach to Kenya's political and economic future, and it is also clear that he was concerned that moving too rapidly to independence might not be the wisest course for the people he represented. He observed that there were at the time few among that group who had the educational qualifications and work experience necessary to fill the top positions in the civil service that would be opened to non-Europeans with the end of colonial rule. Thus he became a supporter, along with the majority of the 14 AEM, of the Kenya National Party (KNP), formed as an alternative to the European-led New Kenya Party (NKP), as a multiracial vehicle for leading Kenya to independence. Four AEM did not agree to go along and formed the Kenya Independence Movement (KIM) to demand a rapid transition to independence under exclusively African leadership. The multiracial or nonracial approach of the KNP was rejected by Odinga, Mboya, Kiano, and Lawrence Oguda (South Nyanza) as they called for "undiluted democracy" immediately in the form of one person, one vote. For Moi, this split produced his first opportunity for leadership. He and his fellow KNP-supporting colleagues expelled Odinga from the AEMO and Moi was chosen to replace him as chairperson of the organization.[11]

This first taste of leadership proved fleeting and not very influential. While the colonial state registered the KNP, the party did not gain strong backing from Kenya's African majority. The masses in Nairobi and other urban centers backed the more radical stand of KIM, and by the end of the year, some KNP supporters, particularly representing central Kenya, moved to back the KIM. The Moi-led AEMO came to support the KIM demands for rapid independence under African leadership at the first of three Lancaster House conferences (Lancaster House I) in early 1960.[12] Moi and his KNP colleagues chose unity over division at the important discussions in London while remaining alert to the potential difficulties of moving Kenya immediately to *uhuru*. Significantly, Moi took no leadership role at the conference as Ngala was chosen as leader of the AEMO delegation with Mboya as secretary. Moi loyally followed their lead at the conference while his most influential contribution came through small group meetings with European and Asian delegates that helped lay the foundation for future cooperation.

Perhaps most consequential for Moi was the way the critical constitutional plan for the immediate way forward was imposed. SofS Iain Macleod presented his plan to African delegates and the three other delegations at Lancaster House on Friday morning February 12. They were to consider it and meet with Macleod in the afternoon to either accept or reject his proposals. Unknown to Moi and his colleagues, the SofS did not give the same plan to all delegations. When he met the African delegation first in the afternoon, Ngala expressed a desire for further negotiation on several points. Macleod rejected this demand and started to leave the room where the delegates had assembled. Ngala and Mboya quickly accepted every detail of Macleod's plan which the latter then sweetened by adding additional seats to the proposed LegCo. While the Asian delegation also accepted Macleod's plan, the NKP delegates (who had received a slightly different plan) were not able to do so. It was only on the following Monday that Michael Blundell, the NKP delegation leader, accepted Macleod's scheme based on the final agreement as to details.[13]

The African delegation returned from Lancaster House I victorious as it was now clear that European settler political dominance was over, and the country would be independent under African leadership for a short period of time. The solidarity of the delegation had played a huge part in this. Nevertheless, the AEMO delegates did not achieve all of their demands (e.g., the immediate release of Jomo Kenyatta), and they had also been outmaneuvered by Macleod. It is clear that this experience stayed in the mind of Moi as well as others. Solidarity was important, but in these kinds of negotiations, stubborn holding to positions could possibly have borne more fruit. This was the first of several instances where Moi realized that relying on the good faith of the British government could be dangerous. This would be demonstrated to him as the implementation of the new constitutional arrangements moved forward in 1960–1961.

## POLITICAL LEADERSHIP IN A TIME
## OF RAPID CHANGE

Moi and the other AEM faced a hectic and challenging period of time in the months following their return to Kenya. This included the reshaping of the council of ministers with three AEM taking portfolios, the preparations for the election to a new LegCo promised at Lancaster House, and political realignment in the formation of colony-wide African political parties. Moi played a part in all these, but less as a mover and shaker than as a politician who responded to national and local pressures and concerns in finding a political home and grasping a leadership position.

Moi was immediately caught up in the negotiations surrounding the entry of AEM into the council of ministers and the intrigue and political infighting accompanying the attempt to form a mass nationalist political party. For the former, the leadership of the colonial state felt that Kalenjin and Kamba LegCo members should be among the new ministers due to their communities' service during the active phase of the Mau Mau war.[14] Moi was thus considered for a ministerial post, but the colonial establishment regarded Taitta Toweett, a Kalenjin elected in 1958, as better educated and more articulate. If four new African ministers had been appointed, Toweett would have taken a portfolio, but in the end, only three were chosen. Moi was not among them, though Toweett was appointed as assistant minister for agriculture.[15]

Political realignment and the formation of national parties took longer to work out. It began at an African Leaders Conference held at the end of

March. The AEM were to report to other African political leaders on the London conference, and some of the AEM wished to use the meeting at Kiambu to launch a national political party (to be known as the Uhuru Party). This was to be brought about by leaving some of the AEM out of leadership positions, notably Mboya. According to Special Branch reports, the leaders of this plot were Odinga and Kiano, both then strongly opposed to Mboya. They organized a secret meeting at Kiano's Nairobi residence to finalize their plan on March 22. Moi was one of several AEM to be invited. Mboya and a group of his supporters crashed the meeting as it started, and it came to little. Nevertheless, Odinga and company continued to plot for a new party, without Mboya involved in leadership, prior to the Kiambu meeting on March 27. A list of potential officeholders was prepared. James Gichuru was to be president, keeping the seat warm for Kenyatta, Odinga vice president, Ngala general secretary, and Moi treasurer. This slate of officers did not come into operation at the meeting as Mboya was able to give himself an important part in planning the new party, now to be called the Kenya African National Union or KANU.[16]

The delayed founding of KANU presented Moi with challenges and opportunities. His association with Odinga, as in the April 1959 meetings in London, produced an opportunity for leadership. However, a key question on this occasion was how his constituents, as well as those Kalenjin now represented by Toweett, would react to a nationalist political party led by Kikuyu and Luo and potentially dominated by Kenya's then most populous ethnic communities. The first half of 1960 thus proved a challenge for Moi. Was he to maintain a political stance wedded to rapid independence for Kenya, land reform in the then white highlands and African land units, an end to racial segregation, and Africanization of the public service? As Dr. Lynch perceptively demonstrated, Moi was forced to desert the radical nationalist and modernizing political stance of Odinga, Gichuru, and Mboya who came to lead KANU upon its formation in mid-May, and to move closer to those politically conscious Kalenjin who helped form the Kalenjin Political Alliance (KPA). Moi thus paid more attention to local issues such as Kalenjin land claims and fear of Kikuyu and Luo domination.[17] A further factor may be seen in the KANU leadership slate announced in May. Moi did not attend the May 14 and 15 meetings, but he was chosen to be Ngala's deputy as assistant treasurer of the new party. This did not please Toweett and other Kalenjin who left the meetings early, and within a week, Moi turned down the post.[18] If a report by the Kenya Intelligence Committee is to be believed, Moi was still uncertain in terms of his future political alliances at the start of June. It stated that Moi seemed undecided "whether to remain an orthodox nationalist and to follow in the footsteps of Oginga Odinga or to come out openly in favour of the Kalenjin alliance."[19] By the end of the month, he had made his choice.

Moi now turned his attention to leadership of the KPA, and he, Toweett, Tipis (elected in 1958), and Muliro in June formed an alternative to KANU in the Kenya National Democratic Union (KADU). The KPA and the Kalenjin people as a whole were one of the bedrock supporters of the party which claimed to represent the interests of minority tribes. Moi took the post of chairman, joining Ngala (president) and Muliro (vice president) as the top leaders of KADU. A key factor at the time of the party's launch was to expand support while solidifying the backing of the ethnic communities of the leadership, Mijikenda, Luyia, Kalenjin, and Maasai.

Moi was able to consistently deliver the goods in terms of overwhelming support among the Kalenjin for KADU. As suggested above, this was a result of his work as an AEM in articulating issues in the LegCo that touched on his constituents' lives as well as his interaction with influential community leaders. His expanding economic activities also demonstrated his understanding of the rapidly changing economic and social milieu in the Rift Valley province where he became known as a leader who could be turned to for advice and other assistance. As Moi took advantage of opportunities for economic advancement opening at the start of the 1960s, however, he was confronted with contradictions that would mark the rest of his political career and strain his leadership at several points. Opportunities for land and business acquisitions in the white highlands and urban areas quickly opened up. Like other African political leaders of the time, he sought to take advantage of these. At the same time, he was forced to deal with a strongly expressed fear among the Kalenjin and Maasai people that lands that then belonged to them or had been taken for European settlement would now fall into the hands of individuals from other of Kenya's large ethnic communities, most notably the Kikuyu. There is every indication that Moi held decidedly liberal capitalist views at this time, much in line with official British decolonization policy, that any Kenyan should be able to own land or a business in any part of the country, but he had to proceed carefully as many of KADU's core supporters rejected this notion. At a late May 1960 KPA rally, for example, a resolution was approved that lands formerly occupied by Kalenjin in the white highlands should revert to their control.[20] It came down to a question of individual or group rights in terms of property; Moi vacillated on the issue then and later in his career.[21]

This was one of several issues Moi and other KADU leaders grappled with as they sought to solidify the party's support in preparation for the 1961 elections. Advocacy for democracy and civil rights in opposition to what the party leaders viewed as KANU's preference for a one-party dictatorship was critical. KADU joined their rivals in demanding Kenyatta's release from detention, and sought to out-bid the KANU election platform, for example, by promising more years of free primary education.

Moi was very outspoken on these subjects, as he represented KADU's leadership in press briefings and public meetings. By most accounts, he was regarded as the number three leader of the party, as Ngala and Muliro were viewed by most Kenyans as more articulate in Swahili and English as well as having a more extensive formal education. Moi also still had to overcome the perception among the leadership of the colonial state that Toweett was better qualified to be a leader of the Kalenjin than he.[22] Moi worked assiduously to change this perception and, as will be seen, he was largely successful by the end of 1963.

Moi emerged personally strengthened from the 1961 elections, though KADU won only a relatively small share of the popular vote and fewer LegCo seats than KANU. Now standing in his home area of Baringo, Moi overwhelmed his brother-in-law, Eric Bomett. He also had time to campaign for other KADU candidates which boosted his standing among supporters. Ngala, Muliro, and Toweett also enjoyed huge victories, but Moi was well placed to enhance his leadership capabilities and reputation after the elections. Starting in March 1962, Kenyan politics was absorbed with the twin issues of Kenyatta's release and the formation of a new council of ministers. This was because both parties had pledged that they would not take part in the post-election executive unless Kenyatta was freed, but the governor, Sir Patrick Renison, adamantly refused to do so. The political atmosphere soon provided Moi the opportunity to play a major role in breaking this deadlock. He exhibited a coolness under pressure and soon showed himself to be a stubborn negotiator who would not be moved from positions he advocated by cajoling or bullying.

He demonstrated this early on when the governor agreed that KANU and KADU delegations should visit Kenyatta, then detained at Lodwar, in hopes that it might lead to their agreeing to serve as ministers. Moi led the KADU delegation to the March 23 meeting. On that occasion, he pushed back against Kenyatta's call for unity if that meant the existence of only a single political party. That would have meant no leadership position for him and his KADU colleagues, and upon his return to Nairobi he publicly repudiated a statement by KANU that the two parties would work toward cooperation.[23]

Much more significant examples of Moi's negotiating tactics emerged in the long series of talks involved in KADU's agreement to take the lead in forming a post-election government in March and April 1961. For example, Moi forcefully put the KADU case as to the release of Kenyatta from restriction and the formation of a new council of ministers to SofS Macleod at the start of April. In addition to setting a guaranteed date for Kenyatta's release following the appointment of new ministers, Moi also urged that a new house be built for the detained nationalist.[24] Moi and Muliro later represented the party in direct talks with the governor as Ngala was in Egypt and Europe for most of the time preceding the agreement to take up ministries together with the NKP and independent LegCo members, made public on April 19. Three days before KADU's taking the lead in the new council of ministers was finalized, Moi told a meeting in Kapsabet "in strictest confidence," that KADU would form a government within the next two weeks.[25]

These were pressure-packed negotiations marked by strict secrecy on KADU's part and revolving around the issue of Kenyatta's release, a broadening of support for the KADU-led government, and a rapid transition to self-government. Moi and Muliro refused to be rushed by Renison and the Colonial Office (CO), hoping to gain a leg up on KANU and induce members of that party to "cross the floor," to join KADU as Moi, Muliro, and Ngala led Kenya to independence. This was, of course, not the last time that inducing individuals to change parties would be a part of Moi's political calculus. As is well known, KADU's gamble did not succeed as the British government did not agree to any move to independence with a government that did not include Kikuyu and Luo representatives which would be able to work out a satisfactory settlement of property rights focusing on European farms in the white highlands.

Moi joined the new government in his first ministerial experience as parliamentary secretary for the Ministry of Education. While Ngala and Muliro took two of the four ministries allotted to Africans under the Lancaster House I plan, the governor and his advisors chose Toweett for a third as more qualified than Moi. Moi cannot have been entirely pleased with this, but he threw himself into a job he proved well suited for, as a former teacher. In this post, he served under Ngala as minister, and since the latter was kept quite busy as leader of government business in the face of nonstop attacks from KANU members and their allies, Moi had to assume more of the workload in what was now a critical ministry in light of the need to dramatically expand access to primary and secondary education for Africans. When Ngala was elevated to the position of "leader of the house" on November 29, Moi assumed the position of minister in name as well as fact.[26]

This ministerial experience and the accompanying bitter, confrontational politics proved a rugged baptism for Moi and other KADU leaders. It was clear to them by the end of June that their gamble in forming a cabinet had not succeeded.[27] Moi got a taste of this through his involvement in the final stage of negotiations for Kenyatta's release that also involved the start of talks between KADU and KANU leaders on constitutional advance and land and property rights. While Moi and the other KADU leaders had agreed to such talks, they did not wish to start these prior to Kenyatta's release so that their party could claim full credit for it. If it were made after the talks started, KADU members of LegCo and their allies were sure that KANU would convince the Kenyan public that the release was due to KANU pressure at the start of the talks. Ngala and Moi, in separate meetings, convinced Renison to support moving up the date of Kenyatta's release announcement to July 27 when the talks were slated to start. London disappointed KADU by refusing to agree to any announcement before August 4. Moi and others were outraged by this. They felt that they had saved Macleod's bacon by forming a government, and this had led to KANU attacks on KADU leaders for "selling out" to the imperialists and European settlers. Now the British government was unwilling to agree to support KADU.[28]

This seemingly left a bitter taste in Moi's mouth. Over succeeding months, he showed himself suspicious of British motives and fearful that KADU would be abandoned as the CO turned to KANU. This "use and dump" policy must have had a significant impact on Moi; certainly, he himself used it later in his career.[29] Like other KADU leaders, he would undertake negotiations with the British and KANU leaders with circumspection and a belief that KADU would have to rely on its own strategies and energy for any success in the unfolding political arena. Thus the remaining months of 1961 and early 1962 were marked by the solidarity of purpose, the utmost secrecy in developing constitutional and other plans, and a stubborn refusal to compromise, or even give an inch, on fundamental principles.

This was quickly apparent when the so-called Nairobi talks between KANU and KADU began under the governor's chairmanship on August 10. KADU leaders contested every point raised for discussion.[30] The talks broke off on October 6 with the agreement reached only on a joint request to the SofS to convene a conference to plan Kenya's constitutional future. As the talks concluded, moreover, the KADU leadership put on the table a new constitutional plan calling for a federal system of government which would provide democratic safeguards via a system of regional powers and "safeguards in respect of tribal lands and spheres of influence."[31] KADU's constitutional plan, soon known by the term *majimbo* (regionalism), absorbed the attention of party leaders over the second half of 1961, and became a major issue at the constitutional conference (Lancaster House II) in 1962.

Moi was much involved in this process, though he was not among the thinkers or constitutional architects of regionalism. By contrast, he was much at the forefront of presenting the new scheme to the Kenyan public— for example, he first made public KADU's "five principles" that should be safeguarded by a regional constitution. The first was directed to "land titles, including tribal rights," shall be respected and safeguarded in the interest of the people of Kenya. Another principle that would resonate later in Moi's career was balanced development of education, health, and other services so as to ensure all Kenya's people play their part in national life.[32] Moi continued to voice public support for KADU's *majimbo* throughout the remainder of the year and beyond.

The opening of Lancaster House II in February 1962 found Moi and other KADU leaders united in their determination to secure a federal constitution for Kenya. Under Ngala's brilliant leadership, they adopted a no-compromise approach to the conference. They stubbornly refused to reveal the specifics of their constitutional plan and contested any attempt by the British or the KANU delegations to divert them from the hard-line stance they adopted from the first. This was what was referred to as the "basic principles" that had to be agreed upon before the conference could discuss any specific constitutional proposals. Regional governing authorities (six were proposed) and their powers must be entrenched in the constitution. These were fundamental aspects of *majimbo* that must be accepted by the conference.[33] Moi was steadfast in support of this stance which ground the conference to a stalemate. The CO organizers tried to break from this by setting up a series of committees to discuss specific issues; four were initially proposed. Moi led the KADU delegates on the Steering Committee charged with establishing the membership of the committees, their agendas, and meeting times. He rejected the idea that all four committees should start meeting at once, insisting that only the committee on the structure of government should meet. Only after it had decided on the main question of principle could the other committees begin work. KADU refuse to take part in the work of the other three committees.[34]

Such obstructive tactics brought some benefit to KADU in that SofS Reginald Maudling eventually imposed a solution that most conference attendees accepted as a framework for Kenya's self-government and independence constitutions. Moi was one of the KADU representatives who did so reluctantly, but he and other party leaders regarded the outcome of the conference as a victory for KADU and a lesson for the future. Solidarity and hard bargaining could overcome some obstacles, as in this case the opposition of KANU and the British rulers to a federal system. There was still much to be done in working out the details as well as dealing with varied difficulties facing Kenya in the form of secession threats from Somalis in the northeast of the country, labor unrest, and tension over land issues. These and more were to be worked out by a coalition government made up of equal numbers of KANU and KADU ministers that was decided on prior to the departure of delegates from London in early April. Moi now took over the ministry of local government, which turned out to be an influential portfolio as the road to independence seemed sure to be rather difficult to navigate, given differences of view on constitutional and land policy, among others.

## THE CHALLENGE OF LEADERSHIP

In many ways, the period stretching from the end of Lancaster House I until the end of 1963 was critical in defining Moi's emerging leadership skills and his future in Kenyan politics.

These months provided both opportunities and challenges for him amid a tense and turbulent history marked by a continuing recession, challenges to internal security, and an aura of uncertainty surrounding land issues in Kenya. Moi undertook his ministerial duties in what became a characteristic thoroughness of preparation and dedication to hard work. Even the most cursory reviews of his ministerial duties during this period have returned a positive judgment. He impressed European civil servants by always reading the ministerial briefs prepared for him, listening to advice, and asking perceptive questions. He was always well prepared for cabinet and LegCo meetings. In addition, he impressed ministerial colleagues with his forthrightness and willingness to take risks. An important example occurred at a July 9 meeting with SofS Maudlin on his visit to Nairobi; Moi disagreed with the British leader in dramatic fashion. Moi objected against the SofS's rejection of KADU's position that each region in independent Kenya must be able to control its own civil service by insisting that regions must be allowed to recruit their own staff. When Maudling exploded in anger to lecture Moi as if he were a schoolboy, both Moi and Ngala walked out of the meeting.[35]

This blowup was smoothed over, but it won Moi admiration from some of his colleagues for standing by his opinions and demonstrating an independent mindset in the face of a challenge from an influential European, a characteristic of his later career. Moi's success as a minister and as a defender of KADU policies solidified his emergence during the second half of 1962 as a preeminent leader among the Kalenjin. Events in his home area and other Kalenjin-inhabited regions of western Kenya also played a part as he linked the defense of *majimbo* with that of Kalenjin land claims as colonial rule came to an end. Influential elders recognized him as the "Kalenjin spokesman," while at the same time Toweett's star dimmed even though he was also a minister.[36]

Nevertheless, significant challenges remained to be surmounted. Two will be examined here: the Kitale controversy and Moi's defense of regionalism at the time of the third conference at Lancaster House (Lancaster House III). The former erupted in December 1962 as a result of the completion of the Regional Boundaries Commission (RBC) report. The report supported most of KADU's suggestions for establishing six regions that would serve as critical governing units in the self-government and independence constitutions. The commissioners (three former colonial civil servants) recommended against the creation of a Northwestern Region that would link Kalenjin-inhabited districts of West Pokot and Marakwet with the Turkana, Trans Nzoia (a European settled district), and the Luyia-inhibited districts of North and Elgon Nyanza. The regional capital was to be Kitale in Trans Nzoia. The commission put Turkana, Trans Nzoia, West Pokot, and Marakwet in a large Rift Valley Region, thus bringing almost all Kalenjin into the same region as many elders and other leaders had demanded. Moi did not support the latter, however. He recognized that KADU's hopes of electoral success depended on linking Kalenjin and Luyia support in the coming election under the new constitution. He thus led a delegation from the KPA testifying before the commission that the Kalenjin people would be quite happy if some of their numbers shared the Northwestern Region with the Luyia and Turkana.[37] Luyia members of KADU and their leader, Muliro, were outraged by this RBC decision, which rejected Moi's plea, as Muliro had been the primary architect of the scheme that would place Kitale and the Trans Nzoia in a region with most Luyia as the latter ethnic community already made up the majority of the district's population.

Moi joined Muliro and other KADU leaders in seeking to change the commission's recommended regions even though he knew many Pokot and Marakwet approved of the report. Moi realized the necessity of holding the party together in view of the forthcoming election. Thus he supported Muliro and Ngala's call at a December 1 cabinet meeting for the transfer of only the western portion of Trans Nzoia, including Kitale, to what the commission had created as Kenya's Western Region. Moi and Ngala, rather than Muliro, introduced this idea at the meeting called to discuss the commission's report. No consensus could be reached in support of this change, thanks to the opposition of Mboya. As a result, no change in the report could be made when it was officially published, and the Kitale controversy blazed brightly for the whole of 1963 and beyond.[38]

Like Muliro and Ngala, Moi was outraged by this and supported what now became a public campaign for the transfer of Kitale to the Western Region. Amid threats of civil disobedience and potential bloodshed, the crisis came to a head in February and March 1963 when new SofS Duncan Sandys came to Nairobi to settle constitutional issues in dispute. Moi's anger peaked when it became known early in March that Sandys planned to respond to Somali demands for secession from Kenya by extensive changes in the RBC report so as to create a Northeastern Region. Moi viewed this as precedent for solving the Kitale issue in a similar manner, but as KANU ministers remained adamantly opposed to any such change, Sandys and then governor Malcolm MacDonald would not accept the KADU demand.[39] Moi was furious as a result of this decision, and he vehemently expressed his displeasure when leaving a cabinet meeting. He claimed the British government could not be trusted. It had done "everything to please those who were violent and subversive" while "those who were loyal have been brushed aside." He went on: "if the Somali with 85,000 could think in terms of self-determination I do not see why the 1,000,000 Kalenjin should not think the same way."[40] This would not be the last time Moi would link constitutional dissatisfaction with talk of secession and threats of violence.

However, Sandys found a way of dealing with the Kitale question at the next cabinet meeting, and other issues quickly intervened. With the self-government constitution now finalized, Kenya moved to elections and implementation. At the national level of the House of Representatives, the election result was bad for KADU though Moi was returned unopposed. Nevertheless, the party won control of the Rift Valley regional assembly, and Moi took on an added responsibility as the assembly elected him its president. Moi's political profile was substantially enhanced after the inauguration of internal self-government on June 1. The constitution had not detailed the specific duties and powers of a regional president, and Moi made the most of this as well as the fact that in March Sandys had decided that each region should be in control of its own civil service. Moi capitalized on these and other factors to serve as one of KADU's most forceful leaders, pushing for the rapid implementation of the self-government constitution and setting an expansive developmental agenda (as in other KADU controlled assemblies increasing secondary school enrollment). This placed him at the forefront of the political struggle to preserve *majimbo* as the central government, led by Kenyatta as prime minister south from the first to change the constitution so as to do away with devolution by installing a centralized system of administration. A key demand was to alter the majorities required in the upper house for any change in the constitution. Moi's was a clear public voice against the calls for change from Mboya and Odinga.

This was demonstrated as Moi participated in the preparatory talks with the governor and central government ministers during July and August. Moi and other KADU leaders refused to agree to the need for any change to the constitution except those of a technical nature required for the transition to complete independence which had been set for December 12. He boycotted the talks long before KADU officially walked out on August 22. By that time, his public rhetoric had become very heated. For example, he regularly called for not only complete implementation of the self-government constitution but also autonomy for his KADU-led region. With regard to land transfers in the region, Moi warned that these must be made with the consent of the Kalenjin and Maasai people or they would not be recognized.[41]

Moi's militancy thus was a factor that could not be ignored by the Kenya and British governments with Lancaster House III set to open on September 25. Governor MacDonald viewed some of the KADU talk as a bluff in light of the party's weakening political position, but he cautioned his superiors at the CO that the leaders, and Moi in particular, "had great influence with the warrior Kalenjin and Masai tribes" and this could cause trouble if they felt that "Regional rights and responsibilities are being reduced in ways prejudicial to their interests," a situation that could lead to "formidable difficulties in Kenya."[42]

This was the background for the start of Lancaster House III. KADU decided to attend after some hesitation while the Kenya government was represented by a high-powered delegation led by the prime minister and including Mboya and Odinga. Moi remained behind as the most senior KADU leader in Kenya during the conference which lasted until October 18. There were few plenary sessions and almost no discussion between the KADU delegation (Ngala, Muliro, Tipis, Martin Shikuku, and J.M. Seroney) and the Kenya government as deadlock quickly emerged. Kenyatta's government demanded extensive changes for the independence constitution in addition to altering the procedure for amendments. KADU leaders opposed any but technical changes and demanded that the self-government constitution be immediately implemented in full. The resulting deadlock produced two crises in October.[43]

Moi was at the center of the first of these. He and other KADU leaders in Kenya were frustrated by the lack of progress at the conference and deeply worried by reports in the Kenya press that predicted a quick end to the conference with Sandys accepting most of the KANU government's demands. Talk of partition of the country was in the air, but the KANU Nairobi branch publicly rejected the idea in insulting terms. Over the weekend of October 6–7, Moi and other members of the KADU parliamentary group reached a tipping point.[44]

This began with a meeting at Moi's Nakuru residence on October 6 and led to a decision by Moi and a small group to plan a breakaway state. The secession plan included the three regions KADU controlled (the coast and western in addition to the Rift Valley) and the northeast region where Somali had boycotted the recent elections. Moi was to be vice president of the new state with Ngala as president and Muliro prime minister. Moi and fellow planners also considered fomenting violent acts such as destroying roads and bridges, burning the homes of KANU supporters in the regions, as well as robbery and assassination attempts directed toward Luo and Kikuyu.[45]

The KADU parliamentary group did not take up the proposals for secession and violence when it met on October 9. However, the group telegraphed Ngala that the delegation in London should immediately return home, and a map was prepared, showing the boundaries of the "breakaway state" that had originated with Moi's group. This was made public at a Nairobi press conference where Moi took a leading role.[46] It was published on October 10. Moi for one was adamant that Ngala and colleagues return to Nairobi at once and the party undertake immediate action to bring about secession. It quickly emerged, however, that the KADU parliamentary group were divided on the question and that Ngala and Muliro were reluctant to go along with the plan. To cool the crisis, Sandys and MacDonald agreed that Shikuku, the KADU general secretary, should return to Nairobi to tell the parliamentary group what was really happening at the London talks and to counsel patience in awaiting the final decisions of the British government. After lengthy discussions, Shikuku gained agreement from the majority present to put the plans for a breakaway state on hold until the outcome of the talks was known.[46] Moi accepted the party verdict, but he was not completely in accord. Some party members seemed to be unwilling to fight to the last for *majimbo*. These included Muliro, who rejected the position of prime minister in the new state, and Toweett, who did not attend any of the parliamentary group meetings. At the end of the group's meetings, however, intelligence sources claimed that Moi told colleagues to return to their home areas and "prepare the people for the worst" in case the British government made basic changes to the self-government constitution demanded by Kenyatta's government.[47]

It was these and the earlier reports which caused concern in the CO and office of the governor in Nairobi to consider taking even more action: Moi's arrest and detention. The outspoken leader may not have known it, but at the same time that Shikuku's mission to Nairobi was organized, KADU's then constitutional adviser, F. M. Bennett MP, asked CO staff to make no move to arrest Moi at that time. F. D. Webber, head of the East Africa department at the CO telegraphed the deputy governor, Sir Eric Griffith-Jones, to alert him as to Bennett's request. Under the self-government constitution, the governor's office still had the final word in measures such as that. Webber told the deputy governor his personal feeling: "in present rather delicate position better wisdom lies in not (repeat not), e.g. restricting Moi or others at this particular moment." Griffith-Jones agreed that "premature action of this nature might well provide the spark to cause an explosion."[48]

In the end, Moi was not detained, and the British government did bow to the Kenya government threats. Sandys introduced several changes disliked by KADU. However, the delegation returned to Kenya having gained a promise from the prime minister to implement the constitution in full and consoled themselves with the fact that the procedure for amendment had not been altered as radically as Kenyatta's delegation had demanded. KADU leaders now had to try to make the best of this and decide what path to follow in the coming months.

Moi played a critical role in this drama as KADU faced the possibility of a split and dissolution. The parliamentary group met over three days following the return of Ngala, Muliro, and the others from London. Intelligence sources reported that during the first two days Moi called for a rejection of the

Lancaster House III decisions, "a declaration of the partition of Kenya, and some degree of violence." Moderates, led by Muliro, urged acceptance of the outcome and cooperation with the Kenyatta government.[49] On the third day of the meetings, the moderates emerged in the majority as Moi's views were rejected. Griffiths-Jones reported to the CO that Ngala, who had sat on the fence, now came down on the side of the moderates. Moi and his supporters accepted the majority decision, though with reluctance.[50]

This important episode has largely been overlooked in most accounts of Moi's career. Morton makes no mention of it. Perhaps this was something Moi himself encouraged as he cultivated the image of a man of peace and conciliation both domestically and internationally when president. However, this account suggests that more attention needs to be given to it since it can be said to provide an interesting parallel to the ethnic cleansing 30 years later that is often blamed on Moi. Moreover, it would appear on the surface that Moi's strong stance and adherence to violent rhetoric in 1963 did not harm his career leadership prospects.

His leadership of the Kalenjin was now solidified as a result of the October crisis. This was not lost on MacDonald, who quickly came to view him as the most consequential KADU leader. Ngala's stance had disappointed the governor, and Muliro was seen as lacking the complete support of his ethnic community, something considered to be very important by Kenya's last governor in his attempts to reduce the tension between KADU and the government. Toweett, for example, had gone missing from the parliamentary group meetings, and this hurt him in the eyes of the governor as well as the Kalenjin public. By late November, MacDonald reported to Sandys that he had achieved success in encouraging Moi to take his concerns "with most of his Regional and tribal troubles" directly to Kenyatta instead of relying on the governor as a go-between. Moi and Kenyatta were now "on pretty good terms."[51] It is not too much of a stretch to see this as the start of Moi's political journey toward becoming the prime minister that led to his appointment as the minister of home affairs in December 1964 and as vice president two years later.[52]

## NOTES

1. Most notable is a lack of appreciation of Kenya's historiography. Andrew Morton, *Moi: the Making of an African Statesman* (London: Michael G. O'Mara Books, 1998). Much to be preferred is Dr. Lynch's account. Gabrielle Lynch, *I Say to You: Ethnic Politics and the Kalenjin in Kenya* (Chicago: University of Chicago Press, 2011). The chapter focusing on Moi's career is sub-titled: "The Making of an African Big Man."

2. For further detail see Robert M. Maxon, *Britain and Kenya's Constitutions.1950-1960* (Amherst, NY: Cambria Press, 2011), 117 & 132.

3. Lynch, *I Say to You*, 87–88.

4. For this first African election in colonial Kenya, voters could qualify for from one to three votes. Moi gained 71.88 percent of the votes in the constituency, a larger proportion than any other successful candidate. His future political colleagues Ronald Ngala and Masinde Muliro gained 36.19 percent and 30.61percent, respectively.

5. Lynch, *I Say to You*, 87. She makes a case for his use of patronage then and in later political campaigns. Morton, *Moi*, 59–60.

6. Baring to SofS, secret March 15, 1957. British National Archives (BNA): CO 822/1531. This assessment was made in the immediate aftermath of the election.

7. The British records of these constitutional discussions may be found in BNA: CO 822/1425, 1430, 1431, and 1433.

8. J.V. Prendergast, Kenya Director of Intelligence and Security, Report on AEM Policy Conference, January 13 to 15, enclosure in E. W. Magor to J.L.F. Buist (CO), secret, January 27, 1958, BNA: CO 822/1340.

9. Extract of Special Branch Headquarters Intelligence Summary for July 1958, secret, BNA: CO 822/1340.

10. Record of Meeting Held on April 27 in the CO between the SofS and Constituency Elected Members. Lennox-Boyd to Baring, telegram, emergency, secret and personal, April 28, 1959, BNA" CO 822/1343. Maxon, *Britain and Kenya's Constitutions*, 236–37.

11. "Kenya Africans at Loggerheads," *Times*, August 24, 1959.

12. Kenya Intelligence Committee Monthly Appreciation No. 11/59, BNA: CO 822/1343.

13. These negotiations are detailed in Maxon, *Britain and Kenya's Constitutions*, 321–28.

14. Renison to SofS, telegram, immediate, secret, and personal, March 26, 1960, BNA: CO 822/2015. Sir Patrick Renison took over as Kenya's governor in October 1959.

15. Coutts to Granville Roberts, secret and personal, April 2, 1960, BNA: CO 822/2025 and Kenya Special Branch Headquarters Intelligence Summary No. 3/60, BNA: CO 822/2028. Sir Walter Coutts served as chief secretary and deputy governor under Renison and Granville Roberts was then Kenya's press representative in Britain. Renison to SofS, telegram, emergency and secret, March 31, 1960, BNA: CO 822/2754.

16. The fullest account of these events is found in: Kenya Special Branch Headquarters Intelligence Summary No. 3/60, BNA: CO 822/2028.

17. Lynch, *I Say to You*, 57–61. She made extensive use of Special Branch reports of meetings Moi attended during the period March to June 1960.

18. "Mr. Ngala Not to be K.A.N.U. Officer," *East African Standard* (*EAS*), May 21, 1960.

19. Kenya Intelligence Committee Monthly Appreciation No. 6/60, BNA: CO 822/2100.

20. "Kenya Tribes Rally to Stake Their Claims," *Times*, May 30, 1960. Another demand accepted was that civil servants serving in Kalenjin-inhabited areas should only support policies approved by the KAP as representatives of the local population. See also Lynch, *I Say to You*, 63.

21. For a discussion of KADU's policy and the reaction of the British administration see Robert M. Maxon, *Kenya's Independence Constitution: Constitution-Making and End of Empire* (Lanham, MD: Fairleigh Dickinson University Press, 2011), 65–66.

22. A political fact also influenced this opinion. While Moi won an overwhelming victory in the 1961 election, he gained a relatively modest vote total of 5,225; by contrast Toweett polled 56,445. George Bennett and Carl Rosberg, *The Kenyatta Election: Kenya 1960-1961* (Nairobi: Oxford University Press, 1961), 65–66.

23. Extract from Kenya Intelligence Committee Monthly Report No. 6/61, BNA: CO 822/2102.

24. He also supported KADU's call for money to be provided by Britain for "the resettlement problem," noting that the British government had spent 50 million pounds in defeating Mau Mau, "a useless thing." Secret Record of Meetings held at RAF station Eastleigh on April 3, 1961, between certain Kenya political groups and individuals and the Right Honourable Iain Macleod, BNA: CO 822/2101 and 2107.

25. Extract from Kenya Intelligence Committee Monthly Report No. 4/61, BNA: CO 822/2102.

26. "Concession to Kadu pressure," *EAS*, November 30, 1961; Renison to SofS, telegram, immediate and secret, December 1, 1961, and SofS to Renison, telegram, immediate and confidential, December 5, 1961, BNA: CO 822/2754. He served until April 11, 1962. This fact is presented to reinforce the point made earlier that many newspaper accounts of Moi's career since leaving office make inaccurate references to his colonial-era ministerial record. An example may be taken from a 2017 *Sunday Nation* article focusing on Moi's protege, Nicholas Biwott. In the article, Moi as minister in charge of education is described as taking Biwott to Kenneth Matiba, his permanent secretary, to procure an overseas scholarship for the young man. The writer stated that Matiba was the source for the story, but, if so, the late Matiba's memory betrayed him. As noted above, Moi left the ministry in April 1962; Matiba was appointed acting permanent secretary for education on June 7, 1963. It was not until December 12, 1964, that Moi again held ministerial office, though not in education. Kamau Ngotho, "Unmasking the myth of 'Total Man' Biwott," *Sunday Nation*, November 19, 2017.

27. In mid-July, for example, Ngala complained to Renison that his supporters in LegCo felt that the SofS and governor were "denying them the support which they feel they have right to expect" as KADU's political interests were being subordinated to British political considerations. Renison to Macleod, telegram, emergency, secret and personal, July 20, 1961, BNA: CO 822/1912.

28. The Return of Jomo Kenyatta: A Review of the Period March-November 1961, enclosure in Director of Intelligence to Permanent Secretary, Ministry of Defence, secret, November 22, 1961, enclosure in Renison to SofS, immediate, November 23, 1961, BNA: CO 822/2102.

29. Karuti Kanyinga, "Messy Politics—The Legacy of Moi's Rule," *Nation*, March 4, 2020.

30. The Return of Jomo Kenyatta, BNA: CO 822/2102.

31. Renison to Macleod, telegram, immediate, secret, and personal, October 3, 1961, BNA: CO 822/2237. For an account of the Nairobi talks see Maxon, *Kenya's Independence Constitution*, 48–53.

32. "Kadu Launches Its Blueprint for National Unity," *EAS*, October 14, 1961.

33. Record of First Meeting Held on Wednesday, February 14, 1962, at 10:30 am, BNA: CO 822/2237; extract from K.C.C. Fourth Meeting Held on February 16, 1962, K.C.C. (62) 11, Speech by Mr. Ngala, BNA: CO 822/2242.

34. Record of the Second Meeting of the Steering Committee Held at 3 pm on February 24, 1962, BNA: CO 822/2372.

35. Extract from the Minutes of the SofS's Sixth Meeting with Ministers of the Kenya Government on July 9, 1962, BNA: CO 822/2256.

36. Lynch, *I Say to You*, 85, 91–92.

37. Regional Boundaries Commission, A Meeting with a Delegation from the Kalenjin Political Alliance, held at Nakuru on August 29, 1962, Kenya National Archives (KNA): GO1/2/1.

38. Council of Ministers 58th (Constitutional) Meeting, secret, December 1, 1962, BNA: 822/2538 and KNA: WC/CM/1/12. The governor and his deputy supported the change and Kenyatta raised no objection, but Renison and the CO held that alterations in the report could only be made by unanimous consent of the council of ministers, and Mboya refused to go along with Kitale in Western Region. For the fullest treatment of the Kitale controversy, see Maxon, *Kenya's Independence Constitution*, 142–51 and 164–69.

39. Council of Ministers, Tenth Meeting with the SofS, March 7, 1963, BNA: CO 822/2316.

40. Maxon, *Kenya's Independence Constitution*, 168.

41. "Growing Demands in Kenya for Regional Autonomy," *Times*, July 22, 1963. The paper's correspondent noted a "fiery speech" Moi made in Kericho where he told "a jubilant crowd that he and they were prepared to shed blood if necessary to protect the Rift valley region."

42. MacDonald to SofS, telegram, immediate, secret, and personal, September 20, 1963, BNA: CO 822/3102.

43. For full details see Maxon, *Kenya's Independence Constitution*, 227–53.

44. Ibid., 231–34.

45. Annex to Kenya Intelligence Committee Monthly Appreciation KIMCA (63) (10) for the period October 1 to October 31, 1963, BNA: CO 822/3059.

46. Ibid. "Kenya Division Threat," *Times*, October 10, 1963.

47. Ibid. Acting Governor to SofS, telegram, immediate, secret, and personal, October 11, 1963, BNA: CO 822/3053.

48. Ibid. Acting Governor to SofS, telegram, immediate, secret, and personal, October 12, 1963, BNA: CO 822/3053. Only the British government could make changes to be included in the independence constitution.

49. SofS to Acting Governor, telegram, emergency, confidential, and personal, October 9, 1963, from Webber and Acting Governor to SofS, telegram, emergency, secret, and personal, October 10, 1963, for Webber, BNA: CO 822/3053. Later the same day, Sandys telegraphed Griffith-Jones to warn that unless the situation in Kenya demanded immediate action, the SofS would make the final decision "before arresting or restricting any political personalities." SofS to Acting Governor, telegram, emergency, secret, and personal, October 10, 1963, BNA: CO 822/3053.

50. Annex to Kenya Intelligence Committee Monthly Appreciation KIMCA (63) (10) for the period October 1–31, 1963, BNA: CO 822/3059. Acting Governor to SofS, immediate, secret, October 23, 1963, BNA: CO 822/3053.

51. MacDonald to Sandys, secret, November 29, 1963, BNA: CO 822/3101. It would be wise, of course, not to exaggerate the significance of MacDonald's report as it is clear he sought to inflate his own role in bringing peace and stability to Kenya in much of his correspondence.

52. Moi was the only KADU leader to enter Kenyatta's cabinet at the time. Even such a respected newspaper as *The Guardian* marked Moi's death by a false claim that "at independence in 1963 he became minister of home affairs." "Daniel arap Moi Obituary," *The Guardian*, February 4, 2020.

# BIBLIOGRAPHY

## Primary Sources

British National Archives, London

## Colonial Office Records

CO 822/1340; 1343; 1343; 1425; 1430; 1431; 1433; 1531; 1912; 2015;2025; 2028; 2100-2102; 107; 2237; 2242; 2371-2372; 2538; 2754; 3053; 3059; 3101-3102.
Kenya National Archives, Nairobi
GO1/2/1
WC/CM/1/12

## Secondary Sources

Bennett, George and Carl Rosberg. *The Kenyatta Election: Kenya 1960-1961.* Nairobi: Oxford University Press, 1961.
"Concession to Kadu Pressure." *EAS*, November 30, 1961.
"Daniel arap Moi Obituary." *The Guardian*, February 4, 2020.
"Growing Demands in Kenya for Regional Autonomy." *Times*, July 22, 1963.
"Kadu Launches Its Blueprint for National Unity." *EAS*, October 14, 1961.
Kanyinga, Karuti. "Messy Politics—The Legacy of Moi's Rule." *Daily Nation*, March 4, 2020.

"Kenya Africans at Loggerheads." *Times*, August 24, 1959.

"Kenya Tribes Rally to Stake Their Claims." *Times*, May 30, 1960.

"Kenya Division Threat." *Times,* October 10, 1963.

Lynch, Gabrielle. *I Say to You: Ethnic Politics and the Kalenjin in Kenya.* Chicago: University of Chicago Press, 2011.

Maxon, Robert M. *Britain and Kenya's Constitutions, 1950-1960.* Amherst, NY: Cambria Press, 2011.

———. *Kenya's Independence Constitution: Constitution-Making and End of Empire.* Lanham: Fairleigh Dickinson Press, 2011.

Morton, Andrew. *Moi: the Making of an African Statesman.* London: Michael O'Mara Books, 1998.

"Mr. Ngala Not to be K.A.N.U. Officer, *EAS*, May 21, 1960.

Ngotho, Kamau. "Unmasking the Myth of 'Total Man' Biwott." *Sunday Nation*, November 19, 2017.

## Chapter 5

# Ainsworth after Dark

## *The Pied Piper of African Development in Colonial Kenya, 1895–1920?*

Okia Opolot

John Dawson Ainsworth (1864–1946) was a colonial administrator who enjoyed a long and distinguished tenure (1889–1920) during the early period of Kenya's colonial history. He served in several capacities as a member of the British East Africa Company, a district commissioner (DC), provincial commissioner (PC), and, lastly, the colony's first chief native commissioner (CNC) in 1919.[1] As an administrator, Ainsworth's tax collection methods became the template for the rest of the colony. In 1901, he also founded the East African Agricultural and Horticultural Society.[2] Moreover, in 1912 Ainsworth radically proposed the creation of provincial councils to safeguard African interests, which would also include educated African members.[3]

With such a long administrative career in Kenya, Ainsworth left a paper trail and garnered many friends and foes alike. Ainsworth's critics, mainly European settlers, routinely denounced him for being an overly "pro native" administrative official who promoted African development to the detriment of the European export agricultural sector.[4] As one notable settler, Lord Cranworth (Bertram Gurdon), stated, "Mr. Ainsworth was not a settler's man; he was a native's man pure and simple."[5] *The Leader of British East Africa*, a settler newspaper, declared that Ainsworth's "opinions are tainted with the color of negrophilism."

On the other side of the spectrum, Ainsworth's advocates viewed him in another light. Colonial Office officials regarded Ainsworth as a highly respected expert with "wide experience and knowledge" of Africa.[6] Unlike administration officials, like Dr. Norman Leys, who also had reputations for "pro native fanaticism," Colonial Office officials trusted Ainsworth's judgment.[7] According to Ainsworth's main biographer, Professor Robert Maxon, "he was the man most often turned to in time of difficulty or crisis."[8] He was the man on the spot.

However, despite Ainsworth's apparent "negrophilism," F. H. Goldsmith, who penned an early memoir of John Ainsworth, written mostly by himself, contends that, "there is little doubt that Ainsworth had been unjustly criticized in earlier years for being too 'pro-native.'"[9] He was right. Ainsworth played an important role in the second Maasai Move and came to be associated with the infamous Northey Circular in 1919 that expressly intimated that Africans should be "encouraged" to work for European interests.[10] Moreover, Ainsworth, the reputed defender of African development, viewed Africans as children who had to be civilized.[11]

So, who was John Ainsworth? Was he a strong proponent of African development? Alternatively, was he just another paternalistic administrator hellbent on turning Kenya into a "White Man's Country?"[12] It is difficult to easily reconcile these opposing historical portraits. In fact, Robert Maxon cautions against an over-simplistic evaluation of Ainsworth's motives. He maintains that Ainsworth was actually in favor of nonexploitative African development, but he felt that the administration's overall support for European production ultimately undermined his efforts. As Maxon states,

> He tried to frame policies which would protect African interests, as he defined them, in land and labor, but faced with zealous settler demands which received a more sympathetic hearing than his own advice from the territory's governors, he was not always successful.[13]

In this sense, then, Ainsworth was a casualty of the contradictions of colonial rule in the Kenya Colony. To borrow from Bruce Berman and John Lonsdale, the vacillating opinions of Ainsworth from the CO and European settlers reflected the myriad contradictions of colonial rule in Kenya.[14] Appropriating aspects of Nicos Poulantzas' Marixt interpretation of the state,[15] Berman and Lonsdale contend that the state in Kenya was only relatively autonomous and had to act as a mediator between African and settler production, which led to episodic contradictions.

The political, economic, and social institutions of the colony clearly favored the minority European settlers. However, if the administration engaged in policies concerning Africans that were too exploitative, it faced criticism from the various tentacles of the humanitarian lobby,[16] plus rebukes, and possible sanctions from the Colonial Office. The Colonial Office, during this time period, vacillated between the two development paths in Kenya Colony but ultimately favored the trust principle.[17] These contradictory imperial goals produced episodic administrative challenges in the colony, as evidenced in the case of Ainsworth.

To explore this conundrum of contradictions further, this paper examines Ainsworth's roles in a couple of administrative controversies in Kenya Colony and also delves into his own written communications with the Colonial Office and a series of articles that he wrote for the *Farmers Journal* in 1920 on "native" labor in Kenya. By piecing together Ainsworth's paper trail against the backdrop of labor, the image that shines through becomes a story of, not only development but also race during the early colonial period in Kenya.

Berman has written that colonial administrators maintained a common paternalistic ideology.[18] According to Roger van Zwanenberg, Europeans, "generally believed that they were dealing with an inferior race and civilization who would need hundreds of years before they would 'catch up.'"[19] Europeans believed that they had taken on the "burden" of colonization in Africa to modernize "backward" peoples.

Ainsworth's views were consistent with general European conceptions of Africa at this point.[20] He advanced a vision of African development steeped in Social Darwinist thinking that promoted trusteeship while advancing the interests of white settlers through coercive means.[21] Although Ainsworth did favor African production, he also held prevalent European paternalistic attitudes toward Africans. Regarding African development, Ainsworth stated that, "we must bear well in mind that we cannot . . . leave the black man to go his own way . . . we are bound to do what is humanely possible to raise him to a higher state of citizenship."[22]

As a result, borrowing from Critical Race Theory (CRT), we also contend that the concepts of intersectionality and interest convergence shed more light on some of Ainsworth's contradictory positions that he promoted later.[23] Although CRT, as a theoretical construct, first emerged in the context of the post–Civil Rights era in United States history as a criticism of liberalism, its core tenets have wider implications.

According to CRT, even though racism is deeply embedded within institutions, like the economic structures, judicial system, and laws, there can also be interest convergence where the material interests of opposing groups within a racial hierarchy can overlap on certain issues, which then fosters positive change or justice.[24] In the case of Ainsworth, he was a member of a colonial administration that carried out policies that ultimately favored European settlers, despite the language of trusteeship. However, when certain policies appeared to have the potential to undermine African production, there was a material interest convergence on the part of the administration to push back or defend African production.

In regard to intersectionality, or anti-essentialism, CRT scholars assert that people often have overlapping identities that can function in an asymmetrical or contradictory manner within institutions. On the one hand, Ainsworth was a member of the dominant racial group in Kenya Colony and, as such, he should have been expected to, at least, safeguard their interests. Conversely, he also was a member of the administration that was supposed to provide tutelage to African "children." Moreover, although Ainsworth was English, he came from a working-class background. This social gulf would have separated him from some of the leading settlers in the colony, like Lord Delamere.

This chapter relies upon Robert Maxon's, biography of Ainsworth, *John Ainsworth and the Making of Kenya* and F. H. Goldsmith's, *John Ainsworth, Pioneer Kenya Administrator, 1846-1946*. Both books, particularly *John Ainsworth and the Making of Kenya*, serve as the textual framework for Ainsworth's administrative career and provide insight into some of his motives.

## EARLY CAREER

This section gives a brief sketch of Ainsworth's early administrative career in the East Africa Protectorate (EAP). His actions during this early period show that he was open to treating Africans in a fair manner. In addition, the seeds of thought that later germinated into his promotion of African production began during this early period.

John Ainsworth was born in Manchester, England in 1864. He was educated for about eight years in formal business training.[25] Afterward, he began a career as a trader. At the age of 20, Ainsworth began his work in the Congo, where he served for five years with a trading company in the Congo Free State.[26] In 1889, he joined the Imperial British East Africa Company (IBEAC) organizing foot safaris, as a Transport Superintendent, into the interior from the coastal port of Mombassa.[27] Eventually, the IBEAC transferred Ainsworth further inland to Machakos in Eastern Kenya, as he became a Station Superintendent in 1892.

The move to Machakos was a significant step-up in Ainsworth's career. It was his first administrative appointment under the aegis of the IBEAC, and the experience helped shape his reputation as pro-African. Prior to Ainsworth's tenure at Machakos, company officials poisoned relations with the local Kamba people by consistently allowing IBEAC *askaris* (guards) to steal food and rape women. However, after settling in at Machakos, Ainsworth worked to establish a stable working relationship with the Kamba.[28] In exchange for food, he provided trade goods and commercial contacts, plus opportunities for employment. Ainsworth also invited Indian traders to Machakos, who then introduced currencies, in this case, *Rupees*, into the markets, which helped to initiate cash exchanges.[29] Ainsworth also established a very profitable relationship with a Kamba man, Mzau wa Mwanza, that allowed him to penetrate the local social networks and more effectively govern the area. Ainsworth spoke fondly of Mzau who he mentioned was "subsequently of considerable assistance to me in the administration of the Akamba and what success I ultimately attained in the District was largely due to him."[30] Maxon notes, however, that Ainsworth's treatment of the Kamba probably had more to do with, the fact that, his own forces were too weak to subjugate them militarily.[31]

After the British government assumed control of the EAP in July 1895,[32] the new colonial administration retained Ainsworth as a subcommissioner in Machakos in what would now become Ukamba Province.[33] At this time, Ukamba Province included Ukamba, Kikuyu, Yaita, and Taveta districts, with Machakos as the administrative center. During this early period of colonial rule, administrative duties for officials on the ground typically consisted of maintaining security, suppressing slave trading, and facilitating caravan transport to the Uganda Protectorate.[34]

In pursuance of his duties under the EAP, Ainsworth again displayed traits that distinguished him as someone who was fair in dealing with Africans. For example, in November 1895 a large trading caravan consisting of several hundred Kikuyu porters and Swahili *askaris* encamped near a Maasai settlement in the Kedong Valley. During the course of encampment, the Swahili assaulted Maasai women and attempted to steal some of their cattle. In response, the Maasai attacked the caravan and killed several hundred of the Swahili and Kikuyu. In retaliation for the Maasai attack, IBEAC trader Andrew Dick led an attack on the Maasai that resulted in his own death. Despite the loss of a European life, in what was later known as the Kedong Massacre, Ainsworth ultimately sided with the Maasai and made a less stringent settlement with them.[35]

After a successful stint in Machakos, Ainsworth transferred his headquarters to Nairobi in 1899. At this point, Mombasa was the capital of the East Africa Protectorate. In keeping with the methods he employed successfully with the Kamba, Ainsworth eventually developed a good working relationship with the Maasai who resided at Fort Dagoretti, which bordered both Maasai and Kikuyu territory. He cultivated social linkages with significant leaders among them, more specifically their spiritual leader, the *Laibon* Lenana.[36] In 1906, Ainsworth became the subcommissioner of Naivasha Province and a year later became the provincial commissioner of Nyanza Province. His actions while administrating Nyanza Province solidified his reputation as an advocate of African production.

## AINSWORTH AS DEFENDER

Ainsworth's career ark paralleled the gradual development of the East Africa Protectorate. After 1903, administrative and Colonial Office encouragement of European settlement in Kenya created tensions in the development vision of Kenya as either an African colony or a European settler colony. As mentioned earlier, these were part of the contradictions of colonial rule in Kenya. This anxiety manifested in Ainsworth's promotion of African production and the subsequent criticism that he received from various prominent European settlers. As G. Mungeam states, "Ainsworth had a long acquired the reputation of being a pro-African administrator who strove to protect his people from exploitation."[37]

After the completion of the Uganda railway in 1902, it became the main artery for the transportation of goods in the colony. As a result, the administration began to encourage European settlement as a way of paying off the debt of construction, plus making the railway economically viable.[38] Sir Charles Elliot, the EAP's second commissioner (1901–1904), called for European settlement during his tenure as a way of making the colony profitable. The formal process of land alienation began with the passage of the 1902 and 1915 Crown Lands Ordinances.[39] Initially, Europeans could lease land from the crown for up to 99 years and could buy up to 1,000 acres of land for homestead farming. In 1915, the administration extended land leases to 999 years. All African land became crown land. Between 1906 and 1912, the state demarcated reserve areas for Africans that also hemmed them in as a potential source of labor. In 1906 and 1908, two pledges from the Colonial Office further ensured the exclusivity of the central highland area for European settlers. The "Elgin Pledge," named after the secretary of state for the colonies, the Earl of Elgin (Victor Bruce), reserved the "White Highlands," as the alienated land came to be known for European settlement only. Ultimately, the White Highlands came to encompass approximately seven million acres or approximately 33 percent of arable land in Kenya.

After 1903, Europeans began to flood into the Rift Valley in search of cheap land. With this onslaught of Europeans, Ainsworth sided with Africans, as he championed Kikuyu land rights bordering Nairobi against European settler encroachment.[40] According to Maxon, Ainsworth was "never and ardent advocate of European settlement in Kenya."[41] For example, Ainsworth clashed with Sir Charles Elliot and Lord Delamere (Hugh Cholmondeley), a leading European settler and landowner, over the pace of European land acquisition. Specifically, Ainsworth wanted the Land Office to only issue land grants after land had been mapped which angered many European settlers anxious for land.

Maxon asserts, however, that Ainsworth's attitude toward European land acquisition was more about maintaining administrative control.[42] He did support the idea of economic development in the colony through the European agricultural sector. He felt that the African agricultural sector should complement rather than compete with the European.[43]

As mentioned earlier, by 1909, Ainsworth was entrenched in Nyanza Province. Memorandums Ainsworth submitted to the CO in August 1913 concerning general education for Africans and overall development in Nyanza Province provide elucidation of his views on African development.

Ainsworth favored African development as a means of facilitating trusteeship. As he stated,

> [W]hat we require in East Africa is a general policy for the uplifting and betterment of the natives . . . we must raise the status of the natives and they must be thought to realize that they are citizens of the empire . . . all of this cannot be achieved unless the government . . . accept that a policy of native development is the only sound moral and businesslike way of dealing with the millions of blacks over whom we have asserted our control.[44]

Ainsworth defined acceptable work for African men as "work in your in Reserve at production for yourselves and your community or work outside for wages."[45] Ainsworth's promotion of Africans working for themselves in the reserve areas actually differed from other administrative officials. For example, O. F. Watkins, who followed Ainsworth as chief native commissioner in March 1921, felt that individual African men working on their own private plots could never suffice as true wage labor under the exemptions of the 1920 Native Authority Amendment Ordinance due to the difficulty in proving that Africans had worked.[46]

Ainsworth's ideal of African development emphasized tribal cohesion among the Africans. This meant separate development for Africans within their own reserves. Ainsworth's views on segregation were Social Darwinistic and, specifically, influenced by the thinking of the South African general Jan Smuts during the First World War.[47] As Maxon notes, however, many of the European settlers were actually very critical of segregation, fearing that it would squelch the labor flow from African reserve areas.[48] Later, Ainsworth's thinking influenced much of the Dual Policy of encouraging both African commodity and European production under the governor, Sir Robert Coryndon in 1923.[49]

In Nyanza, Ainsworth encouraged African agriculture and gave away free seeds. His efforts bore fruits, as Nyanza Province eventually became the leader in maize production in the colony.[50] According to the Kenyan historian Bethwell Ogot, Africans responded positively to Ainsworth's initiatives and Nyanza Province soon began producing cotton, groundnuts, and sim sim.[51] As a reflection of Nyanza Province's growing agricultural importance, in

1911 the region exported £66,000 of produce on the railway.[52] Prior to 1908, Nyanza Province did not produce any significant marketable produce carried on the Uganda railway.

To augment crop production further, Ainsworth also encouraged innovations in cultivation methods and tool use.[53] For example, he introduced and promoted the use of European plows pulled by oxen. Ainsworth also pushed for improved communications infrastructure by extending the Uganda railway from Kisumu to Mumias. This eventually occurred with the construction of the Uasin Gishu railway extension, which, ironically, promoted European production.[54]

Perhaps as a reflection of the growing economic power of African production in Nyanza, hut and poll taxes also increased during Ainsworth's tenure.[55] Illustrative of its economic importance, direct taxation of Africans would eventually comprise 85 percent of government revenue.[56] From 1905 to 1910, hut tax revenue in the EAP increased from £29,548 to £118, 473.[57] Perhaps, as a reflection of his commitment to African development, Ainsworth always thought that the level of taxation exacted from the African populace did not match the level of social services and development found in the reserve areas.[58] Buttressing Ainsworth's view, recent work in the field of economic history has shown that British colonies in East Africa, like Kenya and also Uganda, maintained "extractive" economic policies predicated upon high rates of direct taxation and the exploitation of African labor.[59]

The central importance of taxation went beyond mere tax receipts though. The institution of taxation was also a labor inducement. In order to pay the taxes, Africans would have to find some sort of work for wages. Working for wages invariably led to European employment. Ultimately, Ainsworth believed that if Africans prospered in their reserve areas, they would be more amenable to going out of the reserves to work for Europeans. Ainsworth believed that if Africans were to progress, they had to work hard, but the choice of working must be of their own choosing.[60]

Ainsworth's promotion of African commodity production was more of an attempt to achieve fiscally sustainability than part of an elaborate, sinister plan to undermine the European cash crop sector. Regarding African production, there was interest convergence on the part of the administration. Prior to the start of the Great Depression in 1929, African production and taxation buoyed government revenue.[61] It is not surprising that Ainsworth, while he was PC of Nyanza Province, started a short-lived pass registration system for Africans leaving Nyanza to work on European farms. Ainsworth felt that a pass system would help African laborers better secure their wages and strengthen job security.[62] This labor identification system preceded the much-hated *kipande* labor ID system, which came into force in 1920. Ainsworth's pass system only had a brief existence due to the amount of administrative work involved.[63] In defending African production, then, Ainsworth was actually promoting the overall economic well-being of the colony despite the displeasure this caused European settlers.

## AINSWORTH AS "NEGROPHILIST"

By 1912, the increasing influx of European settlers created a growing demand for cheap African labor. Many Europeans employers offered low wages and difficult working conditions that only ensured trouble in acquiring African workers. Ainsworth's promotion of African agriculture angered many settlers because it seemed to them that he was attempting to stem the supply of workers leaving the reserve areas. European settlers criticized Ainsworth's support for African production in Nyanza Province. The criticisms of Ainsworth were consistent with the dominant vision of Ainsworth as a defender of African production.

In 1912, the simultaneous arrival of more European farmers coupled with the development of various government projects, like the Thika extension of the Uganda railway, the construction of a piped water delivery system in Mombasa and the building of the Mombasa harbor works, all served to create the appearance of a labor shortage.[64] Ainsworth actually contended that mistreatment of African laborers by European employers caused the labor shortage. As he stated in a memorandum on the labor crisis, "it is my absolute opinion that most of the present difficulties in obtaining labour are due to causes for which the White and Indian employers are entirely responsible."[65] Ainsworth countered that "if the whites are to maintain a permanent hold over the blacks, it can only be through sympathetic contact."[66]

*The Leader of British East Africa* eventually published Ainsworth's memorandum on the labor shortage, plus a criticism of his position in an editorial and cartoon.[67] The criticism reflected the general settler dissatisfaction with Ainsworth in Nyanza Province. The gist of the critical editorial in *The Leader* was that Ainsworth was protecting African production to the detriment of the European settler economy. The editorial writer believed that Ainsworth was not fair in dealing with European settlers. By promoting African production in Nyanza Province, the editorial asserted that Ainsworth was discouraging Africans from leaving the reserve areas to work on European farms. The editorial concluded by asserting that, ultimately, European settler agriculture was more valuable to the colony. Maxon sees this as the real beginning of settler disapproval of Ainsworth's views on African production.[68]

With the convening of the Native Labour Commission in 1912, settlers took the opportunity to continue public attacks against Ainsworth's policies regarding African production. The acting governor, Charles Bowering, appointed the Native Labour Commission of inquiry on August 13, 1912, to address some of the difficulties European settlers experienced in acquiring African labor.[69] The Native Labour Commission initially convened on September 19, 1912, and published its field of investigation on October 1, 1912.[70] The field of inquiry of the Native Labour Commission report was relatively all-inclusive and addressed labor recruitment, African wages, taxation and employer treatment of workers, indentured labor, taxation, and squatter farming.

Interestingly enough, Bowering did not appoint Ainsworth to the Labour Commission, and, for that matter, only one administration officer served on it. However, Ainsworth did testify before the Labour Commission. In addition to Ainsworth, some notable administration officials who also testified were Dr. Norman Leys, W. McGregor Ross, A.C. Hollis, G. A. Northcote, and M. Beech. Ainsworth's testimony, alongside the testimonies of certain European settlers, reinforced, to the settlers, the negative view of him as a defender of African production.

In his testimony, Ainsworth reiterated that the ill-treatment of African workers and the conflicting demands for African labor during harvest time in the reserves created the labor shortage.[71] Although he was absolutely in favor of Africans working, Ainsworth stated that he emphasized African production in the reserves. He added that he normally instructed his administrative officers not to recruit African laborers for European plantation owners. Nevertheless, he was emphatic that chiefs and elders were "to do everything possible to prevent the loafing propensities of the young men."[72] Because of the "burden" of civilizing Africans, many administrative officials did not feel that the various stereotypes about Africans (that they were culturally backward and lazy) were racist or that the various colonial policies designed to make African work were exploitative.[73] However, in contrast to most European witnesses, Ainsworth did feel that increased wages would push more Africans toward wage employment out of the reserves.[74] In addition, he now spoke out against a pass system and any reduction of the reserves.

In their testimony to the Labour Commission, many settlers accused the administration of retarding labor recruitment. As one settler, J. Boyes, put it, "the Administrative Officer appeared to adopt the line of putting the native first and the settler second."[75] In this regard, Lord Delamere, arguably the most prominent settler in the EAP at the time due to his large scale land holdings and his high political visibility, argued that African labor problems were due, mainly, to the fact that, Africans still maintained access to the land. Subsequently, they had no need for wages. In this direction, he denounced Ainsworth, specifically, for encouraging African production, which he felt slowed their progress toward wage labor. Besides impeding the flow of African labor to European planters, Delamere felt that the development of wealthy African peasants had other unforeseen consequences. According to Delamere, one ethnic group, the Kamba, had profited so well under Ainsworth's tutelage that, "they were now to be found drunk from one end of the country to other."[76]

Another European settler, C. B. Clutterbuck of Njoro, also reinforced Delamere's views of Ainsworth in his testimony to the Labour Commission. According to Clutterbuck, after Ainsworth's appointment as PC in Nyanza Province, he was unable to get any African labor.[77]

The final resolutions of the Native Labour Commission ranged upon a wide number of topics. These included recommendations for a further demarcation of reserves, the appointment of a chief native commissioner, the delimitation of squatter farming, and the elimination of professional labor recruiters and, as mentioned earlier, the proposal that even though the government should not engage in direct recruitment of African labor, specific instructions should be given to encourage African men to work for wages outside the reserve areas.[78] Ainsworth supported many of the recommendations that came out of the Native Labour Commission.

Despite the critical views of Ainsworth by many European settlers, Maxon is clear that "Ainsworth advocated European settlement in both public and private statements and worked for its success."[79] He believed that they could be the engine of economic growth for the colony. He just did not believe that Africans should be coerced into leaving their reserve areas to work for Europeans. This apparent contradiction would reflect Ainsworth's legacy.

## AINSWORTH'S CONTRADICTORY LEGACY

Despite his support of African production, Ainsworth became embroiled in a number of administrative wrangles that dimmed the luster surrounding his pro-African legacy. With the exception of the Maasai Move, the controversies were abuses associated with the exploitation of African labor or the creation of conditions that made it easier for Europeans to gain access to African workers. In all of the cases, the resulting policy implications benefited European settler production.

The notorious Maasai Move, a controversial administrative decision that expanded opportunities for European production, was also important in shedding more light on Ainsworth's Social Darwinistic views on African development. Ainsworth's involvement in the relocation of the Maasai reflected the intersectionality of his identities as both administrator and European. In June 1911, the governor, Sir Percy Girouard, moved a section of the Maasai people from the Laikipia Plateau to the Southern Reserves, despite an earlier 1904 treaty signed between the Maasai and the British administration promising never to move them from Laikipia.[80] By moving the Maasai, Girouard hoped to consolidate them into one reserve and to, more importantly, open up more land for European settlement. Ainsworth, who during this time period was at Nakuru in Naivasha Province, was placed in charge of the move toward the end of August 1911.[81]

Although the move broke an earlier treaty and was a breach of trustee-ship, over which Girouard would later lose his job, Ainsworth supported the move.[82] Maxon suggests that Ainsworth's support was contingent upon the idea that the move south would put the Maasai under one contiguous geo-graphic unit and further consolidate political cohesion under their spiritual leader, Lenana, who subsequently died just prior to the move in March 1911. Despite his support for the move, Ainsworth was aware that many of the Laikipia Maasai did not support it. In fact, they later, unsuccessfully, chal-lenged the move in court in 1912.[83]

Ironically, after the Maasai brought their case to court, Lord Delamere and J. K. Hill, another prominent settler, erroneously accused Ainsworth of instigating the court case in some sort of misguided attempt to protect African interests.[84] Lord Delamere's letter and Ainsworth's response to it shed more light on intersectionality and Ainsworth's Social Darwinistic views. In his accusation against Ainsworth, Delamere stated that,

> I hope this is untrue as I believe in his wrong-headed way Mr. Ainsworth has had the interests of the country at heart. But he has always denied the rights and benefits of the civilization to which he should be a prop and tried to introduce a system which must result in the ultimate demoralization and degeneration of the native to a drinking loafer and it is possible that he has taken up this attitude with regard to the Masai Movement.[85]

Delamere's charge against Ainsworth hinged upon his perceived racial identity as a European, which Delamere questioned. However, in his role as an admin-istrative official, Ainsworth also had to work to promote a vision of African development that, as Ainsworth stated in response to Delamere, "must be sym-pathetic within reason with the object of interesting the people in schemes of self-development and betterment."[86] Significantly, Ainsworth felt that both he and Lord Delamere were ultimately working toward the same goal of the over-all development of the colony. However, Ainsworth differed in that he believed Africans could remain in their reserve areas to work. Ainsworth remained clear in his Social Darwinistic approach to African development as he asserted that,

> with Africans any process of evolution must be gradual; the pace cannot be hurried. I claim, however, that a good deal has been achieved in East Africa in a fairly short time in face of, to the natives strange and worrying conditions.[87]

As he later wrote in an article for the *Farmer's Journal*, Ainsworth, like many humanitarians and administrative officials, believed that "natives are much on par with children and therefore must be taught and brought up as decent and responsible members of state" and otherwise "the result in the case of Africa would be uncontrolled savagery."[88]

The Maasai Move was the first major issue that cast a shadow over Ainsworth's legacy. Afterward, as labor problems became more central in the early development of the colony, Ainsworth subsequently became embroiled in labor controversies that sullied his reputation as a defender of African production.

With the start of the First World War in 1914, military authorities in the EAP organized African labor into military Carrier Corps under the leadership of O. F. Watkins as commander. This led to abuses as, in some cases, chiefs and headmen simply rounded up Africans and sent them into service.[89] In March 1917, Ainsworth became Military Commissioner of Labour.[90] Although Ainsworth was aware of the terrible working conditions for porters, he felt that the military need for the laborers took precedence over these concerns. The use of forced labor was legal due to the emergency created by the war. Ainsworth did work to repatriate back to the reserves porters suffering from health problems. He also ensured that their care facilities, on route home, were adequate.

With the conclusion of the First World War, Ainsworth reached the pinnacle of his administrative career. The governor of Kenya appointed him chief native commissioner in 1918. The position was an advisory position on African policy in Kenya. The CNC did not have direct control over the provincial commissioners regarding policy matters. Despite the lack of real authority, the Convention of Associations criticized Ainsworth's appointment as CNC.[91] Moreover, a leading European settler, E. S. Grogan personally attacked Ainsworth's appointment.[92] Although he was approaching the end of his storied career in Kenya Colony, in his role as CNC, Ainsworth became involved in another labor controversy.

Following the war, Kenya Colony experienced another bout of African labor shortage. The increased profitability of settler products, like coffee and sisal, following the First World War contributed to an atmosphere of heightened demand for African labor. The administration's decision to settle former First World War veterans in Kenya also heightened demands for African labor.[93] With this acute demand for labor from European settlers, Ainsworth, in his new capacity as CNC, embarked upon a meandering road of contradictory policy pronouncements, from June 1918 to January 1919, that anticipated his eventual entanglement in a grand mal forced labor controversy, known as the Northey forced labor crisis.[94] Ainsworth's entanglement in contradictory administration labor policy was a reflection of the tensions surrounding the promotion of the European export sector while also giving lip service to African production.

On October 23, 1919, the new governor, Sir Edward Northey (1919–1922), issued a labor circular, with Ainsworth's name affixed to it, regarding recruitment of African labor. Northey released the circular due to the recurrent shortage of labor occasioned by forced labor recruitment for the Carrier Corps during the war and the increased demands for labor from European settlers coinciding with famine and disease.[95]

In issuing the circular, Northey was following an earlier example set by himself and other administration officials before him. However, in this case, he was also clearly giving priority to European development.[96] This infamous labor circular explicitly stated, "All government officials in charge of native areas must exercise every possible lawful influence to induce able-bodied male natives to go into the labour field."[97] Even though the wording was, seemingly, innocuous, the emphasis on "encouraging" Africans into the labor market hinted at state coercion of African labor for private European interests, a policy that had been previously disavowed in 1914 by the then secretary of state for the colonies, Lewis Harcourt.[98] According to the administration doctor and vociferous gadfly, Dr. Norman Leys, the syntax of "encouragement" or "moral suasion" was, simply, euphemisms for coercion in Kenya Colony.[99]

According to Maxon, although Ainsworth affixed his name to Labour Circular No. 1, October 23, 1919, it was largely the initiative of Northey. Ainsworth, as alluded to earlier, did not favor state recruitment of African labor for Europeans.[100] As he stated, "in this connection it is necessary to bear in mind that any form of forced labor in this country cannot help but have the most disastrous results" because it made Africans detest work in general.[101]

Nevertheless, Ainsworth took responsibility for the circular, as he stated that, "the Circular being over my name I naturally took full responsibility for it."[102] Maxon states that Ainsworth probably drafted the original document while Northey made significant changes to it and then affixed Ainsworth's name to the circular.[103] Maxon sees the final document as more reflective of Northey's views as opposed to Ainsworth's views. Although Ainsworth, like Northey, believed that Africans should not remain "idle" in the reserves, he differed with the governor over the use of coercion.[104] Northey supported an active and assertive government role in recruitment of African labor.[105]

On the other hand, notwithstanding his earlier statements, Ainsworth supported the idea of Africans leaving the reserves to work for Europeans even if the initial impetus to their labor migration was the push factor of coercive communal labor. Communal labor was a type of unpaid forced labor employed in colonial Kenya in the rural African reserve areas.[106] As Ainsworth stated,

Chiefs and Native Authorities can demand that their people undertake such works as roads, irrigation, etc., in so far as such works are for the good of the whole community . . . and in this procedure lay our hope that the young man will prefer to leave their reserves for work outside, one reason being that such work in the reserves is not paid for.[107]

Moreover, although Ainsworth disapproved of government recruitment of labor for private purposes, he accepted government recruitment of labor for government departments. In a separate proposal, Ainsworth had actually supported the creation of licensed labor bureaus to help recruit African labor.[108]

After the release of the Northey labor circular, the two Anglican bishops of East Africa, John Willis of Uganda and R. S. Heywood of Mombasa, and J. W. Arthur of the Church of Scotland issued a memorandum on November 8, 1918, that mildly criticizing the circular, even accepting that some form of coercion was necessary.[109] The bishops issued the statement after consultation and agreement with Ainsworth and the Acting Governor of Kenya Sir Charles Bowring. By this time, Northey, who had recently been injured in a polo accident, was convalescing in England.

The Bishop's Memorandum, as it was called, was hardly a radical critique. The Anti-Slavery and Aborigines Protection Society and the Conference of Missionary Societies, along with other humanitarian organizations, criticized the circular more forcefully. The outcry against the Northey Circular eventually resulted in a parliamentary debate in the House of Lords on July 14, 1920.[110]

With the increased humanitarian criticism of the circular, the administration and the CO called on Ainsworth to submit reports on the working of the Circular. With the crescendo of humanitarian attacks against the labor policy in Kenya, Ainsworth also began to defend, publicly, the administration policy.[111] From these exchanges, Ainsworth, at times, appeared to contradict some of his earlier positions regarding coercion. His responses reflected the intersection of his contradictory roles as an administrator in a settler colony.

In response to the request for comment on the labor circular, Ainsworth compiled a memorandum, originally intended for publication in the *Journal of the African Society,* and sent it to the CO. Regarding the Northey Circular, Ainsworth emphasized that the intent of the labor circular was to encourage Africans to work through lawful means. In a characteristically Social Darwinistic analysis, Ainsworth asserted that prior to colonial rule, Africans lived in a constant state of "raiding and counter raiding, strangers attacked without provocation."[112] Colonialism ended the strife and turmoil, but with the end of raiding, Africans were "becoming slack and indolent and in [a] large number of cases the people are inclined to habits of drinking and immorality."[113] To remedy this situation, Ainsworth prescribed work, but only within the reserves. He saw the Northey Circular as an attempt to instill a work ethic through lawful means. Ainsworth, curiously, added that, although he disagreed with forced labor in principle, he did see its utility in particular cases. Forced labor for state purposes was one of the cases where conscription was necessary. In defense of African development, Ainsworth came much closer to supporting coercion than he had in previous writings. His flirtation with coercion, only for state purposes, was a reflection of the contradictions in the political economy of Kenya Colony.

The CO received Ainsworth's memorandum with obsequious critique. After all, as A. C. C. Parkinson minuted, "it seems odd that an article on natives and native labour prepared by a man of Mr. Ainsworth's wide experience and knowledge should be criticised in any way by our department."[114] Even after the CO had received various complaints from administrative officials highly critical of the Northey Circular, like H. R. Tate, the provincial commissioner for Kikuyu Province, and the administration doctor, Norman Leys, the CO noted that "Ainsworth . . . has shown no sign of misgivings."[115]

Maxon sees Ainsworth's defense of the Northey Circular as more of an example of "soldiering on." As an administrative official, Ainsworth did not want to disagree publicly with administration policy. He also neared retirement and did not want to jeopardize his pension.[116] In reference to his public newspaper debates with critics like Leys, Maxon interprets Ainsworth's actions as an overall attempt to defend British colonialism against critics from the left in England.[117]

His actions later while in semiretirement seem to reinforce Maxon's conclusion. Ainsworth was asked to draw up a draft circular to replace the Northey Circular. In the new draft circular, Ainsworth moved away from Northey's position by clearly stating that the administration should not be involved in labor recruiting. Moreover, in commenting on another criticism of the Northey Circular by H. R. Tate, Ainsworth stated concretely "I would add that I am definitely opposed to any form of recruitment by the State for private undertakings."[118] Moreover, after the CO eventually removed Northey from office, Ainsworth commented that the new governor, Sir Robert Coryndon, would be more favorable to African interests than Northey had been.[119]

The forced labor crisis surrounding the Northey Circular concluded when the secretary of state for the colonies, Winston Churchill released a despatch on September 5, 1921, that disavowed forcing Africans to work for private citizens.[120] By this point, Ainsworth was retired. Although he still retained his reputation as a defender of African rights and production, his historical legacy was mixed.

## CONCLUSION

The divergent historical views of Ainsworth reflect the difficulty in assessing the true motives behind the actions of public figures in Kenya's colonial history.[121] Ainsworth, like Archdeacon Walter Owen of Nyanza Province, was an administrator who was well known for his strident defense of African interests and was equally disliked by many European settlers.[122] Despite this public image, though, his actual support for African rights was ambivalent and contradictory and consistently led to curious missteps.[123] However, in contrast to Archdeacon Walter Owen, Ainsworth's public role as an administration officer tempered his official statements regarding Africans' development. Despite his defense of African production, he was also associated with a number of administration policy moves intended to favor the European agricultural sector over African production. Ironically, in terms of African production, Ainsworth's thinking was more in line with humanitarian groups, like the Anti-Slavery and Aborigines Protection Society who promoted land ownership and free labor as the principal components of the *mission civilatrice* in Africa.[124] But, of course, Ainsworth was an administrator in an African colony that also contained a minority of European settlers. Although the administration professed trusteeship, the colonial policies supported the European agricultural sector, hence the contradictions of colonial rule in Kenya Colony. Ainsworth's legacy also reflects the intersection of the overlapping identities that he was forced to maintain as a European administrative officer. In his role as an administrator, though he promoted African production, Ainsworth maintained the prevalent paternalistic attitudes regarding Africans that were steeped in Social Darwinistic thinking. On the other hand, as Professor Maxon states of Ainsworth, "within the limits imposed by his experience, education, and financial situation, he worked to uphold African interests and prevent what he saw as the dangers of white supremacy."[125]

## NOTES

1. Robert Maxon, *John Ainsworth and the Making of Kenya* (Lanham, MD: University Press of America, 1980), 335–37. The CNC was more of an advisory position. The CNC did not have any powers of the Provincial Commissioners and staff. He was mainly supposed to supervise policy regarding Africans in the colony and represent "native" policy to the government.

2. G. H. Mungeam, "John Ainsworth," in B. E. Kipkorir, ed., *Biographical Essays on Imperialism and Collaboration in Colonial Kenya* (Nairobi: Kenya Literature Bureau, 1980), 38.

3. Maxon, *John Ainsworth and the Making of Kenya*, 248–49.

4. Mungeam, "John Ainsworth," 49.

5. Quoted in Maxon, *John Ainsworth and the Making of Kenya*, 130.

6. Minute by A.C.C. Parkinson, July 23, 1920, Colonial Office [hereafter CO] 533/233, The National Archives, London.

7. Minute by A. C. C. Parkinson, May 17, 1921, CO 533/274, The National Archives, London.

8. Maxon, *John Ainsworth and the Making of Kenya*, xii.

9. F. H. Goldsmith, *Johns Ainsworth: Pioneer Kenya Administrator, 1864-1946* (London: Macmillan & CO LTD, 1955), 103.

10. Opolot Okia, "The Northey Forced Labor Crisis, 1920-1921: A Symptomatic Reading," *International Journal of African Historical Studies* 41 (2) (2008): 263, note 4; Opolot Okia, "In the Interests of Community: Archdeacon Walter Owen and The Issue of Communal Forced Labor in Kenya, 1921–1930," *Journal of Imperial and Commonwealth History* 32 (2) (2004): 19–40.

11. "Natives Work and Wages," *The Farmers Journal*, August 12, 1920.

12. "White Man's Country" is a reference to Elspeth Huxley's biography of a leading European settler, Lord Delamere. See, Elspeth Huxley, *A White Man's Country: Lord Delamere and the Making of Kenya* (New York: Praeger, 1968).

13. Maxon, *John Ainsworth and the Making of Kenya*, xii.

14. See John Lonsdale and Bruce Berman, "Coping with Contradictions: The Development of the Colonial State in Kenya, 1895-1914," in John Lonsdale and Bruce Berman, *Unhappy Valley: Conflict in Kenya and Africa, Book One* (Athens: Ohio University Press, 1992).

15. Nicos Poulantzas, translated by Patrick Camiller, *State, Power, Socialism* (New York: Verso Books, 2000).

16. The humanitarian lobby consisted of political, religious, and social organizations such as the British Foreign and Anti-Slavery Society, the Aborigines Protection Society, The Conference of British Missionary Societies, and the Church Missionary Society that consistently petitioned the British government to effect changes or reforms in colonial policy in the late nineteenth and early twentieth century. Controversial events such as the Congo reform movement, the Chinese slavery controversy in South Africa, and various forced labor issues in Africa formed the constituent outlines of humanitarian protests. Kevin Patrick Grant, "A Civilized Savagery: British Humanitarian Politics and European Imperialism in Africa 1884–1920" (Ph.D. thesis, University of California Berkeley, 1997), 29. See also, Suzanne Miers, "Slavery and The Slave Trade as International Issues, 1890–1939," in Suzanne Miers and Martin Klein, eds., *Slavery and Colonial Rule in Africa* (London: Taylor and Francis, 1998), 16–38.

17. Robert Maxon, *Struggle for Kenya* (Rutherford, NJ: Farleigh Dickinson University Press, 1993), 19.

18. Bruce Berman, *Control and Crisis in Colonial Kenya: The Dialectic of Domination* (Athens: Ohio University Press, 1990), 105.

19. Roger van Zwanenberg, "The Background of White Racialism in Kenya," *Kenya Historical Review* 1 (1973): 9.

20. Maxon, *John Ainsworth and the Making of Kenya*, 131–32.

21. On this Social Darwinistic thinking see, Mahmood Mamdani, *Citizen and Subject: Contemporary Africa and the Legacy of Late Colonialism* (Princeton: Princeton University Press, 1996); van Zwanenberg, "The Background to White Racialism in Kenya," 6.

22. "Black Man and the White Man in East Africa: Some Suggestions for the Future Based Upon Past and Present Requirements and Experience," MSS.Afr.S.382, Papers of John Ainsworth, Bodleian Library, Oxford.

23. For more on Critical Race Theory, see Eduardo Bonilla-Silva, "Rethinking Racism: Toward a Structural Interpretation," *American Sociological Review* 62 (3) (June 1997): 465–80; Richard Delgado and Jean Stefancic, *Critical Race Theory* (New York: New York University Press, 2012); Derrick Bell, *Faces at the Bottom the Well: The Permanence of Racism* (New York: Basic Books, 1993); Kimberle Crenshaw, Neil Gotanda, Gary Peller, Kendall Thomas, Eds. *Critical Race Theory: The Key Writings that Formed the Movement* (New York: The New Press, 1995).

24. Delgado, *Critical Race Theory*, 20–25.

25. Maxon, *John Ainsworth and the Making of Kenya*, 1.

26. Mungeam, "John Ainsworth," 38.

27. G. H. Mungeam, *British Rule in Kenya, 1895-1912* (Oxford: Clarendon Press, 1966), 1.

28. Maxon, *John Ainsworth and the Making of Kenya*, 4.

29. Goldsmith, *Johns Ainsworth: Pioneer Kenya Administrator*, 13.

30. Ibid.

31. Maxon, *John Ainsworth and the Making of Kenya*, 14. According to Maxon, Ainsworth, essentially, established a tributary relationship with certain sections of the Kamba.

32. The creation of the East Africa Protectorate on July 1, 1895, over the area between Mombasa and the Rift Valley was the culmination of a series of agreements between Germany and Great Britain starting in 1886 that split up the region of East Africa into German-controlled Tanganyika and British controlled Kenya (EAP) and Uganda. For more on this creation of the EAP consult, John Galbraith, *Mackinnon and East Africa: A Study in the "New Imperialism"* (Cambridge: Cambridge University Press, 2009); G. H. Mungeam, *British Rule in Kenya, 1895-1912: The Establishment of Administration in the East Africa Protectorate* (London: Clarendon Press, 1966); W. R. Ochieng, ed., *A Modern History of Kenya, 1895-1980* (Nairobi: Evans Brothers Limited, 1989).

33. Berman, *Control and Crisis in Colonial Kenya*, 98. At this early juncture, Ainsworth's recruitment into the colonial administration was a reflection of the haphazard recruitment strategy at this early point. By 1907 the CO required recruits to have a university degree which would have excluded Ainsworth.

34. Goldsmith, *John Ainsworth: Pioneer Kenya Administrator*, 32.

35. Mungeam, "John Ainsworth," 43; Maxon, *John Ainsworth and the Making of Kenya*, 61–63.

36. Maxon, *John Ainsworth and the Making of Kenya*, 107. Part of the growth of this relationship between Olenana and Ainsworth and the British in general was the gradual "creation" of Olenana as chief of the Masai.

37. Mungeam, "John Ainsworth," 49.

38. M. Sorrenson, *Origins of European Settlement in Kenya* (Nairobi: Oxford University Press, 1968), 23–36, 63, 233–34.

39. Ibid.

40. Mungeam, "John Ainsworth," 45–46.

41. Maxon, *John Ainsworth and the Making of Kenya*, xii.

42. Ibid., 80.

43. Ibid., 130–31.

44. Memorandum Dealing with Certain Proposals for the General Education of Natives in Native Districts in the East African Protectorate," April 30, 1913, CO 533/130, The National Archives, London.

45. Ainsworth to H. J. Read, June 7, 1921, CO 533/273, The National Archives, London.

46. This issue caused embarrassment for the CO. On October 27, 1920, the Undersecretary of State for the Colonies stated that "if a native has been fully employed in cultivation for himself for three months, he is exempt from the provisions of the Native Authority amendment Ordinance, 1920." Hansard Debate, Extract, October 27, 1920, Box/141, British and Foreign Anti-Slavery Society [hereafter BFASAPS], Bodleian Library, Oxford.

47. Maxon, *John Ainsworth and the Making of Kenya*, 311.

48. Ibid., 315.

49. Berman, *Control and Crisis in Colonial Kenya*, 200–01.

50. Anthony Clayton and Donald Savage, *Government and Labour in Kenya, 1895-1963* (London: Frank Cass, 1974), 42.

51. Bethwell Ogot, "British Administration in Central Nyanza District of Kenya, 1900-1960," *Journal of African History* 4 (2) (1963): 255.

52. Goldsmith, *Johns Ainsworth: Kenya Pioneer*, 76.

53. Maxon, *John Ainsworth and the Making of Kenya*, 217.

54. Ibid., 224.

55. Ibid., 218. In 1906–1907 the tax receipts from Nyanza were 305,849 Rupees. By 1912 this figure had increased to 865,137 Rupees.

56. Roger van Zwanenberg, *Colonial Capitalism and Labor in Kenya* (Nairobi: East African Literature Bureau, 1975), 75.

57. John Ainsworth, PC Nyanza to Secretary, April 30, 1910, Provincial Commissioner [hereafter PC]/Nyanza Province [hereafter NZA]/2/3, KNA, Nairobi.

58. Maxon, *John Ainsworth and the Making of Kenya*, 267.

59. Ewout Frankema, "Colonial Taxation and Government Spending in British Africa, 1880-1940: Maximizing Revenue or Minimizing Effort," *Explorations in Economic History* 48 (2011): 139–41; 144–46.

60. "Black Man and the White Man in East Africa: Some Suggestions for the Future Based Upon Past and Present Requirements and Experience," MSS.Afr.S.382, Papers of John Ainsworth, Bodleian Library, Oxford.

61. Van Zwanenberg, *Colonial capitalism and Labour in Kenya*, 75; Sharon Stichter, *Migrant Labour in Kenya: Capitalism and African Responses, 1895-1975* ((Harlow, Essex: Longman Group LTD, 1982), 70. By the 1930s, however, following the collapse of the peasant sector during the great depression, African prohibition

from coffee growing, and preferential marketing for certain European products, the European sector thrived and the old European clamors for cheap African labor became part of folklore.

62. Maxon, *John Ainsworth and the Making of Kenya,* 354.

63. Ibid., 281.

64. Clayton and Savage, *Government and Labour in Kenya,* 55.

65. Quoted in Maxon, *John Ainsworth and the Making of Kenya,* 225.

66. Maxon, *John Ainsworth and the Making of Kenya,* 226.

67. Ibid., 227.

68. Ibid.

69. Clayton, and Savage, *Government and Labour in Kenya,* 55–64.

70. The terms of reference were to enquire into the reasons for the shortage of African labor utilizing evidence from both employer and employee; examine the effect of the Administration upon the labor question and to look into wages and other subjects which affected labor.

71. East Africa Protectorate [hereafter EAP], *Report and Evidence of the Native Labour Commission, 1912-1913* (Nairobi: Government Printer, 1913), 135.

72. Quoted in Robert Maxon, *Johns Ainsworth and the Making of Kenya,* 234.

73. Van Zwanenberg, "The Background of White Racialism in Kenya," 9.

74. EAP, *Report and Evidence of the Native Labour Commission,* 135.

75. Ibid., 39.

76. Ibid., 109.

77. Quoted in Maxon, *John Ainsworth and the Making of Kenya,* 233.

78. Maxon, *John Ainsworth and the Making of Kenya,* 333–35.

79. Robert Maxon, "John Ainsworth and Agricultural Innovation in Kenya," *Kenya Historical Review* 1 (2) (July 1973): 157.

80. For more on the Maasai Move see, Lotte Hughes, *Moving the Maasai: A Colonial Misadventure* (London: Palgrave Macmillan, 2006).

81. Goldsmith, *John Ainsworth: Pioneer Kenya Administrator,* 82.

82. Maxon, *John Ainsworth and the Making of Kenya,* 238.

83. Ibid., 239.

84. Ibid., 246. The administration, however, thought Dr. Norman Leys was the instigator behind the court case.

85. Quoted in Goldsmith, *John Ainsworth: Pioneer Kenya Administrator,* 85.

86. Quoted in Goldsmith, *John Ainsworth: Pioneer Kenya Administrator,* 86.

87. Quoted in Goldsmith, *John Ainsworth: Pioneer Kenya Administrator,* 87.

88. "Natives Work and Wages," *The Farmers Journal,* August 12, 1920.

89. Clayton and Savage, *Government and Labor in Kenya,* 82.

90. Ibid., 86.

91. Ibid., 341.

92. Ibid., 342.

93. Maxon, *Struggle for Kenya,* 145. The Soldier Settler scheme was an attempt to increase the size of the settler population by giving the First Word War veterans land at nominal rates. Problems arose because a portion of the soldier settlers were given land in Laikipia that lacked adequate water and was too far away from the railroad.

94. See, Memorandum Regarding a Meeting on the Labour Question, September 18, 1918, CO 533/273, The National Archives, London; Native Labour for Government Requirements, Circular No. 4/1, CO 533/233, The National Archives, London.

95. Maxon, *Struggle for Kenya*, 145.

96. Native Labour for Government Requirements, Circular No. 4/1, CO 533/233, The National Archives, London.

97. Labour Circular No. 1, 23. Labour Circular No. 1, October 23, 1919. The full copy of the circular and other materials was reprinted in Great Britain, *Despatch to the Governor of the East Africa Protectorate Relating to Native Labour and Papers Connected Therewith*, Cmd. 873, (August 1920), 6–8.

98. Minute by Harcourt, June 15, 1914, CO 533/1148, The National Archives, London. In 1914 after a public controversy over the report of the 1912 Native Labour Commission that African labor should be "encouraged," Harcourt agreed with the Anti-Slavery and Aborigines Protection Society that encouragement of African labor for private persons was tantamount to slavery and would not be tolerated. See also, Buxton to Harcourt, June 11, 1914, CO 533/148, PRO, London; Butler to J.H. Harris, June 17, 1914, Box G 132, File: Labour and Land, British and Foreign Anti-Slavery Society and Aborigines Protection Society [hereafter BFAS/APS], Rhodes House Library, Oxford.

99. Minute by A. C. C. Parkinson, May 17, 1921, CO 533/274, The National Archives, London.

100. John Ainsworth to Acting Chief Secretary, January 2, 1920, Papers of Elspeth Huxley, Box 1/3, Bodleian Library, Oxford.

101. Education of Natives in Native Districts in the East African Protectorate," April 30, 1913, CO 533/130, The National Archives, London.

102. Quoted in Goldsmith, *Johns Ainsworth: Pioneer Kenya Administrator*, 102.

103. Maxon, *John Ainsworth and the Making of Kenya*, 364.

104. Ibid., 368.

105. Ibid., 368, 372.

106. See, Opolot Okia, *Labor in Colonial Kenya after the Forced Labor Convention, 1930-1963* (New York: Palgrave Macmillan, 2019); Opolot Okia, *Communal Labor in Colonial Kenya: The Legitimization of Coercion, 192-1930* (New York: Palgrave Macmillan, 2012).

107. "Memorandum RE A Meeting on the Labour Question," September 18, 1918, CO 533/273, The National Archives, London.

108. Maxon, *John Ainsworth and the Making of Kenya*, 273.

109. Clayton and Savage, *Government and Labour in Kenya*, 113.

110. Great Britain, *Parliamentary Debates, Lords*, 5th ser. Vol. 41 (1920), No. 60.

111. Maxon, *John Ainsworth and the making of Kenya*, 377–81.

112. "Some Notes Regarding Africa," June 8, 1920, CO 533/233, The National Archives, London; Memorandum on Native Labour Circular, May 3, 1920, CO 533/233, The National Archives, London.

113. "Some Notes Regarding Africa," June 8, 1920, CO 533/233, The National Archives, London.

114. Minute by A.C.C. Parkinson, July 23, 1920, CO 533/233, The National Archives, London.

115. Minute by W. Bottomley, December 1, 1920, CO 533/247, The National Archives, London.

116. Maxon, *John Ainsworth and the Making of Kenya*, 381.

117. Ibid., 415.

118. Ainsworth to Acting Chief Secretary, January 2, 1920, Papers of Elspeth Huxley, Box 1/3, Rhodes House Library, Oxford.

119. Maxon, *John Ainsworth and the Making of Kenya*, 415.

120. Great Britain, *Despatch to the Officer Administering the Government of Kenya Colony and Protectorate Relating to Native Labour,* Cmd. 1509 (September 1921).

121. See, for example, the literature on the hidden transcripts of Archdeacon Walter Owen. Okia, "In the Interests of Community," Leon Spencer, "Christianity and Colonial Protest: Perceptions of W. E. Owen, Archdeacon of Kavirondo," *Journal of Religion in Africa* 13 (1) (1982): 47–60; Nancy Uhlar Murray, "Archdeacon W. E. Owen: The Missionary as Propagandist," *International Journal of African Historical Studies* 15 (40) (1982): 653–70.

122. See, Opolot Okia, "In the Interests of Community: Archdeacon Walter Owen and the Issue of Communal Labour in Colonial Kenya, 1921-30," *The Journal of Imperial and Commonwealth History* 32 (1) (2004); Nancy Murray, "Archdeacon W. E. Owen: Missionary as Propagandist," *International Journal of African Historical Studies* 15 (4) (1982).

123. Leon Spencer, "Christian Missions and African Interests in Kenya, 1905-1924," (Ph.D. Diss., Syracuse University, 1974), 56.

124. See, Kevin Patrick Grant, *A Civilised Savagery: Britain and the New Slaveries in Africa, 1884-1926* (New York: Routledge, 2005).

125. Maxon, *John Ainsworth and the Making of Kenya*, 439.

## BIBLIOGRAPHY

Bell, Derrick. *Faces at the Bottom the Well: The Permanence of Racism.* New York: Basic Books, 1993.

Berman, Bruce. *Control and Crisis in Colonial Kenya: The Dialectic of Domination.* Athens: Ohio University Press, 1990.

Berman, Bruce and John Lonsdale. "Coping with Contradictions: The Development of the Colonial State in Kenya, 1895-1914." In *Unhappy Valley: Conflict in Kenya and Africa, Book One* by Bruce Berman and John Lonsdale, 77–95. Athens: Ohio University Press, 1992.

Bonilla-Silva, Eduardo. "Rethinking Racism: Toward a Structural Interpretation." *American Sociological Review* 62, no. 3 (June 1997): 465–80.

Clayton, Anthony and Donald Savage. *Government and Labour in Kenya, 1895-1963.* London: Frank Cass, 1974.

Crenshaw, Kimberle, Neil Gotanda, Gary Peller, Kendall Thomas, Eds. *Critical Race Theory: The Key Writings that Formed the Movement.* New York: The New Press, 1995.

Delgado, Richard and Jean Stefancic. *Critical Race Theory.* New York: New York University Press, 2012.

Frankema, Ewout. "Colonial Taxation and Government Spending in British Africa, 1880-1940: Maximizing Revenue or Minimizing Effort." *Explorations in Economic History* 48, no. 1 (2011): 136–49.

Galbraith, John. *Mackinnon and East Africa: A Study in the "New Imperialism."* Cambridge: Cambridge University Press, 2009.

Goldsmith, F. *Johns Ainsworth: Pioneer Kenya Administrator, 1864-1946.* London: Macmillan & CO LTD, 1955.

Grant, Kevin. *A Civilised Savagery: Britain and the New Slaveries in Africa, 1884-1826.* New York: Routledge, 2005.

Hughes, Lotte. *Moving the Maasai: A Colonial Misadventure.* London: Palgrave Macmillan, 2006.

Huxley, Elspeth. *A White Man's Country: Lord Delamere and the Making of Kenya.* New York: Prager, 1968.

Mamdani, Mahmood. *Citizen and Subject: Contemporary Africa and the Legacy of Late Colonialism.* Princeton: Princeton University Press, 1996.

Maxon, Robert. *John Ainsworth and the Making of Kenya.* Lanham, MD: University Press of America, 1980.

———. *Struggle for Kenya: The Loss and Reassertion of Imperial initiative.* Rutherford, NJ: Farleigh Dickinson University Press, 1993.

Miers, Suzanne. "Slavery and The Slave Trade as International Issues, 1890–1939." In *Slavery and Colonial Rule in Africa*, edited by Suzanne Miers and Martin Klein, 16–38. London: Taylor and Francis, 1998.

Mungeam, G. *British Rule in Kenya, 1895-1912: The Establishment of Administration in the East Africa Protectorate.* London: Clarendon Press, 1966.

———. "John Ainsworth." In *Biographical Essays on Imperialism and Collaboration in Colonial Kenya*, edited by B. Kipkorir. Nairobi: Kenya Literature Bureau, 1980.

Murray, Nancy. "Archdeacon W. E. Owen: Missionary as Propagandist." *International Journal of African Historical Studies* 15, no. 4 (1982): 653–70.

Ochieng, William, ed. *A Modern History of Kenya, 1895-1980.* Nairobi: Evans Brothers Limited, 1989.

Ogot, Bethwell. "British Administration in Central Nyanza District of Kenya, 1900-1960." *Journal of African History* 4, no. 2 (1963): 249–73.

Okia, Opolot. "The Northey Forced Labor Crisis, 1920-1921: A Symptomatic Reading." *International Journal of African Historical Studies* 41, no. 2 (2008): 263–93.

———. "In the Interests of Community: Archdeacon Walter Owen and The Issue of Communal Forced Labor in Kenya, 1921–1930." *Journal of Imperial and Commonwealth History* 32, no. 2 (2004): 19–40.

Poulantzas, Nicos. *State, Power, Socialism.* Translated by Patrick Camiller. New York: Verso Books, 2000.

Sorrenson, M. *Origins of European Settlement in Kenya.* Nairobi: Oxford University Press, 1968.

Spencer, Spencer. "Christian Missions and African Interests in Kenya, 1905-1924." Ph.D. diss., Syracuse University, 1974.

Stichter, Sharon. *Migrant Labour in Kenya: Capitalism and African Responses, 1895-1975.* Harlow, Essex: Longman Group LTD, 1982.

van Zwanenberg, Roger. *Colonial Capitalism and Labor in Kenya.* Nairobi: East African Literature Bureau, 1975.

———. "The Background of White Racialism in Kenya." *Kenya Historical Review* 1 (1973).

*Chapter 6*

# Challenge to African Democracy

## *The Activism and Assassination of Pio Gama Pinto*

Godriver Wanga-Odhiambo

African democracy has faced great challenges over the years, including ethnic cleansing, mass dislocations of people, and political assassinations. Consequently, many nation-states are in a state of "political ICU," gasping for life. This work attempts to go beyond both Eurocentric and Afrocentric views in the analysis of independent nation-states, using as a case study the first political assassination in post-independent Kenya: that of Pio Gama Pinto.

This work serves to illuminate Pinto's selfless heroism and his belief in equality, having paid the ultimate price for standing up against colonialism, neocolonialism, capitalism, and any kind of imperialism. People who stand for equality and equitable distribution of resources are often derided as communists. Did Pinto's morality and socialist ideology rub the authorities the wrong way? If so, did that motivate his killing, and by whom? What was the hand behind the curtain? Pinto was not only a nationalist but also a Pan-Africanist and an internationalist; did that fact make him an easy target for neocolonialists and their sympathizers in postcolonial Kenya? These are some of the questions that we are still seeking answers for today.

The post-independent state has often ignored the work and historical contribution of Pinto. By inquiring into the life and assassination of the Kenyan freedom fighter, this work seeks to contribute to the historiography of Kenya's post-independent state. This historical approach also puts into perspective the contributions of South Asians toward the liberation of Kenya. The unpacking of Pinto's role in liberation—not only in Kenya but in Africa and beyond—reveals that Pinto was a revolutionary and an internationalist much like Ernesto "Che" Guevara, and understanding Pinto's role and history is more crucial than ever.

## BACKGROUND AND NATIONALISM

Asian migration into East Africa predates the colonial period. Asian migrants came in different waves at different times, but the majority came from different parts of India. The migrants to colonial Kenya included Muslims, who were divided into various sects such as the Shia and Sunni, among others. Also, in Kenya were the Memons and various sects of the Hindus such as the Vanik and the Oswals. Among the Asians were also found those of Christian faith; this group mainly consisted of Goans, who formed less than 10 percent of the Asian community in Kenya by 1962.[1] They came from a tiny Portuguese colony of Goa. Today Goa is a separate state located south of Maharashtra in India. Many Goans during the colonial period disliked being classified as Indians; they downplayed their Indian background even though they spoke an Indian language. They were of mixed ancestry, having intermarried with the Portuguese and adopted Portuguese names such as D'Souza (or de Souza).[2] They were well educated and modeled their social life on the Western lifestyle. It was to this group that Pio Gama Pinto belonged.

During the colonial period, this group held clerical jobs in banks and the civil service, served as teachers in mission schools, and worked as lawyers. They spoke English, Portuguese, and the Asian vernacular known as Konkani, which is remarkably close to the Marathi language. Some became involved with politics and supported the struggle for independence. For instance, Pio Gama Pinto was a trade unionist, journalist, and champion of African nationalism; Fitzval R. S. de Souza was a lawyer, journalist, and founding member of the Kenya Freedom Party; and John Maximian Nazareth was a legislative councilor and the president of the East African Indian National Congress.[3] These three contributed so much to issues of equality and independence in Kenya.

The decolonization movements in Africa in the 1950s and 1960s were launched with great hope, seeking not only to end colonization but also to solve Africa's tragic socioeconomic and political issues. Unfortunately, after African states achieved independence from their colonizers, their incipient democracies faced grave challenges. These have included ethnic rivalries and conflicts, ethnic cleansing, the intimidation and forceful evictions of people, and political assassinations. However, it is important to note that ethnic and other conflicts were started by colonialism and imperialism as a way to maintain their grip.

The first assassination in Kenya after independence was that of Pio Gama Pinto. Pinto saw the dangers of imperialism and neocolonialism, and devoted his whole life fighting for the true meaning of independence, which included economic, political, social, and cultural independence. His assassination, a mere two years after independence, set in place a troubling trend in Kenya's political scene. Pinto's assassination in 1965 was followed by that of T. J.

Mboya in 1969 and that of J. M. Kariuki in 1975. Others would follow later.

His assassination and the historical "forgetting" of his role have led to many still-unanswered questions: What was the role of Pinto? What has been Pinto's place in people's memory, and how have people (freedom fighters, family, friends, and contemporary admirers) chosen to remember him? Where does he stand as a symbol of nationalism and as a rallying political symbol in the intense political division of postcolonial Kenya? What political symbolism if any that has grown around Pinto's patriotism compared to those of early independence leaders such as Jaramogi Oginga Odinga and Dedan Kimathi who stand out as images of defiance against the oppression of any kind and continue to inspire political actions such as "voting block power" rebellion in Kenya? Nicholas Githuku also raised similar questions in his analysis of the role and legacy of Dedan Kimathi.[4]

These unanswered questions extend beyond Pinto's life to the political life of Kenya. What are the implications of the discovery of the cover-up transcripts of Pinto's murder, botched trial, and adamant refusal of inquiry into his assassination? Why did the independent state frustrate efforts to publish Pinto's biography, especially in the mid-1960s and the 1970s? Why was his history ignored by his own country? This omission exposes the problem of writing the history of the freedom fighters who played a crucial role in decolonization, particularly those seen as radical. Pinto's wife Emma Pinto shared this view in her letter to June Milne in 1972:

So few people have the generosity of looking at the African Revolution from an African point of view that quite often the "inside Africa" opinions are not always, as the indigenous people see it. I hope and pray that your Publishing House does not "lift" newspaper articles to tell the truth about Africa, but rather from the locals themselves—and not necessarily by any means from those at the helm now. The work was done by unsung heroes who still toil in the background and [are] often trampled by limelight seekers.[5]

## THE CASE OF PIO GAMA PINTO

Pio Gama Pinto was a Kenyan Goan born on March 31, 1927, in Nairobi. Pinto went to school in India when he was eight years old and spent nine years studying there. At 17 years old, while still in India, he started agitating against the caste system and the poverty evident in the Raj state. As a student, Pio was involved in Goan Liberation, he helped with the formation of the Goa National Congress. After his studies, he joined the Indian Air Force briefly and soon became a journalist, protesting against Portuguese rule, which kept so many Goans in poverty.

While in Bombay working at the Post and Telecommunication Company, he took part in the general strike as a trade unionist and got a glimpse of the power of mass action and organization. His revolutionary activities and connections in Bombay put him at risk for arrest. When the Portuguese realized his role, they planned to deport him to their West African colony of Cape Verde, fortunately, Pio came to know about it, so he returned to Kenya in 1949.

## NATIONALIST

Despite the years he spent away from his native country, Pinto had always kept the plight of Kenya in mind. Before his return to Kenya, Pinto pressurized Pandit Nehru, the leader of India, to help in the decolonization of Kenya. His efforts bore fruit and in 1948 India established its High Commission in Nairobi. Nehru appointed its first commissioner, Apa Pant, an Oxford-trained lawyer, with instructions to do all it would take to help Kenya decolonize. When Pinto returned to Kenya in 1949, he worked with Pant closely (and in secrecy). For instance, Pinto was able to transport Pant to Kiambu in the middle of the night and—with Senior Chief Koinange presiding, in the presence of 12 Kikuyu elders, and in a full traditional ceremony—Pant was made an elder of the Kikuyu community to honor his contributions to the Kenyan people.[6] The colonial government investigated Pant and raided his office and residence several times in search of incriminating evidence or weapons, all in vain. The coordination between India and the pro-independence forces in Kenya only ended when Pinto was arrested, and Pant recalled.

His return to Kenya in 1949 had marked a new era in his life. At first, he held a series of clerical jobs but soon began to get involved with local politics, working to dislodge the colonial government.[7] In addition to working with Nehru's commission, during the Mau Mau Uprising in the early 1950s, Pinto supported the insurgents with money and arms. In the 1950s, he also served as a secretary to the Kenya Indian Congress, an organization devoted to the legal equality of Indians and Europeans in Kenya. He also worked closely with the leaders of the Kenya Africa Union, led by Jomo Kenyatta. The KAU was the largest African nationalist organization in

Kenya, but after the Mau Mau Uprising, the organization was banned and Kenyatta and others; Bildad Kaggia, Achieng Oneko, Fred Kubai, Kungu Karumba, and Paul Ngei (known as the Kapenguria Six) were imprisoned.[8] As the organization went underground, Pinto assisted in the formation of KAU "study circles" to continue the work and dedication of the organization. This prevented the movement from disintegrating following the trial and imprisonment of the Kapenguria Six. During the trial, he assisted in the defense of Jomo Kenyatta and the other prisoners and appealed to his solicitor friends such as Dennis Pritt and Achharoo Ram Kapila among others, to take up political cases when no money was forthcoming.[9] Meanwhile, he maintained a close liaison with British Members of Parliament, whom he kept posted on the situation in Kenya, pointing out the atrocities committed by the colonial government.

Pinto's ceaseless work for independence attracted the attention of the colonial authorities, and he was arrested during 1954s "Operation Anvil" only five months after his marriage, though mostly targeted Kikuyus in Nairobi.[10] Pinto was detained at the notorious Takwa Special Detention Camp at Manda Island under emergency regulations that had been declared by Sir Evelyn Baring in 1952.[11] Pinto was accused of three crimes, "1 that he had knowledge of illegal arms traffic, 2 that he had assisted Mau Mau in drafting documents and arranged for the printing of membership card of the 'African Liberation Army' and 3, that he had given assistance to the non-militant wing of the Mau Mau in planning its subversive campaign."[12]

Later, in February 1958, Pinto was transferred from Manda Island to Kabarnet in Baringo District, under Restriction Order. While in detention, the colonial administration tried to break his spirit and constantly made a joke of him as being the only "Asian Mau Mau." The colonial administration hoped he would become an informant, but this never happened. He became a crucial figure (with Achieng Oneko) in reenergizing inmates once they discovered the colonialist move to demoralize them and sow division.[13]

Pinto was released toward the end of 1959. Upon release, he continued with the struggle, at the same time he took care of the widows and orphans of his comrades, those lost in the struggle by collecting clothing, funds, and food to redistribute to such families. Furthermore, in 1960, just a few months after being released, Pio formed another organization, the East African Goan League; the Portuguese wanted the British colonialists to ban the organization but failed. The British colonial masters had refused Pio to see Kenyatta; however, due to his shrewdness, and using the East African Goan League, the group applied for permission to see Kenyatta. The British accepted, nobody expected Pinto in Maralal. But everyone was surprised to see Pinto at the head of the Goan delegation that had gone to see Kenyatta.[14]

## JOURNALISM

After release from prison, Pinto realized that the media was key to the struggle for independence and justice, especially to disseminate information and to counter propaganda by the colonial state. Back in 1952, he had resigned his post with the Kenya Indian Congress to work as the editor of the *Daily Chronicle* and a correspondent for the Press Trust of India and All India Radio. Now, he was determined to resume his journalistic efforts. In 1960, he resumed publicity work with the KAU, now reconstituted as the Kenya African National Union (KANU). That same year he cofounded *Sauti Ya KANU* (Voice of KANU), KANU's newspaper. The newspaper was vital to KANU's success in the upcoming elections. In 1961 and 1962 he petitioned help from Nehru, who provided funds to establish the Pan-African Press. Pinto held the position of manager in the press, which advocated tirelessly for trade unions, rights, and independence in such publications as *Sauti Ya Mwafirika* (Voice of African) and the *Pan-African Paper*.[15] His efforts were rewarded in the legislative elections of 1961–1963, in which KANU won first legislative power and then, with the transition to independence in 1963–1964, control of the executive branch as well.

Pinto was a journalist and a political activist. He combined these roles in letting the world know about the situation in colonial Kenya. He wrote for Indian newspapers, connected with African liberation movements not only in Kenya but also Mozambique and supporters in United Kingdom, under the umbrella of the Movement for Colonial Freedom (MCF). The MCF included members of the House of Commons, and representatives from various colonial countries living in Britain. There were specialists and MPs who took a keen interest in issues going on in the colonies. The MCF established Standing Committees, each with an MP chairman, they met weekly. These Standing Committees were for various regions such as South East Asia, Caribbean, West Africa, Central Africa, South Africa, and East Africa. The various committee chairmen included Stan Awbery, Jennie Lee, Tony Benn, Leslie Hale, and Fenner Brockway, and that last two who worked with Pinto closely. The Standing Committees closely followed what was happening in the colonies, suggesting actions and maintained close links with the liberation movements, even when operating under difficult circumstances. In Kenya, their contact person was Pinto who worked until his arrest and after his release.[16]

Thus, he sent regular cuttings of newspapers and wrote letters tirelessly about atrocities in colonial Kenya to many people, among them Kenyans in United Kingdom, as well as British MPs and the Kenya support groups in United Kingdom, using a cover address of Mrs. Ela Reid.[17] For instance, he sent letters to the support groups and Fenner after Mr. John Tameno informed him of the colonial government's efforts to create antagonism between the Kikuyu and the Masai. The colonial state had encouraged the Morans to carry out raids on the Kikuyu in the Aberdares region and other places. These reports were sent secretly through the diplomatic bag of the Indian High Commission.

Pinto worked together with other members of the British Parliament who were anti-colonialists. For example, he worked with Fenner and Hon. Leslie Hale, who came to Kenya at the invitation of KAU to investigate and report on the arrest of Jomo Kenyatta and other members of Kapenguria Six. Pinto worked tirelessly with these two gentlemen, as eulogized by his friend Fenner:

> In 1952 Leslie Hale and I had to be protected not from Mau Mau but from Europeans. We stayed in the home of a friendly Indian, day and night soldiers occupied the gardens to protect us from threats of assassination. Nevertheless, we were continuously active during our stay to bring peace and recognition of the right of the African people to self-government, and Pio was one of the most dedicated helpers. He was a young journalist in Nairobi and would come to us several times a day with news and make contacts for us with influential people to enable us fulfill our mission.[18]

It is evident that Pio worked diligently with his friends in the British Parliament. It was due to his resilience and encouragement that Fenner was able to establish in England the aforementioned "Movement for Colonial Freedom." Fenner was captivated by Pinto's commitment and ability to mobilize support for the decolonization of other African countries. To him, Pio was a friend and a comrade with shared ideals of freedom of mankind, hence on hearing of his death, Fenner commented: "I was sad both because of his service to freedom and for his wife and children. I died a little myself when I heard the news."[19] Pinto's connections in the United Kingdom were wide, and he also worked closely with Mr. Kingsley Martin and Mr. Colin Legum, especially in his efforts of trying to set up the Tribune Press. His efforts were recognized and later awarded a posthumous award by the International Organization of Journalists for his contributions in journalism to the liberation of African countries.

## SOCIAL JUSTICE WORK

When Pinto returned to Kenya in 1949, he began a decade and more of work on issues of social justice for the good of his fellow Kenyans. One important issue was the colonial state's dispossession of the Kipsigis and the Kamba peoples of their ancestral lands. Throughout the twentieth century, Africans had been evicted from their traditional lands, which were then given to foreign tea companies for tea production. For example, in 1952, Pinto wrote a letter to Fenner indicating how the colonial government evicted the Kipsigis people from their lands in order to create room for the African Highlands Produce Company.[20] When the Kipsigis contested the forceful removal from their land at Kimilot and resettlement in an arid area designated LRM 778, an area of only 7,650 acres, Pinto joined forces with Joseph Daniel Otiende, another nationalist and freedom fighter, to help build the Kipsigis' case. The court ruled in favor of the Kipsigis (a rare occurrence in colonial times), but the colonial government ignored the court decision and proceeded with their plan for dispossession, using armored cars and prison labor to demolish the huts of the Kipsigis people. Pinto continued to advocate for land rights, writing to British contacts and others to advance the case for national land rights. Throughout the 1950s, Pinto solicited the support of international actors in Britain, India, and elsewhere. One frequent correspondent was Fenner Brockway, a British Member of Parliament, antiwar activist, and anti-colonialist.[21] Brockway had been born in British India and returned home to become a leader of progressive causes.

His work on land rights often required personal sacrifices. For instance, during his tenure as the editor of the *Daily Chronicle*, the East Africa Royal Commission on Land asked for evidence of land ownership of the Kikuyu people. This was a difficult task, seeing that most leaders either were arrested or had gone to fight in the forest. Pinto, whose work ethic was legendary, sometimes working until 5:00 a.m., knew that he could not investigate the land claims while working full time at the *Daily Chronicle.* Therefore, he resigned from his editorial job and dedicated himself full time to documenting the Kikuyu claim. For three months, he read through the Carter Commission Report and other documents, took statements from Kikuyu elders in the villages, and wrote a memorandum report/response to the Carter Land Commission.

Pinto worked to bring various Kenyan communities and factions together in the struggle for land rights, trade unions, and social justice. His goal was the inclusion of as many communities as possible to create unity and a broad base for independence and justice. For example, originally KANU barred non-Africans from membership. Pinto thus assisted in the formation of the Kenya Freedom Party, which was open to non-Africans as well as Africans. It shut its doors only when KANU allowed non-African members as well. Furthermore, during the First Lancaster House Conference of 1960—in which the new Kenyan constitutional framework was being constructed—Pinto tried to bring the Asian community into the process to bolster the unity of all Kenyans. And during the 1963 elections, Pinto found that KANU's chapter in the Central Province had denied the former Mau Mau member Bildad Kaggia a slot on the legislative ballot. Kaggia had fallen out with KANU leader Jomo Kenyatta because of Kaggia's relentless advocacy for the poor and landless, and the KANU leadership attempted to exclude him from the new legislative branch. Pinto brought together allies such as Mbiyu Koinange, Joe Murumbi, Fred Kubai, Achieng Oneko, and J. D. Kali to advocate for Kaggia's inclusion. Together, the group went to Kandara and talked to the elders who had been poisoned against Kaggia. Pinto reiterated Kaggia's role in fighting for Kenyans and reminded the elders of Kaggia's many years in detentions in support of Kenyan rights and independence. KANU relented and allowed Kaggia on the ballot. He swept all the votes except one to be KANU nominee, won the elections and Kaggia served in Kenya's very first independent legislature, the National Assembly, as well as serving in ministry positions.

Pinto himself showed little interest in running for the National Assembly. He served in an honorary capacity on the KANU Nairobi election committee. In 1963, Pinto was elected member of the Legco, the interim legislature before full independence and the creation of the National Assembly. And it was the only pressure from his friends that made him run for office and became a Specially Elected Member of the House of Representatives in 1964. Jaramogi Oginga Odinga commented on his appeal, especially in the face of his Portuguese heritage: "Anyone who met Pinto forgot his pigmentation because his work and deeds left no doubt that he was a Kenyan Nationalist. He had immense organizational powers and ceaselessly went around bridging all gaps in our defenses."[22]

Pinto was involved in many other initiatives over the years. He established the Lumumba Institute in 1964 with the mission of training party officials. And he continued to advocate for the poor and railed against the greedy capitalist and neo-imperialist forces that threatened the health of the newly independent republic: "Kenya's Uhuru [freedom] must not be transformed into freedom to exploit, or freedom to be hungry, and live in ignorance. Uhuru must be Uhuru for the masses—Uhuru from exploitation, from ignorance, disease, and poverty. The sacrifices of the hundreds of thousands of Kenya's freedom fighters must be honored by the effective implementation of KANU's policy—a democratic, African, socialist state in which the people have the rights, in the words of KANU election manifesto, 'to be free from economic exploitation and social inequality.'"[23] His opposition to the newly unleashed forces of capitalism in Kenya put him at risk, but Pinto's advocacy for social and economic justice never wavered.

## INTERNATIONALIST AND PAN-AFRICANIST EFFORTS

Pinto's struggle against oppression was not confined to Kenya only. His activities were broad, and he had a vision unlike any other nationalists in Kenya, then or now. For instance, in East Africa, Pinto was a member of the East African Central Legislative Assembly, an arm of the East Africa High Commission, and forerunner of the East African Common Services Organization (EACSO), and was a close associate of President Julius Nyerere. He constantly visited Dar es Salaam and Kampala and supported the creation of some sort of federation for economic development among the three member states of Kenya, Tanganyika, and Uganda. His (and Nyerere's) efforts yielded fruit when the EACSO was succeeded by the East African Community. He was also among the committee of nine members of Organization of African Union (OAU) that strategized the liberation of other colonies in Africa.

Indeed, Pinto was an Internationalist and a Pan-Africanist. He was relentless in his decolonization activities worldwide. For example, he worked with many liberation movements and freedom fighters/nationalists such as Jonas Savimbi in Angola, Mario de Andrade of Partido Africano da Independencia da Guinie e Cabo Verde (PAIGC) in Guinea Bissau, and Chedi Jagan in Guyana.[24] Pinto also worked for the decolonization of Mozambique. In 1961, Pinto assisted in the formation of Mozambique African National Union, which later joined Frente de Libertacao de Mozambique (FRELIMO) (Mozambique National Liberation Front) in 1962 led by Eduardo Mondale in the struggle against Portuguese colonization. Mozambique was under a severe colonial grip and could not allow any nationalist activities to take place; hence, FRELIMO was proscribed. But Nyerere being a true Pan-Africanist allowed FRELIMO to be headquartered and operate from Dar es Salam, where Pio was a frequent visitor helping with logistics. Pio was committed to the cause of Mozambique liberation.[25]

Additionally, he assisted nationalist and political refugees from South Africa, Mozambique, and Angola to find their ways to countries where they could organize resistance movements—hence his close association with Nyerere and Kwame Nkrumah of Ghana who were at the forefront of such initiatives. Pinto, like many other activists such as Che Guevara, did not like being contained behind office walls or congress. He once confided to his friend Fitz De Souza just a few weeks before his assassination that his wish was to resign from his parliamentary seat and retire to Lindi or Mtwara, Tanzanian towns situated at the border with Mozambique, to assist the FRELIMO freedom fighters. However, his friends would not let him go; they convinced Pinto that his work was needed in the Kenyan parliament; little did they know he was already a marked man.

His internationalism is further evident in his activities and interest in his home state of Goa (India); he was strongly associated with the struggle against Portuguese fascism in both Goa and Africa. To counteract Portuguese propaganda about the supposed benefits of Portuguese rule, Pinto started a Konkani paper in Nairobi called *Uzwod*, whose main objective was to raise awareness of the social and political realities of Portuguese rule in Goa. Additionally, upon his release, he formed the East African Goan League and used this organization to invite delegates to Kenya from Goa in May 1961. Lucio Rodrigues and Dr. Laura D'Souza led this group, which consisted of cultural ambassadors and performers who upheld the self-respect and dignity of East African Goans and their culture, besides highlighting the dire situation of the Portuguese colony of Goa. Pinto was a founder member of the Goa National Congress, which aimed to liberate Goa from Portuguese rule. He organized another trip to India in 1961 and was accompanied by Mwinga Chokwe, the Coast chair of KANU and Hon. Tom Mboya, the general secretary of KANU. They met the Goan nationalists and Mboya spoke eloquently, telling the government of Nehru that while it was eager to liberate Africa, it needed to push out the Portuguese imperialists within India itself.[26] Pinto and other delegates even advocated for military resistance to Portuguese rule. They offered to organize an international volunteer brigade to liberate Goa; that pushed Nehru into action, and he would eventually order the troops that, thanks to Pinto and delegates like Nsilo Swai and Lakshmi Menon, liberated Goa in 1961. Pinto later went to Delhi for the celebration of the liberation of Goa. He continued to work on setting free other Portuguese colonies in Africa too. Once again, in 1964, he was a delegate to the Delhi meeting that brought together nationalists from all Portuguese colonies to plan their liberation.

In South Africa, he supported the struggle against apartheid[27] and even helped to organize resistance activities in solidarity, leading to the launching of the Van Riebeeck Movement in many countries. This was to counteract the Van Riebeeck Day annual celebrations started by the apartheid regime as a festival to honor the arrival of the Dutch in South Africa on April 6, 1652. Pinto organized resistance to this celebration. For example, he organized Africans and Asians in Kenya to observe the Van Riebeeck Day on April 6, but in a defiant way. He was able to bring in members of the Kenya African Union and the Indian National Congress to support this initiative. Participants observed the day in diverse ways: they wore black in solidarity with people mourning in South Africa, those who could not afford black clothing were encouraged to use a black feather as a visible emblem of mourning; and those who went to places of worship offered prayers for South Africa, the African National Congress, and the dismantling of apartheid policies.[28] His initiatives to celebrate the Van Riebeeck Movement extended to Nigeria and Northern Rhodesia; due to his great lobbying ability, the colonial state in Kenya was afraid of the general meeting called by KAU to observe Van Riebeeck Day and denied permission for the meeting, though it took place in areas such as Nyanza.

Pinto's agenda was the general decolonization of Africa; he was against the oppression of African people and did all he could to oppose it. As early as the 1950s, he worked to establish ties between affected territories, believing that unity against oppressors—regardless of regional boundaries—was the best way to dismantle colonialism. In a letter to Mr. Fenner Brockway dated March 10, 1952, Pinto wrote, "You will observe from the cuttings I have enclosed that steps are being taken to link East Africa with the Federation to the South. Mr. J. Otiende, the general secretary of KAU, has already addressed a communication to the Nyasaland African Congress with a copy to N. Rhodesian African Congress on the subject of establishing closer liaison with their respective organizations."[29] By 1953, the colonial state started to monitor Pinto, so he started to use the address of his brother Rosario Gama Pinto for access to his mails. The pressure was intense. Nevertheless, Pinto continued with his communication among the territories and with friends in Britain's House of Commons. Pinto corresponded with several members of the House of Commons regarding the brutality of colonial rule in Kenya. He would forward newspaper cuttings to Mr. Fenner Brockway, who would disseminate the information. For example, writing to Mr. Douglas Rogers, on January 22, 1953, Fenner a member of the House of Commons stated, "I enclose letters from Pinto which accompanied the cuttings. There is some good stuff in them. You can quote from them but I do not think you should give Pinto as the authority for them. Say the information comes from Nairobi from a reliable source."[30]

In the course of his internationalist efforts, it is alleged that Pinto met with African –America, Malcolm X when he visited Kenya. Malcolm visited many African countries such as Egypt, Nigeria, and Ghana; his visit to Kenya is shrouded in mystery. However, Mickie Mwanzia Koster in her work, "Malcolm X, the Mau Mau, and Kenya's New Revolutionaries: A Legacy of Transnationalism," indicates that Malcolm X visited Kenya in October 1964, where he had an opportunity to learn from Kenyan nationalists about Kenya's independence and the Mau Mau struggles.[31] Malcolm embraced the freedom struggle. From Koster's work, it is convincing that Malcolm met Pinto, since he was heavily influenced by Pinto. Nonetheless, it is a sad coincidence that Malcolm X was murdered on February 21, 1965, in New York, only three days before Pinto was murdered in Nairobi.[32]

## SOCIALISM

Pinto was an able politician of great tact and subtlety. He embraced diplomacy and did not force his opinions on others but remained very firm and resolute, a gentle lion, so to speak. Among the questions surrounding his murder is whether his socialist beliefs made him a target. Pinto had his own version of socialism that he advanced unapologetically. His socialist views scared many, and especially the West.

For decades, opponents of socialism had used the scare tactic of calling them communists, and Pinto was subject to the same accusations. His best friend, the then Vice President Murumbi, clarified Pinto's beliefs: "To me Pio was a Socialist. He lived by his socialist beliefs in thought and deed. . . . he was a friend of the downtrodden, the poor, and above all faithful to his friends who suffered imprisonment for the cause of freedom. He gave all he had to help the poor; he gave but asked nothing in return, he died a pauper."[33] Indeed, Pio was known to have given half of his salary to orphans and Mau Mau widows. It was noted that on the day of his release from detention Pinto had no shoes, having given his only pair to another prisoner who was released.

Pinto disagreed with some leaders in as far as redistribution of land was concerned in independent Kenya. Pio was annoyed that the land bought from the Europeans as part of the independence deal was not given to those who lost the land, especially the Mau Mau.

This was because few chosen Kikuyus got the land. Additionally, some Europeans were also sold the land at an extremely high price while many other Africans remained poor and squatters in their own country. Pio was willing to sacrifice personal gains for what he believed in, and he did not want to enrich himself. Such beliefs were the seeds of disagreement with Kenyatta, who believed in entitlement and believed the seeds of independence belonged to the county, to himself and those close to him.[34]

Its Pio's idea of being against land grabbing that brought him close to Jaramogi Oginga Odinga. According to Fitz, who himself had turned down Kenyatta's idea to get land in Laikipia, Pio would equate the thousands of acres in the Highlands as having exchanged hands from "white Lord Delamare with a black Lord Delamare." According to Pinto, Leaders should lead by example and not grab things.[35]

Pio believed in a helping hand—that is what socialism meant to him. Nonetheless, his approach to socialism acknowledged the need for a mixed economy. He did not support wholesale nationalization of industries; he knew the nation was young and there was little to nationalize anyway. It is apparent that he adhered to the "African Socialism" philosophy of Julius Nyerere, a philosophy that the West confused with communism.

Pinto wanted the government to play a key role in economic and social reconstruction. His wife Emma said, "People have used words like 'communist' and 'socialist' to describe Pio. I feel at his core he was a humanist."[36] It bothered him greatly to see people suffer, and he believed in dignity and respect of humanity. His life was based on the cardinal virtue of equality and goodwill. He wanted to build a society in which the difference in wealth between the rich and the poor was minimal (a point of view that put him in conflict with Kenyatta) and where the poor were neither oppressed nor ignored. He believed in the establishment of rent-controlled urban areas as a way of protecting tenants from exploitative property owners. In addition, he supported the establishment of free health and free education services. His was a pragmatic socialism that sought to support the poor and create healthy societies in Africa once they were rid of the oppressive colonialism of their past.

## THE ASSASSINATION AND TRIAL

On February 24, 1965, Pinto was killed in his driveway, his 18-month-old daughter Tereshka strapped in the back seat of his car. Four shots were fired at close range, apparently by one man. Two of the bullets struck Pinto, killing him.

Who could have killed Pinto? Who would benefit the most? Answering these questions became difficult because friends and family believed that it was a political assassination, and Pinto himself had told them he had often been followed. With this in mind, his friends collected and burned all his unpublished writings. Any piece of paper with Pinto's writing found in his house was destroyed.

The investigation and trial yielded up two possible suspects for the murder. Kisilu Mutua and Thuo Chege were petty criminals who had been drafted into intimidation work by a shadowy "security agent" they knew only as "Sammy." On the day of the assassination, Sammy had taken them in a taxi to Pinto's house, where they were intended to "scare" Pinto away from his political and trade union activities. Having just gotten out of the taxi, another car drove up and shots were fired, killing Pinto. Kisilu Mutua and Thuo Chege were shuttled back into the taxi and driven away. Later they were given instructions to meet Sammy at a familiar rendezvous that night, but when they arrived, three police detectives met them. At the station, police reservist Patrick Shaw—a dreaded holdover from the colonial administration—had them record their statements; but a few days later they were forced by police officers to sign a new statement, and this is the statement that was used at the trial.[37]

The trial was presided over by Chief Justice A. J. Ainsley and three assessors who would ultimately determine their guilt or innocence. The defendants insisted that they had been framed and that the police should track down "Sammy." The principals were also aware that Patrick Shaw—the police official who had prepared the second statement—had been implicated in many unresolved murders in Kenya. As a result, the assessors found both men innocent. Thuo Chege was released, but on July 17, 1965, Justice Ainsley convicted Kisilu because he was present at the crime scene and thus likely to have aided and abetted the killer. Ainsley sentenced him to hang, but this sentence was commuted to a life sentence on appeal. Kisilu spent 35 years and few months in jail before being exonerated and released in 2001.

Because neither the true assassins nor the ones who hired them have ever been identified, theories about the cause of and responsibility for Pinto's assassination have continued to circulate and be debated. Did Shaw do the dirty work for the government or for the neocolonialists? Could it be possible that capitalists saw young progressives/freedom fighters or nationalists who believed in economic freedom as a threat? Could his death be linked to that of Patrice Lumumba, taking the period of death into consideration?

While questions persisted, the government of President Kenyatta and the KANU party refused to open an investigation into the evidence, trial, and sentencing. Pinto's brother Rosario Pinto campaigned stridently for intervention but was continually rejected. He wrote to the Parliamentary Group Meeting through their chair, Hon. Ronald Ngala, for an inquiry, but the secretary of the Parliamentary Group responded, "The President explained that the letter was understandably emotional but said that the matter had been dealt with in court and that constitutionally the Government could not interfere."[38] When this failed, Rosario wrote a letter directly to President Kenyatta on July 20, 1965. He was categorical and reminded Kenyatta of Pinto's personal relation to the president, stating,

I am not at all happy with the outcome of the trial which caste aspersion on the country and the people as a whole. I sincerely hope you will kindly consider this appeal with a view to remedying this unhappy situation which might encourage similar assassinations. . . . There is no need to eulogies my brother's contribution towards your present exalted office sufficient to that he, supported by a band of loyal and sincere personalities, managed to keep away many contenders from your chair during the time of your restriction thereby incurring their enmity and intrigues for life. If for no other reason but this and his contribution in many fields towards the attainment of independence, this tragedy should warrant an impartial enquiry.[39]

Kenyatta did not take action and Rosario subsequently appealed directly to KANU, the ruling political party. On October 8, 1965, he wrote another letter to the secretary general of KANU, Hon. T. J. Mboya, requesting an enquiry. His letter stated, "I very strongly protest to the violent methods used to liquidate true nationalist after achievement of independence. This is unparalleled with events in our neighboring states. In fact, it is yet unbelievable and disgusting to say the least. . . . I shall be most grateful if you discuss this petition with the Executive."[40]

Many African ambassadors and other luminaries, including the foreign ministers of Tanzania and Ghana, asked the Kenyatta government to set up an enquiry of the murder of this son of Africa, but Kenyatta and his government remained tight-lipped. Rosario's pleas were denied, and the government seemed in no hurry to honor Pinto, either through a more thorough inquiry or in any other way. Soon after Pinto's death, the Nairobi City Council had plans to honor his memory by renaming the former Grogan Road, Pio Gama Pinto Road; however, the Kenyatta government intervened and prevented it. Associates of Pinto were harassed. For instance, Ambu Patel, owner of *New Kenya Publisher* and a supporter of the independence struggle had collected a lot of material on Mau Mau fighters and political detainees with an aim of publishing a book. He had many materials on Kimathi, Pinto, and others. Unfortunately, Ambu Patel faced threats from the Kenyatta government as part of a crackdown on anyone with material and support of Mau Mau ex-fighters. Fearing to lose his precious material, Patel retreated to India, taking his materials with him. Unfortunately, the material seems to be lost, in an effort to safeguard it from the hostile Kenyatta regime.[41] The hostility toward Pinto's inquiry continued after Kenyatta's death. During President Daniel Arap Moi's rule, anybody who attempted to write on Pinto was harassed. Such was the fate that befell Shiraz Durrani, Kenyatta's lawyer. Shiraz was interrogated several times by the Special Branch in September 1984, by Fredrick Mukangu. He was taken to the notorious Nyayo house 24th floor because of an article he wrote on Pinto that appeared on the *Standard Newspaper* on September 17 and 18, 1984. Some of the questions asked were ridiculous such as, "are you the one who wrote the article? Why did you write on Pinto? Are you a historian?"[42] It seems both the Kenyatta and Moi governments tried their best to erase Pinto's legacy, ironically, it's Moi who eventually set Kisilu free for the murder in 2001.

Many questions remain unanswered to this day. Pinto's wife Emma, old and ailing, eventually died in October 2020, and went to her grave without any answers. Nevertheless, as historians, it is our responsibility to keep the legacy of Pio Gama Pinto alive. It is not too late to probe more deeply into the assassination and those who might be responsible.

## CONCLUSION

Pio Gama Pinto was a key figure in the independence of Kenya and the struggle against oppression worldwide. Though his life was cut short, and he was unable to carry out all of the plans and dreams he had for Kenya, Mozambique, and so many other suffering communities, his friend Fitz De Souza acknowledged he died with "his boots on."[43] It is no wonder that Julius Nyerere argued bitterly with Kenyatta for condoning Pinto's cover-up. Pinto was mourned everywhere and many young African nations were in shock. Many leaders of African countries contributed to the education fund for his children set up by Hon. Joseph Murumbi, and other countries helped in resettling the grieving family. For example, Ambassador A. M. Gobba of the United Arab Republic issued tickets for the family from Nairobi to London via Cairo en route to Canada, while the Egyptian minister for guidance, Mr. Mohamed Fayek, agreed to host the family for one week in Cairo, while on their way to resettlement.[44]

Pinto gained the love of Africans everywhere and Kenyans in particular for his nationalism and efforts to free Kenya from colonial control. He was a journalist who founded KANU's newspaper and a social activist who lobbied for traditional land rights and workers' unions. He was equally an internationalist who worked for other oppressed colonies and reached out to both colonial and postcolonial powers to invite their cooperation. As a socialist, he remained focus on the well-being of the poor.

Nevertheless, Kenya just like other post-independent nations saw a bitter and sometimes violent struggle between socialism and capitalism. Consequently, capitalism won with the ardent support of the West, basically the United States and the United Kingdom. These outside pressures made President Kenyatta and his successor Moi to violently suppress those advocating for an alternative path, especially those advocating for socialism. As such, opponents were exiled, imprisoned and many just disappeared. Therefore, in the end, the hidden hand of neo-imperialism/capitalism won, and the aims of Mau Mau and other freedom fighters were suppressed, producing contradictions of democracy and capitalism. Pinto seems to have been a casualty of the clash between capitalism and socialism. However, his death and that of J.M. did not end the quest for justice, equality, and land issues.

Today, the fight against injustice continues. Interethnic rivalry, the lack of a social contract between leaders and citizens, and the continued blight of assassinations (including that of T. J. Mboya just four years after Pinto) plague Kenya and other African nations. These political assassinations have bedeviled the nation and driven further internal divisions among Kenyans today, reinforcing stereotypes, suspicions, and the entitlement ideology—ideas that have continued to shape postcolonial politics of identity as seen in periodic electoral violence, the dislocation of peoples, and the senseless killing of ordinary citizens that has marked Kenya's postcolonial epoch. Such narrow identities frustrate not only the forging of a nation but also the thriving of democracy in Kenya. We are living in a moment of "Not Yet Uhuru" since independence has brought no real change; instead, it has created more division and trauma, as the fruit of independence has benefited only a few. Democracy has failed; people still vote along with ethnic blocks, party lines, or regional affiliations rather than for ideas or principles.

Desperation has set in politically. Do votes matter or did we just exchange "white imperialism" with mild "black imperialism." The failure of democracy and its ensuing frustration is today captured in all Kenyan aspects of life. This is witnessed among different ages and in different modes, be it songs or slogans like "Bado Mapambano" (the struggle continues) and *"Utajua Ujui"* (loosely translated as "clueless"), depicting the helplessness but also the optimism and resilience among people linking the past and the present while depicting the socioeconomic and political struggles of ordinary citizens in Kenyans as one people.

The struggle for unity, the well-being of ordinary people, and justice continue. For those individuals and groups of people who are standing up for what is right, Pinto remains a symbol of the oppressed and an example of ordinary Kenyans questioning authoritarian and corrupt regimes. Kenya's democracy is in a "political ICU," and Pinto continues to offer ideas and a sense of dedication to the generations now fighting to get the postcolonial state out of its current socioeconomic inequalities and political thuggery. His resilient spirit is captured as much in the epitaph engraved in his tombstone:

*"If I have been extinguished, yet there arise; A thousand beacons from the spark I bore."*

## NOTES

1. Godriver Wanga-Odhiambo, *The Political Economy of Sugar Production in Colonial Kenya: The Asian Initiative* (New York: Lexington Books, 2016), 15.

2. George Delf, *Asians in East Africa* (London: Oxford University Press, 1963), 9.

3. Robert Gregory, *Quest for Equality: Asian Politics in East Africa 1900-1967* (New Delhi: Orient Longman Ltd, 1993), 18.

4. Nicholas Githuku, "The Unfolding of Britain and Kenya's Complex Tango: An Uneasy Return to a Critical Past and its Implications," in *Dedan Kimathi on Trial: Colonial Justice and Popular Memory in Kenya's Mau Mau*, ed. Julie MacArthur (Athens: Ohio University Press, 2017) 284–316.

5. Shiraz Durrani, ed., *Pio Gama Pinto: Kenya's Unsung Martyr 1927-1965*(Nairobi: Vita Books, 2018), 13.

6. Apa Pant, *Undiplomatic Incidents* (Hyderabad: Sangam Book, 1987), 26–28.

7. KNA: MAC/KEN/71/1 Pinto Pio da Gama, 1927-1965, Public Meetings and the Pan-African Press.

8. Durrani (ed.) *Kenya's Unsung Martyr*, 29. See also E.S. Atieno Odhiambo and John Lonsdale, eds., *Mau Mau and Nationhood: Arms, Authority and Narration* (Athens: Ohio University Press, 2003), 38.

9. KNA: MAC 920.938 PIO. Pio Gama Pinto: Independent Kenya's First Martyr, Socialist and Freedom Fighter.

10. Robert M. Maxon, *East Africa: An Introductory History*, 3rd ed. (Morgantown: West Virginia University Press, 2009), 253.

11. William R. Ochieng, ed., *A Modern History of Kenya 1895-1980* (Nairobi: Evans Brothers, 1989), 189.

12. Durrani, ed., *Kenya's Unsung Martyr*, 28.

13. Shiraz Durrani, "Pio Gama Pinto: Some Facts about the life of a great leader and a Patriot Journalist," *Sauti ya Kamukunji* (University of Nairobi Student Union, 1984), 8.

14. Fitz de Souza, *Forward to Independence: My Memoirs* (Middletown: Fitzval R. S. de Souza, 2019), 238.

15. KNA: MAC/KEN/71/1, Pinto's letter to KANU for candidacy for KANU ticket for Specially Elected Seat, May 29, 1963.

16. Douglas Rogers Archives, letter from Douglas Rogers to Stan Newens, MP, House of Commomns, Westminister, S.W.I.

17. Douglas Rogers Archives-London, Pinto's Letters to Fenner Brockway, January 12, 1953.

18. Durrani, *Kenya's Unsung Martyr,*188–89.

19. Ibid., 189.

20. KNA: MAC/KEN/71/1, Letter to Brockway dated March 10, 1952.

21. KNA: MAC/KEN/71/1, Letter to Brockway, March 10, 1952.

22. KNA: MCA 920.938 PIO, *Pio Gama Pinto Independent Kenya's First Martyr*, 6.

23. Durrani, *Kenya's Unsung Martyr*, 35.

24. Ibid., 159.

25. De Souza, *Forward to Independence*, 240.

26. KNA: MAC 920.938 PIO, *Pio Gama Pinto Independent Kenya's First Martyr*, 31.

27. KNA: MAC/KEN/71/1, Pinto's letter to Brockway, March 10, 1952.

28. Ibid.

29. KNA: MAC/KEN/7/1, Pinto's letter to Brockway, March 10, 1952.

30. KNA: MAC/KEN/7/1, Letter from Brockway to Douglas Rogers, January 22, 1953.

31. Mickie Mwanzia Koster, "Malcolm X, the Mau Mau, and Kenya's New Revolutionaries: A Legacy of Transnationalism," *Journal of African American History* 100 (2015): 250–71.

32. Durrani, *Kenya's Unsung Martyr*, 159.

33. KNA: MAC 920.938 PIO, Pio Gama Pinto Independent Kenya's First Martyr, 9.

34. De Souza, *Forward to Independence*, 235.

35. De Souza, *Forward to Independence*, 250.

36. Emma Pinto as quoted in *Kenya's Unsung Martyr*, 3.

37. Kamau Ngotho, "The call that brought freedom to Kenya's longest serving prisoner," *Daily Nation* (Nairobi), July 29, 2017.

38. KNA: MAC/KEN/71/1, Extract of Minute no. 63/65, Late Pinto Brother's Letter.

39. KNA: MAC/KEN/71/1, Rosario's Letter to Kenyatta, July 20, 1965.

40. KNA: MAC/KEN/71/1, Rosario's Letter to T.J. Mboya, October 8, 1965.

41. Durrani, *Kenya's Unsung Martyr*, 16.

42. Shiraz Durrani, Special Branch Questions September 1984.

43. KNA: MAC 920.938 PIO, Pio Gama Pinto: Independent Kenya's First Martyr: Socialist and Freedom Fighter, 32.

44. KNA: MAC/KEN/71/6, Letter from Mr. A. M. Gobba, February 3, 1967.

# BIBLIOGRAPHY

## Primary Sources

Douglas Rogers Archives, London.

Kenya National Archives (KNA), Nairobi.

KNA: AG/52/451, Republic vs. Kisilu son of Mutua.

KNA: KEN/71/4, Pinto, Pio da Gama, Report on Pinto's Assassination.

KNA: KEN/71/5 Pinto, Pio da Gama Funeral and Memorial Services, 1965.

KNA: MAC/KEN/7/1, Pinto Pio Da Gama, 1927-1965, Public Meetings and the Pan African Press.

KNA: MAC/KEN/71/6, Pinto, Pio da Gama: The Pio Pinto Fund, 1965–1967.

KNA: MAC/KEN/71/7, Pinto, Pio Da Gama 1927–1965, Tributes.

KNA: MAC 920.938 PIO, Pio Gama Pinto Independent Kenya's First Martyr.

## Secondary Sources

Atieno, Odhiambo E.S. and John Lonsdale, eds. *Mau Mau and Nationhood: Arms, Authority and Narration.* Athens: Ohio University Press, 2003.

Bravo, Philip. "The Case of Goa: History, Rhetoric and Nationalism." *Past Imperfect* 7 (1998): 125–54.

Delf, George. *Asians in East Africa.* London: Oxford University Press, 1963.

De Souza, Fitz. *Forward to Independence: My Memoirs.* Middletown: Fitzval R. S. de Souza, 2019.

Durrani, Shiraz, ed. *Pio Gama Pinto: Kenya's Unsung Martyr 1927-1965.* Nairobi: Vita Books, 2018.

———. "Pio Pinto: Some Facts about the Life of a Great Leader and Patriotic Journalist." *Sauti ya Kamukunji*, Nairobi. Vol. 1, no. 8, University of Nairobi, May 1984.

Githuku, Nicholas. "The Unfolding of Britain and Kenya's Complex Tango; An Uneasy Return to Critical Past and Its Implications." In *Dedan Kimathi on Trial:*

*Colonial Justice and Popular Memory in Kenya's MauMau*, (ed.) Julie MacArthur. Athens: Ohio University Press, 2017, 284–316.

Gregory, Robert. *Quest for Equality: Asian Politics in East Africa 1900-1967*. New Delhi: Orient Longman Ltd, 1993.

Koster Mickie M. "Malcolm X, the Mau Mau, and Kenya's New Revolutionaries: A Legacy of Transnationalism." *Journal of African-American History* 100, no. 2 (2015): 250–71.

MacArthur, Julie, ed. *Dedan Kimathi on Trial: Colonial Justice and Popular Memory in Kenya's Mau Mau*. Athens: Ohio University Press, 2017.

Maxon, Robert M. *East Africa: An Introductory History*, 3rd edition. Morgantown: West Virginia University Press, 2009.

Ngotho, Kamau. "The Call that Brought Freedom to Kenya's Longest Serving Prisoner." *Daily Nation* (Nairobi), July 29, 2017.

Ochieng, William R., ed. *A Modern History of Kenya 1895-1980*. Nairobi: Evans Brothers, 1989.

Pant, Apa. *Undiplomatic Incidents*. Hyderabad: Sangam Books Ltd, 1987.

Wanga-Odhiambo, Godriver. *Political Economy of Sugar Production in Colonial Kenya: The Asian Initiative in Central Nyanza*. New York: Lexington Books, 2016.

## Chapter 7

# Eastlands, Nairobi

## *Memory, History, and Recovery*

### Betty Wambui

Eastlands, Nairobi, has a rich history and heritage that has often gone unrecognized in Kenya. It was the first Urban Home for Africans in colonial Kenya. It later became home to much of its lower and middle classes. Its historical status as a material site of City and National memory, as the home of Sheng, the center of matatu culture, contemporary and veteran musicians, sports icons, many Kenyan politicians, and pop culture is rapidly being lost. Similarly, its significance is undervalued, forgotten, and erased. This chapter explores challenges to identity, community, and belonging in Eastlands, Nairobi. It attempts to make a case for the use of urban space, memory, and history to mitigate dangers posed to identity and community by historically unanchored urbanity and sociopolitical neglect. More ambitiously, it claims that such negligence not only misses the important opportunity but also risks much including national fracture while also referring to Kenya's 2010 constitution.

The first section details the spatial and human character of Nairobi moving generally from its colonial past to the present. The second part examines the impact of the topography and settlement patterns in creating and reproducing conditions of structural inequality and deprivation. Here and indeed throughout the chapter, I direct attention to residents' strategies for survival in the face of historical and global pressures that are seen for example in colonial policy, state inaction, intense policing, and gentrification. The final section addresses the possible direction for a wholesome revitalization of the area's community in an era of urban renewal and gentrification.

The underlying argument I make is that this work invokes a necessary discussion as urban environments and architecture change. My case is especially an important one as population needs and relations evolve in transformed emerging spaces that are central to self, identity, community, and belonging. It is my view, that recommendations such as those I offer my conclusion have the potential not only of reclaiming and centering marginal spaces such as those rapidly deteriorating in Bahati, Jerusalem, Jericho, Kaloleni, Makongeni, Mathare, Kibera, Mukuru, Korogocho, and elsewhere in the city; but also of engaging the 2010 Kenyan Constitution. If successful, this work will ensure both the inclusion and visibility of marginalized, disenfranchised populations. My call then serves as an invitation to participate and actualize commonly conceived and executed initiatives that honor marginalized histories and communities.

## HISTORY LEADING TO GROWTH OF EASTLANDS

*The right to the city is like a cry and a demand . . . a transformed and renewed right to urban life*

*Henri Lefebvre*

Nairobi is the capital city of Kenya. It acquired its modern significance during the colonial period (1885–1963). Part of this interest was derived from colonial Britain's need for a functional terminal. As a stopover between the East African Coast (Mombasa) and the Interior (Kampala) amid the construction of the East African Railway. The date of its inception is often offered as 1899. Kenya itself was officially declared a colony in 1920 and its commercial and financial importance to the East Africa Protectorate was recognized in 1905. Early in this and prior history, Nairobi grew as an informal market center. Consequently, it expanded as a railway depot with access to cold water whose value was entirely utilitarian. In this settlement, "European settlers appropriated large tracts of land displacing . . . local African population with no provision for resettlement."[1] This practice of displacement and appropriation of land occupied by vulnerable populations such as low-wealth populations in low-income areas or public spaces such as animal parks, riverbanks, and tropical forests is one that continues to date. At each juncture, these practices threaten home and identity in small and large ways.

From its beginning, the city grew rapidly. Observe the numbers emerging out of a collaboration between the United Nations Centre for Human Settlements (UN-Habitat), the United Nations Environment Programme (UNEP), and the Nairobi City Council (NCC) below in evidence.

Table 7.1    Nairobi Population 1901 to 2015

| 1901 | 8,000 |
|------|-------|
| 1948 | 118,000 |
| 1962 | 343,500 |
| 2009 | 3.1 million |
| 2015 | 3.8 million (projection) |

*Source*: United Nations Environmental Program (UNEP),
2007. https://na.unep.net/atlas/datlas/sites/default/
files/unepsiouxfalls/atlasbook_1135/Kenya_Screen
_Chapter5-End.pdf. Retrieved, 1/1/2021

## RESIDENTIAL PATTERNS

In Nairobi, which resulted from a history of arrogation, appropriation, and expansion, one observes a certain pattern of segregation and exclusion. From early on, the city spatially came to be divided into four broad sections—the Central Business District (Town), European Nairobi (Westlands), Asian Nairobi (Southlands), and African Nairobi (Eastlands). These physical areas were geographically and culturally different from each other in ways that architecture would eventually mark as distinct. Bruce Githua in "Rational Utopias/Irrational Dystopias? Sites and Services in Eastlands, Nairobi" quotes the Kenya Uganda Railway and Habours (K. U. R. and H.) engineer R. O. Preston in 1898. This was a year before the railhead arrived at the site of what would eventually grow into Nairobi. Githua observes as Preston does in "Plan of Survey at Foot of Hill and Edge of Plains" the topographical contrasts in the area. These are ones that would eventually be woven into racial, ethnic, sexual, and class experiences across the emergent city. Specifically, in talking about Eastlands, Githua points out that "The site was located at the junction where the flat, grass-covered Athi plains meet the first rise leading up to the heights of the Aberdare Mountain range." Preston's report describes it as "a bleak, swampy stretch of soppy landscape, windswept, devoid of human habitation of any sort, the resort of thousands of wild animals." This picture of what was to become Eastlands stood in contrast to Parklands which was on the higher, cooler ground. This latter European part of Nairobi was one which Preston saw as "one magnificent stretch of impenetrable forest."[2]

In the emerging polity, one shaped in response to this topography, resource distribution also flowed in accordance to a division structured by race, class, and even gender. These ordered the distribution of resources such as water, parking, recreational facilities, public and sanitary facilities. These distinctions and the discrimination underlying them were to mark the city in ways that echo privilege and disadvantage to these contemporary times. Early on, a pattern of directing social and economic resources away from

Eastlands but more generally from low-income neighborhoods to higher income areas of the City was naturalized. Githua quotes W. T. W. Morgan, an urban geographer who points out that "Accommodating the higher socio-economic class on the higher ground quickly became an enduring pattern in Nairobi's socio-spatial structure."[3] Consequently and intentionally, better residential areas were and continue to be located "on elevated ground, [in the west and north] (with) well drained and formally wooded and friable red soils. Cheaper housing is confined to the extremely level plain in the eastern side with its intractable black clay soil."[4] This construction of difference that has contemporary consequences was and is in accordance with original City plans, as Githua points out. Maybe, in part because of these structural and institutional patterns, by the 1990s, about half of the City's population was living in unplanned settlements that persist to date.[5] Significantly for our discussion, although patterns of informal settlement areas characterized Nairobi's development generally, a higher concentration of such settlements and low-income neighborhoods with higher human populations per square feet compared to the rest of the City came to characterize Eastlands. This might explain the way in which Winnie Mitullah in her paper "Slum Reports: The case of Nairobi, Kenya" (2003) locates and describes Eastlands as being

> in the marginalized fringe of and away from the CDB, [it] is a low-income densely populated area (50–300 people a hectare) with the core region of NCC housing and new institutional housing estates (Race Course, Ngara, Shauri Moyo, Pumwani, Mathare Valley, Eastleigh, Kariobangi, Kaloleni, Bahati, Jericho, Mbotela, Dandora)—by words for urban deprivation and disadvantage, reaching densities of 200 to 300 people per hectare in 1980.[6]

Various Researchers have compared population densities in Eastlands with other areas across Nairobi. Such comparisons reveal that there are significantly more people per square kilometer in the eastern part of Nairobi than in other parts of the City. Both the "Nairobi Inventory"[7] report and the article "Land Use Management, Challenges for the City of Nairobi"[8] offer us similar data on these densities. One could, for example, compare area in relation to population density per square kilometer across the city. As an exercise, compare, for example, the data provided for Makadara, Starehe, and Pumwani—all in Eastlands, to other parts of the City below. This exercise quickly highlights the larger number of persons in Eastlands in comparison to other parts of the City. The overpopulation noted, one that typifies Eastlands, and which is partially explained by the area's history and a prevalent sense that it is in some ways cheaper to live here than elsewhere, has consequences for the delivery of healthcare, education, security, and other services. It also

**Table 7.2**    **Division Area in Square Kilometer Population Density**

| Division | Area (km²) | Population | Population Density (km²) |
|---|---|---|---|
| Langata | 223 | 286,739 | 1284 |
| Embakassi | 208.3 | 434,884 | 2088 |
| Westlands | 97.6 | 207,610 | 2127 |
| Kasarani | 85.7 | 338,925 | 3955 |
| Dagoretti | 38.7 | 240,509 | 6215 |
| Makadara | 20.1 | 197,434 | 9823 |
| Pumwani | 11.7 | 202,211 | 17283 |
| Starehe | 10.6 | 234,942 | 22164 |
| NAIROBI | 696.1 | 2,143,254 | 3079 |

An Inventory of the Slums in Nairobi (unpublished report). *Source*: Pamoja Trust, 2009 https://static1.squa respace.com/static/58d4504db8a79b27eb388c91/t/58e6ad4820099eff43a39103/1491512661162/Nairo bi_slum_inventory_jan_09.pdf, Retrieved 16th December 2015

informs a sense of self for residents and the possibilities, even the shape of communities.

## TEXTURE AND TOPOGRAPHY: IMPACT OF HISTORICAL PATTERNS ON SELF AND COMMUNITY

Most scholars agree that gentrification occurs when low or at least lower income neighborhoods are invaded, taken over by individuals, groups, and members of higher classes with greater resources. These capture local spaces and push long-standing/living populations out. That is, gentrification occurs when capital comes into neighborhoods, oftentimes low or lower wealth neighborhoods, displaces its residents, and disrupts their identities. It reshapes social patterns and communities, transforming their histories, relations, and spaces into commodities and consumables. These are often replaced with what oftentimes appears to be something better—improved housing, tighter policing, safer streets, and so on. It is this process that is taking place across Nairobi but most significantly in Eastlands.

The process of structural development that is replicating across Kenya most especially in Nairobi evidences this impression. In fact, associated changes are often touted as both desirable and good. While this might indeed be so, accompanying gentrification, at least as it often takes place in this era of capital travel, and as it is taking place in Eastlands requires critique. Here, it seems most often to work not only as an expression of contempt of the poor but also as a source of their displacement. Worryingly, it acts toward an erasure of memory of resident selves, agency, history—particularly of resistance, sociopolitical solidarity, resilience, and unity. It is this that I would like to concentrate on at this stage. That is, a consideration of the way in which for this part of Nairobi, gentrification has come at the cost of histories that are central to Nairobi's urban identity, Kenya's political one.

In this discussion, I will think of identity as certain historical and material continuity. Identity enables the creation and sustenance of cohesive relations and neighborhoods in which there is a sense of loyalty, place attachment, and social networks. The neighborhood and the social cohesion it enables are themselves central to individual and community identity. It is these deep psychological, social, and political levels of the individual and community that are destabilized when Eastlands' identity is threatened with the kind of gentrification and residential invasion that is producing an untethered trans-mutation. That is, when this area is changed from a living community and replaced with a transitory survival space so that rather than being a home space,[9] it, as is happening, is made into merely an interim lodging area, a transit place. This change is occurring when, and as disconnected nonlocal and sometimes uncaring local money, meets residential real estate fashioned as opportunity. Together, they operate in detached ways to determine the shape the area is taking. As this disaster happens, in sections, residents are pushed out and replaced. In others, construction fails to respect home space as communal space, green spaces as part of home spaces, play and gathering spaces as integral to the character of such life. It instead replaces these with tight spaces with little light and room for movement or basic comfortable liv-ing. In these new fabrications, residents squeeze in to sleep, can barely cook, or spend time together indoors or near home. If our identities, as some authors have argued, rely on our interaction with space and others who share it, then the disruption these dynamics signify threatens both any sense of belonging and the kind of reflection that allows for a nurturing of identity since both the political economy and the architecture send out messages of alienation and rejection.[10]

Checking the disruption that is happening here and reclaiming essential identities means that we must remember that Eastlands grew because of European practices of segregation within this country that was in its start con-ceived of as a settler colony. As Aldo Rossi has noted, "Cities tend to remain on their axes of development, maintaining the position of their original layout and growing according to the direction and meaning of the older artifact."[11] It is from this understanding that we need to start any project of remembrance, rejuvenation, and restoration. A little bit of this social history first.

I find it both interesting and relevant that in the Nairobi of this past cen-tury, this city in its location and design, existed as an entrepot and adminis-trative capital in the service of colonialism that fit one type of colonial city in urbanists' taxonomies.[12] As a settler colony, its structure fits another—a city divided along a racial-ethnic hierarchy with indigenes at the bottom.[13] Consequently, for an extended period in this part of the British Kenya colony,[14] Africans were forced into close proximity in their living and industrial working quarters as they were not welcome as full residents elsewhere in the city. Even their labor ambitions were discouraged if seen to exceed the limits of what was constructed as their racial proscription. As a result, while ethnic Africans may have had limited cultural contact in previous traditional times, colonial invasion expanded and even forced such interaction. Land, despite resistance, was grabbed from indigenous peoples.[15] Forced by expulsions and migration, or other pressures directed to them, including rapid rapture and transformations of their economies, indigenes were drawn into modern capital markets. They entered these latter mainly as industrial or service laborers. Displacement, expulsion, and disruption led many of them into travel and residency in emerging cities such as Nairobi, Mombasa, Nakuru, Kisumu, and so on. In these newly emerging cities that were regulated by the color bar, most Africans generally entered non-African parts of the city as manual workers, oftentimes mainly as subordinate menial workers.

These elements of segregation are particularly visible in Nairobi where indigenous identities and experiences were tightly proscribed by colonial law and colonial architecture. Both of these (the law and architecture) allow a mapping that tracks racial, ethnic, sex, and class discrimination in living arrangements and quarters. Of special interest to me is the impact and character of this in Eastlands. This area stood in everyday vivid contrast to other parts of Nairobi. Materially, it documented in stone, brick and mortar, wood, cardboard, and eventually plastic, the existence and occupation of Eastlands by a new emerging kind of indigenous African who while forced into subjugation and subordination by colonial practices inside and outside of this area was nonetheless among those familiar and mainly equal in this part of the city. As indigenous Africans were mainly situated into living proximity among those whom they were forced to consider as similar to them, they impressively created out of their racial-ethnic subordination, exclusion, and oppression, a membership and social cohesion that captured and subverted newly emerging senses of ethnicity, race, gender, and class. These are elements of identity that would, through and post colonialism, become central to identity and belonging.

Let us digress from the general topic and focus on some aspects of some of the differences at play for a minute. One notes that in the making of Nairobi, sex and gender gained certain character. For example, it was well known that colonial administration discouraged male labor from bringing wives and children to the city. Explanation seems both an unwillingness to contend with the existence of indigenous family units in the city and discouragement of a sense of permanency as a means of further dehumanizing the Kenyan African.[16] Nairobi was instead mainly presented as a male province for indigenous persons who were encouraged to be transitory, and whose sexuality colonial administration sought to regulate. Toward this end, red-light districts housing "bad" African Women who served "sexually uncontrollable" indigenous men were clearly delineated in city planning and administration. The other category of women openly allowed in the city were those engaged in traditional commerce. These occupied an ambiguous space of not quite women. While more detailed studies[17] about these have been undertaken, my point here is that Nairobi's urban experience materialized most concretely in Eastlands or its environs, in places like Pangani and Majengo which served to construct understandings of sex and gender as they emerged in the period, creating "good" and "bad" women as well as a particular version of femininity, men and masculinity. Good women were of course those who married and stayed in rural areas primarily as agricultural labor, raising the next set of industrial labor. Bad women were those who dared follow men or independently went to the city. In this world that colonialism sought to build, long distanced relationships were introduced into the landscape and reflected in Eastland's architecture as were split families, nucleus families, and various forms of intimate partnerships.

Similarly, let us discuss class for a moment. While class[18] would eventually provide impetus for mobilization and class division itself would over time be challenged; in the period, class was racialized and the lowest of this was associated with a spatial location to the east of the city. This locational restriction served as a constraint to physical movement as well as an inhibition to ambition and dreams. Indigenous Africans, who were presented as of lower class, could only properly be housed in Eastlands in places such as Railways, Kaloleni, Makongeni, Bahati, and so on. Class locations much as racial categories were naturalized, and for the African; made a source of humiliation and powerlessness in ways that were meant to break and alienate the indigene as fully as possible. As to "race," if racial narratives require that "other," then it is to populations clustered in Eastlands that European and Asian Nairobi stood in contrast. Within the sociopolitical topography, these contrasts beget, racial discourses were fleshed and developed in response to practical experience much as ethnicity within this urban space was sometimes liquidated sometimes solidified ultimately producing a particular urban character structured around racial, class, sexual, and gender experiences woven by and around politics, language, religion, music, and sports.

In reflecting on the Eastlands' experience that is captured by discussions such as the ones above, one realizes that at this area's heart is a historical familiarity with exclusion, privation, forced proximity, otherness, and resilience. Less obvious yet maybe more significant is also that in these experiences and in responses to them, is an explanation of the character of the country and its political resistance. Interesting to me, looking at Eastlands, one finds that political exclusion, especially for individuals who lived in this part of the City, much as for rural folk who were losing their traditional resources such as land,[19] a particular experience of urbanity offers an explanation for political resistance. And so one finds that in Kenya's emerging cities, Nairobi in particular, Eastlands specifically, it is enforced residential proximity of individuals from various—sometimes prior to this hostile—communities that provided opportunity and impetus for the dialogue that revealed common experiences, similar interests, a naming of oppression and the oppressor. These in turn resulted in agitation and popular movements that gave the country and the world the Mau Mau and strong labor organizations[20] that persist to this day as well as broad-based political involvement that continues to vibrate to date.[21]

In a sense then, as I claim above, Kenya as a modern nation-state began in Eastlands. It began in this space where forced proximity encouraged Kenyan Africans to address questions of fairness and justice, of the shape that political systems should take, to reflect on social and political organization, on the need for a coalition and the role of sex, class, and ethnicity within a framework of Nationalism, Pan Africanism, and the reality of Globalization. Giving credence to the value of nurture and environment in emergence, we see many examples of local and national leaders that at least for a period lived in Eastlands and were launched into national prominence from this space. These include Jaramogi Odinga, Mwai Kibaki, Simeon H. Ominde, Tom Mboya, Maina Wanjigi, Charles Rubia, Muthoni Likimani, Beth Mugo, and many more. These individuals were often associated with multiple varied sociopolitical parties and organizations as well as Kenya's vibrant Labor Movement including groups such as a COTU-K (Central Organization of Trade Unions—Kenya)[22] which were fired up in Eastlands. Struggle often finds expression not only in political activism but also in the creative arts and sports which are sometimes used as mediums for cultural and sociopolitical critique. This work of imaginative contemplation and inventive reflection is integral to individual and cultural identity. Predictably, Eastlands has tended to be the fertile soil from which many creative artists and sports persons have emerged. These include artists such as Kabaka Williams, Fadhili Williams, Mama Kayayi (Mary Khavere), Mzee Ojwang (Benson Wanjau), Mama Njeri, Othorongogo,[23] satirists such as Wahome Mutahi, many soccer players on popular teams such as Gor Mahia and Leopards, boxers such as Kenya's Hitsquad,[24] James Omondi (Demosh), Conjestina Achieng and many more.[25]

While this is a uniquely rich history with resonance not just citywide but also nationally and internationally, it is not clear to me that there have been any efforts to carefully and systematically archive the histories that these lives and their communities materially signify even with the resources that for example devolution in the Kenyan 2010 Constitution has provided. In fact, what has become obvious to me rather is the promotion of rapid unchecked gentrification without attention to the impact of this on irreplaceable communal and national histories and identities. Tragically, modernity and sovereignty as it has been ushered in by years of negligence, the penetration of global forces and thoughtlessly implemented policy following the 2010 Constitution have contributed to the dilution, minimization and erasure of identity, memory and social cohesion by some of the very forces that the communities and individuals in Eastlands stood against less than a century ago. This is tragic given the histories, experiences, and sacrifices that these spaces and relations signify. At the same time, it may also be the case that it is here, in this area and others like it, because of experiences like these, that critiques and challenges to gentrification as an attack on self and community, as an agent of disturbing forces of global capital take place. It may be here, that questions like these take their deepest poignancy and their greatest urgency, as this area both grows in terms of human populations, and deteriorates in regard to class, class division, ethnicity, and ethnic hostility.

## EVOCATION: MINING HISTORY

A sociopolitical survey of the colonial era presents Eastlands in relation to the rest of the City very much like Baltimore, Maryland, to Washington D.C. It was Black Kenya's home or bedroom in relation to British colonials and the Asian community working and residential spaces. That is, while there were some Africans who functionally lived in other parts of Nairobi, that population was low and their presence in those other parts of Nairobi was understood as exceptional—necessary though undesirable.

In these other locales much as in Eastlands, Africans were there at the behest of the colonial master and were especially seen as alien, as foreign to the dominant sociopolitical culture that imperial power sought to install. The subordination and reduction of those marked by Africanness even with the limitations and restrictions that colonialism instituted across the city, stands in interesting contrast to their place in Eastlands. It was clearly understood that Eastlands was the African's Nairobi. Those Africans who worked outside the area were expected to travel back to their "hoods after their delivery of service and labor outside of it. In those after work hours, to the extent that they could, Kenyan Africans resumed their humanity in Eastlands. For those lucky enough to have or to be allowed families in the city, it is here that they were mainly expected to house them.[26] Sometimes in conformity with the British Policy of divide and rule in this settler colony, African neighborhoods were apportioned by ethnicity. One, therefore, for example, finds that places like Bahati and Makadara were mainly populated by those of the Kikuyu ethnic group. Kaloleni had higher numbers of those of Luo ethnicity. Eastleigh had a majority of Cushite or Arabic origin persons and so forth. There were also, of course, mixed ethnicity estates such as Makogeni which housed Railway Employees, Kunguni and Mbotela, then later Maringo which housed many city employees, and so on. Of note, nevertheless, is that in spite of efforts to discourage the development of cross- or trans-ethnic[27] identities and social cohesion, these nonetheless emerged as individuals and groups were united by experiences of race and racialization. Indeed, it seems to me that as a result of these racial histories and experiences, in Eastlands, Africans found and built a community with people who looked much like them and with whom they were forced into close proximity. Additionally, from here, urban spaces were also developed racial and ethnic identities that extended back into rural areas, ones that have persisted in their colonially modified forms to the present in ways that have sometimes become politically dangerous.[28]

Of special interest to me in thinking through these and other emerging contemporary patterns of place and relations, is the outcome of contact in the colonial era. The fact is that while in the colonial era Africans of all classes (to the extent that there was class mobility) and ethnic groups as they were developing[29] were forced into contact, to commune with each other as they lived and worked together, produced a certain sense of self and solidarity with neighbors. Independence, however, as it was engineered, brought about a separation both in relation to ethnic groups and class. A little on this.

As the British left, newly empowered political elites (petit-bourgeois) worked to secure economic opportunities and a political competence that enabled them to replace the colonial master both in parliament (politically) and in their residence (socially). Ideologically, it seems that this effort was, unfortunately, successful. Consequently, while there was a "racial change" in dominance, there was little ideological and practical change in the new wielders of power. Indeed, in addition to international pressure to conform to modern order, meaning a certain "westernity" characterized by a privileging of capitalism and a façade of political choice, too few attempts were made to replace the ideological persuasion of the colonial master that determinedly sought to disrupt solidarity and diminish group identities. Instead, there seems to have been a wholehearted adaptation of the worst excesses of the exiting elite.

In real spatio-physical ways, local elites replaced the British in ways that are documented in the physical maps of Nairobi.[30] It is this new political class that took over Westlands, moved into parts of Asian Nairobi, and left those sections of Nairobi such as Eastlands that continued to be "othered" and occupied by those less affluent and less politically connected. With this type of a faulty transfer of power, an exit of the British as a ruling power from Kenya and their compromised replacement by newly appointed leaders from newly formed, organic communities that had developed through the struggle for Independence,[31] a sociopolitical and economic chasm took a new shape and grew. Additionally, certain tasks were left undone, most importantly, that of finding ways to witness to the special unique community(ies) that had emerged in the midst of, and in part as a response to, colonial oppression. This includes the work of remembering and memorializing the mobilization with which Kenyan Africans in this part of the country had responded to marginalization and rejection. It remains undone ways that squander opportunities to build deep, thoughtful national identities that offer critical alternatives to colonial constructions. My argument here works on two scales. First is a proposal to undertake the work of documenting, preserving, and promoting Eastlands in Nairobi's and the country's memory as the home of Independence and national identity. This assignment has been left dangerously long unattended. Second is a radical claim that as long as the work remains undone, the resulting aperture feeds into a pattern of marginalization and alienation for communities such as those associated with Eastlands that runs from colonial times to the present in a manner that requires remedy.

## THE PRESENT

This proposal's urgency is pressed by new economic activity occurring in Eastlands. It is an activity that comes as mentioned above, both with desirable advantages and dangerous disadvantages. A daily informs us, "Nairobi's Eastlands set for facelift with plan to build 80,000 houses."[32] Reading this kind of a headline may lead one to breathe a sigh of relief thinking that what is finally happening is that financial resources are finally being directed to this long-starved part of the City. This is not the whole story. Certainly, there is more money being invested in the area from both local and international sources[33] but we need to ask the kinds of questions many of its residents who have learned to be skeptical are anxiously asking: why are they not transparently involved in planning and visioning the future of their communities? Who is investing and why they are investing here at this point? These questions are particularly pertinent when one considers the promises attached to this financial flow in this and other articles, reports, and statements. First, that the new investments will be ones that will involve "private-public" investment partnerships. Second, that reconstruction will and has begun to transform the area from one populated by limited occupancy courtyard houses, mansions, bungalows, and limited floor multirooms homes to high population high-rise apartments that eerily expands high-density occupancy. Third, that the new houses will not be city-owned (where the city is obliged at least in large parts of this low to middle-income area to protect equal, fair, affordable, rent-controlled, public access) but rather that the new housing would be private individually owned units.

Still, at face value, these publicized commitments accompanied by an understanding of the history and shape of Nairobi tell us certain things. First, and most obviously, is the fact that the architecture of this highly populated part of the City—much of it periodic, distinctive, historically significant—will be and is, unprotected, changing. For a start, as private individuals invest in the area without curation or archival sensitive supervision, many of its old buildings will be and are being taken down to be replaced by new storied ones in part because the area is seen as, and remains a less "modern," "underdeveloped" part of Nairobi that some see as a resource to exploit. Second, the area's convenient location in relation to the Central Business District makes its real estate attractive to investors and Central Business District operators as Nairobi's already large population continues to expand. This positionality also makes it vulnerable in this era of capital morality and maximum profit ideology. Indeed, its very locational convenience makes it susceptible to those interested in its appropriation; an interest that has in the past been checked by bureaucratic negligence as well as a subliminal political understanding of the historical existence of this area as a protected, accessible, public good. This status is under threat by a creeping change in local value systems and perceptions that make privatization and the vulture capitalism that underlies it here seem not only palatable but also common sense.

Unfortunately, also for Eastlands' population and archives, with the economic and architectural changes that are taking place within and around it—housing, schools, churches, community centers, commercial spaces, and so on—that have stood witness to more than a hundred years of Kenya's history in this African Part of the City face the threat of demolition and in fact are in instances being torn down. This is alarming to the population that currently occupies this space, many of whom have long histories of family, community, and personal survival here, of labor and sociopolitical solidarity, of practices of neighboring and neighborhood. Other dangers are also at play. For instance, "development" as it is unfolding seems to pose for these residents and the country a threat of loss of sociopolitical history, a danger to historical sites, and with this, a loss of community, local and national memories. This is in part so, since these have not to my knowledge been carefully archived, documented, protected, or preserved in this part of the city.[34]

My opinion, in view of the foregoing, is that as new forms of money flow into Eastlands and gentrification takes place, the work of raising critical attention becomes particularly urgent. It is partially this that I underscore in this chapter. I am arguing that if, as seems the case here, the impact of locational neglect and gentrification is the dismantling of neighborhoods and communities, this is of serious concern if we value social cohesion where "Social cohesion is about getting by and getting on at the more mundane level of everyday life. ...The point to note is that it is the neighbour- hood which is likely to be the site for many of these mundane routines and for the ongo-ing 'repair work' and 'normalization.'"[35] It is this that is not only under threat, but which is being dismantled as we speak in Eastlands. In addition to the social and mental health issues provoked by these changes, there is a real danger of tensions spilling over from expanding ghettoization[36] and invasive gentrification rubbing jowl to jowl in a manner that makes both repair and normalization untenable given the size of the city. The parallel evolution of these spaces and populations, and the risk of explosion as the exploitation and disadvantage that characterizes both processes threaten to tear the body politic apart, hangs latent with the dissolution of intimate relations anchored in place and community attachment.

Various studies and authors, such as Robert D. Putnam[37] and Forrest and Kearns recognize as I do the value of neighborhoods. Some note how neighborhoods offer an opportunity for neighborhooding and neighborliness through the maintenance and strengthening of connectedness. Some of this happens through, for example, community organizations, institutions, and associations. The erosion and collapse of these has a seriously negative impact on civic and political engagement.[38] The argument that many authors make is that if "our dispositions" both social and political—in the sense of both our character and habits as well as our outlooks—are influenced by our neighborhoods as the three suggest, then vibrant engaged communities are the foundation for active-involved citizens and a necessary basis for the existence of the nation-state. This kind of connectedness seems to have been Eastland's most unique quality and its most valuable contribution to the city and nation. Whatever else Eastlands has historically lacked—racial equity, class parity, consistent political access—there has never been any doubt that Eastlands' communities are vibrant and politically engaged. This makes what is happening in Eastlands particularly egregious if in Kenya, much as in the United States that Putnam documents, a trend toward apathy is produced and constructed by the deconstruction of the neighborhoods and communities. As could easily happen with thoughtless reconstruction, this remodeling and reconstruction of the area may become the first step toward the dismantling of Kenya's identity as the product of a certain historical past. To temper this outcome, it is important that we consider the possibilities and challenges before us.

## THE CHALLENGES

To recap, if, prima facie, gentrification involves economic penetration of physical and social neighborhoods, and a transformation that is presented as an improvement on the status quo, one may easily see how such a change may be attractive at some level to Eastlands residents and sociopolitical administrators as a quick fix in the face of histories of poverty and deprivation. Unfortunately, this is a solution that in view of historical global practices and processes whose miasmas are felt here such as colonialism, neocolonialism, neoliberalism, challenged sometimes failed political governance, structural adjustments, recessions, and so forth is of concern. These extractive, exploitative processes, which have produced disenfranchisement, exclusion, poverty, and multiple other ills here and elsewhere, seem also to frame some of the suggested solutions. They, these processes and proposed solutions, are also the ones which enable unchecked license that allows a swooping in, to the benefit of a few from the very mechanisms they initiate as populations are displaced and replaced. Here as elsewhere, they threaten identities and allow for histories and memories to be erased and rewritten, communities to be destroyed and reconstructed in manners that cause paradigm shifts that replicate global money flows and consumption patterns that expose vulnerable communities such as those found in Eastlands, to profound harm.

Given Kenya's history, and our moment which is one consisting of transitions between past practices and contemporary ones, we find in Eastlands a space that is occupied by many ethnic groups that are mainly oral epistemic transmitters. In their traditions, cultures, practices, lived experiences, we are faced with the struggles of communities that have emerged from the melding and blending of various peoples who do not have a history of western literary documentation in a world where this latter is dominant. These are oral peoples whose lives and experiences deserve to be honored and remembered in ways that pay homage to them and their time in wholesome ways. Amid the unique, rich and distinctive diversity these communities epitomize, I see part of the challenge before us one of thinking of home, community, and belonging in subaltern ways. As one of figuring out how to preserve in Eastlands; a living place, an active memory, among peoples who do not have a culture of "literary material archiving" while also nurturing the relations all of this symbolizes.

In Eastlands' communities, historically, culturally, economically, spaces such as churches and town halls do not act as archival spaces in the ways that they do in the modern west, but rather as living congregational ones. Indeed, even in personal spaces such as homes, many Kenyan Africans are not socialized to archive in the ways that many westerners are. Hence in comparison to many western households, many homes do not keep well-organized, labeled photo albums or even audio or visual recordings of family or community events.[39] Western archives also draw from articles of sentimental value which provide material full of archival significance. These may include antiques such as furniture, clothes, and jewelry that may be passed from generation to generation in the West. Cultural, class, and practical circumstances do not

nurture these kinds of habits or patterns, especially in low-income neighborhoods generally. Let us linger for a minute on this matter. As we pointed out
at the beginning of our chapter, one needs to remember that Eastlands much
as the rest of Kenya is right on the Equator, it is part of Tropical Africa.
This means that beyond the challenge of curation, personal or professional,
untrained attempts at preservation of material are challenging as the weather
in this region encourages the speedy decay, decomposition, corrosion, of
natural materials which is what many sociopolitical and cultural artifacts are
made of. More specifically as we focus on Eastlands is an issue that we had
raised earlier on, one that generally confronts low-income populations around
the world—that of storage space and use. Low-income persons oft cannot
afford to keep functional items in their homes without using them. This is in
part because they need to utilize such items and also because they do not in
their limited living spaces have the room for nonfunctional preservation. If
used as such (functionally), there is a high chance of property that may be of
archival significance, wearing, and breaking.

Another factor that offers a challenge to archiving as a site of history and
belonging is a cultural one. The virtue of sharing and giving finds interesting
form at the intersection of culture and class in Eastlands. These virtues (sharing and giving) are promoted in many African communities as well as this
one. In fact, they are the ones that many low-income communities around the
world encourage. Because low-income persons have an intimacy with lack
and need, they consider it a vice, to hold on to items that they do not immediately functionally need when another could benefit from their giving. This
means that many items that could in affluent circumstances be preserved and
archived exchange hands multiple times as they are recycled to their fullest
extent. This is of course commendable, though it leaves us with the question
that I posed above—that of determining how to archive in ways that offer a
window that contributes to history and belonging in respectful and wholesome manners given this community's identities and cultures.

Further, as one attempts to work with communities in Eastlands and envision a method of archiving their worlds and experiences, other questions
emerge. For example, how are we to deal with the elderly? How do we work
with bodies whose eyes, ears, minds have touched and been touched by history? What happens to this group with the loss of their traditional role as
transmitters, many times oral, of wisdom? Alternatively, how can we sustain
them in such roles? What is the place of these valuable members of society
given the tools and mechanisms provided by contemporary architecture and
technology? Other questions arise with the youth. These are often young people disconnected from the histories that their elders are attached to and more
connected to emergent ones. They are focused on futures that do not easily
connect to and or coexist with their communal pasts. When this is so, how do

we seduce, entice, and persuade them to value these histories and experiences especially when because of poverty and popular associations of these spaces with shame, humiliation, violence, deprivation, subordination, loss, criminality, disease, inefficiency, failure, they want to forget these locations of their beginnings and move on to futures that have been very effectively sold to them as detached from these pasts—as more attractive, as ones whose charm is in part their blindness to what seem like embarrassing histories that need to be forgotten? How do we recover pride in history and vanishing communal identities in younger generations who have been convinced that a certain kind of historical amnesia, a certain alienation, is freedom and opportunity?[40]

What happens to orality as an alternative site of knowledge production, as a method of knowledge accumulation and preservation? How do we engage it within the practicalities that this project reveals? More generally what do our reflections here, and as this work continues, tell us of the cost of modernization—of affluence and the need for privacy which drives the emergence of new gentrified architectural spaces?[41] What is valued? Who determines what is important, where are such values really being produced? At what cost?

## CONCLUSION AND VALUE OF STUDY

Though it is impossible to adequately answer the questions this work raises here, these queries nonetheless in their raising offer a chance to critique affluence and gentrification generally, but more particularly in the shape of forces directed to Eastlands; and similar areas especially in comparison to other parts of lived cities—in the case of Nairobi, Westlands. This study also provides an opportunity to review the value of social connections, especially as these are threatened by the influx and displacement that happens with new activity in low- or mixed-income areas such as Eastlands. I think that particularly significant is the chance in its course, to reflect on and promote the sense that Eastlands, as is often the case in low-income areas, has mainly been a place where authenticity and community are valued. That is, though more work is required on this, to discover the ways Eastlands though currently threatened, has persisted and its communities survived. In this consideration, it seems to me that its existence is explained by histories and memories of ways in which by necessity, many are made aware of each other and the value of communal relations. This chapter argues that one important element of this task is that of reviving and archiving context-relevant histories so that we keep alive in engaged memory, an awareness of how vitally connected individual, ethnic and community identities are, in this space.

In the kind of investigation and memorialization I invite or, the dialogue it may elicit, I see several openings. For example, there are chances to develop new economic opportunities that may contribute to the revitalization of Eastlands. These should be ones that dignify the spaces, places, and occupants of the area. For example, this discussion might inspire the creation of small locally run community museums and archives that celebrate the individuals, organizations, and communities that are rooted here. These are spaces that would be of interest to educational institutions locally and internationally. Around them, one can see small business enterprises growing to provide local tour guides, bed and breakfast lodgings, food canteens, entertainment centers, and so forth. It may also encourage the creation of small local breweries that safely brew and thoughtfully serve indigenous brews alongside organic local dishes. As this is happening, urban farming may be expanded in Eastlands. Another focus may be the character of policing. Given the internal openness of many Eastlands' communities, a change of the police force into one more community-friendly would best start here. Educationally, in response to larger class sizes and the challenges of effectively teaching and counseling, Eastlands would be a good place to start well-structured peer-to-peer guided mentoring as well as explore the shape of community schools. This is a project that would be enriched by the revitalization of school and community libraries as well as Social Halls. All of these spaces are ones that could also be used as happens elsewhere in the world, as adult literary spaces where locally organized relevant discussions on for example housing, health, tax, the constitution, the environment, education, orality, tradition, and so forth take place. Organized community cleaning up that takes ownership of neighborhood environments and holds the City Council and resident businesses accountable is another area that would be of interest.[42] This of course connects also to health delivery and wellness promotion which itself would also benefit from a revival of community sports fields which should be protected and assigned local coaches and guardians to keep afterschool and weekend activities going.

I think that one of the most vital aspects of this reflection is the realization memory offers us regarding identity. It is a reminder to the city and the country that while class and ethnic divisions have been naturalized by politics and economics in the recent past, Kenyan Africans were not always undesirably divided by class or ethnicity. In addition, the sense that it is increasingly necessary to pay attention to the role of grassroot organizations including ones that might be mobilized for example by local chiefs and other administrative officials whose availability in the face of the 2010 Kenyan Constitution makes them attractive partners if enthusiastic and committed. Finally and imperatively is the awareness that the initiatives suggested above and elsewhere can only be undertaken if the shape that Eastlands now takes is drawn with the consultation and participation of its residents at every level and on every subject. Involvement might range from questions such as deciding the shape of its constituencies to that of deciding which and whether to protect historical sites. As debates are undertaken regarding how to interact with history, which histories to promote and protect, concerning the naming of community issues and deliberations on whether and how to address and prioritize these, it is important to remember that although the mechanisms for these kinds of discussions are present and available in the 2010 Kenyan Constitution, these have not so far been effectively engaged, and they should be, if we want to keep the heart of the city, of the country, not only beating but also included in its health and growth.

## ACRONYMS

CBD—Central Business District
COTU-K—Coalition of Trade Unions—Kenya, largest such with about two million members
NCC—Nairobi City Council
SRC—Salaries and Remuneration Committee, established by 2010 Kenyan Constitution
UNEP—United Nations Environmental Programme
UN-Habitat—United Nations Centre for Human Settlements

## NOTES

1. (United Nations Environmental Program(UNEP) 2007), Jane Barr—Principal Editor Chris Shisanya—Editor.
2. Bruce Githua. "Rational Utopias/Irrational Dystopias. Sites and Services in Eastlands Nairobi." *Planum: The Journal of Urbanism* 26 (1/2013): 3–4/18.
3. Ibid., *Platum*, 5/18.
4. Ibid., *Platum*, 6/18.
5. See aerial view of Nairobi in United Nations Environment Programme: Environment for Development's "Population and Urban Growth," atlas in this link: https://na.unep.net/atlas/webatlas.php?id=395.
6. Winnie Mitullah. "Urban Slums Reports: The Case of Nairobi, Kenya." *Understanding Slums: Case Studies for the Global Report on Human Settlements* (2003): 3. http://erepository.uonbi.ac.ke:8080/xmlui/handle/123456789/54284.
7. Irene Wangari Karanja and Jack Makau. "An Inventory of the Slums in Nairobi," http://www.irinnews.org/pdf/nairobi_inventory.pdf, 2009, Accessed on December 16, 2015.
8. Maurice Onyango Oyugi and Owiti A. K'Akumu. "Land Use Management Challenges for the City of Nairobi," *Urban Forum* 18, no. 1 (January 2007): 94–113, (Online).

9. Ironically, I am finishing this chapter in the middle of the global crisis we have termed SARS II/Corona Virus Pandemic/COVID-19. Part of the resolution to this crisis has been suggested as a slowdown sometimes lockdown to which citizens across the world have been invited to "stay home." The challenge to do so is currently being felt and observed in areas such as Eastlands in which home-making spaces have been purloined, fractured, eliminated, destroyed, and remanded.

10. Experienced in unemployment, under employment, perennial unemployment, and the powerlessness that accompanies economic and political exclusion.

11. Aldo Rossi and Peter Eisenman. *The Architecture of the City* (Cambridge, MA: MIT Press, 1982), p. 59.

12. Gareth Myers. *African Cities, Alternative Visions of Urban Theory and Practices* (London and New York: Zed Ltd., 2011).

13. David M. Anderson and Richard Rathbone. *Africa's Urban Past* (Oxford, UK: James Curry Ltd., 2000).

14. Keep in mind that this region was referred to as the East Africa Protectorate until 1920, then as the Protectorate of Kenya until independence in 1963.

15. Think of the communities whose containment made Nairobi possible. These include the Dorobo, Maasai, Kikuyu, and Kamba.

16. My maternal aunties and uncles remind us often during family gatherings of how they were smuggled into the city then transported into Eastlands as part of a grocery shipment. My friend Faith Maina talks too of a story that her Mother told often of getting a temporary permit to visit her Father for a week and the fear that resulted when she extended the visit by a few days and one of white city officials found her illegally present in her husband's house.

17. See, for example, John Lonsdale. "Town Life in Colonial Kenya," in *Nairobi Today. The Paradox of a Fragmented City* (Dar es Salaam, Tanzania: Mkuki na Nyota Publishers Ltd., 2006); Kathy Sheldon. *Courtyards, Markets, City Streets. Urban Women in Africa* (Boulder, CO: Westview Press, 1996); Tabitha Kanogo. *African Womanhood in Colonial Kenya, 1900-50* (Athens: Ohio University Press, 2005); Luise White. *The Comforts of Home: Prostitution in Colonial Nairobi.* (Chicago: University of Chicago Press, 1990); Claire Robertson. *Trouble Showed the Way: Trade in the Nairobi Area, 1890-1990* (Bloomington: Indiana University Press, 1997); and Iris Berger and Claire Roberstson (eds.). *Women and Class in Africa* (New York: Homes and Meier, 1986). This is only a sample of available scholarly work.

18. This category is perhaps more complex than it has been presented here (and warrants more intellectual scrutiny). But let it suffice to note here that while there were gradations relative exceptions to the class statuses including among Africans, the lowest of this was reserved for Black Africans.

19. Of course, some, if not many of these folk same ones losing land upcountry.

20. A close history of the beginnings of the Labor Movement, activists such a Harry Thuku and the influence of Pan Africanists such as Marcus Garvey deserves more careful treatment that this chapter allows.

21. For evidence of this, refer to Election Patterns and Statistics in. for example, the last four election cycles and even prior. Additionally, if there was an equivalent of a Nielsen's company it would be interesting to see how many people watch the news. It does seem to me as if the numbers are high. In many homes, listening to the 1:00

p.m. news and watching the 7:00 p.m. and 9:00 p.m. news are respected traditions; as is dissecting it that night with Family and discussing it the next day with friends and colleagues at the market, bus stop, street corners, Pubs and so on. The buying of Dallies as a source of news while reduced, seems to still be going strong.

22. Founded in 1965, this is the descendant to labor organizations that emerged in the colonial period such as significantly, the Kenya Federation of Labor and African Workers Congress (KFL-AWC). For a history of the union, visit its webpage at: http://cotu-kenya.org/history-of-cotuk/.

23. Important work is being done on Kenyan Comedy. For example, on the web, see: Charles Kebeya. "Historicizing Kenyan Comedy," in *Itineration, Cross-Disciplinary Studies in Rhetoric, Media and Culture*, Web. Available by following the following link: http://tundra.csd.sc.edu/itineration/kenyan-comedy.

Another Article that I think interesting:

"The Evolution of Kenyan Comedy: Why aren't we laughing?" to be found on Owaah, 12th May 2014. This is a Website whose submissions are anonymous. Link: http://owaahh.com/the-evolution-of-kenyan-comedy-why-arent-we-laughing/.

24. Roy Gachuhi. "Remembering the days when Kenya's 'Hit Squad' ruled the boxing world." Daily Nation, 29th August 2014, (Web) http://www.nation.co.ke/sports/TalkUp/Kenya-Hit-Squad-ruled-the-boxing/441392-2434988-1094pmf/index.html.

25. There is a unique need to develop a deeper understanding and archive both the creative arts and artists through the colonial period.

26. Again, colonial policy discouraged the sustenance of Family Unions in the City from Married Unions to Dependent Relationships. There are many stories of men, women, and children running afoul of their employers and administrative over-lords for attempting to reunite in the City. There is also a growing body of literature that documents the development of Nairobi's red-light districts especially Pangani and the colony's encouragement of this as a way of controlling indigenous men and women by way of regulating sexual appetites and desires as well as their fulfillment.

27. Ngugi wa Thiong'o would of course call this cross or transnational cohesion.

28. Infamously, note the ethnic animosity with roots in British colonialism, watered by postcolonial leadership that is commonly admitted in the country to have contributed to what are commonly referred to as ethnic, tribal, or postelection clashes following the National Elections December 2007, and which resulted in a historic trial of the Ocampo Six at the International Court of Criminal Justice at the Hague starting with the application for summons by Prosecutor Luis Ocampo.

29. Ethic groups as they currently stand are as many things as possible, most of all products of historical moments and experiences. As such, ethnic identity as it operates in Kenya is in part a response to colonial encounter and pressure, much as it talks to group historical and sociocultural locations. Consider, for example, the Luyia, the Kikuyu, and so on. It is this complex mix that indigenous communities have inherited under the problematic rubric of ethnic identity or tribe.

30. In addition to United Nations Environmental Program. Kenya: Atlas of our changing Environment. UNEP, Nairobi, Kenya (Web) 2009; Irene Wangari Karanja and Jack Makau. "An Inventory of the Slums in Nairobi," (Web), 2009; see also:

Martina Vogel. History of Urban Planning of Nairobi—http://www.studio-basel .com/assets/files/029_NRB_ATLAS_11_planning_dr.pdf. This covers the period 1906–2008; Samuel O. Owuor and Teresa Mbatia. Post Independence Development of Nairobi City, Kenya. Paper presented at Workshop on African capital Cities Dakar, September 22–23, 2008. (Web) https://profiles.uonbi.ac.ke/samowuor/files/2 008_dakar_workshop.pdf; Dennis Mwaniki, Elizabeth Wamuchiru, Baraka Mwau, Romanus Opiyo. Urbanisation, Informality and Housing Challenge in Nairobi: A Case of Urban Governance Failure? Conference Paper—"The Ideal City: between myth and reality. Representations, policies, contradictions and challenges for tomorrow's urban life" Urbino (Italy) August 27–29, 2015. (Web) http://www.rc21.org/ en/wp-content/uploads/2014/12/G2_Dennis-Mwaniki.pdf; and Claire Medard. "City Planning in Nairobi: The Stakes, the People, the Sidetracking," in *Nairobi Today. The Paradox of a Fragmented City* (Dar es Salaam, Tanzania: Mkuki na Nyota Publishers Ltd., 2006). There are of course many other good discussions available.

31. See note xviii above.

32. Nicholas Waitathu. "Nairobi's Eastlands set for facelift with plan to build 80,000 houses." (Standard Newspaper, 11/19/2013) Web Link—https://www.sta ndardmedia.co.ke/business/article/2000098092/nairobi-s-eastlands-set-for-facelift-with-plan-to-build-80-000-houses. More recently, Gilbert Koech. "Eastlands to get radical facelift under urban renewal proposals," in The Star Newspaper. https://www. the-star.co.ke/counties/nairobi/2019-11-25-eastlands-to-get-radical-facelift-under-u rban-renewal-proposals/.

33. Another interesting discussion part of which may connect to diasporic remittances.

34. The loss here is in my opinion equivalent to that which has raised hue and cry in Iraq and Syria. In material terms, the destruction will include that of homes and offices of social and political activists some of whom became historically significant politicians as well as those of creative artists and sports personalities, sites of historical events, and so on. These spaces are important not only for those individuals who occupied them but also for the community synergies that flowed in and out of them as resistance and freedom were strategized. I consider this an outrage made worse by the cavalier attitude of its agents. It is difficult to listen to or read narratives of this change as development without thinking about Walter Rodney's *How Europe Underdeveloped Africa* (London: Bogle-L'Ouverture Publications, 1972).

35. Ray Forrest, and Ade Kearns. "Social Cohesion, Social Capital and the Neighbourhood—Ray Forrest, Ade Kearns, 2001." *SAGE Journals. Urban Studies*, January 1, 1996, 2127 https://journals.sagepub.com/doi/abs/10.1080/0042098012 0087081.

36. I find the definition offered by Tommie Shelby in "Justice, Work, and the Ghetto Poor," in *Urban American Philosophy—An Introduction*, Chris Keegan (ed.) (United States of America: Cognella Academic Publishing, 2016) useful even for Kenya—"a ghetto is a predominantly black, metropolitan neighborhood with a high concentration of poverty"—p. 143.

37. Robert D. Putnam. "Bowling Alone: America's Declining Social Capital." *Journal of Democracy* 6, no. 1 (1995): 65–78. doi:10.1353/jod.1995.0002.

38. Conclusion drawn from the United States where most of the studies are conducted as well as 35 other countries according to Robert D. Putnam in "Bowling Alone: America's Declining Social Capital," *Journal of Democracy* 6, no. 1 (Jan 1995): 65–78.

39. This kind of documentation is changing with widespread access to new communication technologies especially that of the phone and applications such as WhatsApp as well as storage capacities such as cloud.

40. In thinking about alienation, read a good introduction to the topic in: Lewis R. Gordon. "Existential Dynamics of Theorizing Black Invisibility," in *Urban American Philosophy—An Introduction*, Chris Keegan (ed.) ( United States of America: Cognella Academic Publishing, 2016).

41. It is important to admit that in part, new apartments are replacing old homes in Eastlands in response to "consumer demand." Many residents do not want to share toilets and bathrooms. They do not want to live in homes with open courtyards where their neighbors can see their comings and goings. Very much like in the more affluent part of the city, they want a level of privacy that they see provided by the construction of walls around them and their nuclear family. These walls have become associated with class advancement so that few ask what is shut out by the walls only as often happens, what seems to be held in and held up.

Roy Gachuhi. "Remembering the days when Kenya's 'Hit Squad' ruled the boxing world." Daily Nation, 29th August 2014, (Web) http://www.nation.co.ke/sports/TalkUp/Kenya-Hit-Squad-ruled-the-boxing/441392-2434988-1094pmf/index.html.

42. This has already started in places such as Dandora. The Pandemic has forced a reconsideration of education across the world as has the #BlackLivesMatter movement on policing as mentioned earlier.

## BIBLIOGRAPHY

Allport, Gordon Willard. *The Nature of Prejudice*. Basic Books, New York, C. 1979.

Anderson, David M. and Rathbone, Richard. *Africa's Urban Past*. Oxford, UK: James Curry Ltd., 2000.

Anonymous. "The Evolution of Kenyan Comedy: Why aren't we laughing?" to be found on Owaah, 12th May 2014. This is a Website whose submissions are anonymous. Link—http://owaahh.com/the-evolution-of-kenyan-comedy-why-arent-we-laughing/.

Berger, Iris and Robertson, Claire (eds). *Women and Class in Africa*. New York: Homes and Meier, 1986.

Bodenhausen, G. V. and Richeson, J. A. Prejudice, stereotyping, and discrimination. In *Advanced Social Psychology*, R. F. Baumeister and E. J. Finkel (eds.), pp. 341–83. Oxford University Press, 2010.

Forrest, Ray, and Kearns, Ade. "Social Cohesion, Social Capital and the Neighbourhood—Ray Forrest, Ade Kearns, 2001." *SAGE Journals. Urban Studies*, January 1, 1996. https://journals.sagepub.com/doi/abs/10.1080/00420980120087081.

Gachuhi, Roy. "Remembering the days when Kenya's 'Hit Squad' ruled the boxing world." Daily Nation, 29th August 2014 (Web) http://www.nation.co.ke/sports/TalkUp/Kenya-Hit-Squad-ruled-the-boxing/441392-2434988-1094pmf/index.html.

Githua, Bruce. "Rational Utopias/Irrational Dystopias. Sites and Services in Eastlands Nairobi." In *Planum. The Journal of Urbanism.* No. 26 v. 1/2013. Available online: LINK MISSING AT THIS STAGE.

Gordon, Lewis R. "Existential Dynamics of Theorizing Black Invisibility." In *Urban American Philosophy—An Introduction,* Chris Keegan (ed.). United States of America: Cognella Academic Publishing, 2016.

Greven, Katharina. "Hip Hop and Sheng in Nairobi." Creating Identity Markers and Expressing a Life Style. In *Hip Hop and Social Change in Africa.* Msia Kibona Clark and Mickie Mwanzia Koster. New York, USA: Lexington Books, 2014.

Kanogo, Tabitha. *African Womanhood in Colonial Kenya, 1900-50.* Athens: Ohio University Press, 2005.

Karanja, Irene Wangari and Makau, Jack. "An Inventory of the Slums in Nairobi," 2009 Available Online: http://old.sdinet.org/media/upload/documents/Nairobi_slum_inventory_jan_09.pdf.

Kebeya, Charles. "Historicizing Kenyan Comedy." In *Itineration, Cross-Disciplinary Studies in Rhetoric, Media and Culture,* Web. Available by following the following link—http://tundra.csd.sc.edu/itineration/kenyan-comedy.

Koech, Gilbert. "Eastlands to get radical facelift under urban renewal proposals." In The Star Newspaper. https://www.the-star.co.ke/counties/nairobi/2019-11-25-eastlands-to-get-radical-facelift-under-urban-renewal-proposals/.

Lonsdale, John. "Town Life in Colonial Kenya." In *Nairobi Today. The Paradox of a Fragmented City.* Dar es Salaam, Tanzania: Mkuki na Nyota Publishers Ltd., 2006.

Medard, Claire. "City Planning in Nairobi: The Stakes, the People, the Sidetracking." In *Nairobi Today. The Paradox of a Fragmented City.* Dar es Salaam, Tanzania: Mkuki na Nyota Publishers Ltd., 2006.

Mitullah, Winnie. "The Case of Nairobi" in Understanding Slums: Case Studies for the Global Report on Human Settlements, Earthscan for Habitat, 2003. Available online: mirror.unhabitat.org/pmss/getElectronicVersion.aspx?nr=1156&alt=1 OR http://erepository.uonbi.ac.ke:8080/xmlui/handle/123456789/54284.

Morgan, W. T. W. (ed). *Nairobi City and Region.* Oxford: Oxford University Press, 1967.

Mungai, Mbugua Wa-. "Hidden $ Centz: rolling the wheels of Nairobi matatu." In *Nairobi Today. The Paradox of a Fragmented City.* Dar es Salaam, Tanzania: Mkuki na Nyota Publishers Ltd., 2006.

Mungai, Mbugua Wa. "Innovating 'AlterNative' Identities. Nairobi's Matatu Culture." In *Media and Identity in Africa,* Kimani Njogu and John Middleton (eds.). Edinburgh, Scotland: Edinburgh University Press, 2009.

Mwaniki, Dennis, Wamuchiru, Elizabeth, Mwau, Baraka, Opiyo, Romanus. Urbanisation. "Informality and Housing Challenge in Nairobi: A Case of Urban Governance Failure?" A Conference Paper for "The Ideal City: between myth and reality. Representations, policies, contradictions and challenges for tomorrow's

urban life" Urbino (Italy) August 27–29, 2015. (Available on Web) http://www.
rc21.org/en/wp-content/uploads/2014/12/G2_Dennis-Mwaniki.pdf.

Myers, Gareth. *African Cities, Alternative Visions of Urban Theory and Practices.*
London and New York: Zed Ltd., 2011. Available Online—http://www.stellenbo
schheritage.co.za/wp-content/uploads/Garth-A.-Myers-African-Cities_-Alterna
tive-Visions-of-Urban-Theory-and-Practice-Zed-Books-2011.pdf.

Ochieng, Crispino C. "Affordability of Low-Income Housing in Pumwani, Nairobi,
Kenya." *Archnet-IJAR, International Journal of Architectural Research* 1, no. 2
(July 2007): 35–44. http://www.archnet-ijar.net/index.php/IJAR/article/viewFile/
14/14.

O'Shaughnessy, Emma. "African Urban Discourse: Invisible and Reflexive Practice
in African Cities." *Postamble, (Re) reading the African Urban Landscape* 4, no.
2 (2008). Available online: http://postamble.org/wp-content/uploads/2016/09/em
mafinal.pdf.

Owuor, Samuel O. and Mbatia, Teresa. Post Independence Development of Nairobi
City, Kenya. Paper presented at Workshop on African capital Cities Dakar,
September 22–23, 2008. (Web) https://profiles.uonbi.ac.ke/samowuor/files/2008_d
akar_workshop.pdf.

Oyugi, Maurice Onyango and K'Akumu, Owiti A. "Land Use Management
Challenges for the city of Nairobi." *Urban Forum* 18, no. 1 (January 2007):
94–113 (Available Online) https://www.researchgate.net/publication/226926143
_Land_use_management_challenges_for_the_city_of_Nairobi.

Putnam, Robert D. "Bowling Alone: America's Declining Social Capital." *Journal of
Democracy* 6, no. 1 (1995): 65–78. doi:10.1353/jod.1995.0002.

Rakodi, Carole (ed.). *The Urban Challenge in Africa: Growth and Management
of Its Large Cities.* Tokyo; New York; Paris: United Nations University Press,
1997.

Robertson, Claire. *Trouble Showed the Way: Trade in the Nairobi Area, 1890-1990.*
Bloomington: Indiana University Press, 1997.

Rodney, Walter. 1972. *How Europe Underdeveloped Africa.* London: Bogle-
L'Ouverture Publications.

Rossi, Aldo and Eisenman, Peter. *Architettura Della Città (The Architecture of the
City).* Diane Ghirardo and Joan Ockman (Translation) Graham Foundation for
Advanced Studies in the Fine Arts, Institute for Architecture and Urban Studies.
Cambridge, MA: MIT Press, 1982. ©1982—Available Online at—https://www
.academia.edu/36535410/Aldo_Rossi_-_The_Architecture_of_the_city.

Shelby, Tommie. "Justice, Work, and the Ghetto Poor." In *Urban American
Philosophy—An Introduction*, Chris Keegan (ed.). United States of America:
Cognella Academic Publishing, 2016.

Sheldon, Kathy. *Courtyards, Markets, City Streets. Urban Women in Africa.* Boulder,
CO: Westview Press, 1996.

United Nations Environmental Program. Kenya: Atlas of our changing Environment.
UNEP, Nairobi, Kenya, 2009. Available online: http://www.unep.org/dewa/africa/
kenyaatlas/.

Vogel, Martina. History of Urban Planning of Nairobi—http://www.studio-basel.com/assets/files/029_NRB_ATLAS_11_planning_dr.pdf.

Waitathu, Nicholas. "Nairobi's Eastlands set for facelift with plan to build 80,000 houses." (Standard Newspaper, 11/19/2013) Web Link—https://www.standard media.co.ke/business/article/2000098092/nairobi-s-eastlands-set-for-facelift-with-plan-to-build-80-000-houses.

White, Luise. *The Comforts of Home: Prostitution in Colonial Nairobi.* Chicago: University of Chicago Press, 1990.

*Chapter 8*

# Plagues and Pestilences in Late Nineteenth-Century Samburuland

George L. Simpson Jr. and Peter Waweru

This chapter examines a turbulent period in the history of the Samburu people of northern Kenya. It focuses on roughly a quarter of a century when these pastoralists and their herds suffered from a series of ecological disasters, which the authors contend posed an existential threat to the Samburu. The Samburu had emerged as a discrete ethnic group only in the middle of the nineteenth century with a distinct gerontocratic age-set system that facilitated their transhumant exploitation of cattle and small stock in the semiarid lands that they inhabited.[1] Shortly afterward, during the time when the *Tarigirik laji,* or age-set, were warriors (c.1865–c.1879), the herders, as well as neighboring groups in the Lake Turkana basin, made their initial sporadic contacts with African traders and ivory hunters who trekked long distances from the Somali coast at Kismaayo as well as Swahili and Zanzibari merchants and Kamba caravans. Unfortunately for the Samburu and other groups, goods were not all that were exchanged as the inhabitants of the region came into touch with the new world. Outsiders also brought with them microorganisms that would have a catastrophic effect on the human and animal population in the form of deadly diseases. Moreover, the impact on the Samburu was such that it left them particularly vulnerable so that they would more readily come under British colonial rule in the generation that followed this tumultuous time.

The series of disasters that now befell the Samburu still evoke bitter and painful memories and informants describe the time apocalyptically as the *mutai,* or end of things.[2] While, to Samburu, the term *mutai* refers specifically to the epizootics that devastated them, one can also understand the period in its broader ecological context and include the droughts, famine, and plagues (not to mention battles) of this time that were all inextricably related.[3] However one expresses the idea, the halcyon days of prosperity remembered by the herders that had characterized their early years of existence as a distinct community had come to a close. Nevertheless, the central argument advanced by the authors in this study is that in their sufferings the Samburu shared and overcame a common set of ecological challenges during this time that ultimately contributed to their sense of constituting a unique corporate identity and sharing a remembered past. Ultimately, this sense of community would help to shape their subsequent responses to the challenges they faced in the colonial period and even to this day.

## A TIME OF CHOLERA

The first of the contagions to have an impact on the Samburu was cholera, which struck the neighboring Maasai around 1869. James Christie, a physician at Zanzibar who investigated the course of the dreadful epidemic, directly correlated the spread of the disease with trade and perceptively concluded that "the tracks of commerce and of cholera are identical." Coastal traders told the doctor that the Maasai had contracted the bacillus during a raid north of Laikipia on the "Soma-Gurra," a people who lived between the Laikipiak Maasai and Boorana. Equating this group with the "Samburu" of Thomas Wakefield and Charles New, who had established Methodist missions on the Kenya coast in the 1860s, Christie concluded that the cholera epidemic had hit the Boorana and Samburu before it moved into Maasailand.[4] In fact, the outbreak seems to have had only a relatively minor direct impact on the Samburu and their neighbors in northern Kenya; however, the historian Neal Sobania collected no traditions to back Christie's contention concerning the Samburu and Boorana.[5]

Nonetheless, if one accepts that cholera was a factor in destabilizing the Maasai who were already clashing with one another over grazing lands, then it did have a significant indirect impact on the Samburu. Not long after its spread, Maasai civil strife had kindled again to full flame with the Laikipiak suffering a crippling blow at the combined hands of the Purko and Kisongo sections near Naivasha in around 1875 or 1876. By the conclusion of the decade, that is, at about the time of the promotion to warrior status of the *Marikon laji* (c.1879–c.1893), these events redounded northward into Samburu and nearby Rendille domains where Laikipiak elements sought cattle and clashed with the herders. While the Maasai were able to advance into the southern marches of Rendille country, the Samburu and Rendille repelled their initial forays in the vicinity of Mount Marsabit.[6]

Meanwhile, with the collapse of Laikipiak power, the Turkana began making headway moving southward all along the eastern side of Lake Turkana. Enhancing the ranks of the Turkana were refugees from the Laikipiak as well as the Loosekelai Maasai, who had likewise been defeated in the Maasai time of troubles. Other individuals, especially women, and small groups who were caught up in the rising tide also seem to have been incorporated into Turkana society. Nonetheless, one should not overstate Turkana might as the Samburu were ultimately able to check the surge into their domains. Furthermore, the death of the dynamic Turkana diviner-*cum*-military chieftain Lokerio sometime after 1880, as well as the rivalries that developed among pretenders for power, would undermine what proved to be a short-lived Turkana ascendancy.[7]

While these events were occurring, Europe moved a step closer to northern Kenya. A Royal Geographical Society expedition led by the Scottish explorer, Joseph Thomson, made its way through Maasailand, and reached Lake Baringo in 1883. On his journey, Thomson learned of a large saline lake lying farther north, which he called "Lake Samburu," and posited that the mountains of the "Lykipia range" formed its eastern shore. He wrote further that "a great plain with numerous large volcanic mountains and isolated ranges" made up the country between Baringo and the saltwater lake. Concerning the people living in the region, the Scotsman recorded only that the "Wakwafi" dwelled there and that "the natives [had] no canoes." Thomson, who became the youngest recipient of the Society's Gold Founder's Medal for his efforts, did not himself go to the north, but he inspired others to explore the unknown land by declaring, "Clearly there is a region of great interest and importance here, the exploration of which will be a rich reward to the adventuresome traveler; and I can only say I shall envy the man who is first in the place."[8]

An unlikely respondent answered Thomson's call.[9] In 1888, Samuel Teleki, a wealthy Hungarian aristocrat and close friend of the ill-fated Habsburg Crown Prince Rudolf, led a caravan of 278 men, which constituted the first European expedition to reach northern Kenya.[10] Ludwig von Höhnel, a young, Austrian lieutenant, also accompanied Teleki. The large party arrived at the southern tip of Lake Turkana in late February, just before the *Ing'ering'erwa*, or long rains of March and April, with drought prevailing. The area was "unable to satisfy the wants of the most modest savage" according to Teleki, or "*Bwana Tumbo*," as the Africans called the rotund Hungarian.[11] Thus, it is not surprising that the Europeans never actually visited any "Burkeneji," or Samburu, encampments.[12] Nor did they engage in trade with the pastoralists. Teleki wrote that he had observed small numbers of the herders on the slopes of Ol Doinyo Ng'iro; however, Höhnel commented on having merely seen the light of a fire burning on Mount Kulal. Both Europeans additionally noted Samburu as well as others who were living among the Elmolo fishers and hunters who dwelled at Lake Turkana. The Austrian, in particular, remarked on the many Samburu women who had taken up residence with the Elmolo.[13]

The two travelers blamed the Turkana threat for their caravan's inability to establish contact with a Samburu community that had taken refuge in the highlands. Their guide on this stage of the safari, "Lembasso," was a Samburu who had been traveling in the southern part of Samburuland. Lembasso explained that the district was unsafe because of raiding parties and that one such group had recently passed along the southeastern shore of Lake Turkana. A Samburu woman who had escaped from Turkana captivity confirmed Lembasso's account, and told Teleki and Höhnel that the Turkana were raiding and plundering Samburu and Rendille alike. The Austrian officer termed the Turkana "triumphant," and declared that they feared none of the local inhabitants of the region. While the travelers emphasized the violent conflicts then occurring between the African groups, it is nonetheless worth noting that Höhnel mentioned that the Samburu also bartered with the Turkana for cereal.[14]

## CATTLE PLAGUES AND HUNGER

There is apparently another reason why the Samburu sought sanctuary on the mountain slopes. On Marsabit, Ng'iro, and Kulal, their cattle could be kept isolated from an outbreak of contagious bovine pleuropneumonia (BPP), which was sweeping the region by the time of the initiation of the *Marikon*. There they hoped to weather the storm.[15] The Samburu herders themselves called the bacterial disease, *lkipei*. BPP, transmitted by inhaling infected droplets from coughing animals, resulting in inflammation of the lungs and pleurae, pain in the chest and joints, fluid buildup in the thoracic cavity, and ultimately death in as few as 10 percent and as high as 70 percent of the cases. Sources remember it as causing the infected beast to have labored breathing and to face into the wind. After an animal's death and upon slaughtering it, the Samburu found that its lungs were rotten, its thoracic cavity was full of pus, and that the carcass gave off a revolting stench.[16] Unfortunately for the Samburu, their attempt to quarantine their stock did not keep the *lkipei* at bay. Höhnel thus recorded a Maasai account that

> the murrain from which oxen have been suffering for the last ten or twelve years was introduced by an ox which had been stolen from Samburuland. The disease, which seems to be rapidly spreading and in some Masai districts is universal, threatens the very existence of the people, who, as before stated, can think of no mitigation but the breeding of sheep.[17]

All the same, it seems more likely that the disease spread in the opposite direction. BPP had first appeared in South Africa in the 1850s, from where it moved northward to reach Maasai herds already by the following decade. The epizootic seems nonetheless to have become endemic in East Africa so that Thomson had commented on it when he visited the lands south of the Samburu in 1883. Accordingly, the Maasai tradition recorded by the Scot may well reflect a recrudescent outbreak of the disease.[18]

As BPP raged, the Samburu meanwhile faced growing pressure from neighboring ethnic groups. Added to the Turkana threat from the west was the growing strength of Daarood Somali pastoralists in the east who had penetrated the west bank of the Jubba River in significant numbers already from the 1830s. The Darood tide, which pushed members of the Hawiiye clan of Somalis before it, and an outbreak of smallpox, were crucial to the collapse of Warra Daaya power in lands between the Daua and Tana rivers over the next half century. Besides their conflict with these Oromo-speakers, the Somalis were clashing with Boorana over water and grazing. This conflict flared especially from the 1870s. Rendille traditions likewise record that it was around that time that they and their camel herds were driven from the Lorian Swamp. Throughout the destabilized frontier, the Samburu and Rendille also feuded with the Boorana, who were often allied with Gabbra camel-herders. Remnants of the Laikipiak Maasai, too, renewed their raids on the Rendille and Samburu with greater success than they had achieved initially. To wit, the Laikipiak reached the environs of Mount Marsabit in the late 1880s, and it was only with great difficulty that the Rendille were able to overcome the Maasai onslaught. At about the same time, that is, just before the initiation of the *Terito laji* (c.1893–1912), the Samburu repelled Laikipiak raids that endangered their highland communities on Ng'iro and Kulal.[19]

While the outbreak of *lkipei* and raids menaced the Samburu, a still worse disaster was by this time befalling the pastoralists. It came in the form of *lodua*, or rinderpest, and was so cataclysmic in its impact that to this day Samburu interprets it in apocalyptic terms as a punishment from Nkai, or God, for their iniquities.[20] Indeed, the epizootic set in motion radical changes that rent the very fabric of the community. The disease had devastating consequences for a regional economy recovering from the BPP contagion, and it wiped out entire herds sometimes literally overnight. This, in turn, undermined indigenous social institutions and political authority among the Samburu. Moreover, it exacerbated interethnic tensions and often led to the severance of bond partnerships between the Samburu and their neighbors or to reciprocal raiding and violent clashes. Death and hunger had profound psychological repercussions for the Samburu as well. Ultimately, the rinderpest outbreak was of crucial importance to the breakdown of the ecological balance and turned nature against man.[21]

To appreciate fully the consequences of the disease, which has measles as its closest human relative, one must first understand its pathology. Rinderpest is an acute, viral contagion with an incubation period that can be as brief as three or as long as nine days. Healthy animals become ill after they come into direct contact with the infected excretions from diseased beasts. It manifests a wide variety of symptoms including the sudden onset of fever, depression, a loss of appetite, abdominal pain, loss of milk production, diarrhea, difficulty in breathing, nasal and lachrymal discharges, as well as ulcerative and necrotic lesions of the mucous membranes of the mouth, tongue, and throat. The illness especially strikes cattle and feral animals including buffalo, antelopes, and giraffes. Mortality rates can be as low as 30 percent, but may also approach 100 percent with death occurring within 4–12 days of the onset of the disease. Other domestic animals such as camels, sheep, and goats rarely get the disease as they have an innate resistance to rinderpest. If they do contract it, the symptoms are not always apparent and the effects are much less severe.[22]

Although some might accept a divine interpretation for the advent of rinderpest in Africa, a more mundane explanation is that the virus was a by-product of the colonial encounter in Northeast Africa. Rinderpest appeared first at the Red Sea port of Massawa in 1887 in some diseased cattle that the Italians had shipped from India via Aden for troops about to invade Ethiopia. It spreads like wildfire throughout Ethiopia in 1888, and was recorded in Italian Somaliland in 1889. The epizootic reached Samburu herds from Boorana cattle not long after Teleki and Höhnel visited the region. It continued its spread southward into Maasailand by 1891 and within five years had reached the southern tip of Africa at Cape Colony.[23]

In its wake, the plague left unparalleled devastation. Neal Sobania depicts the effects of rinderpest from a poignant Rendille account:

> When it started it only took three days to finish all the Samburu cattle. On the fourth day only people were left; none of their animals were left. What remained was only one cow. Before the disease people had a great number of cattle . . . but after three days they were left with nothing except themselves.[24]

Peter Waweru, too, has recorded a similar heartrending tradition of animals dying "so swiftly that a herd of cattle that appeared healthy when let out of the pen in the morning would all die before the sun reached overhead."[25] Another tale concerns the game afflicted by the virus so that "dozens of the wild creatures would stand, heads lowered pitifully and too exhausted to move even when touched by an observer."[26]

With the death of as many as 95 percent of their cattle, the Samburu lost their principal means of sustenance and the bony hand of famine wreaked a cruel toll on the human population as well. Some abandoned pastoralism to "become Dorobo" and live by hunting and gathering, while other destitute

Samburu found refuge with neighboring communities such as the Dasanech and Elmolo. Previously, the pastoralists had managed to live in harmony with their environment. Now, they found themselves at the mercy of forces beyond their control, and fatalistically accepted Nkai's judgment.[27]

The eyewitness account of William Astor Chanler gives some idea of the desolation wrought by rinderpest. In 1893, the New Yorker made an abortive journey from Embe Country north of Mount Kenya toward Lake Turkana. Baluchi traders told him that famine was raging along his intended route all the way to Dasanechland. The Harvard drop-out, who became a friend to Theodore Roosevelt, learned further of a "plague" between Lake Turkana and Mount Kilimanjaro that had just "exterminated vast herds of buffalo and had even destroyed a large number of antelope, [yet] had apparently left the zebra untouched." The American's caravan, which included the returning Höhnel, bore witness to the suffering of the local population when it encountered 50 starving hunter-gatherers that August along the seasonal Seya River on the northeastern extension of the Laikipia Plateau.[28] Nevertheless, Chanler gave an eyewitness description of the Lorroki Plateau as, "contain[ing] hundreds of square miles of the most magnificent pasture land I have ever seen. The country is well watered, and the climate as healthy as any portion of the world I have yet visited." He added significantly that, "This country is now *uninhabited* as the Masai have vanished with the death of their cattle."[29]

A Samburu who had "become Dorobo" told the American adventurer that the pastoralists had suffered defeat at the hands of the Maasai and their animals had died from the epizootic. The cattle-herders were thus left in "semiserfdom to the Rendile" as Chanler understood the relationship of those who acted as laborers with their Rendille *sotwatin*, or patrons who owned the livestock the Samburu tended. He subsequently met with a hundred Samburu *murran*, or warriors, whom he averred, "exactly resembled Masai warriors," and tried to trade with them. The *murran* were eager to exchange donkeys for cattle; however, and since Chanler required camels and horses, they could not do business.[30] Shortly afterward, the expedition suffered twin disasters. First, a rhinoceros gored Höhnel so badly that he had to be evacuated from Lorroki to the coast. Then, 70 out of 85 of the temperamental American's porters and *askari*s, or armed guards, deserted the caravan so that Chanler had to give up his safari, too.[31]

## SMALLPOX AND DROUGHT

The misfortune that befell the Chanler peregrination was nothing compared to the unrelenting calamities that the Samburu faced. Fast on the heels of the rinderpest came *ngeyamara*, or smallpox. The disease, which has a mortality rate of around 30 percent, seems to have been present among the Samburu from the time of the *Tarigirik* age-set, and the Samburu associated its arrival with that of Somali traders.[32] Nonetheless, as humans are its host and the transmission of smallpox requires prolonged face-to-face contact, the contagion apparently had only a minor impact upon the widely dispersed transhumant herders. At the time of the Teleki expedition in May 1888, Höhnel had still noted that "smallpox was rapidly spreading amongst the Reshiat [Dasanech]" from the Arbore, or in other words in the region just north and west of their historic cradleland in "Wato."[33] It was at that time also that the area suffered two successive years without rainfall, so that, by 1890, wretched survivors of the devastation caused by *lodua* and raiding increasingly became clustered together in northern Samburuland. This allowed the epidemic to assume alarming proportions among a population that had not experienced a major outbreak of smallpox for some time so that both adults and children fell victim to the scourge.[34] In addition, a parallel eruption of *ngeyandisi*, or yellow fever, only exacerbated the death toll. Survivors were left not only with ugly pitted scars all over their bodies but no doubt with psychological wounds as well.[35]

Besides disease, nature also visited further plagues on the region. There is a well-known saying that when it rains, it pours—but unfortunately it did not do so for much of the period in question. That is to say that at the time when the *Terito* became *murran*, a prolonged drought gripped Samburuland. A locust invasion occurred in 1894 as well that made a mad harvest of anything green throughout a huge swath of East Africa stretching from northeastern Uganda to Tanzania. There are reports that in the latter region, not even hard pineapple and palm leaves were spared. Helge Kjekshus describes conditions in Tanzania thus, "The fields of maize and rice were devoured. The wells had to be covered against locusts and the houses tightly closed against them."[36]

The destruction of the ecosystem had further deleterious consequences. Carnivores survived the plagues, but found their normal sources of food dramatically diminished. They therefore increasingly preyed on the enervated Samburu and their domestic animals. The Samburu remember instances when hungry lions and hyenas became bold enough to enter homesteads and carry off people.[37] With so many grazing animals having perished, land reverted to bush, which in turn allowed for the spread of tsetse flies as well as the *ndigana*, or disease in livestock, and human sleeping sickness they harbor.[38] The delicate balance that the pastoralists had so long cultivated truly had been irrevocably shattered by the 1890s.

Beset by such a daunting host of maladies, those who survived became, in the words of a Samburu informant, "the poorest of the poor."[39] Whatever their ethos of pure pastoralism and their aversion to hunting and gathering, empty stomachs allow no rules. Accordingly, Sobania has recorded oral traditions such as one that tells that during the *mutai* the desperate Samburu "speared a rhinoceros and ate it; speared an elephant and ate it. All the things which live in the bush they ate."[40] The starving people collected roots and picked esculent wild fruits such as *lenang'ayo, sogotei, lposan*, and *lipupoi*. Another of their choices was the small but succulent and sour fruit that grows on the *musigio* tree (*Rhus natalensis*)—the leaves of which also provided fodder for goats.[41]

Another casualty of the *mutai* was a breakdown in the peaceful relations between the Samburu and their neighbors. The region witnessed significantly more frequent and deadly raids and counter-raids in the aftermath of the ecological catastrophe. Violence became more organized and extensive as *murran* sometimes traveled long distances to steal livestock for food or to begin to reconstitute lost herds. Furthermore, because the disasters had dramatically undermined traditional social structures, there was a loss of social control. Often, the Samburu *lpayiani*, or elders, no longer could contain the restless warriors.[42]

Communities, such as the camel-centered Rendille and the Ariaal, who herded both cattle and camels, had fared far better than had the bovicentric Samburu in the face of the rinderpest and the initial smallpox epidemic. The more diversified, mixed economy of the Dasanech, which combined millet cultivation and fishing with stock-raising, likewise proved in better shape to overcome the adversities than the Samburu means of subsistence. The institution of *gedech*, whereby refugees tended Dasanech animals in exchange for sheep and goats allowed laborers to reconstitute lost herds.[43] While needy Samburu thus were able to exploit long-standing associations with these groups, as Chanler's observation concerning the supposed servile status of the Samburu to the Rendille illustrates, there simply were too many pauperized pastoralists to be absorbed. Moreover, the temptation to obtain livestock through raiding proved too great for some *murran* to resist so that the long-standing alliance between the Samburu and Rendille became severely strained in a milieu of escalating conflict. As a matter of fact, many an unscrupulous Samburu client apparently turned *ltombon* (Rendille for "thief" or "bandit") and filched animals from his patron.[44] When a decade after it had struck the Samburu, smallpox ravaged the Rendille, the symbiotic relationship between the groups could finally begin to be restored. By that time, many of the Samburu were immune to the virus and took the place of Rendille herders who had succumbed to the disease. Even so, stock theft did not come to an abrupt end as the loss of Rendille warriors left their stock poorly defended.[45]

Samburu relations with some of the other neighboring ethnic groups generally were more confrontational in this period. The Turkana, who were relatively unscathed by the disasters and who were still a significant threat, coped much better than these ethnic groups.[46] The Samburu remember the Turkana as taking advantage of the Samburu's weak position by attacking them, killing men, women, and children, and capturing much of what was left of their few surviving cattle.[47] The Turkana advanced onto Lbarta Plain, and their raids reached Mount Kulal and the Koroli Desert.[48] Elsewhere, reciprocal raiding occurred between the Boorana and Gabbra on one side and the Samburu, Rendille, and Dasanech elements on the other in the region that today constitutes the borderlands between Ethiopia and Kenya. Thus, for example, the historian Paul Robinson has recorded a Gabbra tradition of a major raid at "Sake" in southern Ethiopia in 1894 in which Samburu *murran* captured a large number of their small stock before withdrawing to Mount Kulal. Nonetheless, the Oromo-speaking groups ultimately got the better of the Samburu and Rendille. In the words of the Kenyan historian Paul Goto Boorana, cavalry became "a scourge" to their pastoral enemies, and the Boorana came to hold the Samburu in contempt. The fighting contributed to the already-in-progress Samburu migration from Wato especially to mountain refuges in northern Kenya as well as to the concurrent expulsion of Rendille from their most northern domains. Filling the vacuum, Boorana and Gabbra occupied territory in the East Lake Turkana Basin as far south as Marsabit and the Chalbi Desert by the first decade of the twentieth century.[49]

While the above comments emphasize the hostile nature of interactions among the groups living in the frontier in the wake of the *mutai*, one should be aware that peaceful relations continued. This chapter has already noted that the Samburu maintained bond partnerships with the Rendille and Dasanech, and the Samburu continued to marry individuals from other ethnic groups even while raids continued. Indeed, such peaceful ties were significant because they allowed for the exchange of animals. As a consequence, the Samburu were able to parlay small stock for cattle from not only traditional "friends" such as the Rendille and Dasanech, but also from "enemies" including the Boorana and Turkana.[50]

## CONCLUSION

In conclusion, this study has examined how the latter part of the nineteenth century was one of continuing crises for the peoples who inhabited what is today northern Kenya. Indeed, the authors contend that this time became a defining period for the Samburu as a distinct ethnic group. They had survived the *mutai*, yet ecological disasters and interethnic violence had profoundly left their mark on the community. Samburu herds suffered particularly from contagious BPP and rinderpest epizootics while the pastoralists themselves likewise endured epidemics. Drought and locust invasion exacerbated the already grave conditions. As a consequence, the period became a time of hunger and death. All the while, a new Turkana ascendancy replaced the hegemony of the Laikipiak in the northwest, and Somali incursions brought an end to Warra Daaya power further east. The intense strains contributed to conflict within internal Samburu institutions and brought new tensions to the relationship between warriors and elders while the community as a whole often clashed with its neighbors. Finally, the herders began to quit their domains in Wato and to return especially to highland refuges in what is today northern Kenya, where they would soon encounter the first official representatives of the British Empire and fall under colonial rule in the first decade of the twentieth century. The Samburu's memories of this common historical experience of ecological challenge had nonetheless helped create a sense of corporate identity that would gird them for the difficult times to come.

## NOTES

1. George L. Simpson, Jr. and Peter Waweru, "Becoming Samburu: The Ethnogenesis of a Pastoral People in Nineteenth-Century Northern Kenya," *Journal of the Middle East and Africa* 3, no. 2 (2012).

2. Peter Waweru, "Ecology Control and the Development of Pastoralism among the Samburu of North-Central Kenya: 1750-1909," (M.A. Thesis, Kenyatta University, 1992), 148–50.

3. Neal Walter Sobania, "The Historical Tradition of the Peoples of the Eastern Lake Turkana Basin c.1840-1925," Ph.D. Thesis, University of London, School of Oriental and African Studies, 1980), 133–4.

4. James Christie, *Cholera Epidemics in East Africa* (London: The Religious Tract Society), 198–9, 200–2, 211–2, 225–38, and 471; and T. Wakefield and Keith Johnson, "Routes of Native Caravans from the Coast to the Interior of Eastern Africa, Chiefly from Information Given by Sádi Bin Ahédi, a Native of a District near Gázi, in Udigo, a Little North of Zanzibar," *The Journal of the Royal Geographical Society of London* 40 (1870): 303–39. See also E.G. Ravenstein, "Somal and Galla Land; Embodying Information Collected by the Rev. Thomas Wakefield," *Proceedings of the Royal Geographical Society and Monthly Record of Geography* 6, no. 5 (1884): 267; and E.S. Wakefield, *Thomas Wakefield: Missionary and Geographical Pioneer in East Equatorial Africa* (London: The Religious Tract Society, 1904).

For an excellent secondary account on Christie's work on Zanzibar, see Charles Miller, *The Lunatic Express* (New York: Penguin, 2001). The cholera epidemic seems to have originated in the Indian Ocean island that David Livingstone described as "Stinkbar" on account of the stench he experienced there. Dr. Christie related that,

"Cholera . . . took a total of 50,000 lives during outbreaks of 1858 and 1869 . . . one-sixth of the island's population." It is the Zanzibari traders who were responsible for the spread of the disease. Ibid., 36.

5. Sobania, "The Historical Tradition," 133. Sobania and Paul Spencer posit that the "Soma-Gurra" were Garre Somalis. Ibid.; and Spencer, *Nomads in Alliance: Symbiosis and Growth among the Rendille and Samburu of Kenya* (London: Oxford University Press, 1973), 154.

6. Sobania, "Defeat & Dispersal: The Laikipiak & Their Neighbours at the End of the Nineteenth Century," in Thomas Spear and Richard Waller, eds. *Being Maasai: Ethnicity and Identity in East Africa* (London: James Currey, 1993), 105; "The Historical Tradition," 134–9; and Waweru, "Ecology Control, 167–8.

7. John Lamphear, "Aspects of 'Becoming Turkana': Interactions & Assimilation Between Maa- & Ateker-Speakers," in Spear and Waller, *Being Maasai*, 98–100; and Lamphear, *The Scattering Time: Turkana Responses to Colonial Rule* (Oxford: Clarendon Press, 1992), 33–40; and Sobania, "The Historical Tradition," 139–41.

8. Joseph Thomson, *Through Masai Land: A Journey of Exploration among the Snowclad Volcanic Mountains and Strange Tribes of Eastern Equatorial Africa* (Boston: Houghton, Mifflin, and Company, 1885), 532–3; and Robert M. Maxon and Thomas P. Ofcansky, *Historical Dictionary of Kenya* (London: The Scarecrow Press, 2000), 244. For brief secondary accounts of the famous expedition see the chapters on Thomson in Nigel Pavitt's *Kenya: The First Explorers* (New York: St. Martin's Press, 1989) and Pascal James Imperato's *Quest for the Jade Sea: Colonial Competition around an East African Lake* (Boulder: Westview Press, 1998), 33–47.

9. Two historians suggest that Prince Rudolf had territorial ambitions in East Africa. See Monty Brown, *Where Giants Trod: The Saga of Kenya's Desert Lake* (London: Quiller Press, 1989), 95; and Imperato, *Quest for the Jade Sea*, 47; and *Arthur Donaldson Smith and the Exploration of Lake Rudolf* (Lake Success, NY: Medical Society of the State of New York, 1987), 13.

10. Brown, *Where Giants Trod*, 95 and 107. For the Teleki expedition, see Imperato, *Quest for the Jade Sea*, 49–78.

11. Samuel Teleki, "Count Teleki's Discoveries in Eastern Africa," *Scottish Geographical Magazine*, 5, no. 2 (1889): 99. The African members of the caravan used the nickname to refer to the supercilious Hungarian's big belly. See Frederick Jackson, *Early Days in East Africa* (London: Edward Arnold & Co., 1930), 125–7.

12. The Samburu call themselves *loiborgineji*, or "people of the white goats," and the appellation is what some of the first European travelers corrupted into "Burkeneji" as they identified the Samburu whom they encountered.

13. Teleki, "Count Teleki's Discoveries," 99; and Ludwig von Höhnel, *Discovery of Lakes Rudolf and Stefanie* (London: Frank Cass & Co. Ltd., 1968), 2: 76, 106–11, and 137.

14. Teleki, "Count Teleki's Discoveries," 99; and Höhnel, *Discovery*, 2: 74, 101–7, 115–6, 215, and 237.

15. Sobania, "The Historical Tradition," 143–4; and Richard Waller, "*Emutai*: Crisis and Response in Maasailand 1883-1902," in Douglas H. Johnson and David M. Anderson, eds. *The Ecology of Survival: Case Studies from Northeast African History* (London: Lester Crook Academic Publishing, 1988), 102.

16. Nongiso Lekume, Oral Interview (O.I.), March 1991. Cf. Sobania's description of pleuropneumonia in "The Historical Tradition," 142.

17. Höhnel, *Discovery*, 1:240.

18. Sobania, "The Historical Tradition," 143–4; Waller, "Emutai," 86–8; John Ford, *The Role of Trypanosomiasis in African Ecology* (London: Clarendon Press, 1971), 337; and Thomson, *Through Masai Land*, 357–80.

19. Sobania, "The Historical Tradition," 155–61 and 165–9; Edmond Romilly Turton, "The Pastoral Tribes of Northern Kenya 1800-1916," (Ph.D. diss., University of London, 1970), 71–85; Günther Schlee, *Identities on the Move: Clanship and Pastoralism in Northern Kenya* (Manchester: Manchester University Press, 1990), 42–3; and The Impact on East Africa of the Galla and the Somali, Rhodes House, Oxford, Mss. Afr. s. 520.

20. Lepari Lesakwel, O.I., April 1991.

21. Helge Kjekshus, *Ecology Control and Economic Development in East African History: The Case of Tanganyika, 1850-1950* (Berkeley: University of California Press, 1977), 126.

22. Waller, "*Emutai*," 86–91; and Gordon R. Scott, "The Murrain Now Known as Rinderpest," *Newsletter of the Tropical Agriculture Association* 20, no. 4 (2000): 16. See also G.M. Mugera, et al., *Diseases of Cattle in Tropical Africa* (Nairobi: Kenya Literature Bureau, 1979), 1; and George J. Losos, *Infectious Tropical Diseases of Domestic Animals* (New York: Churchill Livingston Inc., 1986), 549–613. Another earlier version has it that the British introduced the disease into Sudan in 1885 with infected cattle they had obtained at Black Sea ports to feed the relief expedition to save Charles Gordon from Mahdist forces at Khartoum. See R.W.M. Mettam, "A Short History of Rinderpest with Special Reference to Africa," *Uganda Journal* 5 (1937): 22.

23. Waller, "*Emutai*," 88; Scott, "The Murrain," 14–16; Richard Pankhurst and Douglas H. Johnson, "The Great Drought and Famine of 1888-92 Northeast Africa," in Johnson and Anderson, *The Ecology of Survival*, 69; and Sobania, "The Historical Tradition," 153–4.

24. Sobania, "The Historical Tradition," 153.

25. Kirima Leleina, O.I., April 1991. The Samburu claim that the disease, which in this case they call *lopet*, failed to manifest any noticeable symptoms before the cattle became ill. Perhaps *lopet* was a particularly virulent form of rinderpest, as the Turkana use the term for the virus. C.A. Turpin, "The Occupation of the Turkwel River Area by the Karamojong Tribe," *Uganda Journal* 12 (1948): 161–5.

26. Mettam, "A Short History of Rinderpest," 23.

27. Sobania accordingly cites a Samburu historical tradition that states, "God finished it like that, because God finishes things like that." "The Historical Tradition," 154.

28. William Astor Chanler, *Through Jungle and Desert: Travels in Eastern Africa* (London: Macmillan, 1896), 230, 237–8, and 350. See also Brown, *Where Giants Trod*, 121–36; and Imperato, *Quest for the Jade Sea*, 79–102.

29. The emphasis is that of the authors. See Chanler to The Directors, Imperial British East Africa Co., September 22, 1893, enclosure in McDermott to Under Secretary of State Foreign Office, November 22, 1893, Public Record Office (P.R.O.), Kew, Foreign Office (F.O.) 2/59.

30. Chanler, Through Jungle and Desert, 281–2, 306, and 316–7. Paul Spencer points out that the American was "a careless ethnographer." Indeed, Chanler's comment that "all negroes are notoriously fond of bright-colours" speaks volumes about his understanding of Africans. Ibid., 308; and Spencer, *Nomads in Alliance*, 155.

31. Imperato, *Quest for the Jade Sea*, 87–90; and Brown, *Where Giants Trod*, 133–5.

32. Lparikir Leshoranai, O.I., March 1991.

33. "Wato" is an unidentified place that likely lies between Lake Turkana and Chew Bahir. Höhnel, *Discovery of Lakes Rudolf and Stefanie*, 2: 207. Teleki, too, commented that smallpox had depopulated much of the region. Teleki, "Count Teleki's Discoveries," 99.

34. Neal Sobania, "The Historical Tradition," 162, 175–6, and 190. Richard Waller points out that "under normal conditions, pastoral populations are too widely dispersed for diseases like smallpox to become endemic and they have, therefore, no acquired immunity." Waller, *"Emutai,"* 91.

35. Baine Lengarawuiti and Mary Lewoso, O.I.s, March 1991.

36. Kjekshus, *Ecology Control*, 139; and Martin Falkenstein, "Long Ways: Ethnicity, Market Integration and Urbanization among the Ariaal and Rendille of Northern Kenya." (Ph.D. Thesis, Bielefeld University, 1997), 84. Accounts of the locust infestation can be found in John Lamphear, *The Traditional History of the Jie of Uganda* (Oxford: Clarendon Press, 1976); and John Iliffe, *A Modern History of Tanganyika* (Cambridge: Cambridge University Press, 1979).

37. Samayo Lekairab, O.I., March 1991.

38. According to a paper submitted at a colonial meeting on the subject, the encroachment of fly continued in some cases into the 1930s. E.F. Whiteside, "The Control of Animal Trypanosomiasis in Kenya," (Nairobi: I.A.C.E.D. Symposium, 1958), 1. See also Waller, "'Clean' and 'Dirty,' Cattle Disease and Control Policy in Colonial Kenya, 1900-1940," *Journal of African History* 45, no. 1 (2004): 47–8.

39. Kirima Leleina, O.I., March 1991.

40. Sobania, "Disaster and Recovery" (Nairobi: Historical Association of Kenya, 1978), 9.

41. Charles Lenalongoito, O.I., March 1991. A list of such "wild foods" eaten for sustenance during drought and famine can be found online at Ethiopia: Famine Food Guide Field Guide at http://www.africa.upenn.edu/faminefood/objectives.htm accessed June 12, 2012.

42. Waller, *"Emutai,"* 93; and Paul Wesley Robinson, "Gabbra Nomadic Pastoralism in Nineteenth and Twentieth Century Northern Kenya: Strategies for Survival in a Marginal Environment" (Ph.D. diss., Northwestern University, 1985), 351–5.

43. Sobania, "The Historical Tradition," 206–8.

44. Siamanda Leshoranai, O.I., March 1991; Chanler, *Through Jungle and Desert*, 290; Falkenstein, "Long Ways," 81–2; and Sobania, "The Historical Tradition," 187–9.

45. Sobania, "The Historical Tradition," 192–8; Falkenstein, "Long Ways," 86–7; and Spencer, *Nomads in Alliance*, 157–8. For a primary account, see Alfred

Arkell-Hardwick, *An Ivory Trader in North Kenia: The Record of an Expedition through Kikuyu to Galla-Land in East Equatorial Africa* (London: Longmans, Green, and Co., 1903), 241.

46. Sobania suggests that it was the Turkana's transhumant herding that kept their cattle isolated and consequently safe from the rinderpest. "The Historical Tradition," 175.

47. Lebaa Lebarsoloi, O.I., April 1991.

48. The Scattering Time, 46; and Turton, "The Pastoral Tribes," 331.

49. Robinson, "Gabbra Nomadic Pastoralism," 116–20, 354–5, 382, and 388–9; Paul Goto, "The Boran of Northern Kenya: Origins, Migrations and Settlements in the Nineteenth Century" (B.A. Thesis, University of Nairobi, 1972), 65; Sobania, "The Historical Tradition," 177; and Falkenstein, "Long Ways," 86.

50. Weliwel Letato, O.I., March 1991.

## BIBLIOGRAPHY

Arkell-Hardwick, Alfred. *An Ivory Trader in North Kenia: The Record of an Expedition through Kikuyu to Galla-Land in East Equatorial Africa.* London: Longmans, Green, and Co., 1903.

Brown, Monty. *Where Giants Trod: The Saga of Kenya's Desert Lake.* London: Quiller Press, 1989.

Chanler, William Astor. *Through Jungle and Desert: Travels in Eastern Africa.* London: Macmillan, 1896.

Christie, James. *Cholera Epidemics in East Africa.* London: The Religious Tract Society, 1904.

Falkenstein, Martin. "Long Ways: Ethnicity, Market Integration and Urbanization among the Ariaal and Rendille of Northern Kenya." Ph.D. Thesis, Bielefeld University, 1997.

Ford, John. *The Role of Trypanosomiasis in African Ecology.* London: Clarendon Press, 1971.

Goto, Paul. "The Boran of Northern Kenya: Origins, Migrations and Settlements in the Nineteenth Century," B.A. Thesis, University of Nairobi, 1972.

Höhnel, Ludwig von. *Discovery of Lakes Rudolf and Stefanie.* 2 Vols. London: Frank Cass & Co. Ltd., 1968.

Iliffe, John. *A Modern History of Tanganyika.* Cambridge: Cambridge University Press, 1979.

Imperato, Pascal James. *Arthur Donaldson Smith and the Exploration of Lake Rudolf.* Lake Success, NY: Medical Society of the State of New York, 1987.

———. *Quest for the Jade Sea: Colonial Competition around an East African Lake.* Boulder: Westview Press, 1998.

Jackson, Frederick. *Early Days in East Africa.* London: Edward Arnold & Co., 1930.

Kjekshus, Helge. *Ecology Control and Economic Development in East African History: The Case of Tanganyika, 1850-1950.* Berkeley: University of California Press, 1977.

Lamphear, John. "Aspects of 'Becoming Turkana': Interactions & Assimilation Between Maa- & Ateker-Speakers." In *Being Maasai: Ethnicity and Identity in East Africa*, edited by Thomas Spear and Richard Waller, 87–104. London: James Currey, 1993.

———. *The Scattering Time: Turkana Responses to Colonial Rule.* Oxford: Clarendon Press, 1992.

———. *The Traditional History of the Jie of Uganda.* Oxford: Clarendon Press, 1976.

Losos, George J. *Infectious Tropical Diseases of Domestic Animals.* New York: Churchill Livingston Inc., 1986.

Maxon, Robert M. and Thomas P. Ofcansky. *Historical Dictionary of Kenya.* London: The Scarecrow Press, 2000.

Mettam, R.W.M. "A Short History of Rinderpest with Special Reference to Africa." *Uganda Journal* 5 (1937): 16–27.

Miller, Charles. *The Lunatic Express.* New York: Penguin, 2001.

Mugera, G.M. et al., *Diseases of Cattle in Tropical Africa.* Nairobi: Kenya Literature Bureau, 1979.

Pankhurst, Richard and Douglas H. Johnson. "The Great Drought and Famine of 1888-92 in Northeast Africa." In *The Ecology of Survival: Case Studies from Northeast African History*, edited by Douglas H. Johnson and David Anderson, 47–70. Boulder, CO: Westview Press, 1988.

Pavitt, Nigel. *Kenya: The First Explorers.* New York: St. Martin's Press, 1989.

Ravenstein, E.G. "Somal and Galla Land; Embodying Information Collected by the Rev. Thomas Wakefield." *Proceedings of the Royal Geographical Society and Monthly Record of Geography* 6, no. 5 (1884): 255–73.

Robinson, Paul Wesley. "Gabbra Nomadic Pastoralism in Nineteenth and Twentieth Century Northern Kenya: Strategies for Survival in a Marginal Environment." Ph.D. Dissertation, Northwestern University, 1985.

Schlee, Günther. *Identities on the Move: Clanship and Pastoralism in Northern Kenya.* Manchester: Manchester University Press, 1990.

Scott, Gordon R. "The Murrain Now Known as Rinderpest." *Newsletter of the Tropical Agriculture Association* 20, no. 4 (2000): 14–20.

Simpson, George L. Jr. and Peter Waweru. "Becoming Samburu: The Ethnogenesis of a Pastoral People in Nineteenth-Century Northern Kenya." *Journal of the Middle East and Africa* 3, no. 2 (2012): 175–97.

Sobania, Neal. "Defeat & Dispersal: The Laikipiak & their Neighbours at the End of the Nineteenth Century." In *Being Maasai: Ethnicity and Identity in East Africa*, edited by Thomas Spear and Richard Waller, 105–19. London: James Currey, 1993.

———. "Disaster and Recovery." Nairobi: Historical Association of Kenya, 1978.

———. "The Historical Tradition of the Peoples of the Eastern Lake Turkana Basin c.1840-1925." Ph.D. Thesis, University of London, School of Oriental and African Studies, 1980.

Spencer, Paul. *Nomads in Alliance: Symbiosis and Growth among the Rendille and Samburu of Kenya.* London: Oxford University Press, 1973.

Teleki, Samuel. "Count Teleki's Discoveries in Eastern Africa." *Scottish Geographical Magazine*, 5, no. 2 (1889): 96–100.

Thomson, Joseph. *Through Masai Land: A Journey of Exploration among the Snowclad Volcanic Mountains and Strange Tribes of Eastern Equatorial Africa.* Boston: Houghton, Mifflin, and Company, 1885.

Turpin, C.A. "The Occupation of the Turkwel River Area by the Karamojong Tribe." *Uganda Journal* 12 (1948): 161–65.

Turton, Edmond Romilly. "The Pastoral Tribes of Northern Kenya 1800-1916," Ph.D. Dissertation, University of London, 1970.

Wakefield, E.S. *Thomas Wakefield: Missionary and Geographical Pioneer in East Equatorial Africa.* London: The Religious Tract Society, 1904.

Wakefield, T. and Keith Johnson. "Routes of Native Caravans from the Coast to the Interior of Eastern Africa, Chiefly from Information Given by Sádi Bin Ahédi, a Native of a District near Gázi, in Udigo, a Little North of Zanzibar." *The Journal of the Royal Geographical Society of London* 40 (1870): 303–39.

Waller, Richard. "'Clean' and 'Dirty,' Cattle Disease and Control Policy in Colonial Kenya, 1900-1940." *Journal of African History* 45, no. 1 (2004): 45–80.

———. "*Emutai*: Crisis and Response in Maasailand 1883-1902." In *The Ecology of Survival: Case Studies from Northeast African History*, edited by Douglas H. Johnson and David M. Anderson, 73–114. London: Lester Crook Academic Publishing, 1988.

Waweru, Peter. "Ecology Control and the Development of Pastoralism among the Samburu of North-Central Kenya: 1750-1909," M.A. Thesis, Kenyatta University, 1992.

Whiteside, E.F. "The Control of Animal Trypanosomiasis in Kenya." Nairobi: I.A.C.E.D. Symposium, 1958.

*Chapter 9*

# The Evolution of Imperial Social Development Policy and Practice in British Sudan

## *A Comparative Case Study of the Gezira and Zande Schemes*

Joseph M. Snyder

Lord Hailey's social revolution signaled a new trend in British colonial thought in which the colonial project's ostensible purpose pivoted away from the traditional and paternalistic methodology built into the framework of early twentieth-century British trusteeship.[1] Instead, beginning in the late 1930s, the metropole adopted a more ameliorative approach that resembled a technocratic vision of a modern, "forward-looking" "partnership."[2] This revolution of the colonial space came soon after the promulgation of Hailey's *African Survey* in 1938 and had the effect of revising the objectives of the colonial project. Administration would no longer be subsumed by the manifold exigencies inspired by the need to maintain law and order; rather, as the need for pacification subsided and partly in response to popular unrest during the recovery years, a paramount concern became the social emergence of indigenous peoples: to be achieved, it was supposed, by virtue of the mechanisms of scientific and social research.[3]

The Parliament legislated this doctrinal deviation when it passed the Colonial Development and Welfare Act of 1940 (CDWA), which superseded the Colonial Development Act (CDA) of 1929. Whereas Hailey's *Survey* can be said to have provided the ideological stimulus for development, the CDWA transformed the rhetoric of social policy into reality by adding the crucial element of capital. Not only did the act commit the British government to the subsidization of projects designed to improve colonial living standards, but it also provided for an annual outlay of up to £500,000 for colonial research, which the British government used to fund the Colonial Research Committee, itself chaired by Lord Hailey.[4] The CDWA acknowledged "that social and economic progress in the colonial areas required distinctive and separate treatment."[5]

For British Sudan, however, there was a problem. The framework for the relationship between Sudan and London was shaped by the statutes and provisions outlined in the Anglo-Egyptian Condominium Agreement of 1899. Under that Agreement, Britain administered Egypt and Sudan as a single entity, with the latter being considered an exotic appendage of the former. Though this arrangement came to an end with Britain's abrogation of the Condominium Agreement in 1922, it was reimposed in 1936 with the Anglo-Egyptian Treaty of Alliance, a conspicuously paternalistic document, given the ostensible trajectory of imperial policy away from paternalism. The treaty reaffirmed the essential paradigm of metropolitan governance: oversight of Sudan fell within the purview of the Foreign Office (FO), not the Colonial Office (CO).[6]

In terms of the CDWA, this distinction was vital. Since the CO had no role in its administration, Sudan could not tap the Act's 10-year £120 million development fund. In effect, this was the perpetuation of an earlier restriction imposed under the Colonial Development Fund established by the CDA of 1929. As so often had been the case, Khartoum found itself once again on the short-end of the funding stick.[7] Awareness of this did nothing to take the sting out of persistent exclusion, however, as Civil Secretary Douglas Newbold complained: "[The Sudanese] *are* loyal, witness 1914–1918 and 1940–1944, but to what? A remote abstraction, a Condominium. And as regards butter, the Egyptians dangle large pats in front of them while Britain legalistically denies them Imperial Preference, eligibility for Colonial Development Fund, and so on. Little wonder that some of the Sudanese intelligentsia say, "We admire British culture and justice, but what do we get out of the British connection?"[8] The British government recognized that allowance had to be made for those territories that did not fall under the aegis of the CO. In the case of British Sudan, this translated into a £2 million grant-in-aid to fund further development.[9]

The revision of its social development agenda suggests that the British government had become preoccupied with improving the conditions of the people living in the Empire. The shift away from earlier forms of trusteeship was in the main caused by three events which pressurized the colonial space. The shift began with the Great Depression and its Empire-wide implications, which gave rise to the welfare state, an essential pillar of social development. In 1938/9, the Royal Commission on the West Indies investigated strikes, lockouts, and general unrest among the laboring populations in the West Indies, the Rhodesian Copperbelt, and in the plantations of Burma and

Malaya, marking a major turning point in the conversion of the Colonial Service to a development policy more in line with the welfare of colonial peoples.[10] The Second World War was an important and contradictory watershed for the Empire. War catalyzed a development and welfare strategy that emphasized and promoted social emergence while it drained the Empire of its resources, both human and financial, and delayed the program's full implementation. The war simultaneously stressed the imperial supply chain, which dovetailed into an increased demand by London for colonial resources in the name of imperial and national interests.[11]

This study builds on the historiography of pre- and postwar colonial development in British Sudan. In its consideration of the evolution and influence of social development on the Gezira Cotton-Growing Scheme, it shares space with Arthur Gaitskell's seminal *Gezira: A Story of Development in the Sudan*, M. W. Daly's *Imperial Sudan: The Anglo-Egyptian Condominium*, and Alden Young's *Transforming Sudan*. As a comparative survey of social development in British Sudan, this study also adds to the historiography of Southern Sudan's Zande Scheme, including Conrad Reining's *The Zande Scheme: An Anthropological Case Study of Economic Development in Africa* and Dunstan M. Wai's *Southern Sudan: The Problem of National Integration*. More broadly, this study intersects with the historiography of colonial development in the British Empire. In particular, its focus on social development, welfare, and technocratic intervention in the late-colonial period is part of a discourse that includes J. M. Lee's *Colonial Development and Good Government: A Study of the Ideas Expressed by the British Official Classes in Planning Decolonization, 1939-1964*, Joseph M. Hodge's *Triumph of the Expert: Agrarian Doctrines of Development and the Legacies of British Colonialism*, James Midgley and David Piachaud's *Colonialism and Welfare: Social Policy and the British Imperial Legacy*, Mark Duffield and Vernon Hewitt's *Empire, Development, and Colonialism: The Past in the Present*, and Michael Havinden and David Meredith's *Colonialism and Development: Britain and Its Tropical Colonies, 1850-1960*. This study departs from the prevailing historiographies in that it is a direct comparative analysis of the largest and most ambitious agricultural development schemes undertaken in British Sudan.

## EMERGENT SOCIAL DEVELOPMENT IN WARTIME NORTHERN SUDAN

As the post-Depression, wartime rhetoric of social development intensified in London, it found a direct corollary in Sudan in the form of "Schedule X," a pilot scheme for social development embedded within the Gezira Irrigation

Scheme.[12] Promulgated by the Gezira Advisory Board[13] in 1940, the Schedule formalized the government's social development program by laying out the blueprint for a program of "Sudanization" (i.e., the devolution of authority in the field to Northern Sudanese), as well as a directed program of agricultural education.[14] This was not the first time a social development scheme along these lines had been proposed at Gezira, however. But the Sudan Plantations Syndicate (SPS), the private body responsible for managing the scheme on behalf of the colonial government, had earlier proven intransigent, citing concerns that devolution would negatively affect efficiency and result in decreased revenue.

While there was little reason to suppose that the Syndicate's position in 1940 had changed, the British were committed to devolution and decentralization, as Newbold indicated in a letter to R. C. C. Mayall, Governor of Gezira Province: "unless the Sudanese can soon have more intelligent participation in the Scheme than that of a laborer, we are bound to have trouble."[15] To convince the SPS, Khartoum did two things: first, it addressed the Syndicate's concerns over lost revenue by agreeing that any such loss could be partly or wholly made up by the dilution of the Scheme's British staff. Second, it tied the extension of its Agreement with the government to the social development program. In these circumstances, the Syndicate, whose fiscal argument against "Sudanization" had carried the day during the Great Depression, could do little else but agree to the new terms.[16]

Schedule X marks an important moment in the history of social development policy in Sudan. As such, it is worth reproducing here:

> The Government's general policy is to train up a class of small farmers who, when the concession period is ended, can make the best use of the permanent irrigation system established in the Gezira.
>
>     The Government's administrative policy is:
>
> (a) The development of an orderly organisation of village communities controlled by headmen selected by themselves.
> (b) The devolution of civic and agricultural control of the farmers to agents of this organization (e.g. agricultural sheikhs) and the use of village and other councils and of native courts to support and enforce the authority of these agents.
> (c) The gradual substitution of Sudanese for all non-British employees and eventually the use of Sudanese agriculturalists in the field in an advisory capacity.
>
>     The Government's agricultural policy is:
>
> (a) The production of a class of mixed farmers with a permanent stake in the land which they farm. To this end:

(b) The cultivation of food and fodder crops should be given as much importance as the money crop.

(c) Provision should be made for the agricultural education of native agents
and selected farmers.[17]

But the Schedule X design was not immune to the imperatives of war,
which made several aspects of the plan impracticable in the short term. The
Sudan Government lacked the machinery to implement many of the initiatives under the agricultural policy; chief among these was the inability of
the Department of Agriculture to provide trained Sudanese as field inspectors. With the onset of war, money for such diversions was not forthcoming. Further, and despite the loss of many British inspectors to war service,
the process of devolution begun experimentally in the Hosh region of the
Scheme, remained slow, and was shelved entirely until 1943. In the end, during the first few years of the 1940s, Schedule X mainly reflected two things:
the Empire's growing "developmentalist state" mentality, which had become
the handmaiden of social revolution, and the rhetoric that inspired it.[18]

The objectives of self-management had become a more conscious ideal,
and the war aroused considerable nationalist sentiment among the Sudanese,
particularly where the Gezira was concerned. As Newbold noted, there was
increasing interest in the Scheme by the educated Sudanese, and it was only
a matter of time before the tenants themselves "awoke" to its possibilities.[19]
On the ground, a practical stimulus for this came from two directions: the
Graduates' Congress and the Atlantic Charter, both of which require some
comment. Drafted by Great Britain and the United States and agreed upon
by the Allies in 1941, the Atlantic Charter did for the Second World War
what Wilson's Fourteen Points did for the First World War: it provided the
ideological bases for nationalists throughout "the Colonial Melting Pot"
to canalize their energies toward self-determination. In Northern Sudan,
the affirmation of the right of all peoples to choose their own government
seems to have been taken as the unequivocal declaration of the policy, which
translated into a marked increase in the urgency of building up local responsibility.[20] Meanwhile, in the House of Lords, Hailey was himself inspired by
the Atlantic Charter and urged concrete statements about British intentions
vis-à-vis representative institutions in the colonies. "Common prudence,"
he remarked, "forbids us to disregard the more advanced section of opinion,
for it is this element which in the long run will determine the attitude of the
people towards our administration."[21]

In Sudan, the "advanced section of opinion" was constituted of the
proto-representative Graduates' Congress. Based loosely on the concept
and design of the Indian National Congress, the Graduates' Congress
was founded in 1938 as an avowedly apolitical group (doubtless because

Newbold had himself warned the Congress off from politics) of Sudanese graduates of Gordon Memorial College. At the outset, the Congress's objective was the promotion of the "general welfare of the country and its graduates."[22] The government accepted this and likened the Congress to "a semi-public organization interested in philanthropic and public affairs and competent to hold and express opinions on such matters as come within its purview." It caught British officials off guard when the Congress thrust upon them its 1942 "Memorandum," which teemed with political rhetoric. Inspired by the Atlantic Charter, the "Memorandum" called for "a joint declaration [by the British and Egyptian governments] granting the Sudan, in its geographical boundaries, the right of self-determination, directly after the war," the formation of a Sudanese representative body to approve finance and legislation, "[t]he termination of the Sudan Plantations Syndicate contract at its expiration," and "[t]he carrying out of the principle of the welfare of the Sudanese."[23]

The Graduates' Congress' demands were symptomatic of the challenges and opportunities wrought by the war, which the Sudanese thought would make the British more receptive to change. Though the Congress's aggressive demands were rejected and the graduates chastened, it was apparent to the government that Sudan, like other African dependencies, could not be oblivious to the progressive trends of thought and declarations emanating from Great Britain and the United States. In a note to the Governor's Council, Newbold assessed the situation and made recommendations, which reflected the global state of affairs. He noted, for example, the importance of the promulgation of the Atlantic Charter and the consequent commentaries in the world's press and broadcasts. Further, he commented on the fall of Malaya and Burma, which led to several articles in the British, American, and Dominion presses critical of British colonial administration in those areas. He remarked as well on the Congress' "Memorandum" and its demands regarding self-determination.[24] Newbold concluded that, in order for Sudan to get "into step with these forces," the government had to extend the process of devolution, accelerate the "Sudanization" of the administration, and expedite the creation of an Advisory Council for the Northern Sudanese.[25]

These recommendations bore fruit when, in 1944, "five province councils were formed to assist governors in their executive duties and to elect members to the Advisory Council for the Northern Sudan," and the principles of the Atlantic Charter were implemented in the Gezira Scheme by way of the Schedule X conception, a development which paralleled a comprehensive reorganization that created rural district councils and delegated powers to issue local bylaws.[26] In a move that signaled Khartoum's recognition that the economic necessities motivating the SPS were at odds with the notions of advancement and social emergence embedded in the new development policy, the government decided not to renew its agreement when it expired in 1950.[27]

Significant as these changes were, they masked a fundamental flaw. As the government continued to formulate its social-planning agenda, all the decisions were being made *for* the tenants of Gezira rather than *by* them. Despite being at odds with the idea of "partnership" espoused by Hailey, British paternalism had commingled with the agenda of the intelligentsia that comprised the Congress' narrow constituency to stifle the tenants. In the end, it was up to the tenants themselves to make their voices heard and, in 1946, they did so. That year, they "awoke": they went on strike and demanded that the £E1.3M standing in the credit reserve fund (maintained against a possible future slump in the cotton market) be paid out to them forthwith.[28] They complained, among other things, that they had no idea as to the size of the fund and, in any event, had no say in the fund's administration. A Special Gezira Committee for the Advisory Council for Northern Sudan visited the area and recommended that £E400,000 be paid out to the tenants. To this, the government agreed, but it went further. In what were the first concrete steps to associate the tenants of Gezira more closely with the central authority, it "set up the machinery for representation of the tenants in matters particularly affecting their interests as cultivators."[29]

By including the tenants in the formulation of policy, heretofore limited to what the British planned to do and what the Syndicate felt it could reasonably allow, the government closed the last gap in the necessary triumvirate of social development in the Gezira Scheme. With the end of the Syndicate Agreement in 1950 came a convergence of metropolitan theory and colonial praxis, one in which the government and the tenants acted together to attain the same goal, a dynamic mediated by Britain's new army of scientific and technical advisers. That year, the Sudan Gezira Board assumed responsibility for the agricultural and business management as well as the social welfare of the scheme. Below the board was a Gezira Local Committee, comprised of those working and living in the Gezira to give advice "on matters affecting the welfare of the inhabitants," an ambit that included allocation of funds available for social development.[30]

## EMERGENT SOCIAL DEVELOPMENT IN POSTWAR SOUTHERN SUDAN

As the fulcrum of administration began to pivot away from the British and toward the Northern Sudanese, attention turned to the vast expanse of territory beyond the Nuba Mountains Sudan's Black African population called home: the South. Since the reconquest in 1898/9, the British administered

Southern Sudan with little or no reference to the Northern Arabized region. For all practical purposes, it was a territory unto itself; possessed of culture, religion, and heritage that had more in common with the peoples of the neighboring Belgian Congo than those from Northern Sudan.

In 1930, the British acknowledged the South's separate identity with the promulgation of its Southern Policy, the ostensible purpose of which was to safeguard the Southern Black African provinces from commercial exploitation at the hands of the Northern Arabs. In effect, Southern Policy institutionalized what had been the government's administrative principle toward the South all along: benign neglect masquerading as protectionism. This protectionism combined with the remoteness and poverty of the region and with a lack of capital investment by the British on anything beyond bare strategic essentials to produce an economic situation that, "even by African standards, was undeveloped."[31] It was no better off politically, as a commission of inquiry investigating the Southern disturbances of 1955 noted: "in view of later political developments in the Sudan as a whole, [Southern Policy] was not only barren, but was bound to create, and in fact did create, more fear and mistrust in the mind of a Southern Sudanese against his fellow countryman in the North."[32] As a result, a different Sudan existed south of the Nuba Mountains that was backward and tribalized. As the North democratized, the South lingered on under the paternalism of Native Administration; as the economy of the North modernized and flourished, the South's dilapidated infrastructure stagnated and its provincial economy remained de-linked from world markets. For over 40 years, the South continued to be a primitive backwater and had been virtually untouched by modernity.

This began to change somewhat when the Graduates' Congress issued its "Memorandum" in May 1942. In their manifesto, the Northern Sudanese demanded the right to self-determination *within the geographical boundaries of Sudan*. The implications of this were the most far-reaching of any demand made in the document, for it raised a fundamental question: What would an independent Sudan look like? Consider too that the "Memorandum" also demanded the "abolition of ordinances on 'closed areas' and the lifting of restrictions placed on trade and on the movement of Sudanese within the Sudan."[33] This was a broadside against the Southern Policy itself, which used the mechanism of closed districts to prevent any interaction between the Northern and Southern Sudanese, be it political or economic. The proposed abolition of these ordinances raised the bogey of a reconstituted Sudan, one that in all probability included the backward Southerners. In the end, did the South have a future in an amalgamated Sudan, or was it to be left to the mercy of the "instinctively predatory" Arab North when the British packed up and left?[34]

The answer came in 1943, when Dr. J. D. Tothill, the director of Agriculture and Forests in Sudan, submitted a memorandum to Khartoum titled, "An Experiment in the Social Emergence of Indigenous Races in Remote Regions." Based in large part on the results of a tour he conducted of the South's Equatoria Province in 1939, with minor revisions made in 1942, the goal of the experiment was the "complete social emergence and the social and economic stability of the Zande people."[35] As designed, the essence of the so-called Zande Scheme was self-sufficiency. Tothill argued that, in order to plan the orderly emergence of the inhabitants of central Africa as "happy, prosperous, literate communities based on agriculture and participating in the benefits of civilization," it was necessary to break through the impasse in development by making them as self-contained as possible. To this end, he proposed an irrigation scheme anchored by the cultivation of cotton but sustained by various other cash crops. The key assumption was that, by marketing a surplus of these goods to obtain the comparatively small amount of money required for the few indispensable imports they would need, it theoretically allowed the Azande to achieve financial independence.[36]

Built into Tothill's plan was a variety of programs meant to foster the social emergence of the Azande people. Included among the more basic aims were the betterment of the people's health, by virtue of an improved diet and the elimination of the scourge of malnutrition, and the expansion of their educational opportunities.[37] It was to be a gradual process, but over the course of several decades, the educational system was to be expanded so that in time 95 percent of the Azande would be literate. The idea was that schooling would be made available to every Zande boy and girl, starting at the "bush level," continuing up through newly established secondary schools and culminate with the region's first-ever university.[38] Oversight of all of this was to be vested in the Equatoria Projects Board (EPB), which took its functional cue from its Northern counterpart in the Gezira. As the controlling body, the EPB was to operate the various industries for the benefit of the Azande, from those related to cotton-growing to those associated with the processes of palm oil extraction and soap-making.[39] And, reflecting a kind of lessons learned from the Gezira experience, Tothill stressed the necessity of encouraging local participation in the Board. Exclusion, it was implicitly acknowledged, would only breed resentment.

The Scheme's emphasis on social and economic development supported by a framework of partnership exemplified the essential tenets of Hailey's *African Survey* and the ideological revolution it launched. As such, it represents a contrast to the formula of development that inaugurated the Gezira Scheme in 1926. Above all else, irrigation of the Gezira Plain and the cultivation of its "white gold" was an economic/strategic decision, the goal of which was to shore up the British position in both Sudan and Egypt.[40]

In planning the Zande Scheme, however, Tothill eschewed any economic considerations beyond those that contributed to the self-sufficiency of the Azande: the better to insulate them from the volatility of world markets. This principle highlights a significant paradoxical difference between the two schemes: whereas Gezira was intended to integrate Sudan more fully into the global economy, Zande was designed to keep the people detached from it.

It is ironic that the first large-scale development experiment in Southern Sudan should have an introverted and purposefully provincial outlook. It was also a bold and risky project. In a marked departure from standard practice, Tothill discarded the use of experimental or pilot research projects to extrapolate the likelihood of success or failure of the larger endeavor. There would be no testing of feasibility as at Barakat and Tayiba in the Gezira Plain. The Zande Scheme was to be an all-or-nothing undertaking, based largely on the results of cotton-growing in trial plots planted in the Yambio area in 1935.[41]

The design of the Zande Scheme raises several basic questions. Why place a large, resource-intensive irrigation scheme in an isolated, remote corner of southwestern Sudan, thousands of miles inland, removed from harbors and ports, and outfitted with a rudimentary infrastructure? More puzzling still, why single out the Azande, when no such constituent preciseness was applied to the Gezira Scheme? The answers to these questions lay in geography and demography: Not only did the industrious Azande occupy a considerable portion of the largest area of good rainfall in Sudan, but they were also the largest Black African community in the South. Such continuity, it was supposed, could only increase the likelihood of the Scheme's success.[42]

All of this was theoretical, for it must be remembered that Tothill's social emergence experiment was only a blueprint and remained little more than ink on paper until 1944. That year, as the Southern Policy—or "lack of policy" as some administrators bemoaned—came under increasingly heavy criticism from the Northern Sudanese and the Egyptians, the Governor-General Hubert Huddleston convened a meeting of the province governors, the legal, financial, and civil secretaries, and the directors of agriculture, medical, and education to discuss the postwar future of Southern Sudan. During the meeting, it was reported that, developmentally speaking, the region was "being left further and further behind" the North. It seemed that for every Northern advance, the South suffered a corresponding increase in backwardness. This chronic retrogression was in part the result of British interference in Sudan, a fact that inspired a keen sense of guilt among a number of officials.[43] Yet the immediate postwar period removed the limiting factors that had made development in the South unlikely: "not only were the funds for development available, but official opinion both in the South and Khartoum seemed more favorable to a firm development policy."[44]

These elements converged with the political awakening of the North to encourage the British to adopt a more positive policy in the South.[45] It was to be an aggressive program that called for a "more intensive and rapid economic and educational development of the Southern Sudan" to be planned and executed. As suggested during the meeting, the program of advancement was to proceed along two parallel lines of expansion, one for education and one for the improvement of communications, "whether by river, road and rail" as well as "any industrial possibilities." In August 1945, Acting Governor-General T. P. Creed submitted his Despatch No. 89 to Lord Killearn, the British High Commissioner in Cairo.[46] In that document, Creed explained the policy adopted by the Governor-General's Council in the spring of 1944 and emphasized that "our obvious duty [to the people of Southern Sudan] is therefore to push ahead as fast as we can with their economic and educational development on African and Negroid lines, and not upon the Middle Eastern and Arab lines of progress which are suitable for the Northern Sudan. It is only by economic and educational development that these people can be equipped to stand up for themselves in the future." He cautiously concluded "a beginning has been made."[47]

As was often the case with Sudan, however, there was a problem underlying these objectives. Adjusting to a new, forward-looking paradigm of social emergence is a challenging proposition from the outset; more so when the government is divided over the shape that the future should take. As attention turned to Tothill's Scheme, Khartoum struggled with whether the future of the South rested in a united framework with the North or as a federation along Nigerian lines.[48] This uncertainty is apparent in Creed's Despatch to Cairo, in which he noted that the comparative backwardness of the Southern Sudanese threatened their future as "East Africans"—implying that the British considered Sudan's postcolonial configuration as anything but decided.[49]

The Scheme's purpose and subsequent design were entrusted to the Ad Hoc Committee on Zande Projects, which convened in the South in February 1945. Almost immediately, the notion of self-sufficiency on which Tothill's plan depended was abandoned. The Committee justified this by noting that the machinery required to enforce the total prohibition of all imports would be "colossal," and therefore costly. It also stressed that there would be a "general dissatisfaction if cheap and otherwise desirable articles available elsewhere in the Sudan or just over the border were denied to the Azande." It was resolved that "the principle of self-sufficiency could only be accepted as far as local produce and locally made articles could compete with imported goods."[50]

Moreover, the economic imperatives of the EPB sundered ecological considerations. During the first meeting of the Committee, Dr. H. Greene "emphatically warned" of the dangers of erosion risked by the growing of

an annual crop such as cotton and recommended that its cultivation be postponed. The Committee accepted his concerns "in principle," but they were
pushed aside because cotton was seen as the "only industry [. . .] suitable for
immediate adoption as a cash crop by the native [. . .] which would produce a
quick return to the Board with an immediate benefit to the farmer in the shape
of cheap cloth of good quality." At the same time, the cultivation of plantation crops, including coffee, sugar, and oil palms, was jettisoned. In its resolution, the Committee noted that the decision was taken because the Agriculture
and Forest Department lacked the necessary knowledge of the crops "to ask
native cultivators to take them into their local economy." As such crops were
intended to be the bulwark of Tothill's ideal of self-sufficiency, which the
Committee had already done away with, the abandonment of their cultivation
seems a formality.[51]

By 1946, little remained to distinguish the Zande Scheme as a product of
Hailey's social revolution. Not even education, the key to the social emergence of the Azande, survived the corrosive effects of the uncertain future
of Southern Sudan. Whereas Tothill's design stressed the importance of the
spread of education, with universal education from grade school through
secondary school and beyond being achieved within 30 years, the Committee
discarded the idea and instead suggested that "the proposed expansion of
educational facilities for the entire Sudan would provide enough teachers
within 28 years for all Zande children to get an education of village school
standard."[52]

Within a year, the Zande Scheme was no longer recognizable as a bold
experiment in social emergence. Subjected to the imperatives of economics,
it had been reconstituted into something resembling the Gezira Scheme of the
early twentieth century. Essential to understanding this revision of Tothill's
idyll is what Creed hinted at in his Despatch: crippling ambiguity and per-
vasive uncertainty. The blueprint for Zande was ill-defined in the one area
it most needed clarity and precision: the avowed objectives of the Scheme.
Since no one (including Tothill) took the time to precisely define how social
emergence was to be achieved, the administration defaulted to an organic process nudged in the direction of social emergence by way of economic development. With no quantifiable way to appraise its effectiveness, the success
of social emergence in Zande became measurable over time only in terms
of the relative happiness of the Azande.[53] Amid growing ambiguity as to the
future of the South, the British saw negotiating the terms of the project as an
opportunity to turn the Zande Scheme into an economic engine that could, in
time, provide the necessary revenue to finance the region as an independent
state, should that be the eventual outcome of events in the North.[54] The future
of a unified Sudan remained an open question until at least 1947 when, at the
Juba Conference on the Political Development of Southern Sudan, Southern

chiefs expressed concern about the potential political ramifications of union. Although the Dinka chief Gir Kiro admitted, "the Sudan was a single country," the fact that the chiefs were answerable to their people made them cautious.[55] While they had no objection to living "as brothers" with the Northern Sudanese, Chief Cir Rehan wanted first to "wait and learn before joining them" politically. Given these countervailing tendencies, it is not surprising that the Scheme's configuration changed and left little room for immediate social development.[56]

As the Sudan government worked to reconcile these dichotomies in Zande, Khartoum was buffeted by a series of events that pressurized the British position in the South. First among these was the failed renegotiation of the Anglo-Egyptian Treaty of 1936. As *codomini* under that agreement, Egypt and Britain enjoyed a relatively harmonious relationship, albeit one punctuated by periods of discord, such as that which followed the Egyptian Revolution of 1919. The renegotiation of the 1936 Agreement, initiated by the Egyptian Government in 1945, presented a somewhat different dynamic. Soon after talks began in April 1946, positions hardened and negotiations foundered on a fundamental point of contention: Sudanese sovereignty. The overarching disagreement manifested itself in the interpretation of an essential clause concerning the future prospect of Sudanese independence. Given its significance, the "draft Sudan protocol"—the Sidki-Bevin Agreement—is worth reproducing here:

> The policy which the High Contracting parties undertake to follow in the Sudan, within the framework of the unity of the Sudan and Egypt under the common crown of Egypt, will have for its essential objective to assure the wellbeing of the Sudanese, the development of their interests and their active preparations for self-government and consequently the exercise of the right to choose the future status of the Sudan. Until the High Contracting parties can in full common agreement realize this latter objective after consultation with the Sudanese, the Agreement of 1899 will continue and article 11 of the Treaty of 1936 . . . will remain in force.[57]

As written, the clause was open to interpretation, and each *codomini* did so according to its own needs. From the Egyptian point of view, it meant that the King of Egypt was also the King of Sudan. The British, however, interpreted it to mean that the "Egyptians were for the first time conceding the right of self-government and eventual self-determination to the Sudan."[58] Negotiations came to a halt as the discussions degenerated into a stalemate over semantics. Hoping to bring an end to the impasse, which had resulted in unrest in the streets of Cairo, Governor-General Huddleston secured affirmation of the British interpretation of the clause from the Prime Minister's

Office in London. It read in part, "His Majesty's Government . . . are determined that nothing shall be permitted to deflect the Sudan Government, whose constitution and powers remain unaltered by the recent conversations, from the task to which that Government have applied themselves—the preparation of the Sudanese for self-government and for the task of choosing freely what their future status should be."[59]

This failed to placate the Egyptian government which had broken off negotiations. On January 26, 1947, Cairo announced that it would take "the whole question of Egypt and the Sudan to the United Nations," then temporarily headquartered at Lake Success in New York. The subsequent meeting before the Security Council proved unsympathetic toward the Egyptian Government, which listed among its demands "the total and complete evacuation of British troops from Egypt, including the Sudan," and "the termination of the present administrative regime." In its response, the Security Council assumed a noncommittal position, but nevertheless urged caution: "[I]t is difficult for the Security Council to make a decision of any kind now . . . . We do not know what the wishes of the Sudanese people are nor" their aspirations.[60] The Council adjourned without adopting any of the major resolutions and instead encouraged the parties to resume negotiations, all to no avail. Though Cairo may not have achieved its hoped-for ruling, the dispute between the *codomini* managed to do one thing: having raised the issue in the world's largest global forum, the notion of Sudanese independence had, for a brief time, taken center stage.[61]

The discussions at Lake Success signaled the high watermark of the growing interest of politically conscious Sudanese in external affairs, an otherwise predominant feature of the postwar years. In time, this gave place to the concentration of attention on matters of far-reaching importance within their own country. This shortening of focus to domestic affairs in no way obscured the watchfulness of all political elements on external developments, particularly in light of the dissolution of the British Raj; but, on the whole, these took second place to Sudanese solicitude for internal developments which culminated in the final session of the Advisory Council for the Northern Sudan and the promulgation of the *Executive Council and Legislative Assembly Ordinance* in June 1948.[62]

The momentum toward independence had by this time accelerated and the corollary of the concomitant political imperatives found expression in a series of events.[63] First, the British abrogated the Southern Policy, a change of inestimable importance in administration that signaled the government was no longer entertaining the notion of a federated Sudan; no paradigm for advancement was being considered outside the framework of unity. More importantly, however, was a necessary emphasis on economic development, lest the Southerners face virtual enslavement at the hands of the Northern

Arabs. This found resonance in a subsequent event: the funding of a massive development program. This presents an important paradox, since it would only be by virtue of capital provided by the North that the South would be able to perpetuate its development goals beyond 1951, the expiry date of the government's funded development period.[64] Civil Secretary James Robertson pointed out the implications of such an arrangement in a note to the Governor-General's Council: "if the Northern Sudanese are to be asked to spend nearly £E900,000 a year on the South they are surely entitled to some say in its administration."[65] This new reality caused the British to shed their illusions. There would no longer be any ambiguity as to the future configuration of Sudan.

As Khartoum readied for unification, work proceeded apace on key features of the Zande Scheme, including the construction of sawmills at Kateri, Gilo, and Loka in Yambio District. All-weather roads were built, primarily through the use of conscripted Azande labor, to link the principal southern towns and permits to trade were now given to anyone who could meet the commercial requirements.[66] These, however, were for naught without the fulfillment of the most significant aspect of the project: the resettlement of the Azande. Unlike in the Gezira, where the government encouraged tenants to settle the plain through a decades-long process of land settlement, the British uprooted over 100,000 Azande and transplanted them from the rural, tribal homesteads around which they had organized their society to a grid-pattern settlement outlined with roads and dotted with houses.[67] The impact of this 5-year process on the traditions and social life of the agriculturalist Azande was devastating.[68] Indeed, the rubric of modern social emergence reckoned little with the fabric of traditional society and its corrosive effects undermined two mutually supporting aspects of Azande culture: the arrangement of homesteads and the patron-client relationship. The Scheme divided up the Azande and segregated them into units framed by dwellings, collapsing the social organization of the Azande by undermining it where it was weakest: the grouping of homesteads.[69] In doing so, the British broke up extended families, fragmenting the superstructure of relations that kept the Azande economically and socially sound. This process also physically de-linked the clients (the tribesmen) from their patrons (the chiefs or headmen), a challenge made all the worse by the monetization of the economy. For, the Scheme overwrote the imperatives of the Azande barter economy, typically the engine that drove indigenous economies, with the mechanism of cash money. Instead of cattle, land, and foodstuffs allocated by the headmen, the principle of reciprocity became vested in the essential and alien machinery of the Scheme itself: profit and loss.[70] Within this new schema, the paramount chiefs were replaced by bureaucrats and technicians and the interpersonal network of the Azande obliterated, exploding the highly personal elements of the patron-client dynamic and hitting the Scheme where it mattered most: production.[71]

These conditions were described in a letter written in 1954 by Martin W. Wilmington, an eyewitness to the Scheme. His correspondence, addressed to the Department of Agriculture, presents a good comparison of the practice of the Zande Scheme with that of the theory of its underlying social development principles. "While no visitor can help but admire the considerable technical achievements of the Scheme," he observed, "there seems to be too much emphasis on ostentatious technology and not enough on economics and social welfare." He continued, "There is much talk about managerial efficiency and budget balancing but little emphasis on economic policy, social welfare, and progress statistics showing the 'social' rather than the financial yield of the project." Wilmington underscored this with an observation regarding the project's personnel. "One would presume that key positions in the execution of a scheme designed to produce 'social emergence' would be held by economists and social workers. In Zande, the key men are business managers and agricultural inspectors whose concern with the larger social and economic implications of the project must, by necessity, remain a by-product of their work." At the same time, the Sudan Government had done little to set up schools and "other paraphernalia of civilization" to further the social development goals of the project.[72]

At issue here is the structure nourished by the EPB, the charter of which had been reinterpreted so that the social emergence of the Azande was to be realized only *after* the commercial program of the Scheme had provided the means.[73] The result was a growing distance of policy between the Scheme's trading and production divisions, which became two separate entities related only through their headquarters, some 350 miles apart. Coupled with a lack of good local distribution channels, this produced a bewildering state of affairs on the ground. Whereas the products manufactured by the Azande found little interest locally due to relatively high prices, they generated a great deal of interest elsewhere due to a comparatively low price for otherwise high-quality goods. This was not ideal since the price Azande cotton fetched in Khartoum was lower than that purchased locally. For the Azande, this meant little monetary return for their labors. As their dissatisfaction grew, progressively lower crop yields combined with the lack of communal solidarity to signal the terminal decline of the project, less than five years into its operation.[74]

In many ways, this reflects broader challenges confronting the Empire in its efforts at maintaining a sustainable standard of living in its territories. The production and export of primary agricultural products to aid Britain's postwar imperial economy was the model many territories adopted to finance development, including Sudan.[75] The irony of the period is that just as the war and the immediate postwar years renewed pressures for the more intensive utilization of colonial resources, the new development paradigm obliged the British to foster the social emergence of indigenous peoples. The contradictions inspired by this administrative schizophrenia manifested in the negotiated space between colonial theory and practice, the unstable point of genesis for projects like Zande as well as the Tanganyika Groundnut Scheme.[76] Confronted by these incongruities and disconnects, colonial governments from Nigeria to Malaya struggled with balancing raising colonial living standards and welfare with responding to the pressures of metropolitan needs, all to varying degrees of success.[77]

Like many other large-scale agrarian development schemes, the Zande Scheme was a good idea on paper. Imbued with the intentions inspired by Hailey's *African Survey*, Tothill's aspirations were bold, yet the scheme's idyllic design had serious flaws. It is difficult to imagine any government approving a project the size and scale of Zande without even a long-term pilot program to justify the cost, but perhaps most importantly it lacked a crucial element, one that Gezira had in hindsight unknowingly enjoyed: cohesiveness of policy. Indeed, just as the Zande Scheme began its downward spiral, its northern counterpart reached an apogee in social development planning and legislation. In 1950, some four years before Martin W. Wilmington wrote his letter expressing his concerns about Zande, the Sudan Legislative Assembly in Khartoum promulgated the *Gezira Scheme Ordinance*, which became the basis of a new organization of the project. The *Ordinance* called for the Sudan Gezira Board, which replaced the outgoing Syndicate as the administrative organ of the Scheme, to promote social development by any means, "having as [the] main object the benefit of the tenants and other persons living in the Scheme area."[78] To achieve this goal, the *Ordinance* established two bodies: a Social Development Committee with responsibility for the execution of social development and the Gezira Local Committee composed of representatives of the tenants, local government, and departments, under the chairmanship of the governor of the Blue Nile Province. "This body was to submit to the Gezira Board the advice of those living in the Gezira on all matters affecting the welfare of the inhabitants and to make recommendations concerning the allocation of funds available for social development."[79] A similar body, the Zande District Local Advisory Committee (ZDLAC), was formed in the South, but by 1951 its discussions had degenerated into repetition of previous meetings. It was soon abolished due to costly ineffectiveness and though a Social Development Committee was suggested to replace it, the idea never gained traction, partly because of the confusion over how to achieve social emergence.[80]

Beyond the formation of committees, the *Gezira Scheme Ordinance* did something new: using money the Board derived from the sale of cotton, it established a fund specifically set aside for social development activities and embedded into the project's management the essential element of tenant coop-eration. Although these changes disregarded the non-tenant scheme laborers, they crystallized the Gezira Scheme as a model for future endeavors and would influence tenancy arrangements in projects like Kenya's Mwea Scheme.[81]

This is the inheritance of Gezira, started during the austere early days of the British colonial mission in Sudan and slowly transformed into a pioneer-ing mechanism of economic and social development. Today, it encompasses 2.1 million *feddans* and remains operational, some 85 years after the Sennar Dam was completed in 1926.[82] In contrast to this, the Zande Scheme—a product of the experimentalist and technocratic mindset that permeated impe-rial thinking from the 1930s onward—stands as a colossal failure alongside such projects as the Tanganyika Groundnut Scheme and the West African Egg Scheme. But when Zande and the development of the South came to the forefront of the Sudan Government's political agenda in the closing years of the Second World War, the British Empire was in a poor position to prosecute such an ambitious regenerative program. Weakened by war and undermined by its own rhetoric of self-determination, little could be done to resuscitate its mission in the South short of handing it over in *toto* to the developmentalist-minded North.[83] In this respect, Zande as deployed in the far southwestern corner of Sudan represents a confused last developmentalist gasp of an empire that struggled with its legacy even as it accepted the inevitability of its own self-liquidation.

## CONCLUSION

Lord Hailey's ideological revolution left a mixed legacy in British Sudan. The *African Survey* provided the foundational ethos that helped shift the objectives of colonial administration away from the responsibility for law and order and toward a concern for the social development of indigenous peoples.[84] In this respect, the Gezira and Zande Schemes echo contemporary imperial ideology, albeit writ large on the microcosm of the Sudanese land-scape. As such, the projects also reflected the problems of the development agenda. Throughout the Empire, the British confronted obstacles that made it virtually impossible to close the gap between metropolitan theory and colonial praxis, from money and manpower to indigenous resistance. It was left to the Empire's men-on-the-spot, such figures as Newbold, Robertson, and Tothill, to achieve this within the tolerable limits of both London and the Sudanese, which were often at odds. It was a precarious balance, often teeter-ing on the edge of open conflict.

In a sense, these conditions brought about a reckoning for social develop-ment in Southern Sudan when everything the British had hoped to achieve with social policy broke down. On July 26, 1955, a riot broke out at Nzara, the industrial hub and manufacturing center of the Zande Scheme. It began when the new Northern Sudanese general manager attempted to remove from the factory a Zande worker who had earlier insulted one of the Northern Sudanese staff. Shortly beforehand, the general manager had also dismissed 300 of the project's workers.[85] Though it was all over in a few weeks, the suppression of the riot by Northern Sudanese soldiers kindled resentment and anger among the Southerners, some of whom had witnessed the melee in which a number of Azande were fatally wounded. Less than a month later, the Equatorial Corps mutinied at Torit, which dovetailed into a general uprising throughout Equatoria Province.[86]

The riot draws attention to an important aspect of social development in Southern Sudan: the process of Sudanization, whereby trained Sudanese gradually replaced the British managers and administrators of the Zande Scheme. Caught up in the rush to independence between 1951 and 1953, Sudanese from Northern Sudan replaced the British managers and administrators more quickly than planned. The process was riddled with problems from the start. The Northern Sudanese had neither the competence of the Europeans nor the confidence of the Azande.[87] In addition, the Southerners had a long history of distrust of the Northern Sudanese which was fueled by memories of past enslavement by Arab traders and exacerbated by "extreme disappointment and frustration as a result of Sudanization and the consequent fear of political domination."[88] As Southerner grievances mounted, simmering political resentment between the National Unionist Party (NUP) and the Umma Party over Sudan's future as either a federated or independent state spilled into the Southern region, where they politicized the Sudanization of the Zande Scheme and made "rash and irresponsible promises" about the promotion of Southerners into the scheme.[89] As a result, the government accused the South of conspiring against the national interest and threatened to "use the force of iron in dealing with any Southerner who will dare attempt to divide out nation."[90] The tensions this engendered were vented along the lines of the highly charged, ethnicized bifurcation of Sudanese identity.

From the outset, this chapter has sought to demonstrate that the evolution of social development in British Sudan reveals a larger narrative of events, particularly those that prompted ideological changes in Africa during the colonial period. This conceit has obliged a direct comparative analysis of the two largest and most ambitious irrigation projects ever undertaken by the British in Sudan: the Gezira and Zande Schemes. In doing so, it fills a gap in the historiography of British Sudan which helps to contextualize later events, such as the Sudanese Civil War. In looking at these two projects and how they were either the product of, or influenced by, the guiding principles of the British colonial endeavor, the interconnected causal relations of their construction have been made more legible. This allows us to trace the evolution of imperial ideology by looking at the social development agenda. It also reveals how the Gezira Scheme, which was begun as an engine of economic development designed to make Sudan self-sufficient, became a model of social emergence that came to influence future development schemes. It also shows how the reverse happened in Zande: Tothill's idyll, once a paragon of social development that pivoted on the fulcrum of self-sufficiency, became the mechanism by which the British attempted and failed to secure the economic future of the Zande.

## NOTES

1. J. M. Lee, *Colonial Development and Good Government* (Oxford: Clarendon Press, 1967), 45.

2. Joseph M. Hodge, *Triumph of the Expert: Agrarian Doctrines of Development and the Legacies of British Colonialism* (Athens: Ohio University Press, 2007), 17–18 and Arthur Gaitskell, *Gezira: A Story of Development in the Sudan* (London: Faber and Faber Limited, 1954), 222.

3. Lee, *Colonial Development*, 78.

4. Hodge, *Triumph of the Expert*, 180 and Lee, *Colonial Development*, 35.

5. Lee, *Colonial Development*, 84.

6. Muddathir 'Abdel Rahim, *Imperialism and Nationalism in the Sudan: A Study in Constitutional and Political Development, 1899-1956* (Khartoum: University Press, 1986), 85.

7. Harley V. Usill, "Britain's Achievement in the Sudan," *World Affairs* 110, no. 4 (1947), 292.

8. K. D. D. Henderson, *The Making of the Modern Sudan: The Life and Letters of Sir Douglas Newbold, KBE* (London: Faber and Faber Limited, 1953), 399. Emphasis Newbold's.

9. Usill, "Britain's Achievement," 292.

10. Lee, *Colonial Development*, 45.

11. Hodge, *Triumph of the Expert*, 197.

12. Gaitskell, *Gezira*, 208.

13. The body responsible for the coordination of government policy as it concerned the Gezira Scheme.

14. Gaitskell, *Gezira*, 165 and Henderson, *Letters*, 516–17.

15. Henderson, *Letters*, 516.

16. Ibid. and Gaitskell, *Gezira*, 344–53.

17. Gaitskell, *Gezira*, 208 and Henderson, *Letters*, 516–17.

18. Christopher Bonneuil, "Development as Experiment: Science and State Building in Late Colonial and Postcolonial Africa, 1930-1970," *Osiris* 15, no. 2, Nature and Empire: Science and Colonial Enterprise (2000), 265.

19. Henderson, *Letters*, 516 and Gaitskell, *Gezira*, 224.

20. Henderson, *Letters*, 213.

21. Ibid., 559–60.

22. Ibid., 536–37.

23. Ibid., 540–41 and Sir Harold MacMichael, *The Sudan* (New York: Frederick A. Praeger, 1955), 192.

24. Henderson, *Letters*, 554–55.

25. Gaitskell, *Gezira*, 222 and Henderson, *Letters*, 557.

26. *Report on the Administration of the Sudan for the Years 1942-1944 (inclusive)* (Khartoum: Messrs. McCorquodale & Co. [Sudan] Ltd., 1947), 2 and Gaitskell, *Gezira*, 216.

27. Gaitskell, *Gezira*, 216 & 222–23.

28. Ibid., 224.

29. *Report by the Governor-General on the Administration, Finances and Conditions of the Sudan in 1946*, Cmd. 758, 3.

30. *Report of the Select Committee of the Legislative Assembly on the Future Administration of the Gezira 1950*, African and Middle Eastern Division, Library of Congress (hereafter AMEDLOC) HD1741.S85G42.

31. Conrad C. Reining, *The Zande Scheme: An Anthropological Case Study of Economic Development in Africa* (Evanston: Northwestern University Press, 1966), 141.

32. *Report of the Commission of Inquiry into the Disturbances in the Southern Sudan*, 17, AMEDLOC DT108.6.A52 1956a.

33. Henderson, *Letters*, 541.

34. Khartoum Despatch 89, Sudan Archives Durham (hereafter SAD), 664/12/2.

35. William A. Hance, "The Zande Scheme in the Anglo-Egyptian Sudan," *Economic Geography* 31, no. 2 (1955), 150.

36. Reining, *Zande*, 143.

37. Minutes of the Ad Hoc Committee: Zande Projects, SAD 664/12/13.

38. Reining, *Zande*, 144.

39. *The Zande Scheme* (Juba: Publications Bureau, 1952), 1–4, LOC.

40. Gaitskell, *Gezira*, 254.

41. Reining, *Zande*, 135.

42. Ibid., 143.

43. Robert O. Collins, *Shadows in the Grass: Britain in the Southern Sudan, 1918-1956* (New Haven: Yale University Press, 1983), 274.

44. Appendix B, Khartoum Despatch 89, SAD 664/12/9.

45. Ibid., SAD 664/12/2.

46. Ibid., SAD 664/12/9.

47. Ibid., SAD 664/12/2.

48. Sir James Robertson, *Transition in Africa: From Direct Rule to Independence, A Memoir* (London: C. Hurst and Company, 1974), 106.

49. Appendix B, SAD 664/12/2.

50. Minutes, SAD 664/12/12-13.

51. Ibid., SAD 664/12/13.

52. Ibid., SAD 664/12/14 and Reining, *Zande*, 151.

53. Letter from Martin W. Wilmington to Mr. Bayoumi, Department of Agriculture, Khartoum, SAD 929/9/27.

54. Robertson, *Transition in Africa*, 105.

55. *Proceedings of the Juba Conference on the Political Development of the Southern Sudan*, June 1947, 7.

56. Beshir Mohammed Said, *Sudan: Crossroads of Africa* (London: Bodley Head Publishers, 1966), 51.

57. Robertson, *Transition in Africa*, 96 and MacMichael, *The Sudan*, 195.

58. Robertson, *Transition in Africa*, 93–99.

59. MacMichael, *The Sudan*, 197.

60. Ibid., 200–01.

61. Ibid., 202.

62. *Report on the Administration of the Sudan in 1948* (Khartoum: Messrs. McCorquodale & Co. [Sudan] Ltd., 1950), 1.

63. "Southern Sudan Policy," Civil Secretary's Office, Khartoum, December 16, 1944.

64. Hance, "The Zande Scheme," 150.

65. Robertson, *Transition in Africa,* 109.

66. Collins, *Shadows*, 63–64 and Reining, *Zande*, 163–64.

67. J. W. G. Wyld, Aide Memoire to the Zande Scheme and Notes on Progress, SAD 779/5/17.

68. Major Jasper Wyld, "Background to the Development of a Central African Tribe: A Lecture Given to the Institute of Rural Life at Home and Overseas," February 7, 1951, SAD 779/6/55.

69. Reining, *Zande*, 129.

70. Ibid., 179.

71. Ibid., 180.

72. Wilmington to Bayoumi, SAD 929/9/28-30.

73. Minutes, SAD 664/12/13 and Reining, *Zande*, 157.

74. Reining, *Zande*, 171.

75. Alden Young, *Transforming Sudan: Decolonization, Economic Development, and State Formation* (Cambridge: Cambridge University Press, 2017), 96.

76. Lee, *Colonial Development*, 134.

77. Hodge, *Triumph*, 230–31.

78. Gaitskell, *Gezira*, 250.

79. *Report of the Select Committee of the Legislative Assembly on the Future Administration of the Gezira 1950*, AMEDLOC HD1741.S85G42.

80. Reining, *Zande*, 199–200.

81. Maurits W. Ersten, "Controlling the Farmer: Colonial and Post-Colonial Irrigation Interventions in Africa," *The Journal for Transdisciplinary Research in Southern Africa* 4, no. 1 (2008), 221–24.

82. Ibid., 216.

83. Ø. H. Rolandsen, "Discourses of Violence in the Transition from Colonialism to Independence in Southern Sudan, 1955-1960," *Journal of Eastern African Studies* 8, no. 4 (July 2014), 612–13.

84. Lee, *Colonial Development*, 78.
85. *Report of the Commission of Inquiry into the Disturbances in the Southern Sudan During August, 1955*, 21–22, AMEDLOC DT108.6.A52 1956a.
86. Reining, *Zande*, 34 & 215 and Collins, *Shadows*, 332.
87. Collins, *Shadows*, 332.
88. *Report of the Commission of Inquiry into the Disturbances in the Southern Sudan*, 110.
89. Ibid., 112.
90. Ibid., 20–21.

# BIBLIOGRAPHY

## Primary Sources

Manuscripts: Great Britain, Sudan Archives, Durham.
SAD 664/12/2, 3, 9, 10, 12-27. Minutes of the Ad Hoc Committee: Zande Projects, 1945.
———— 779/5/17 and 7/12, 13, 27, 28, 55-60. Original Correspondence, Sudan.
———— 929/9/27-33. Original Correspondence, Sudan.
*Proceedings of the Juba Conference on the Political Development of the Southern Sudan.* 1947.
*Report on the Administration of the Sudan for the Years 1942-1944 (inclusive).* Khartoum: Messrs. McCorquodale & Co. [Sudan] Ltd., 1947.
*Report on the Administration of the Sudan in 1948.* Khartoum: Messrs. McCorquodale & Co. [Sudan] Ltd., 1950.
*Report of the Commission of Inquiry into the Disturbances in the Southern Sudan*, 17, Library of Congress (hereafter AMEDLOC) DT108.6.A52 1956a.
*Report of the Select Committee of the Legislative Assembly on the Future Administration of the Gezira 1950*, African and Middle Eastern Division, AMEDLOC HD1741.S85G42.

## Secondary Sources

Beshir, Mohammed Said. *Sudan: Crossroads of Africa.* London: Bodley Head Publishers, 1966.
Bonneuil, Christopher. "Development as Experience: Science and State Building in Late Colonial and Postcolonial Africa, 1930-1970." *Osiris*, 15, no. 2. Nature and Empire: Science and Colonial Enterprise (2000): 258-281.3.
Collins, Robert O. *Shadows in the Grass: Britain in the Southern Sudan, 1918-1956.* New Haven: Yale University Press, 1983.
Ersten, Maurits W. "Controlling the Farmer: Colonial and Post-Colonial Irrigation Interventions in Africa." *The Journal for Transdisciplinary Research in Southern Africa* 4, no. 1 (2008): 209–36.
Gaitskell, Arthur. *Gezira: A Story of Development in the Sudan.* London: Faber and Faber Limited, 1954.

Hance, William A. "The Zande Scheme in the Anglo-Egyptian Sudan." *Economic Geography* 31, no. 2 (1955): 149–56.

Henderson, K. D. D. *The Making of the Modern Sudan: The Life and Letters of Sir Douglas Newbold*. London: Faber and Faber Limited, 1953.

Hodge, Joseph M. *Triumph of the Expert: Agrarian Doctrines of Development and the Legacies of British Colonialism*. Athens: Ohio University Press, 2007.

Lee, J. M. *Colonial Development and Good Government*. Oxford: Clarendon Press, 1967.

MacMichael, Sir Harold. *The Sudan*. New York: Frederick A. Praeger, 1955.

Rahim, Muddathir 'Abdel. *Imperialism and Nationalism in the Sudan: A Study in Constitutional and Political Development, 1899-1956*. Khartoum: University Press, 1986.

Reining, Conrad C. *The Zande Scheme: An Anthropological Case Study of Economic Development in Africa*. Evanston: Northwestern University, 1966.

Rolandsen, Ø. H. "Discourses of Violence in the Transition from Colonialism to Independence in Southern Sudan, 1955-1960." *Journal of Eastern African Studies* 8, no. 4 (2014): 609–25.

Robertson, Sir James. *Transition in Africa: From Direct Rule to Independence, A Memoir*. London: C. Hurst and Company, 1974.

Usill, Harley V. "Britain's Achievement in the Sudan." *World Affairs* 110, no. 4 (1947): 290–92.

Young, Alden. *Transforming Sudan: Decolonization, Economic Development, and State Formation*. Cambridge: Cambridge University Press, 2017.

*The Zande Scheme*. Juba: Publications Bureau, 1952.

*Chapter 10*

# Illusions about a Boom in Cotton Production in Southern Nyanza during the Depression, 1929–1939

Peter Odhiambo Ndege

When cotton was first introduced as an export crop among peasant farmers in present-day Southern Nyanza,[1] in 1910 its adoption met with very little success. This was because of its unpopularity due to the heavy work it entailed relative to the labor demands of food crops, its inedibility, and the outbreak of the First World War in 1914. Attempts to reintroduce it after the War did not meet expectations primarily because of the contradictions of the dual policy which undermined the development of African agriculture. This policy disbursed the largest proportion of African labor and revenue collected through African taxation to European settler agriculture. During the depression, 1929–1939, the colonial state once again renewed its efforts to intensify cotton production in the belief that it held the greatest promise in bringing about economic development. Consequently, cotton was pushed by the local European administrators who, because of the reluctance of the central government to fund development in African areas, felt collectively responsible for the economic development of the district. They often did this without regard to the realities of the local and the wider situation. Administrators' overoptimism was largely responsible for this. All along this feeling and expectation turned to be illusory. This chapter explains how and why this happened.

The dramatic fall in prices in the United States and Europe was experienced in Kenya soon after October 1929. It worsened the preexisting strains that already characterized the Kenyan colonial economy by this time.[2] These included the agricultural and export orientation of the economy, the internal domination of settler over African agriculture, and also the overreliance of settler agriculture on the financial support and supply of labor by the state.[3] These internal roots of the depression in Kenya had been concealed by the brief economic buoyancy of the 1920s.[4]

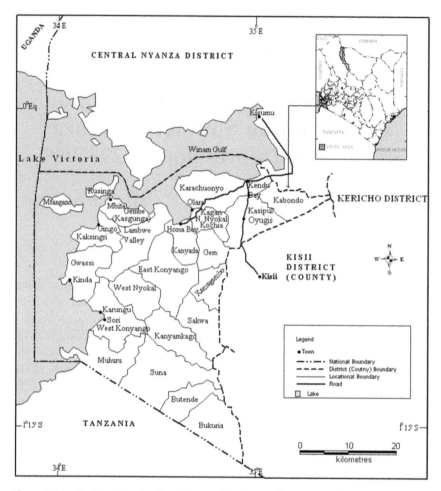

**Figure 10.1 Cotton Growing Locations and Major Buying Centers in South Kavirondo (SK).** *Source*: Drawing by Luka Kanda, Department of Geography Laboratory, Moi University.

The depression posed to the state the challenge of how to raise revenue in the face of the dramatic fall in the value of Kenya's agricultural exports. European settlers were concerned with how to cope with the high costs of production at a time when returns from sales of agricultural produce were rapidly declining. For Africans in SK and the rest of the country, the depression led to a period of extreme reproduction squeeze. As used by Henry Bernstein, this refers to pressures or stresses, which make it difficult for individual families to sustain and reproduce or sustain them economically and socially[5]. During the depression, such pressures included famine, low commodity prices, high taxation, and lack of employment opportunities. These factors influenced Luo peasant farmers' in the area to try and balance between producing cotton for tax and other necessities and food production, a very difficult exercise. As for the colonial state, John Lonsdale has stated that it acted in the depression to save itself first and the settlers only second, and that it was largely able to do so.[6] This implies that Africans came in a distant third.

In order to push commodity production, including that of cotton, the government undertook many measures, including the reorganization of the administrative and agricultural personnel, improvement of cotton-growing methods, intensification of tax collection, the improvement of road and lake transport, the establishment of more cotton-buying posts and increase in cotton prices, and finally, the encouragement of European and Indian entrepreneurs to invest in cotton ginning. The success of these measures initially paid dividends but was soon circumscribed by certain realities.

In 1931 the administration of agriculture in the Province and SK was reorganized for greater efficiency in service delivery.[7] Lynn Watt became the Senior Agricultural Officer (AO) responsible to the Director of Agriculture (DofA) for all departmental activities in the Province. He would also be responsible for agricultural activities in Central Kavirondo (CK) and Bukura. On the other hand, the AOs in Kakamega, North Kavirondo (NK), and Kisumu, CK were to be responsible for activities in their districts under Watt's guidance and in consultation with their respective District Commissioners (DCs) in matters regarding itineraries, often referred to as *Safaris*, and work. With AO's responsibilities and line of action more clearly defined, the DC SK requested for another AO and additional African Agricultural Instructors. In 1932, I. W. Gaddum, together with six African Agricultural Inspectors (AAIs), was posted to the district. Two years later, the number of AAIs increased to seven. The task at hand remained too huge for the local administration.

The administration of the district was similarly improved by the appointment of new chiefs. Most of them had been educated in Christian Mission schools and had previous work experience outside the district. Isaac Ogoma, Obonyo, and Ngome were still retained as chiefs of Kanyada, Kochia, and Kadem, respectively. This was because of their impressive work in relation to cotton-growing during the 1920s. Each of these chief's had their own cotton farms. They also encouraged their subjects to grow the crop. The new set of chiefs included Daniel Ojijo and Paul Mboya, both in Karachuonyo, and Gideon Magak of Mumbo/Kasipul. Each chief was to be assisted by a team called *Milangos*. As assistant chief, Daniel Ojijo keenly promoted cotton and other cash crops, as well as the establishment of trading centers. But he soon fell out with the administration on account of his membership of the Young Kavirondo Tax Payers'Association (YKTPA) and the Kavirondo Native Chambers of Commerce (KNCC). The colonial administration never tolerated chiefs' participation in these political organizations.

The administration's favorite was Paul Mboya who was appointed chief of Karachuonyo in 1935.[8] He improvised an efficient tax collection system and popularized the block or group system of cotton-growing whose operation is detailed below. Gideon Magak who was appointed chief of Mumbo in 1933 belonged to the league of the new chiefs. He not only promoted cotton-growing but also Robusta Coffee after Africans were finally allowed to grow with it.[9] The South Nyanza Local Native Council (LNC) which was established in 1925 provided an important local government institution in which the chiefs were members. Chiefs were expected to use it for mobilizing resources for the promotion of cash crops through tax revenue. These remained insufficient as its powers were limited and a disproportionate amount collected was used for the development of European settler agriculture.

With the DofA and the district administration now reorganized, cotton-growing was intensified and extended to new areas. The colonial state relied primarily on chiefs and Local Native Councils (LNCs) to buy and distribute seeds, provide land for seed trials and demonstration farms, and also to spread the necessary propaganda. At a meeting in April 1935, Provincial Commissioners (PCs) held the opinion that production had not adequately increased in African areas because of the apathy of the producers themselves. Consequently, they resolved to increase the power of chiefs under section 8 of the Native Authority Ordinance.[10] This piece of legislation empowered chiefs to use force to compel people to grow cotton and root crops. However, more often AO, AAIs, and chiefs preferred to use propaganda as they toured the district to popularize cotton-growing. Armed with both these means, the administration used trial and error methods to push cotton in inland locations like Kabondo, Mumbo, Kanyidoto, and Suna parts of which later turned out to be unsuitable for cotton production. Apart from lack of adequate knowledge about the soil conditions of all parts of the district, the AO was impelled to borrow rain gauges from Christian Mission stations and dispensaries at the SK administrative headquarters in Kisii to get correct readings of rainfall variations to ensure that cotton was grown in suitable areas.[11]

The extension of cotton-growing areas also required the improvement of cotton-growing methods to increase the quantity and improve the quality of cotton. During the 1931/32 season, standardized spacing sticks were distributed to improve the spacing of cotton and other crops. AOs and AAIs also established correct planting periods. These were between June and September, although June plantings were found to give the best cotton yields. Surprisingly, in line with indigenous Luo agricultural practice of intercropping, which was earlier disparaged, the AI and AAIs now encouraged cotton growers to plant leguminous crops like groundnuts and sesame between lines of cotton crops.

In addition, the AO and AAIs introduced the block or group farming system. By this system, large farms measuring from 50 acres were established by roadsides. Individuals were then allocated a quarter of an acre each on which to plant cotton. The method's advantages included ease of supervision and the teaching of appropriate methods of cotton cultivation by AAIs. Second, it led to all cotton being planted at the same time thereby facilitating rapid marketing. Third, individual *shambas* in the block were uniformly clean and well cultivated. Furthermore, Gaddum reported that the block system made it easy to estimate various acreages under the different *Milangos*, also known as headmen, who assisted chiefs, and thereby encouraged competition. The method was also intended to "encourage the apathetic" workers who saw the results attained by their more energetic neighbors.[12] But the block system had its disadvantages as well. DC KL Hunter reasoned in 1935: "A man at present sand witched in the middle is limited in his area by that fact alone."[13] Hunter planned to move away from it. But more important, many cultivators did not like the block system because it was alien to indigenous Luo land tenure. According to the indigenous Luo tenure system, each family had its own land which was distributed to each household under the management of each wife. Indigenous Luo land ownership was only communal at the lineage level. At the family level, it was individualistic. Hunter was therefore right to argue that the block system stifled the individual's initiative and effort in cotton-growing. His attention was also focused on transport.

In 1932, the DC and the LNC requested the Public Works Department to take over the upkeep of the Kisii-Kendu Road in order to make it an all-weather road. Hitherto, the road was maintained by a local labor force including those convicted of nonpayment of tax. During the year, the LNC also planned to allocate some grant for the maintenance of the Homa Bay-Marinde-Kamagambo Road, including the extension to Sare, into a motorable condition. By this time, very few lorries plied the roads. Oxcarts and head porterage continued to be the means of transport. It is rather ironical that W.O. Sunman, the AO Kisumu, discouraged the use of lorries in transporting cotton.[14] His reasons were that their use would be an obstacle to cotton inspection at cotton-buying centers and the possibility of the lorry owner inducing the cotton grower to sell cotton to him at a lower price, leading to the producer's exploitation. Instead, he recommended the continued use of the conventional methods: head porterage, oxcarts, and draught animals, including oxen and donkeys. Sunman suggested the building of more buying posts to reduce the distance the cultivators traveled and thus obviate the use of lorries. The condition of lake transport also required improvement. The pier at Kendu Bay, the major port, including the causeway approach to it, was quite bad, particularly during the rainy season during which the pier was underwater. The conditions at Karungu, Mohuru, and Homa bays were even worse. The improvement of these port facilities as was the case with roads was undertaken though not satisfactorily because of lack of revenue.

Funds collected from the Hut and Poll Tax and the LNC rates were very insufficient. Between the late 1920s and 1935, the Hut and Poll Tax was 12 Shillings. With 93,271 taxable males according to the Census Register, the total tax collected in the district was 57,415 pounds. A very negligible fraction of this amount was retained for use in the district. This did not escape the attention of the members of the KNCC. In September 1932, in a Memorandum to the Kenya Land Commission they expressed their concern as follows:

> We are not encouraged to grow cotton because this crop if becoming popular would stop the supply of labor for settled areas. We are not allowed to grow coffee because the settlers would not like us to get rich, for fear of stopping the labor supply. One of the reasons advanced against us is that we do not know how to grow coffee and to find out various diseases. We do not know and did not know many things yet by mere copying we have made cotton industry successful in Uganda.[15]

The tone of this submission illustrates that an incipient petty-bourgeois class had already emerged among the Luo in Nyanza Province. This class was aware of the dynamics of Kenya's political economy and its effects on commodity production and trade as demonstrated by minutes of their meetings and letters to the PC in connection with cotton buying and ginning. Their concerns were sometimes shared by the local British administrators.

For example, in his own submission to the Kenya Land Commission later the same month, DC C.E.V. Buxton stated that SK had missed a fair chance of development because of lack of funds, absence of economic objective, and lack of roads.[16] In 1933, the unfair disbursement of funds led the Joint Luo-Abasuba and Kisii-Abakuria LNC, possibly with Buxton's advice, to petition Sir Phillips Cunliffe Lister, the secretary of state for the colonies as follows: "We cannot at present afford to pay a higher LNC rate, that of Shs, 2/= (including tax) and we lack services which we believe to be necessary for the development of the South Kavirondo Reserve."[17] As the largest proportion of the Hut and Poll Tax was used to support development in the European sector of the economy, and in view of the fact that the Native Betterment Fund, which was proposed in 1934 failed to be implemented due to settler opposition, the only other source of revenue for the development of the district was through the cotton tax.

This tax was levied in accordance with the Cotton Rules of 1923. In 1932, 1 cent tax was levied per 1 pound of seed cotton. As this proved insufficient, the tax was increased to 100 shillings payable at every buying post. The rationale behind the cotton tax was that it was used to pay AAIs for their work in the promotion of cotton-growing. Although this tax was ostensibly paid by the ginners, in reality, the burden fell on growers who were paid less than the amount of the tax. The Provincial Commissioner (PC) Nyanza regretfully noted that unlike taxes imposed on European produced coffee, pyrethrum, sisal, and butter, which was used to develop these very industries, cotton "is the only crop on which tax is collected without some corresponding benefit to growers."[18] Although Provincial and District administrators sympathized with the cotton growers' plight and even pleaded their case, the government refused to abolish the cotton tax. The tax was only reduced in SK in 1933 and 1934, when production was very low due to poor prices and bad weather.[19]

Cotton prices fluctuated a lot but remained low throughout the depression. On March 12, 1928, about one year before the depression cotton-buying companies, Small and Company, Foulkes and Company, and the British Cotton Growers Association were each reported to have paid an average of 18, 17, and 20 cents, respectively, for 1 pound of second grade cotton at their various buying centers.[20] In January 1930, cotton prices in NK fell to 12 cents per pound at the ginneries and 13 cents per pound at buying posts. By 1932, the prices fell further to 8 cents at Asembo Bay in CK. When cotton-buying commenced at Kendu Bay in mid-October the same year, the price was 10 pence per pound and even lower at other buying posts distances away.[21] Prices in SK were 1 cent less than in areas close to Sio port where cotton was ginned at the time, because of transport charges there by lake. When buying commenced in October 1933, prices at cotton-buying stores were between 6/50 and 7 shillings. This reduction resulted in many growers' reluctance to pick their cotton. Some reared their livestock in the cotton fields.[22] By 1934, the situation had not improved much. In the district, prices commenced at 6/50 shillings and rose to 9/50 per 100 pounds. Once again most producers considered these prices too low to make them bother with picking and taking cotton to the buying centers. What lowered prices even further was that 1/50 below ginning price was deducted for every 100 pounds of cotton sold.[23] In February 1934, the DC Kisii pointed out that Small and Company did not pay cotton producers the specified price of 8 cents per pound.[24] Other licensed buyers did the same. This was an indication that cotton marketing continued to face problems in spite of the Cotton Rules of 1923. Cotton-buying centers were far between. This forced cotton producers to travel very long distances. Further, as happened before the depression, Africans were excluded from cotton purchasing.

Although more buying centers were established by 1934 in new areas like Homa Bay, Rangwe, Nyangweso, and Oyugis, the Luo in SK were dismayed by the fact that cotton-buying licenses were granted only to Asians. These included the Nyanza Commercial Company and Small and Company. This concern was particularly expressed by members of the KNCC.[25] Between 1932 and 1934, they held meeting with the PC, S.H. Fazan to whom they also sent a memorandum. In one of their letters to Fazan, they graphically stated that the government's discrimination against them was "a piece of casting sand in the eyes of Kavirondo Traders." In another meeting they requested the government to allow the LNCs to collect funds for the erection of ginneries run by African traders. Their alternative suggestion was that Indian ginnery owners should employ African agents to buy cotton from producers.

The issues raised by the members of the KNCC demonstrate that as a petty-bourgeois class, they had accommodated commodity production and trade. At the same time, they were critical of some of its aspects that did not work for them and for the rest of the peasant producers. They were agitating for greater and equal participation in all aspects of cotton production. Nyanza PC Fazan refused to support their demands, in particular, their suggestion that Indian ginners employ Africans as cotton-buying agents. To this, Fazan stated that "the extent to which ginners wish to employ natives at their buying posts is a matter for the ginners themselves and I do not propose to interfere with their discretion in the matter."[26] He believed that Africans were not yet ready to engage in cotton trade because they were not yet "efficient and trustworthy." On his part, Hunter, the SK DC, argued that African leaders' demand that they be allowed to participate in cotton trade, being "a veiled assertion that they were not obtaining a fair return to their products" required careful thought by the government.[27] As will be seen below, the colonial state would simply revise the Kenya Cotton Rules of 1923 to exercise even greater control over cotton production and marketing and thereby stifle the emergence of capitalists in Luo land.

Many Luo peasants in cotton-growing areas of SK had come to terms with the fact that cotton was inextricably twinned with the production of the other crops. The depression and the persistent drought, locust invasions, low prices, taxation, and increasing demand for imported goods between 1929 and 1934 had simply intensified their capture into the commodity, and inescapably, cotton production. During this period, recourse to the Mumboist millenarian protests had been weakened by the detention and deportation of its leaders in the early 1920s. However, the administration remained wary of the recrudescence of the protest movement well into the 1930s.

Nonetheless in the end AOs' and chiefs' initiatives led to an increase in acreage under cotton production and the quantities of cotton produced. In 1934, alone the system had led to the increase in the area under cotton in SK to 5,500 acres. It, therefore, led to a huge increase in the quantity of cotton produced. For instance, during the 1935/36 season 2,708,000 pounds of seed cotton was produced. During the next cotton season the amount increased to 5,000,000, slightly over 100 percent.[28] This made SK attractive to Indian and European entrepreneurs for the establishment of cotton ginneries. In this, they were encouraged by the local colonial administrators, particularly the DC Hunter.

Before the establishment of ginneries at Kendu Bay and Homa Bay in 1934 and 1937, respectively, as discussed in detail below, all the cotton that was bought from these ports were transported across the Nyanza Gulf to the gins that had been established earlier in CK and NK.[29] The British Cotton Ginnery Association has established the first ginnery in Asembo in CK before the First World War but closed it after only two years because of insufficient cotton supplies. Later, in 1923, Captain Gordon Small established a second ginnery at Samia in NK, operated it briefly and sold it to Indian brothers who decided to retain the name of the company. Two years later in 1925, Folkes and Company who were already operating a ginnery in Kampala were licensed to operate a ginnery at Nambale, also in NK. The same year the British Cotton-Growing Association secured a lease to operate a ginnery at Malakisi in NK. After five years, they sold it to Messrs. Valtaldas and Company of Jinja, Uganda. It appears, therefore, that Indian entrepreneurs possessed better skills in the operation of ginneries. Apparently, they acquired the skills from long experiences with cotton in Uganda.[30] But most importantly, the absence of ginneries in SK was thought by the PC and the DC to be an obstacle to cotton production in the district.

Due to the additional cost of transporting cotton to Samia, the PC Nyanza proposed in February 1932 that a ginnery be established at Kendu Bay. He rightly believed that by minimizing transport costs, which were usually borne by producers, this would improve their earnings.[31] But because of insufficient cotton in SK at the moment the idea was shelved. The DC and AO SK revived the idea two years later in March 1934.[32] Although H. Wolfe the Deputy Director of Agriculture, Plant Industry (DDofAPI), was in support, the PC opposed it. He argued that the establishment of a ginnery in the district was not justified at the time in view of the inadequate quantity of cotton. He, further, argued that, in spite of efforts to encourage cotton production, the total output in SK for 1934 was only 65,225 pounds and that this was still short of 1,000.000 estimated earlier by the DC.[33] It was only after the DC SK and his AO had provided further supportive statistical proof that to justify the establishment of a ginnery that the Director of Agriculture ((DofA) gave his approval. He immediately informed the colonial secretary that a ginnery should be established at Kendu Bay for the following reasons.[34] First, a substantial area in SK was suitable for cotton-growing. Second, the total population of the cotton-growing area, which was approximately 75,000, was high enough to produce sufficient amounts of cotton. Third, that a ginnery in the area would minimize transport costs. The fourth reason was that Messrs. Small and Company who purchased cotton in the area had already surpassed the required output of 2000 bales of ginned cotton. Finally, and quite importantly, Wolfe, the DDofAPI), in a meeting with DC and AO SK and the local chiefs, discussed the matter and resolved that indeed a ginnery at Kendu Bay would boost cotton production in the district. Thereafter, on April 24, 1934, the DC took the initiative and granted Messrs. Small and Company the permission to establish the ginnery on conditions which were verbally communicated to them at a meeting in his office.[35] This led to a lot of acrimonies as the DC appeared not to have observed the procedure that such grants were the responsibility of the DofA.[36] In the end, and to save the government's face, the lease was approved on the following special conditions: First, any other company would not be issued with a permit to erect a ginnery within the locations that of Karachuonyo, Mumbo, and Kabondo in which Small and Company had monopoly cotton-buying rights; second, the minimum price for the buying of seed cotton would be fixed by the DofA, to which price the Company had to adhere; and finally, the Company was to pay for five African cotton instructors a sum of 35 Shillings each for six months each year.[37] It is of note that whereas the first condition was meant to be an incentive for the Company, the last condition illustrates the government's reliance on the Company to finance the African Instructors under the charge of the European AOs responsible for the promotion of cotton-growing in the district. Overall it also shows hitches in the bureaucracy delayed the colonial government's own policies and projects. An inspection visit by the representative of the London-based Empire Cotton-Growing Corporation (ECGC) during the year revealed other teething problems countrywide generally and in Southern Nyanza.

One month before Small and Company was granted the lease, Governor Sir Joseph Byrne had requested the ECGC for assistance in the development of the cotton industry in the colony.[38] The assistance touched on specific ways of increasing cotton production. The Governor requested for funds to hire the necessary personnel for the purpose: 3 AOs, 3 Assistant AOs, and 60 African Agricultural Instructors. The request was considered but rejected in the end. Instead, the Corporation sent its agent S. Milligan to visit the country in mid-1935.[39] His object was to analyze the country's cotton potential. Milligan's major recommendation after touring cotton-growing areas in the country was that the development of successful cotton-growing required thorough research in all its aspects, which in turn required facilities.

With regard to SK, which was then lumped together into one area with CK, Milligan reported that the area was still in probation but had better prospects for cotton-growing in localities closer to the lake; that of those further away in the higher altitudes were not so promising.[40] He further noted that the climate in the entire area was not ideal for cotton-growing due to the occurrence of distinct dry periods, adding rather optimistically that "this may not be a disadvantage as cotton is none the worse for such, provided the weather is sunny and overcast."[41] In addition, he noted that planting days have yet to be determined but would vary for different locations. He was agreeable to the use of the Block system and suggested that the SP seed variety instead of the existing N.17 should be used as it was the most suitable for the area.[42] He strongly recommended that the appointment of two additional AOs for SK and CK was essential to promote cotton production in the two districts.

As a consequence of Milligan's recommendations, the Kenya government sent an AO to the ECGC's station at Baberton in South Africa for nine months to study cotton selection and experimental methods and lint examination techniques.[43] Samples of cotton from different areas in the country were also sent to the Imperial Institute for examination. Reports about their quality were encouraging. Cotton variety, spacing, and inter-planting trials for SK and CK were increasingly being carried out at the Agricultural Experimental Farm at Kibos. Finally, the visit and recommendations influenced the Kenya Government to revise the Kenya Cotton Rules of 1923 and to promulgate The Kenya Cotton Ordinance and Rules of 1937, which established even greater control on all aspects of the cotton industry.[44]

The significance of Milligan's visit and recommendations were first that it demonstrated the Kenya government's determination to stimulate cotton production by Africans to raise revenue during the depression. The ECGC's refusal to finance the scheme implied that the cost of cotton production in British colonies, including Kenya, had to be borne by the colonies themselves. Milligan's recommendations further show that the ECGC was most concerned about the quantity and the quality of cotton exports from Kenya than anything else. The outcome of all this was that, in the interest of its own self-sufficiency during the lean depression years, the colonial state in Kenya, which was always financially hamstrung, relied on its own local administrators and financial resources from taxes in the cotton-growing areas to do all they could to push the crop. For this reason, Milligan's recommendations were not adequately implemented. Hence the rather uncertain circumstances under which the ginnery at Kendu Bay was licensed.

The granting of the Ginnery lease at Kendu Bay had an immediate impact on the quantities of cotton produced and sold in the district. As shown in table 10.1, seed cotton production in Southern Nyanza increased from 951,569 pounds in 1934 to 2,708,337 pounds in 1936 and 4,425,514 pounds in1937. Between 1936 and 1937, cotton production increased by 53 percent. Correspondingly cotton sale during the 1934–1935 season alone was 951 pounds, which surpassed CK's 525,605 pounds.[45] This phenomenal increase in sales led DC Hunter to report that in 1935 Karachuonyo people were enthusiastic about cotton production. He cited the example of one man who received a total of 500 Shillings for his cotton sales alone that year.[46]

**Table 10.1  Seed Cotton Sales in Pounds from Buying Posts in Southern Nyanza, 1935–1937**

| | Year | | |
|---|---|---|---|
| Store | 1935 | 1936 | 1937 |
| Kendu Ginnery | 522,029 | 1,294,228 | 1,492,306 |
| Miriu | | | 249,217 |
| Kabondo | | 25,027 | 64,100 |
| Doho | | | 133,064 |
| Oyugis | 12,286 | 51,002 | 73,563 |
| Rangwe | 22,946 | 96,923 | 152,788 |
| Kochia | 144,899 | 350,542 | 602,200 |
| Homa Point | | | 159,045 |
| Homa Bay | 246,143 | 474,627 | 823,475 |
| Mirogi | | 43,442 | 7,489 |
| Kabwai | | 99,633 | 63,922 |
| Kasigunga | | | 60,000 |
| Rusinga | | 93,307 | 107,445 |
| Mfangano | | | 32,768 |
| Kaksingri | | | 109,284 |
| Karungu | 3,266 | 83,376 | 98,438 |
| Gwassi | | 22,763 | 36,136 |
| Muhuru | | 73,467 | 71,174 |
| Suna | | | 89,100 |
| **Total** | **951,569** | **2,708,337** | **4,425,514** |

*Source*: Nyanza Province Daily Correspondence Reports, Cotton: Monthly Returns, 1930-1963.

There were a few more like him whose efforts were not acknowledged in other cotton-growing locations like Kanyada and Kochia. Chief Obonyo of the latter Location had used proceeds from his cotton farm to build a brick house and purchase a car. Hunter, the DC, attributed this increase in peasant farmers' incomes to the fact that prices had risen slightly since the opening of the 1935/36 season from 12 Shillings to 14/50 for grade A cotton at Kendu Ginnery and 1/50 and 3/50 at stores with grade B cotton ranging from 4/- to 6/-. Much as price increases were an incentive to more peasants to grow cotton, other factors were also responsible. One was the increase in the number of cotton-buying centers from 6 in 1935 to 12 in 1936 and 19 in 1937. The other reason was peasant farmers' attempts to cope with the reproduction squeeze already referred to above.

In spite of the increase in cotton production and sales in the district and the dominant position Small and Company occupied, all was not well with the cotton business as far as the company was concerned. The managers soon realized that the ginnery was operating below its capacity: only two to three months in a year and then lying idle for nine months when there was no cotton to be ginned. Therefore, in May 1937, they requested to be allowed to install a modern machine which would produce oil from locally grown groundnuts and a maize mill within the precincts of the ginnery. This request would be delayed by the provision in the Kenya Cotton Rules of 1923 which prohibited the use of the ginnery lease for any other purpose.[47] After much pleading, the DofA begrudgingly conceded to this request. Meanwhile, the overall increase in cotton production and sales convinced the administration about the need for a second ginnery at Homa Bay, hardly 20 miles from Kendu Bay.

Because of the controversy previously experienced with the Kendu Ginnery lease, the PC and DC SK were both determined to pay more attention to the rules and procedure regulating granting ginnery leases. As with the ginnery in Kendu Bay already detailed above, the major issues for consideration included the following: first, whether the actual and potential cotton production and sales really justified a second ginnery, and second, the best criteria to be used in vetting the applicants to determine their suitability.

As for the first consideration, Sunman, the AO at Kisumu, advised that the decision to establish a second ginnery in SK should be premised on calculations that carefully took into account the 1935/36 and 1936/37 cotton production figures.[48] This, he believed, would ensure that the establishment of a second ginnery at Homa Bay did not lead the Kendu ginnery output to fall below 2000 bales. Although he was convinced that the six ginneries already established in the whole of Nyanza Province operated economically, he advised that "the number of ginneries in Nyanza should be kept to a minimum lest we fall to a certain degree into the over-ginned state of Uganda."[49] In a quick response, the AO Kisii submitted the required figures of actual and estimated cotton productions in Homa Bay for the two seasons.[50] These were 474,627 pounds in 1935/36 for Homa Bay alone and 2,708,337 pounds for the whole district. The estimates for the 1936/37 season were 800,000 pounds for Homa Bay and 5000,000 for the whole district. The estimates for the 1937/38 were 1000,000 pounds for Homa Bay and 7,500,000 for the whole district. The AO Kisii further estimated that seed cotton produced totaled 6,000 bales which would be divided into two halves between the two ginneries. But as argued below, though used to convince the DofA to license the lease for the Homa Bay Ginnery, the estimates were quite overoptimistic as they did not take into account certain realities which unfolded almost immediately.

When the tender for the ginnery was advertised in late 1937, a total of 39 companies applied, out of which, 19 and 16 were already based in Kenya and Uganda, respectively.[51] Most of these applicants had in 1936 applied for a ginnery at Rangala in CK.[52] The list reflected the membership of traders engaged in the processing and sale of agricultural product in Kenya and Uganda and demonstrates its domination by Indians. It further illustrates the fact that British firms at the time mostly dominated the export and import sectors of the colonial economy, particularly commerce and therefore explains why out of the total applicants very few showed interest in cotton ginning. These included Smith Mackenzie of Mombasa, Gethin, and Dawson of Kisii, A. Bauman and Company of Nairobi, Liverpool of Uganda, John L Riddoch of Kisumu and the Settler-owned Kenya Farmers Association based in Nakuru. It is interesting to note that Small and Company who had been granted the lease at Kendu Bay applied once again for consideration for another lease at Homa Bay. It is also interesting to note that only one Luo from SK applied. This was Daniel Ojijo, former assistant chief of Karachuonyo and a member of the Kavirondo Native Chambers of Commerce. He was most likely fronting for other members and traders like John Paul Olola who was already operating a ghee manufacturing firm in Kadem and Aduwo Nyandoje who owned businesses and property in Kisumu. Olola and Nyandoje were, respectively, secretary and chairman of the Kavirondo Native Chambers of Commerce. Their single application implied that the commercial consciousness among the Luo petty bourgeoisie in the district was only nascent at the time. The reason for this was that the colonial state limited African participation in the economy to producing specific commodities like cotton which they then sold to Indian middlemen and European firms. The state therefore deliberately stifled the emergence of African capitalism.[53]

The big numbers of companies that applied for the ginnery license in Homa Bay indicated their optimism and high hopes regarding the prospects of the development of the cotton industry in SK in spite of their commercial engagements elsewhere in East Africa. John L. Riddoch was finally awarded the lease once more, amid allegations of favoritism by the Indian community. But the lease particularly demonstrated Riddoch's own optimism about the prospects of cotton in the district. The fact that Riddoch, who operated the businesses in Nyanza Province, considered cotton ginning as a means to build his business empire further implied that he estimated the prospects in the industry to be quite bright. Like the local administrators, however, he failed to accurately read the underlying realities that would face cotton production in the district and the rest of Kenya. These included the labor, financial, infrastructural, and marketing strictures which faced the cotton industry in the country and in SK, in particular. The situation was exacerbated by the outbreak of the Second World War in 1939.

During its first year of operation the Homa Bay Ginnery bought a total of 1,144,119 pounds of seed cotton which amounted to 37.5 percent of all the cotton in SK,[54] below what had been earlier estimated. Being a shrewd businessman with long experience in the Province Riddoch expected that worse conditions were in the offing. In June 1938, he already planned to form the Homa Bay Ginners Limited to take over his ginnery interests although he would still maintain control at the Company by holding more than 59 percent of the shares. He would run the Company in association with British citizens from Uganda who possessed a lot of experience in cotton ginning and selling.

In January 1939, Riddoch wrote a lengthy letter to the Director of Agriculture in which he attributed the shortfall to adverse weather conditions, bad cultivation, and careless picking by the growers and lack of supervision by AO because of frequent staff changes.[55] In a tone that pointed an accusing finger at the government, he stated that having committed himself to a large capital expenditure at the invitation of the government it was its duty to supervise the cultivation of cotton in the area allotted to the Ginnery in the most efficient manner. He was keen to add that apart from the purchase of a top range ginnery equipment, he also contributed by paying the cotton tax at all buying stations, toward the payment of African Agricultural Instructors as required by the 1937 Cotton Rules. The outbreak of the Second World War in 1939 worsened the situation for all the stakeholders in the cotton industry: the peasant producers, and owners of the Ginneries, the colonial state and Britain.

The War altered the fortunes of cotton-growing in the district and the other cotton-growing areas in the rest of the country. The British and Kenya colonial states were forced to use their scarce resources for, and to put the greatest emphasis on, the production and requisition of cereals and livestock to feed warfront soldiers and the recruitment of young men to assist in the fight against the enemies of the British Empire: the Germans, the Italians, and the Japanese. These developments dimmed the earlier optimism and overzealousness of the local administration in cotton production.

This chapter has argued that much optimism about the prospects of cotton production in Southern Nyanza efforts to achieve the plan faced many crises and contradictions which colonial authorities in Kenya never successfully resolved. The difficulties included the identification of areas suitable for cotton production; the supervision and inspection of the entire process of cotton production; its purchase from peasant producers who had to transport it to the buying stations; its ginning and marketing overseas, and the necessary, though controversial, establishment of the Kendu Bay and the Homa Bay ginneries in SK. As representatives of the colonial state, the DofA and the Department's officials at the Provincial and District levels, on the one hand, and the PCs and his district officials, on the other hand, were not united as agents of the colonial state regarding the promotion of cotton-growing in the area. They differed in matters pertaining to the details of policy. The colonial state in Kenya and the capitalist interests in Britain as represented, for example, by the ECGC, did not always get along, as expected. This is demonstrated by the Corporation's refusal to approve Governor Byrne's request for financial and human resource assistance to facilitate the development of cotton-growing, in Kenya. During the depression and particularly after 1934, the initiatives of both the peasant cotton producers and the administration led to the increase in cotton production, which in turn raised too much enthusiasm and optimism to invest in cotton production. This increase only lasted up to 1938. The outbreak of the Second World War in 1939 led to cotton's neglect. Production failed to meet the required quantity, quality, and export value as anticipated. As for the local inhabitants, their adage *"pamba oluoro chilo,"* that cotton abhors dirt, became a metaphor for the crises that faced cotton production. Unfortunately, the post-War and postcolonial governments do not appear to have learned from the experiences before 1939.[56]

## NOTES

1. Shortly before the imposition of colonial rule in 1903, the area was referred to as Ugaya District. Then in 1909, two years after the administration headquarter was transferred from Karungu to Getembe, Kisii and the Luo were incorporated within South Kavirondo District. In 1948, the name of the district was changed to South Nyanza District by which it was known until 1961 when the Gusii had their district, Kisii District. Today the Luo of Southern Nyanza inhabit Homa Bay and Migori counties, following the adoption of the 2010 Constitution which provided for devolved government. They are still part of the larger Nyanza region. For the sake of convenience, South Kavirondo (SK) is used here throughout.

2. See B. Jewsiewicki, "The Great Depression and the Making of the Colonial Economic System in the Belgian Congo," *African Economic History* 4 (1977): 153–62.

3. Roger Van Zwanenberg, "Kenya's Primitive Colonial Capitalism: The Economic Weakness of Kenya's Settlers up to 1940," *Canadian Journal of African Studies* 9 (1975): 277–92; Roger Van Zwanenberg, "The Development of Peasant Commodity Production in Kenya, 1920-1940," *Economic History Review* 27 (1974): 442–54; and also, Richard D. Wolff, *The Economics of Colonialism: Britain and Kenya 1870-1930* (Nairobi: Transafrica Publishers, 1974).

4. This aspect of Kenya's economy is discussed by Robert Maxon, "The Years of Revolutionary Advance, 1920-1929," W.R. Ochieng' (ed.), *A Modern History of Kenya 1895-1980* (Nairobi: Evans Brothers, 1989), 71–111.

5. Henry Bernstein, "African Peasantries: A Theoretical Framework," *The Journal of Peasant Studies* 6 (1979).

6. John Lonsdale, "The Depression and the Second World War in the Transformation of Kenya," in David Killingray and Richard Rathbone (eds.), *Africa and the Second World War* (New York: St. Martins, 1986), 96–99.

7. Acting Director of Agriculture to AOs Bukura, Kakamega, Kisii 16th March 1931, Kenya National Archives (KNA): KNA/AGR/1/179.

8. District of South Kavirondo, Political Record Book, Character of Chiefs. KNA: DC/SK/3/1.

9. Ibid.

10. Minutes of PCs Meeting, April 9, 1935, KNA: Central Province Daily Correspondence and Reports (CPDCR).

11. Colony and Protectorate of Kenya, *Department of Agriculture Annual Report*, 1934. Nairobi: Government Printer, 1934 and Major B. W. Bond, District Officer Kisii, "Development Scheme: South Kavirondo." Memorandum to the Kenya Land Commission, 11th May 1932. Colony and Protectorate of Kenya, *Kenya Land Commission, Evidence,* Volume 111. Nairobi: Government Printer, 1934.

12. Gaddum, AO SK to Deputy Director of Agriculture (Plant and Industry), 7th November 1933, containing progress report about his visit to Kanyada, Kochia and Karachuonyo from October 25th to 30th. KNA: DC/KSI/7/1.

13. South Kavirondo Annual Report (SKAR) 1935. KNA: DC/KSI/1/4.

14. Sunman to Deputy Director of Agriculture, 26th March 1932, Daily Correspondence and Reports, 1930–36, KNA: PC/NZA/2/1009.

15. Memorandum by the Native Chamber of Commerce before the Kenya Land Commission on the 6the September 1932, Page 2146. Colony and Protectorate of Kenya, *The Kenya Land Commission, Evidence*, Volume 111. Nairobi: Government Printer, 1934.

16. Evidence by Major C. E. V. Buxton, DC SK. Before the Commission at Kisii, Kenya Land Commission, Colony and Protectorate of Kenya, *The Kenya Land Commission, Evidence*, Volume 111 (Nairobi: Government Printer, 1934), 2346.

17. Memorandum to Sir Phillips Cunliiffe Lister, Secretary of State for the Colonies, 7th December 1933, Political Record Book, 1930–1940, KNA: DC/KSI/3/5.

18. PC Nyanza to Colonial Secretary, 31st May 1937. Ibid.

19. PC Nyanza to Colonial Secretary, 10th October 1934. Ibid.

20. Reports of price changes cited here are as recorded in the Nyanza Province Annual Reports, NKARs, CKARs, and SKARs, and also NK Monthly Agriculture Reports for the depression years, KNA: AGR/KSM/1/822.

21. SKAR. 1932, KNA: DC/KSI/1/4.

22. Colony and Protectorate of Kenya, *Department of Agriculture Annual Report, 1933* (Nairobi: Government Printer, 1933), 136.

23. AO to Deputy Director of Agriculture 23rd March 1934, KNA: PC/NZA/2/12/58.

24. DC Kisii to Small and Co, 21st February 1934: Cotton Monthly Ginning Returns: KNA, Nyanza Daily Correspondence and Reports, 1930–63.

25. These are contained in the Meeting of the Executive Committee of the Native Chamber of Commerce, 16th November 1932, Minutes of the General Meeting of the Kavirondo Chamber of Commerce, 10th August 1934 and 31st December 1935, and Letter from the chairman, Kavirondo Native Chamber of Commerce to Acting PC, Fazan, 18th June 1936. KNA: PC/NZA3/20/79.

26. PC to Chairman, Native Chamber of Commerce, KNA: PC/NZA3/20/79.

27. SKAR. KNA: DC/KSI/1938, KNA: DC/KSI/1/4.

28. SKAR. 1936. KNA: DC/KSI/1/4.

29. This and the following information about the establishment of ginneries in earlier years are contained in Hugh Fearn, *An African Economy: A Study of the Economic Development of Nyanza Province of Kenya, 1903-1953* (London: Oxford University Press, 1961).

30. Robert G Gregory, *South East Asians in East Africa: An Economic and Social History, 1890-1980* (Boulder: Westview Press, 1993).

31. PC H.R. Montgomery to Director of Agriculture, 29th February 1932, Daily Correspondence and Reports, 1930-1963, Cotton, Kendu Ginnery. KNA: AGR/NZA.

32. DC SK to PC Nyanza, 19th March 1934, Ibid.

33. PC Nyanza to Director of Agriculture, 7th March 1934, Ibid.

34. Director of Agriculture to the Colonial Secretary, March 1934, Ibid.

35. DC SK to Messrs. Small and Co., 24th April 1934 and DC to Messr. Small and Co. 7th May 1934. Ibid.

36. Director of Agriculture to PC Nyanza 19th July 1934. Ibid.

37. Conditions for the Lease of the Kendu Ginnery, Kendu Ginnery Lease, KNA: PC/NZA/2/12/58.

38. This request and the discussions that accompanied it are contained in a British Colonial Office file titled, Stimulation of Native Exports, CO533/410.

39. For details about S. Milligan's visit see Colony and Protectorate of Kenya, S. Miligan, *Inspection Note on the Kenya Cotton Crop in November and December, 1939* (Nairobi: Government Printer, 1936).

40. Ibid., 12–13.

41. Ibid., 13.

42. Ibid., 15.

43. Colony and Protectorate of Kenya, *Department of Agriculture Annual Report* (Nairobi: Government Printer, 1933), 193.

44. Colony and Protectorate of Kenya, *Proclamation, Rules and Regulations: The Kenya Cotton Ordinance and Rules, 1937* (Nairobi: Government Printer, 1938).

45. AO Kisii to Deputy Director of Agriculture PI 13th January 1935, KNA: PC/NZA/2/12/58.

46. SKAR. 1935. KNA: DC/KSI/1/4.

47. Small and Company to Director of Agriculture, Kendu Ginnery Lease, KNA: PC/NZA/2/12/58.

48. AO SK to AO Nyanza 3rd March 1936, Ibid.

49. AO Nyanza Province to Deputy Director of Agriculture Plant and Industry,16th June 1936, Ibid.

50. AO Kisii to AO Nyanza, 11th January 1937, Ibid.

51. For the full list and names of the Companies that applied see Homa Bay Ginnery, KNA: PC/NZA/2/12/65.

52. S. H. Fazan, Applications for a Ginnery at Rangala, Agriculture, Cotton Proposed Ginnery, Daily Correspondence Reports, 1930-1963. KNA: PC/NZA/2/1009.

53. Details about the emergence of rural African capitalists among the Gusii who are Luo neighbors in Southern Nyanza is discussed in the following works: Robert M Maxon, "Stifling Capitalism in Rural Africa: The Gusii Coffee Industry in Kenya, 1932-1949," *Journal of Third World Studies* 11 (1994): 317–50. For its discussion in the whole of Kenya, see Gavin Kitching, *Class and Economic Change in Kenya: The making of an African Petite-Bourgeoisie* (New Haven and London: Yale University Press, 1980).

54. W Lyne Watt Agriculture Officer to PC, 13the June 1938 and PC Tomkinson to Colonial Secretary, Nairobi, 4th July 1938, KNA AGR/2/1.

55. John L Riddoch to Director of Agriculture 10th January 1939. Homa Bay Ginnery, PC/NZA/2/12/65.

56. Independent Kenya's attempts to revive cotton in Central Province have been critically assessed by Alfonso Peter Castro, "Sustainable agriculture or sustained error? The Case of Cotton in Kirinyaga, Kenya," *World Development* 26, no. 9 (1998): 1719–1731.

# BIBLIOGRAPHY

Berman, Bruce. *Control and Crisis in Colonial Kenya: The Dialectics of Domination.* London: James Curry, 1990.

Berman, Bruce and John Lonsdale, "Coping with the Contradictions: The Development of the Colonial State I Kenya, 1895-1914." *Journal of African History* 20 (1979): 487–505.

Bernstein Henry. "African Peasantries: A Theoretical Framework." *Journal of Peasant Studies* 6 (1979).

Castro, Alfonso Peter. "Sustainable Agriculture or Sustained Error? The Case of Cotton in Kirinyaga, Kenya." *World Development* 26, no. 9 (1998): 1719–31.

Character of Chiefs, South Kavirondo Political Record Book. KNA: DC/KSI/1/4.

Colony and Protectorate of Kenya. *Department of Agriculture Annual Report.* Nairobi: Government Printer, 1933.

———. *Kenya Land Commission, Evidence*, Volume 111. Nairobi: Government Printer, 1934.

———. *Proclamation Rules and Regulations: The Kenya Cotton Ordinance and Rules, 1937.* Nairobi: Government Printer, 1937.

Cotton. Monthly Agricultural Reports. Kenya National Archives (KNA) KNA: AGR/KSM/1/822.

Homa Bay Ginnery. KNA: PC/NZA/2/12/65.

Fearn, Hugh. *An African Economy: A Study of the Economic Development of Nyanza Province of Kenya, 1903-1953.* London: Oxford University Press, 1961.

Gregory, Robert G. *South East Asians in East Africa: An Economic and Social History, 1890-1980,* Boulder: Westview Press, 1993.

Jewsiewicki, B. "The Great Depression and the Making of the Colonial Economic System in the Belgian Congo." *African Economic History* 4 (1977): 153–62.

Kendu Ginnery Lease. KNA: PC/NZA/2/12/58.

Kitching, Gavin *Class and Economic Change in Kenya: The making of an African Petite-Bourgeoisie.* New Haven and London: Yale University Press, 1980.

Lonsdale, John, "The Depression and the Second World War in the Transformation of Kenya." In *Africa and the Second World War*, David Killingray and Richard Rathbone (eds.). New York: St. Martins, 1986: 96–99.

Maxon, Robert, "The Years of Revolutionary Advance, 1920-1929." In *Modern History of Kenya 1895-1980*, W.R. Ochieng' (ed.). Nairobi: Evans Brothers, 1989: 71–111.

————. "Stifling Capitalism in Rural Africa: The Gusii Coffee Industry in Kenya, 1932-1949." *Journal of Third World Studies* 11 (1994): 317–50.

Memorandum to Sir Phillips Cunliiffe Lister, Secretary of State for the Colonies, 7th December 1933, South Kavirondo Political Record Book, 1930–1940, KNA: DC/KSI/3/5 KNA: DC/KSI/3/5.

Miligan, S. *Inspection Note on the Kenya Cotton Crop in November and December, 1939*. Nairobi: Government Printer, 1936.

Minutes of Meetings of the Kavirondo Native Chamber of Commerce, 1931-1951. KNA: PC/NZA/20/79.

Ndege, Peter Odhiambo, Struggles for the Market: The Political Economy of Commodity Production and Trade in Western Kenya, PhD Thesis West Virginia University, 1993.

South Kavirondo Annual Reports. KNA: DC/KSI/1/4.

Talbott, I.D., *Agricultural Innovation in Colonial Africa: Kenya and the Great Depression*, Lewiston: The Edwin Mellen Press. 1990.

Wolff, Richard D. *The Economics of Colonialism: Britain and Kenya 1870-1930*. Nairobi: Transafrica Publishers, 1974.

Zwanenberg, Roger Van. "The Development of Peasant Commodity Production in Kenya, 1920-1940." *Economic History Review* 27 (1974): 442–54.

————. "Kenya's Primitive Colonial Capitalism: The Economic Weakness of Kenya's Settlers up to 1940." *Canadian Journal of African Studies* 9 (1975): 277–92.

*Chapter 11*

# Community Development in Post-Independence Malawi

## *Deciphering Some Local Voices*

Gift Wasambo Kayira

In 1998, a team of government officials and Concern Universal consultants arrived at Wovwe Rice Scheme in Northern Malawi. The group helped to establish a farmers' organization, the Wovwe Water Users Association (WWUA).[1] Wovwe Rice Scheme was established in the late 1960s. Inspired by the late colonial period development imaginations, it operated as a settlement scheme under the supervision of the Department of Agriculture officials until 2002 when the Malawi government devolved the management of the scheme to farmers. Before then, however, the government rehabilitated canals, water intake points, and several other dilapidated irrigation facilities.[2] With the association in place, experts boasted that they had secured the success of the scheme through grassroots participation.

Ten years after these changes, the once rehabilitated scheme fell back to its original state, and by 2014 it was under a new phase of rehabilitation. Conflicts among farmers challenged the very existence of the association. Claims to "indigeneity" over land almost drifted it back to the pre-scheme era.[3] Besides, farmers defied the rigid constitutional rules governing the association's activities and shifted their allegiance to parallel indigenous structures of authority. If experts perceived community participation as a workable alternative to expert-driven rural development initiatives, the Wovwe experience was the opposite of this thinking.

This chapter uses the Wovwe case to analyze the lived experiences of local people who participated in community-based development projects in postcolonial Malawi. Although we have a good understanding of how local African societies contested the expert-driven rural development projects of both the colonial and the immediate postcolonial present, we have limited knowledge of local initiative and how it manifested through self-help and other community-driven development projects. This chapter contributes to local histories of development by drawing on the experiences of the local people who participated in and managed the Wovwe rice irrigation scheme of Northern Malawi. Since its establishment in the 1960s, the scheme operated under expert guidance until the early 2000s when the government devolved its management to local farmers. The chapter reflects on how experts helped to establish a farmers' organization and how farmers contested this sense of trusteeship when the new management of the scheme proved ineffective. Contrary to expectations that community-managed projects arrest the difficulties associated with expert-driven top-down development projects, the Wovwe is a story of management shortfalls, financial hardships, and water shortages. Farmers took advantage of these challenges and contested the authority of the new management team to which expert trusteeship was passed. They disobeyed constitutional rules, withheld their labor toward the maintenance of scheme facilities, and appealed to traditional more than the formal leadership channels. The study puts the Wovwe within a deeper history of community development in Africa and shows how some people who were more marginal to power negotiated their involvement in the development process and often triumphed.

More broadly, the chapter contributes to local histories of development, a new area in historical research that emphasizes understanding the development process through the eyes of local people as opposed to state, non-state, or international actors and experts. Over the last decade, mainstream historiography on development histories focused on the latter group in ways that reinforced the modernizer's view of the world.[4] Where the agency of the local people was acknowledged, the aim was often to show the specific problems they caused, which forced experts to act on their behalf. Development history remained the domain of experts although scholars such as Monica Beusekom, Dorothy Hodgson and, later, Rohland Schuknecht, were already pointing to how local Africans negotiated their involvement in expert-driven colonial development projects.[5]

The rise of studies focusing on local histories of development during the first two decades of the twenty-first century has further helped us to understand the "development project."[6] We now have a fair understanding of how social engineering development programs became spaces where the power to shape the economic habits of the local people was contested in ways that revealed the agency of the subalterns. That agency, however, mostly played out within the framework of expert-driven projects such that much of the existing analyses display an opposition between development experts and project beneficiaries. We have limited experience of local initiatives manifesting through self-help and other community-driven development interventions.[7] If expert-driven projects were patronizing and less empowering for the local people, to what extent did community-driven projects of the post-1990 era arrest these shortfalls, and how did they shape the local experience? This chapter addresses these questions by drawing lessons from a community-driven irrigation scheme in Malawi. It shows how similar power dynamics that manifested in the expert-driven projects of the colonial and the early postcolonial period in Africa played out at Wovwe among seemingly equal actors—the local communities.

One aspect explaining such common experience centers on the enduring principle of trusteeship, the idea that development is a project of experts who seek to direct the social and economic progress of others. The Wovwe experience shows that although experts were not involved in the day-to-day running of this community-driven project, their presence was not eliminated. Expert trusteeship manifested at different levels. First, experts retained control over the conceptualization and establishment of the farmers' organization. The intentions planners held were benign and reflect what Li has described as the "will to improve."[8] They believed they had the responsibility to ensure that the scheme improved the lives of the people entrusted to the care of the state.

Such intentions notwithstanding, this top-down intervention undermined what Pat O'Malley has elsewhere described as the "authenticity of indigenous governance."[9] More significantly, experts planted the Wovwe association within a society that valued respect for traditional leadership more than a farmer organization. Second, experts passed the mantle of trusteeship to specific categories of people, notably members of the association's Board of Trustees (BOT) and the Secretariat. The latter became a target of farmers' opposition in ways that remind us about similar political dynamics of the colonial-era development projects. Demotivated with management shortfalls and ecological challenges, farmers undermined the scheme rules and put confidence in chiefs whom they considered as their legitimate leaders.

The first section of the chapter highlights the long history of contemporary community-based development practice and reiterates, as other scholars have done, that the drive toward it in the post-1990 era did not lack a deeper historical antecedent. Throughout the colonial period in Africa, British technocrats and administrators had campaigned for community development schemes as a strategy of improving the welfare of Africans. They did so with a sense of trusteeship that aimed at improving Africans without destabilizing community life. The second section discusses attempts the postcolonial state in Malawi made to integrate local Africans in the development process between the 1960s and 1970s. In this way, it shows how the Wovwe experience, which is discussed in the third and last sections, represented the climax of earlier attempts to achieve a participatory development process in the country. The study is based on oral interviews conducted among Wovwe farmers and some selected documents.

## COMMUNITY DEVELOPMENT DISCOURSE
## IN AFRICA: A HISTORY

Political economy scholars in Africa typically place rural development ideas and practices under two opposing frameworks of modernization on the one hand, and community-driven development, on the other. Under the former, development experts or government officials directed the development process through a top-down approach.[10] This state-led development regime played out after independence in Africa until the economic crisis of the late 1970s became clear. From the 1980s, advocates of neoliberalism condemned this state-led development for its failure to arrest poverty. Instead, they advocated for market liberalism.[11] The latter, which argued for the removal of the state from the development process, among others, found a home within the World Bank and the International Monetary Fund. Emerging in the mid-1980s, the neoliberal development philosophy emphasized private sector initiatives, redefinition and reduction of the role of the state, promotion of new decentralized, stakeholder-driven and community-based management institutions.[12]

In the 1990s, scholars further criticized this development regime. Other than its failure to arrest poverty among societies in the Global South, they argued, the development project had only promoted particular political ambitions while widening the inequality gap in rural areas.[13] For example, James Ferguson reduced development projects to anti-politics machines, a weapon which the state used to wield control over rural societies.[14] James Scott condemned the "high state modernism" that characterized expert-driven development projects for stifling local initiative.[15]

On his part, Arturo Escobar suggested a post-development intervention with the indigenous communities taking control of the development process through their own knowledge and skills.[16] In the last decade, other scholars, whom Jeff Grischow conveniently calls the "social capitalists," have joined such scholars as Escobar to celebrate the power of social capital.[17] These scholars regard social capital as a force of cohesion binding communities together as they shaped their own economic futures through indigenous-based development institutions and networks. This distrust with expert-driven development coincided with the second wave of democratization in Africa (occurring from the 1990s) and gave meaning to the community development initiative of the post-1990 era. The practice emphasized community participation in development projects in ways that would empower the local people as actors and managers of development projects. At the center of the community development philosophy was the assumption that once empowered, beneficiaries would have the incentive to manage their projects more efficiently, sustainably, and equitably than does a centrally financed government agency.[18]

This reading of history in which community development follows the disappointment with the 1960s and 1970s expert-driven rural development projects is misleading. Scholars of development histories have illustrated the deeper historical antecedents of contemporary community development practice. As Cowen and Shenton remind us, "the policy of community development was not rooted in some 'post-colonial' fantasy of an imagined community of the poor," taking over the control of the development process.[19] Community development in Africa had a deeper historical context, dating back to the early twentieth century. Politicians, bureaucrats, and individuals with an informed opinion within the British Empire, for instance, discussed these ideas as part of the broader debates on Britain's economic activities in Africa. At issue was how to frame an economic policy that would improve the welfare of Africans without destabilizing their communal life. Worried that capitalist activities were creating individualism among African communities, members of the Fabian Society—an intellectual body which advocated for the interests of the working class in Britain and the exploited societies in the colonies—put their hope in African cooperation and community to achieve both colonial order and economic progress.

The Fabians, who had a tremendous influence on the Labour Party Government's colonial policy, emphasized collectivism, with British officials slowly guiding Africans toward progress as communities or individuals within communities.[20] This was also a necessary intervention to protect Africans from the ravages of capitalism.[21] As early as 1926, the Labour Party, which appeared to have embraced well the Fabian message, advocated for agricultural cooperatives, designed to assist Africans in their economic undertakings by producing and marketing their products as communities.[22]

Following the onset of the Great Depression in the 1930s, there was a renewed commitment toward grouping Africans into cooperatives. This campaign would facilitate both the production and marketing of African products in a hostile economic environment without destabilizing community life. Similar efforts to organize communities into vibrant cooperatives came after 1940 following the passing of the Colonial Development and Welfare Act. The Act in question apportioned metropolitan funding toward colonial development and research. The postwar economic crisis also caused a similar level of urgency. Well-organized African cooperatives would help produce raw materials such as cotton that would feed metropolitan industries.

Community development became an official colonial policy of the British Labour Party Government in 1949.[23] Many of the rural development projects framed in the 1940s, however, already had cooperatives as a central component. One example was the Sukumaland development project of Tanganyika, which Rohland Schuknecht has described at length. Planned in the 1940s, the project grouped Africans into cooperatives directed at producing food crops and cotton that would better their lives and feed cotton industries of the economically troubled Britain. The project also had the aim of ecologically stabilizing the animal and human population. The Sukumaland project achieved none of these aims because farmers were less willing to participate in such top-down managed projects. Cotton production increased but through extensive production outside the scheme. Besides, the cooperative movement became politicized and helped to shape the Tanganyika African Union (TANU). The TANU was a political party that campaigned for African independence from the British.[24]

In the 1950s, however, much of British tropical Africa witnessed a surge of compulsory community settlement schemes. Hodge has observed that the confidence experts previously held—of improving African societies through western expertise while promoting production and marketing cooperatives—had collapsed.[25] The government turned to force and propaganda to promote agricultural change. In colonial Malawi, for example, the government experimented with village land improvement and community settlement schemes in the 1950s. Under these schemes, the state consolidated and rearranged the otherwise fragmented African land. Diversion ditches, terraces, and other soil conservation strategies such as contour bands were constructed in the marked land. The 1949 Natural Resources Ordinance, which spelled out harsher punishments for those who refused to comply with "sound" agricultural husbandry, gave shape to a land-use component of these schemes.[26] Besides, the government resettled some selected African families—especially those in environmentally sensitive areas—in state-developed schemes.[27] The state envisaged that by bringing farmers together, it would be possible to guide them toward progress through production and marketing cooperatives that fostered active farmer participation in the development process. This would be in line with the 1953 Nyasaland District Councils Ordinance, which sought to empower Africans to take an active role in local government affairs as opposed to relying on nonelected chiefs.[28]

Almost all the settlement schemes failed to attract African farmers, and others resisted forced land-use measures.[29] The top-down strategies inherent in them did not win the confidence of local people. The government authorities relied on chiefs to convince their subjects about the benefits of the changes in question. As Peter McLoughlin notes, however, chiefs did not always wield control in rural areas. As a result, there was a disconnection between the "official mind" and local aspirations.[30] Moreover, considering the soil and land conservation campaign as a less rewarding exercise personally, some chiefs took no pride in persuading Africans to move into these schemes.[31] Thinking exceptional, land planning executed through meticulous technical detail, and propaganda campaigns would work out a miracle, government officials ignored the sociological aspects of the reforms. There were minimal consultations with the local people such that matters to do with household economics—household food needs, new labor demands the consolidated plots presented—were often ignored.[32] Besides, coming in the 1950s when Africans opposed the Federation of Rhodesia and Nyasaland, the disturbances these schemes caused in resettling Africans were interpreted in political terms.

The 1950s events, however, represented a temporary shift away from the previous goals of organizing farmers into cooperatives to facilitate their active participation in development projects. Other parts of British Africa, notably Kenya, remained relatively on track with farmer-centered development projects. As Cowen and Shenton note, community development practices of the colonial era in Kenya gave rise to the "Harambee" self-help projects after independence where communities, grouped in cooperatives, took a more active role in improving their lives. Between 1965 and 1984, "37,300 Harambee projects were completed, contributing some 12 percent of national gross capital formation."[33] Many of these extended to nonagricultural ventures. With Southern Rhodesia (Zimbabwe), Kushinga Makombe has documented the community development program as it evolved between the 1960s and the 1970s. In consultation with foreign experts from the American Agency for International Development (USAID), the Native Affairs Department (NAD) officials reorganized African communities into communal self-help organizations charged with the responsibility of planning and executing rural development projects through a participatory approach.[34] The program had an element of "consultation," detailed plans on rural housing, and nonagricultural enterprises such as those of cooperate retail trade.

Such experiences corroborate Immerwahr's view that the United States did not just engage with the global world as a "broadcaster of some monolithic culture [but also] as a sympathetic enabler of village level democracy, plurality, and local knowledge."[35] As early as 1954, for instance, a Community Development Division was established within the U.S. foreign-aid agency. In addition to providing aid, the division had deployed staff to over 20 countries, where 47 community development programs were attempted.[36] The quest for community was as much significant a cause to pursue as was the famous modernization drive. It "preached the values of grassroots democracy and recognized the ways in which traditional institutions could protect their members from the economic and political shocks of modernization."[37] Not surprisingly, Immerwahr describes the community development drive of the post-1990 era as "community development reanimated."[38]

That said, expert-driven and top-down strategies of achieving rural development characterized much of Africa in the 1960s and 1970s. Colonial community development interventions shared a similar weakness. The interlude of the 1960s to 1970s rural development, however, should not cloud our judgment about the similarities between the colonial and the post-1990 community projects. "As admirable as these ideals [on community development] may be," notes Hodge, "it is hard not to notice the uncanny resemblance to earlier colonial doctrines."[39] More noticeable are the strategies of bringing about rural progress, emphasizing both cooperation and community life. Again, as the Wovwe case will show, the aims and intentions of experts manifesting themselves in reorganizing societies into active agents of the development process remained the same. Colonial administrators and other experts played the role of trusteeship in the past. Under the post-1990 era, members of the community, mostly those who seemed to command the confidence of the local people, emerged as new trustees. Even with that, experts and planners from non-state and government departments took an active role in reorganizing communities and setting up farmers' organizations in line with expert wisdom. Colonial administrators and the more contemporary experts, therefore, are united in their faith in the principle of trusteeship.

Experts who established the Wovwe Water Users Association in post-1990 Malawi were not different from those colonial administrators in Kenya who helped to organize farmers into cooperative schemes, which became the basis of Harambee projects. Nor were their intentions different from those of the officials under the NAD in Southern Rhodesia whose "commitment to 'consultation'. . . was not [always] based on the premise that rural inhabitants could make a contribution to evolving policy and practice but on the assumption that given time, they would come to see the wisdom of official designs."[40] Local participation, whether for the distant colonial past or the contemporary present, evolved within the confines of experts' designs, and they both share similar weaknesses. As the Wovwe case will show, the contemporary community development projects display how local people contested these projects in ways that reveal the very fault lines of experts' development designs.

## RURAL DEVELOPMENT AND LOCAL PARTICIPATION IN MALAWI, 1960s–1980s

After independence in 1964, the government of Malawi abandoned the heavy-handed approach which had previously characterized the 1950s development campaign. However, the will to include local Africans as active agents of the development process continued. As early as 1964, the government had established "Farm Clubs" first experimented in Lilongwe, Dowa, Kasungu, and Mchinji districts.[41] Farm clubs had a committee, clubhouse, and demonstration plots which agricultural extension officers supervised. They accessed credit from existing credit facilities to purchase agricultural inputs such as fertilizer and seed, and agricultural technology, in the form of work oxen. The Farm Clubs later evolved into "Village Planning Committees," which supervised one to three villages. The Village Planning Committees had the mandate to consolidate plots to "allow for better use of ox-drawn implements."[42] The approach, moreover, was in line with the state plans to enhance local participation in the development process, which it hatched as early as 1965.[43] In that year, the government introduced the District Development Committees (DDCs), followed by the Area and Village Action Groups (AVAGs) in 1966.[44] These committees represented the government's attempts to decentralize development activities in the country. In practice, the structure did not empower the local people as active agents of the development process. It was the government experts that managed the rural development projects in the country through a top-down approach.

Such was the case with the 16 irrigation/settlement schemes the government established between 1967 and 1979. The state deployed its experts to manage the projects and assist farmers to produce rice through scientifically proven methods. In some schemes such as the Wovwe, the Republic of China deployed its technical staff who lived in the schemes where they cultivated selected model rice plots. In that way, the local farmers would learn by emulation.[45] Besides, the government deployed the Malawi Young Pioneers who also cultivated some selected plots that would serve similar purposes as those by the Chinese farmers.[46] On average, farmers or families were allocated a plot of between 0.3 and 1.5 hectares, which they worked using family labor or work oxen. The hectarage steadily decreased with the increasing farmer population. At Wovwe, the Chinese Mission could hire out tractors to willing farmers to assist with the plowing of fields and transportation of harvested rice. To facilitate rice marketing, a state-marketing board, ADMARC, elected its depot at the Scheme. Rice was produced twice every year, during both the rainy (December–April) and dry (June–November) seasons.[47]

The emphasis on the top-down administrative structure, however, should not be exaggerated. The schemes also aimed at promoting local participation. Farmers were grouped into clubs, and some became members of the land-allocation committees. Although nominally weak to influence real change, land-allocation committees, which had several other subcommittees, were empowered to ensure equitable distribution of scheme plots and mobilize labor toward the maintenance of scheme canals. As noted, operating within the top-down administrative machinery, such structures were less empowering.

Besides, the Wovwe scheme, like others in the country, was marked by high, farmer-turnover rates.[48] Farmers often resented the strict discipline which the government staff enforced and often looked to the scheme as a part-time venture with which to raise some income when alternative sources of income were unavailable. The dawn of neoliberal reforms, which coincided with the second wave of multiparty politics after the 1994 General Elections, provided an opportunity to empower farmers fully in ways previously not possible. In the rest of the discussion, the chapter reflects on the experiences of farmers at Wovwe following the power devolution of the post-1990 era.

## COMMUNITY DEVELOPMENT IN THE POST-1990 ERA: LESSONS FROM WOVWE

Efforts to bring about irrigation reforms at Wovwe Rice Scheme started in the mid-1990s and coincided with first, the reintroduction of multiparty politics in the country in 1994, and second, the 1992–1993 famine.[49] While the latter provided an impetus toward democratic reforms in the agricultural sector, the former forced the government to revive irrigation agriculture to achieve food security. Thus, although there was a break in the political landscape of the country—in that there was a shift from authoritarianism to political pluralism—the policy of encouraging smallholder agriculture remained relatively intact and tilted toward placing ordinary farmers as active agricultural actors. In 1996, the government targeted the Wovwe Rice Scheme as one among three schemes earmarked for power devolution under the Irrigation Management Transfer (IMT) program. The other two schemes included Domasi and Nkhande schemes in Zomba and Chikwawa Districts of the Southern Region of the country. With funding from the Food and Agricultural Organisation (FAO) and the Danish International Development Agency (DANIDA), preparatory work started at Wovwe.[50] The project stalled when DANIDA pulled out following disagreements with the Malawi government over the mismanagement of aid and other corrupt practices. Denmark suspended aid to Malawi and closed its Malawi embassy in 2001.[51] Nevertheless, it managed to offer training to different subcommittees set up during the previous era.

The government resuscitated these plans in 1998 when it secured funding from the International Fund for Agricultural Development (IFAD) and launched a Smallholder Flood Plain Development Programme (SFPDP). As before, the program aimed at rehabilitating the schemes and building institutional capacity. Having subcontracted Concern Universal, the SFPDP established the Wovwe Water Users' Association (WWUA), whose constitution the government approved in 2002.[52] Among other aspects, the constitution aimed at safeguarding the economic interests of farmers and prescribed rules and regulations regarding access to plots in the scheme, as well as its maintenance.[53] Again, for the first time in the history of the scheme, it also provided for the payment of membership and water fees for any participating farmer.

The association procured the water abstraction rights from the National Water Resources Board, an exercise it accomplished under the agency of the SFPDP personnel. It also acquired a land lease from the Commissioner of Lands and Valuation, thereby securing the scheme from outside interference.[54] The constitution also provided for an elaborate leadership structure that differed from the previous one. Farmers had the powers to decide their own affairs. All members of the executive and other subcommittees were answerable to farmers who, together, made up the General Assembly. The only independent body was the Board of Trustees (BOT), an advisory arm but which legally owned the farmer's organization.[55] What emerged, therefore, was an elaborate formal institution with well-articulated structures of authority. With these reforms in place, a community-driven scheme emerged set to arrest previous shortfalls. This optimism soon waned as the management team faced opposition from farmers, making progress difficult to achieve.

Financial mismanagement and water shortages triggered many of the contestations under discussion. For instance, a 2007 Audit Report showed that the treasurer had failed to reconcile MK1,600,000 (an equivalence of US$13,300.00 at the time) collected in water fees, despite receiving training on bookkeeping.[56] The report ruled out corruption but emphasized inappropriate accounting skills as a contributing factor to the treasurer's failure to account for the money. Ordinary farmers criticized the executive for misusing the organizations' money. Many of them refused to pay for water rights and membership fees. One farmer said: "we cannot continue paying water fees. We do not see the benefits of it all. The executive simply misuses our money. All they do is to attend senseless meetings in Lilongwe and Blantyre [the major cities of the country]."[57] Farmers were unwilling to honor water fees obligations not because they felt that water was a free commodity as some scholars have observed elsewhere, but rather because they had lost confidence in the way the association handled their finances.[58]

As a result, conflicts emerged between the executive committee of the association and ordinary farmers over the use of resources. Ordinary members demanded the General Assembly's meeting to have the executive committee clarify monetary concerns. The General Assembly failed to convene twice because the Traditional Authority (T/A) of the area did not turn up for the meeting.[59] As provided under the WWUA constitution, T/A Wasambo was a member of the BOT, alongside some religious and political leaders. Although the BOT legally owned the scheme, as noted, it only played an advisory role. The constitution did not specify who, among the BOT's membership, would hold the position of the chairperson. Evidence shows that T/A Wasambo had always served as the chair.[60] The constitution, however, granted powers to the executive committee, and not to the BOT, to call and preside over all annual general meetings.[61] Similarly, the constitution did not compel members of the BOT to attend such meetings, nor was the traditional leader. In October 2007, the executive committee called for such a meeting to clarify financial concerns in a ceremony accompanied by feasting. As noted, the meeting was postponed, pending the availability of the T/A. When asked to clarify this dilemma, the president of the association, T.A. Mbeye, stated that "this is a very important meeting. We cannot preside over it in the absence of the T/A. Doing this is tantamount to a vote of no confidence in our offices. If the T/A does not turn up, we will keep on postponing the meeting."[62]

The president's opinion coincided with that of farmers for different reasons. One farmer admitted that "we do not want to listen to the executive committee. They [the executive committee members] have eaten [embezzled] our money. What we want is the owner of the scheme [the T/A] to address us and explain how the executive has used the money. If the T/A does not turn up for the meeting, we will not allow the meeting to take place."[63] By falling back on T/A's authority, both farmers and the executive committee breached the constitution, which empowered farmers as the ultimate authority over their affairs through their elected leadership. The General Assembly convened later that year (2007) following the T/A's attendance. Financial issues were clarified but not in ways that eliminated dissent among farmers. Already disappointed with the conduct of the management, farmers refused to provide labor for scheme maintenance. They were also unwilling to clean up the irrigation canals and argued that "the administration should use the water fees to hire people and do the job."[64] The main river supplying water to the scheme and whose silt should have been removed from time to time to prevent water flooding was filled up with silt.[65] Related to the above was the failure to enforce constitutional regulations. Although the rules prohibited those farmers who refused to pay for water rights and membership fees from cultivating rice in the scheme, lacking moral authority, the executive committee rarely enforced such rules.[66] Farmers disregarded scheme rules and regulations and often planted their rice at their own time of convenience and not necessarily that prescribed by the constitution.

Water shortages combined with administrative shortfalls in ways that displayed not only farmers' frustration but also the heterogeneity of the farmers' body. When the government established the scheme in the late 1960s, it designed it to accommodate diverse ethnic groups in the country. This was in line with the political objectives these schemes served—to build the multiethnic Malawi nation through interethnic interaction.[67] Two groups of irrigators settled at the scheme. The first comprised the indigenous farmers who straddled the scheme and their rain-fed fields. These were predominantly Ngonde and Tumbuka peoples whose chiefs negotiated with government officials before converting customary to public land to accommodate the scheme.[68] Several other ethnic groups from different areas of the country joined these original inhabitants. The former group also included members of the MYP described above. Some of the MYP members later permanently settled in the area.

These groups coexisted well during the previous era. At the turn of the twenty-first century, the growing farmer population combined with the challenges of water scarcity to create competition for land and water within the scheme and the Wovwe Valley. At the scheme, these challenges pitted occupants of well-watered plots near the water intake-point against those that cultivated plots at the tail end of the scheme. Such contestations revealed some cracks within the farmers' body when selected groups within the latter category attempted to use claims to indigeneity as a tool with which to negotiate for access to well-watered plots. The indigenous people who occupied poorly watered plots argued that the scheme belonged to chiefs and demanded demarcation of plots using customary law.[69]

Following the mounting challenges of water shortages, some indigenous groups welcomed the post-2002 changes at the scheme as representing an opportunity to ascertain greater control over it through their chiefs. They anticipated the reversion of the scheme and land resources to the pre-scheme era when chiefs had control over land. They became disappointed that chiefs, who should have been sympathetic to their concerns, held no real control over the scheme. Instead, they held back their labor as one farmer affirmed: "Why should we contribute in the same way as though we yield equal benefits from the scheme? Our point has been simple. We have to contribute depending on the benefits we get from the scheme." [70]

Other than withdrawing their labor, there is no evidence of protracted conflicts at the scheme. However, the anxieties point to the growing significance of irrigation agriculture in the context of expanding farmer population and declining sources of livelihood in the neoliberal era. In the past, differences among ethnic groups in the scheme were overlooked. However, water shortages fractured the association along the fault lines of greater claims to indigeneity in the valley. Some farmers believed they had the right to access well-watered plots because they were indigenous to Wovwe or, more specifically, because they came to the valley much earlier than others. In this context, the role of the traditional leader as the guardian of land became increasingly important.

The Wovwe Valley did not lack episodes of open and violent conflicts, however. In 2006, conflicts emerged between farmers in the scheme and their counterparts up in the Wovwe Valley who, through self-initiative, had opened self-help irrigation fields modeled after the Wovwe downstream. Seeking to irrigate their rice, the latter group almost changed the course of Wovwe River, an action that denied their counterparts downstream access to sufficient water supply for their crop. Armed with axes and spears, the farming community downstream matched upward to confront their colleagues. "We buy this water," commented one member while referencing the water fees they paid, "yet our colleagues up there do not. Why then should we be deprived of the water we buy?"[71] The case was handled in time when the local police and traditional leaders from the two sides came to the scene.[72]

Administrative misunderstandings were not the only ones that shaped farmers' perceptions toward the association and its management. There were deep-seated expectations about what power devolution would achieve. If farmers saw the new era as that of economic empowerment, such hopes turned to a mirage. Neoliberal market reforms provided a historical context. To contain a state monopoly in the rural economy, the government withdrew from Wovwe the services of the state-marketing board, ADMARC. ADMARC had, for a long time, facilitated the purchase of agricultural inputs and marketing of rice in the area. This withdrawal created a vacuum, with adverse effects on farmers. One farmer lamented that "we can no longer sell to ADMARC . . . Vendors come from Tanzania with their big [measuring] tins, which are not equivalent to our 20 kg [44.2 lb] tin. We have no option but to sell them our rice at a giveaway price."[73] One Group Village Headman reiterated: "We usually sell our rice to Tanzanian traders right in the field before harvest. At times, we lose it because of failure to pay back *kata-pira* [the practice of paying back the loan twice its original amount]. How we wish we were in the old days when markets for our rice were readily available. Our friends growing tobacco are better off because they have readily available markets."[74]

The SFPDP project attempted to solve the problem of markets by establishing contacts with different buyers such as NASFAM, DARO enterprises, ADMARC, Development Trading Limited, Fadamz and Tambala Food Products. However, none of the above buyers ventured into serious rice business at Wovwe.[75] Similarly, to resolve the problem of access to agricultural inputs, the SFPDP helped to attach farmers to the Karonga Teachers Savings and Credit Cooperatives (SACCO).[76] However, some farmers were unwilling to be part of it, citing, among other reasons, the long distance (about 30 miles) they traveled to process their loans at Karonga Boma. By the close of 2007, the very few farmers attached to Karonga Teachers SACCO had withdrawn. If neoliberalism brought greater participation of the local people in the development process, it also had its dark side for farmers at Wovwe.

## SOME CONCLUDING REMARKS

When studies on the local histories of development emerged in the second decade of the twenty-first century, they were pitched against the shortfalls of the mainstream histories of development whose analysis privileged the modernizer's view of the world. This chapter contributes to this new direction. It uses a community-driven irrigation scheme in Northern Malawi as space where the lived experiences of local people as both participants and drivers of the development process played out. The result is a study that fleshes out first, how the local people contested the power to guide the development process at Wovwe, and second, how similar power dynamics played out among seemingly equal irrigation rice growers. Despite this agency, the study also shows the limits of community-driven development projects during the age of neoliberalism.

The first aspect should be located in the assumption that as the expert-driven management regime retreated from Wovwe, the community would carry out the rule by itself. Experts helped to establish the new government to fill in the vacuum while passing over trusteeship roles to the new managers—particularly the office of the Board of Trustees and the Secretariat. Experts helped to rehabilitate the scheme, train, and establish the farmers' organization/water institution. But the Wovwe experiment failed to register positive results. One immediate explanation for this failure centers on the financial and ecological challenges, as highlighted above. Equally in need of acknowledging, however, is how the farmers' organization at Wovwe represented what O'Malley has described as "an artefact of rule from without" and, therefore, shallowly rooted in indigenous systems of governance.[77]

By appealing to the authority of the traditional leader of the area instead of resolving conflicts through legally sanctioned channels of the association, ordinary farmers challenged the very authenticity of an organization, which was, at best, the brainchild of experts. In requesting for the personal intervention of the traditional leader, farmers were appealing to a traditional chiefly council while setting aside the Board of Trustees. In this way, they questioned experts' wisdom of keeping the indigenous domain outside the formal management structure of the scheme. This chapter, therefore, points to how some people who were more marginal to power were aware of the limitations of the organization that emerged. As actors, they contested it by taking advantage of financial and ecological challenges. To express frustration, they disobeyed the duly sanctioned constitutional rules.

The Wovwe scheme was far from monolithic as advocates of community-based development often assume. For selected farmers, the scheme was a symbol of inequalities because it empowered some while dispossessing others. Such differences became pronounced in the face of water shortages and raised serious questions about who held the right to access scheme land. As noted, to access productive parts of the scheme, some farmers resorted to making claims to indigeneity. Similar dynamics played out within the Wovwe Valley. Left out of the scheme, some selected farmers displayed a rare initiative and established self-help rice schemes in ways that question studies that confine development projects to the initiative of the state, the nongovernmental organizations, and other actors. What is significant here, also, is how this group of local farmers competed for water with their counterparts under the Wovwe irrigation scheme. The question of who held the right to harness irrigation water from the Wovwe River pitted the two groups of farmers against each other. Despite these differences, none of the farmers were immune to the challenges of markets as detailed here. The lived experiences, as discussed in this case study, show that we cannot regard community-based development projects, to use the language of Cooper, as "project[s] of self-evident benefit."[78] The turn toward community-based participatory projects in the late 1980s did not erase the problems associated with colonial or immediate postcolonial development projects. Moreover, this turn displays the hidden hand of experts and the sense of trusteeship that regulates their activities.

## NOTES

1. Malawi Government, SFPDP Project Completion Draft Report, Ministry of Irrigation and Water Development, 2007.
2. Ibid.
3. I am using the word indigeneity in very loose terms to describe those groups that came to the area much earlier than others. The Ngonde people, who problematically fit this description, were immigrants just like so many other groups in the country.
4. See David John Morgan, *The Official History of Colonial Development* (London: Macmillan, 1980), falling in four volumes; Stephen Constantine, *The Making of British Colonial Development Policy, 1914-1940* (London: Frank Cass, 1984); Frederick Cooper, "Modernizing Bureaucrats, Backward Africans, and Development Concept," in Frederick Cooper and Randall Packard (eds.), *International Development and the Social Sciences: Essays on the History and Politics of Knowledge* (Berkeley: University of California Press, 2013), 74–79; Joseph Morgan Hodge, *Triumph of the Expert: Agrarian Doctrines of Development and the Legacies of British Colonialism* (Athens, OH: Ohio University Press, 2007).
5. Rohland Schuknecht, *British Colonial Development Policy after the Second World War: the Case of Sukumaland, Tanganyika* (London: Global Book Marketing, 2010); Monica M. van Beusekom, *Negotiating Development: African Farmers and Colonial Experts at the Office Du Niger, 1920-1960* (Portsmouth, NH: James Currey, 2002); Monica M. van Beusekom and Dorothy L. Hodgson, "Lessons Learned? Development Experiences in the late Colonial Period," *Journal of African History* 41, no. 1 (2000): 29–33.

6. A good representation of this literature was presented in a special issue of the *International Journal of African Historical Studies* 50, no. 1 (2017). See particularly the introduction to the issue by L.A Hadfield and John Aerni-Flessner, "Introduction: Localizing the History of Development in Africa," *International Journal of African Historical Studies* 50, no. 1 (2017): 1–9.

7. The following works noted a similar shortfall: Marc F. S. Kunkel, "Review: Writing the History of Development: A Review of the Recent Literature," *Contemporary European History* 20, no. 2 (2011): 229; Hadfield and Aerni-Flessner, "Introduction," 3.

8. Tania Murry Li, *The Will to Improve, Governmentality, Development, and the Practice of Politics* (Durham: Duke University Press, 2007), 5.

9. Pat O'Malley, "Indigenous Governance," *Economy and Society* 25, no. 3 (1996): 313.

10. Contemporary literature has illustrated the deeper historical roots of the ideas that marked the U.S. postwar development drive where state bureaucrats retained control over the development process. See, for example, Frederick Cooper, "Writing the history of Development," *Journal of Modern European History* 8, no. 1 (2010): 5–23.

11. A good representation of this work is presented by Peter Thomas Bauer who, as early as 1970s, was already campaigning for neoliberalism. See Peter T. Bauer, *Dissent on Development* (Cambridge, MA: Harvard University Press, 1972); see also his *Development Aid: End it or Mend It* (San Francisco: ICS, 1993).

12. Anne Ferguson and Wapulumuka Oliver Mulwafu, "If Government failed, how are we to succeed? The Importance of History and Context in the Present-day Irrigation Reform in Malawi," in Barbara van Koppen, Mark Giordano and John Butterworth (eds.), *Community-based Water Law and Water Resources Management Reform in Developing Countries* (Wallingford: CABI, 2007), 211–227.

13. This view was presented by the post-development scholars, most of whom had been inspired by a turn to the 1990s post-structuralism.

14. James Ferguson, *The Anti-Politics Machine: "Development," Depoliticization, and Bureaucratic Power in Lesotho* (Minneapolis: University of Minnesota Press, 1994), xv, 256.

15. James C Scott, *Seeing Like a State: How Certain Schemes to Improve the Human Condition Have Failed* (New Haven: Yale University Press, 2008), 3–52; 88–89.

16. Arturo Escobar, *Encountering Development: The Making and Unmaking of the Third World* (Princeton, NJ: Princeton University Press, 1995), 15.

17. Jeff D. Grischow, "Rural 'Community,' Chiefs and Social Capital: The Case of Southern Ghana," *Journal of Agrarian Change* 8, no. 1 (2008): 64–93; Fergus Lyon, "Trust, Networks and Norms: The Creation of Social Capital in Agricultural Economies in Ghana," *World Development* 28, no. 4 (2000): 663–681; Michael Woolcock, "Calling on Friends and Relatives: Social Capital," in M. Fay (ed.), *Urban Poor in Latin America* (Washington, DC: World Bank Publications, 2005), 219–238.

18. Ferguson and Mulwafu, "If Government Failed," 225.

19. Michael Cowen and Robert W Shenton, *Doctrines of Development* (London: Routledge, 1996), 293. See the e-copy version of the book whose pages appear differently from the print one.

20. Michael Cowen and Robert Shenton, "The Origin and Course of Fabian Colonialism in Africa," *Journal of Historical Sociology* 4, no. 2 (1991): 154.

21. See Paul Kelemen, "Individualism is, indeed, Running Riot: Components of the Social Democratic Model of Development," in Mark Duffield and Vernon Hewitt (eds.), *Empire, Development and Colonialism* (Woodbridge, UK: Byodell and Brown, 2009), 188–201.

22. See Labour Party, *The Empire in Africa: Labour's Policy* (London: The Labour Party, 1926), 3–5.

23. Cowen and Shenton, *The Doctrine of Development*, 291.

24. Schuknecht, *British Colonial Development Policy after the Second World War*. Elsewhere, Monica van Beusekom has illustrated similar contestations in the Office du Niger irrigation project of the French Soudan (Mali). See her *Negotiating Development*.

25. See Hodge, *Triumph of the Expert*, 16, 208.

26. Wapulumuka Oliver Mulwafu, *Conservation Song: A History of Peasant-State Relations and the Environment in Malawi, 1860-2000* (Cambridge: White Horse Press, 2011), 99.

27. Peter F. M. McLoughlin, "Land Re-organization in Malawi, 1950s-60: Its Pertinence to Current Development," in Sayre P. Schatz (ed.), *South of the Sahara: Development in African Economies* (Philadelphia: Temple University Press, 1972), 128–139, 131.

28. Colin Baker, *The Evolution of Local Government in Nyasaland* (Ile-Ife: University of Ife Press, 1975), 45.

29. The following works comprehensively discuss how these schemes evolved: William Beinart, "Agricultural Planning and the Late Colonial Technical Imagination: The Lower Shire Valley, 1940-1960," in *Malawi: An Alternative Pattern of Development: Proceedings of a Seminar held in the Centre of African Studies, University of Edinburgh, May 24 and 25, 1984*, 93–148; McLoughlin, "Land Re-organization in Malawi," 128–139.

30. McLoughlin, "Land Re-organization in Malawi," 133.

31. Erik Green, "Indirect Rule and Colonial Intervention: Chiefs and Agrarian Change in Nyasaland, ca. 1933 to the Early 1950s," *International Journal of African Historical Studies* 44, no. 2 (2011): 274.

32. McLoughlin, "Land Re-organization in Malawi," 137.

33. Cowen and Shenton, *Doctrines of Development*, 292.

34. Kushinga E. Makombe, "Developing Rural Africa: Rural Development Discourse in Colonial Zimbabwe, 1944-79," in Joseph M. Hodge, Gerald Hödl, and Martina Kopf (eds.), *Developing Africa: Concepts, practices and Twentieth-century Colonialism* (Manchester: Manchester University Press, 2014), 167.

35. Daniel Immerwahr, *Thinking Small: The United States and the Lure of Community Development* (Massachusetts: Harvard University Press, 2015), 3.

36. Immerwahr, *Thinking Small*, 4.

37. Immerwahr, *Thinking Small*, 4.

38. Immerwahr, *Thinking Small*, 13.

39. Hodge, *Triumph of the Expert*, 275.

40. Makombe, "Developing rural Africa, 172.

41. Model Villages in Malawi, Circular No. 3/68, Department of Agriculture, Ministry of Economic Planning, Zomba, 1968, Malawi National Archive (MNA) 15-12-6R/15077. Such an observation checks Kishindo's work which traced the history of Farmer Clubs in Malawi to 1978 when the government rolled them out across the country. The idea of Farmer Clubs should be traced to the early 1960s. See Paul Kishindo, "Farmer Clubs and Smallholder Agricultural Development in Malawi," *Development Southern Africa* 5, no. 2 (2008): 491–507.

42. Model Villages in Malawi, Circular No. 3/68, 1968, MNA 15-12-6R/15077.

43. See Development Plan and Projects (Malawi), 1965-1969, MNA 15-12-6R/15077.

44. The AVAGs comprised local members of the communities with chiefs as chairpersons. See R.A. Miller, "District Development Committees in Malawi: A Case Study in Rural Development," *Journal of Overseas Administration* 9, no. 2 (1970): 131.

45. This was part of the technical assistance program of the Republic of China which came in 1967 following the request of the Malawi Government.

46. Established in 1965, the Malawi Young Pioneers (MYP) was a youth organization which, among others, trained the youth in agricultural skills. Every year, about 700 graduates of the MYP were deployed to agricultural schemes as agents of agricultural change. See D.D. Phiri, *History of Malawi*, Vol. 2 (Blantyre, Malawi: College Publishing Company, 2010), 312–315.

47. Wovwe Irrigation Scheme Notes, MNA/ KRDP/ ID/WV/3/150, 1988.

48. Wiseman C. Chirwa, "Land Use and Extension Services at Wovwe Rice Scheme," *Development Southern Africa* 19, no. 2 (2002): 307–327; W.C. Chirwa, *Wovwe and Adjacent Areas: A Baseline Study,* Report for the World Vision International, Chancellor College, Zomba, 1995.

49. After independence from the British in 1964, Malawi became a *de facto* one-party state under the authoritarian leadership of Dr. Hastings Kamuzu Banda who ruled until 1994. The Malawi Congress Party (MCP), Banda's political party, systematically eliminated opposition parties that competed in the 1964 General Election. The new wave of democracy appears to have had an influence on the irrigation reforms that emerged.

50. Detailed in SFPDP Project Completion Draft Report.

51. Ferguson and Mulwafu, "If Government Failed," 217.

52. Malawi Government, SFPDP Project Completion Draft Report, 6.

53. Wovwe Water Users Constitution, Section 1, Subsection 1.4, 2002; SFPDP Project Completion Draft Report, 23.

54. SFPDP Project Completion Draft Report, 7.

55. Laws of Malawi require that any formal organization should be registered under a Board of Trustees with powers to dissolve such associations following the recommendation of the General Assembly. In essence, it is this Board that legally owned the scheme.

56. The Audit Report, Wovwe Water Users' Association, 2007, cited in SFPDP Project Completion Draft Report.

57. Oral Testimony (Hereafter OT), M. Nyamulera, Gangamwale Village, T/A Wasambo, October 15, 2007.

58. For this earlier view, see Ferguson and Mulwafu, "If Farmers Failed," 843.

59. Researcher's personal observation while collecting data to this study, Wovwe Rice Scheme, October to November 2007.

60. Personal Communication with one of the members of the BOT, Mr. Mwafulirwa, October 11, 2007.

61. WWUA Constitution, Section 5.1, subsection 5.1.1, 2007.

62. Personal Communication with T.A. Mbeye, President of WWUA, October 31, 2007.

63. OT, W. Mlenga, Gangamwale Village, T/A Wasambo, Karonga, October 31, 2007.

64. Personal Communication with T.A. Mbeye, President of WWUA, October 31, 2007.

65. Author's personal observation, October 2007.

66. As stipulated in WWUA Constitution, Section 2.5, subsection 2.5.2, 2007.

67. See Paul Kishindo, "Farmer Turnover at Settlement Schemes: The Experience of Limphasa Irrigation Rice Scheme, Northern Malawi," *Nordic Journal of African Studies* 5, no. 1 (1996): 1–10.

68. Wovwe Irrigation Scheme Working Paper, 1979, MNA 10/7; OT, Senior GVH Kapiyira, T/A Wasambo, Karonga, October 27, 2007.

69. Personal interaction with selected farmers in focus group discussions, Wovwe Rice Scheme, October 24, 2007.

70. OT, B. Msukwa, Bunganiro Village, T/A Wasambo, October 11, 2007.

71. OT, W. Mlenga, Gangamwale Village, T/A Wasambo, October 13, 2007.

72. Personal communication with T. Mbeye, WWUA President, October 11, 2007.

73. OT. M. Nyarweni (nee Ngware), member of WWUA, October 26, 2007.

74. O.T. GVH Mphangwiyanjini, T/A Wasambo, October 27, 2007.

75. O.T, T. Mbeye, WWUA President, October 11, 2007.

76. SFPDP Project Completion Draft Report.

77. O'Malley, "Indigenous Governance," 313.

78. Cooper, "Introduction," 6.

## BIBLIOGRAPHY

Baker, Colin. *The Evolution of Local Government in Nyasaland.* Ile-Ife: University of Ife Press, 1975.

Bauer, Peter, Thomas. *Development Aid: End it or Mend It.* San Francisco: ICS, 1993.

———. *Dissent on Development.* Cambridge, MA: Harvard University Press, 1972.

Beinart William. "Agricultural Planning and the Late Colonial Technical Imagination: The Lower Shire Valley, 1940-1960." In *Malawi: An Alternative Pattern of*

Development, *Proceedings of a Seminar held in the Centre of African Studies.* University of Edinburgh, 24 and 25 May, 1984, 93–148.

Chirwa, Wiseman, C. "Land Use and Extension Services at Wovwe Rice Scheme." *Development Southern Africa* 19, no. 2 (2002): 307–27.

——— *Wovwe and Adjacent areas: A Baseline Study,* Report for the World Vision International, Chancellor College, Zomba, 1995.

Constantine, Stephen. *The Making of British Colonial Development Policy, 1914-1940.* London: Frank Cass, 1984.

Cooper, Frederick. "Modernizing Bureaucrats, Backward Africans, and Development Concept." In Frederick Cooper and Randall Packard (eds.), *International Development and the Social Sciences: Essays on the History and Politics of Knowledge.* Berkeley: University of California Press, 2013, 64–92.

———. "Writing the history of Development." *Journal of Modern European History* 8, no. 1 (2010): 5–23.

Cowen, Michael and Robert Shenton. "The Origin and Course of Fabian Colonialism in Africa." *Journal of Historical Sociology* 4, no. 2 (1991): 143–74.

———. *Doctrines of Development.* London: Routledge, 1996.

Escobar, Arturo. *Encountering Development: The Making and Unmaking of the Third World.* Princeton, NJ: Princeton University Press, 1995.

Ferguson, Anne and Wapulumuka Oliver Mulwafu. "If Government failed, how are we to succeed? The importance of History and Context in the present-day irrigation reform in Malawi." In Barbara van Koppen, Mark Giordano and John Butterworth (eds.), *Community-based Water Law and Water Resources Management Reform in Developing Countries.* Wallingford: CABI, 2007, 211–27.

Ferguson, James. *The Anti-Politics Machine: "Development," Depoliticization, and Bureaucratic Power in Lesotho.* Minneapolis: University of Minnesota Press, 1994.

Green, Erik. "Indirect Rule and Colonial Intervention: Chiefs and Agrarian Change in Nyasaland, ca. 1933 to the Early 1950s." *International Journal of African Historical Studies* 44, no. 2 (2011): 249–74.

Grischow, Jeff, D. "Rural 'Community,' Chiefs and Social Capital: The Case of Southern Ghana." *Journal of Agrarian Change* 8, no. 1 (2008): 64–93.

Hadfield, L.A and John Aerni-Flessner, "Introduction: Localizing the History of Development in Africa." *International Journal of African Historical Studies* 50, no. 1 (2017): 1–9.

Hodge, Joseph, Morgan. *Triumph of the Expert: Agrarian Doctrines of Development and the Legacies of British Colonialism.* Athens, OH: Ohio University Press, 2007.

Immerwahr, Daniel. *Thinking Small: The United States and the Lure of Community Development.* Massachusetts: Harvard University Press, 2015.

Morgan, David, John. *The Official History of Colonial Development.* London: Macmillan, 1980.

Kelemen, Paul. "Individualism is, indeed, running Riot: Components of the social democratic model of Development." In Mark Duffield and Vernon Hewitt (eds.), *Empire, Development and Colonialism.* Woodbridge, UK: Byodell and Brown, 2009, 188–201.

Kishindo, Paul. "Farmer Clubs and Smallholder Agricultural Development in Malawi." *Development Southern Africa* 5, no. 2 (2008): 491–507.

————. "Farmer Turnover at Settlement Schemes: The Experience of Limphasa Irrigation Rice Scheme, Northern Malawi." *Development Southern Africa* 5, no. 2 (2008): 491–507.

Kunkel, Marc F. S. "Review: Writing the History of Development: A Review of the Recent Literature." *Contemporary European History* 20, no 2 (2011): 215–32.

Labour Party. *The Empire in Africa: Labour's Policy.* London: The Labour Party, 1926.

Li, Murry, Tania. *The Will to Improve, Governmentality, Development, and the Practice of Politics.* Durham: Duke University Press, 2007.

Lyon, Fergus. "Trust, Networks and Norms: The Creation of Social Capital in Agricultural Economies in Ghana." *World Development* 28, no. 4 (2000): 663–81.

Makombe, Kushinga, E. "Developing rural Africa: Rural development discourse in colonial Zimbabwe, 1944-79." In Joseph M. Hodge, Gerald Hödl, and Martina Kopf (eds.), *Developing Africa: Concepts, Practices and Twentieth-century Colonialism.* Manchester: Manchester University Press, 2014, 155–78.

McLoughlin, Peter F. M. "Land Re-organization in Malawi, 1950s-60: Its Pertinence to Current Development." In Sayre P. Schatz (eds.), *South of the Sahara: Development in African Economies.* Philadelphia: Temple University Press, 1972, 128–39.

Miller, R.A. "District Development Committees in Malawi: A Case Study in Rural Development." *Journal of Overseas Administration* 9, no. 2 (1970): 129–42.

Mulwafu, Wapulumuka, Oliver. *Conservation Song: A History of Peasant-State Relations and the Environment in Malawi, 1860-2000.* Cambridge: White Horse Press, 2011.

O'Malley, Pat. "Indigenous Governance." *Economy and Society* 25, no. 3 (1996): 310–36.

Phiri, D.D., *History of Malawi,* Vol. 2. Blantyre, Malawi: College Publishing Company, 2010.

Schuknecht, Rohland. *British Colonial Development Policy after the Second World War: The Case of Sukumaland, Tanganyika.* London: Global Book Marketing, 2010.

Scott, James, C. *Seeing Like a State: How Certain Schemes to Improve the Human Condition Have Failed.* New Haven: Yale University Press, 2008.

van Beusekom, Monica M. and Dorothy L. Hodgson. "Lessons Learned? Development Experiences in the Late Colonial Period." *Journal of African History* 41, no. 1 (2000): 29–33.

van Beusekom, Monica, M. *Negotiating Development: African Farmers and Colonial Experts at the Office Du Niger, 1920-1960.* Portsmouth, NH: James Currey, 2002.

Woolcock, Michael. "Calling on Friends and Relatives: Social Capital." In M. Fay (ed.), *Urban Poor in Latin America.* Washington, DC: World Bank Publications, 2005.

*Chapter 12*

# Regime Policing and the Stifling of the Human Rights Agenda

## *Late Colonial and Postcolonial Malawi, 1948–Present*

Paul Chiudza Banda

This chapter adopts the institutional approach to analyze the roles that the Malawi Police Force (MPF),[1] later Malawi Police Service (MPS), has played in the violation of human rights in the country, from the late 1940s to the present. This is despite the commitments made by the successive governments in signing international covenants aimed at promoting the human rights agenda. I argue that the discussion of the history of Malawi's human rights struggles should be understood within the frameworks of the processes of decolonization and the global Cold War. Both had significant influences on the operations of the late colonial and postcolonial states. While there have been various efforts, by the Malawi government and other bilateral donor countries and agencies to improve the situation, especially in the post–Cold War era, the outcomes have not been very impressive largely because of the political and economic considerations of those that wield power, who also influence the operations of the country's police.

## BACKGROUND AND CONTEXTUALIZATION
## OF THE STUDY

The notion of "human rights" was named as such because they belong to the human species. In theory, such rights are supposed to be shared and enjoyed equally by everyone regardless of sex, race, nationality, and economic background.[2] While such rights have historical antecedents set over hundreds of years, this study, as have many recent studies on the subject, including those by Micheline Ishay and Lone Lindholt,[3] among others, concentrates on the period following the Universal Declaration of Human Rights (UDHR) by the United Nations (UN) in 1948.[4] It analyzes how the declaration was extended to the then British protectorate of Nyasaland (now Malawi),[5] and the challenges associated with its implementation in the country. This study particularly focuses on Civil and Political Rights (CPRs). It also acknowledges the importance of Economic, Social, and Cultural Rights (ESCRs).

To conduct this analysis, the chapter adopts the institutional approach, rather than an ad hoc and generalized perspective. I settled for the MPF (later MPS), as a state institution. Among other responsibilities, the police are charged with the responsibility of protecting human rights. In civilized human societies, the police have responsibilities to protect people (as individuals) and their properties and to bring order and harmony. While serving under the authority of a state, the police are there to protect people's rights within the boundaries of the law, and to coerce citizens to conform to agreeable rights for the general welfare of a given society.[6] The justification in studying the operations of the police lies in the fact that the police as an institution[7] is manned by individuals, who are bound to make mistakes, to be abused or misused, and to the detriment of the citizens at large. In such cases, the police could, instead of protecting the individual rights of the citizens, be used to invade or violate the rights of the citizens, including such acts as spreading terror, instilling fear, invade individuals' privacy, subverting the popular will, and keep in power unconstitutional regimes.[8]

In this study, the focus is on both the physical and nonphysical aspects of institutions. The police force is a physical institution. It also has nonphysical or subjective aspects, such as the various constitutional amendments, rules and regulations, and the political climate, that guided its operations. In doing so, connections have been made between the subjective or ideal aspects of the states under study, and whatever has over the years become the "realism" of their actions and policies. In other words, the mentality of the leadership, usually is reflected in the operations of the various institutions under their watch. In most African states, the police as an institution have historically played several roles in society, including the maintenance of law and order; involvement in paramilitary operations; regulatory activities, such as involvement in rural development projects; and regime representation (including linking the central government to its citizens).[9]

The conceptualization of human rights has two main perspectives. Some argue on its universality, while others argue to the contrary. Those who have written from an Africanist or non-Western perspective, including Bonny Ibhawoh, Josiah A.M. Cobbah, Adamantia Pollis, Peter Schwab, and Raimundo Pannikar, among others, argue that the conceptualization of human rights was of Western origin, and that its values cannot be applied or accepted universally. They question whether there is one culture whose values could be elevated to speak for the entire humankind. They argue further that the "universalization" of human rights, especially in the former European colonies, simply represents residues of the colonial experience, where the constructs of the culture of the colonizer dominated over the colonized. They argued that African culture is communal in nature, and thus does not fit into the individualism championed by the Western-influenced human rights initiative. Raimundo Pannikar argued further that even in the Western world itself, there are some differences within fields such as Theology, History, and Marxism, over the conceptualization of human rights.[10]

This chapter argues against such culturally influenced conceptualizations. Firstly, over the years, it has encouraged African leaders, including those in Malawi, to infringe upon the rights of their peoples, while ignoring the internationally agreeable norms. It has given loopholes to such leaders to select ("pick and choose") what they felt was beneficial toward prolonging their reigns or regimes, and disregarded concepts that were a threat to their own political positions. Furthermore, such scholarship depicts African culture as static and African societies as being closed, that have over the years not been influenced by Western or international values, including the protection of human rights. The civil rights (including life, liberty, security, no arbitrary arrest, fair trial, and equality) and political rights (including freedom of expression, political participation, assembly, association, conscience, and religion) that were championed by the UDHR, from Articles Three to Twenty-One, are rights that although being of Western conceptualization are now gaining "universal" acceptability.[11] Furthermore, during the era of decolonization, African nationalist leaders, including those from Malawi and elsewhere, also made extensive reference to the UDHR, invoking the right to "self-determination," to justify their own demands for independence and inclusion in the colonial enterprise.[12] It would also be unfair to argue that African people do not deserve or do not have interests in such individual rights, simply because they have historically had elements of communalism. And as argued by Rhoda E. Howard, the argument that Africans have always had a communal mentality often overlooks the fact that even before formal contacts with the West, Africans were already differentiated along such concepts as wealth, age, gender, enslavement, kinship, religion, and other such socioeconomic concepts.[13]

## THE BRITISH EMPIRE AND THE EXTENSION OF HUMAN RIGHTS IN THE POST–WORLD WAR II ERA

Our understanding of the extension or lack thereof of human rights in British overseas colonies should be located within the complex process of decolonization, an era synonymous with the post–World War II era.[14] The decolonization of British territories was complicated by the onset of the Cold War, especially the threat posed by the global spread of communism from the Eastern bloc (led by the USSR and in part, by Communist China).[15] These eastern powers, just like the United States, had intentions to exert their influence in the former European territories in Africa and Asia (the so-called "Third World"), seeking, as Michael Latham has argued, to control the direction of global affairs and define modernity by extending their socioeconomic systems abroad. While the Americans championed capitalist-driven modernization, the Eastern bloc championed a socialist path to development. They would do so by taking advantage of the high levels of poverty and instability that had ensued during the process of decolonization.[16] In other words, the Cold War was not merely an ideological warfare, rather it also had geopolitical connotations with the two main "warring powers" seeking to exert their influence across the globe.[17] During the same era, as highlighted above, the international community, led by the UN, was committing itself to the protection and respect of human rights for all. It would be the colonized societies, that, as argued by Roland Burke, played some of the most important roles in bringing the UDHR into practice and making the declaration a "universal" document. They were in the forefront quoting from the UDHR in the fight for independence, and after independence, seeking international recognition for the newly created nation-states.[18]

In the British Empire, the initial tilt toward the extension of Bills of Rights to the overseas territories in the post–World War II era, started with the signing of the European Convention on Human Rights (ECHR) in 1950. The British government was one of the signatories and eventually ratified it in March 1951. While some at the Colonial Office (CO) were willing to extend the ECHR to Britain's overseas territories, there was also a reluctance by many, who felt that if the process had been accelerated it would have contributed to widespread demands for independence by nationalist leaders. As such, in most territories, the terms of the ECHR and indeed those of the UDHR were not immediately extended.[19] Even when the UDHR came out, the British authorities were reluctant to extend it to their colonies, especially due to the clause of "self-determination," which would have undermined Britain's hold on its empire.[20] As Simpson (2001) posited, there were fears at the CO that a full acceptance and adoption of the UDHR in the overseas territories could have fueled an anti-colonial crusade. Furthermore, doing so would have indirectly invited the UN to embark on supervising the affairs of colonial governments.[21]

In the case of Malawi, the most basic move by the colonial authorities, in as far as extending the Bill of Rights was concerned, was opening doors for some form of African representation in the Legislative Council (Legco). This began in the mid-1950s when a limited number of educated Africans were nominated to represent fellow Africans. Other than that, there was no constitutional documentation that indicated the rights of Africans. Previously, the Legco had, since its inception in 1907, been manned by Europeans, mainly the colonial officials, European capitalists, European missionaries (where the missionaries were supposed to represent the interests of Africans), and Asian representatives (to represent the group of Indians in the country). By the end of 1953, there were three Africans on the Legco, against six unofficial European representatives, which often meant that government bills could easily be passed.[22] The lack of proper representation thus denied many Africans their political rights to elect their own political representatives, at least until after the 1961 general elections.

The delay in extending the Bill of Rights was influenced by among the many reasons: the British government's economic interests in the British Central Africa region (now Zambia, Zimbabwe, and Malawi). There were also fears of the threat posed by the global spread of communism. Lastly, other British authorities were unwilling to hand over political power to Africans. From such fears, between 1953 and 1963, Malawi was included in a new political entity called the Central African Federation (CAF). The CAF brought together the three British Central African territories.[23] Although the main arguments advanced by the colonial authorities were that the CAF was for the welfare and development of the Africans, sentiments from Sir Roy Welensky, who became the second prime minister of the Federation (1956–1963), indicated that there was a desire by the European settlers and the British government, to maximize the exploitation of mineral resources in the two Rhodesias and Nyasaland. They argued that there was no need to accelerate political development for the Africans, as that would have "naturally" flowed when there was economic health or development (i.e., that without economic health, there could be no political development).[24]

The other motivation for establishing the federation had been to establish a strong state, essential for hampering the spread of communism. The talks to establish the federation accelerated in the aftermath of the Second World War, especially following the infiltration of communism in Asia, leading to the outbreak of such wars as the Korean War (1950–1953). The "official mind" at the time was that territories in the Middle East and Africa would have been the next target or destination, hence the need to form a buffer against the global spread of communism.[25] The British government established several committees where reports were generated throughout the 1950s, aimed at finding ways and means to counter the influence of communism in the British territories.[26] As Britain retained vested interest in the CAF, in 1954, the government established the Federal Security and Intelligence Bureau (FSIB). The bureau's task was to oversee the maintenance of security and monitor the threat posed by the spread of communism. Its headquarter was in Salisbury, Zimbabwe, the designated capital of the federation.[27]

The FSIB collaborated with territorial police intelligence agencies in the violation of human rights. The police officers were quick to use maximum force, to eliminate all forms of anti-federation agitation. For instance, in Malawi, in 1953, 11 Africans were shot dead by the police in the southern province district of Thyolo, as they protested the establishment of the federation, while many others (72) were also severely wounded. No police officer was ever tried for committing the outright murders. At the same time, due to continued agitation against the CAF, by the leading nationalist movement, the Nyasaland African Congress (NAC), the police began refusing to give permission for holding public rallies, thereby denying the Africans their political rights.[28] Such developments were taking place at a time when colonial police commissioners and authorities at the CO in London were negotiating on how best to wean the colonial police forces from control by the central government. The commissioners often feared that increased central government control, or indeed political interference, would have led to the creation of a "police state."[29]

On March 3, 1959, Governor Sir Robert Armitage declared a State of Emergency,[30] acting on an intelligence briefing from the Nyasaland police, on allegations that the NAC leadership had planned to conduct nationwide violence, and to murder Europeans in the country. Under "Operation Sunrise," the security forces arrested the top leaders of the NAC, including Dr. Hastings Kamuzu Banda, the man who became Malawi's leader between 1964 and 1994. The police placed the agitators in detention centers in Nyasaland and Southern Rhodesia. Many were never given fair court trial, probably because they were no clear-cut charges in which to implicate them, in the process violating their rights against arbitrary imprisonment. By the end of April 1959, over 1,000 Africans were detained, while over 2,000 others were also convicted of political offenses. The NAC was outlawed, and it seized to exist as a political entity. The police also killed over 51 protestors across the country. As in previous cases, no police officer was ever tried and convicted.[31]

A British government instituted a commission of enquiry, led by Lord Patrick Develin, hence "the Devlin Commission," condemned the actions of the police officers. The report concluded that Nyasaland had *de facto* become a "police state."[32] According to Philip Murphy (2010), the use of the term "police state" by the Devlin Commission, referring to the tough and punitive measures employed by the security forces, was very embarrassing for both the British and Nyasaland governments, as during the Second World War and later during the Cold War that form of terminology had been more associated with the fascist and communist regimes, and their associated human rights abuses, thereby posing serious questions about how colonial affairs were being handled at the time.[33]

It is interesting, to note from confidential dispatches exchanged between colonial officials in Nyasaland, Southern Rhodesia, and London that although they were worried about the violation of human rights, they were not willing to adhere to the principles of both the UDHR and the ECHR. They were concerned with "cleaning up the mess" that took place in Nyasaland. This included legalizing the police operation, to an extent of evoking Article Fifteen of the ECHR, which gave powers to the states concerned to declare emergency rules and regulations where necessary.[34]

In the same vein, Iain Macleod, the Secretary of State for the Colonies, also seemed equally concerned about the dent which the Nyasaland unrest had inflicted on the British government, especially the abuse of human rights, in contravention of the ECHR. In a dispatch to the prime minister, Rt. Hon. Harold Macmillan, he expressed his worries as follows:

> There are now about 470 men detained under Emergency Powers, 380 of them in Nyasaland, and 90 in Southern Rhodesia. The leaders are at Gwelo in Southern Rhodesia. There had been a fairly swift release of detainees until a short time ago, but the rate of releases has fallen and indeed, to my disappointment, the number of persons in detention has started very slowly to rise again. I am sure we must do everything we can to achieve a substantial reduction very swiftly. For myself, I do not believe that we can possibly justify for long the continuance of the Emergency. We would have no chance of defending our action if we could be brought before the Human Rights Commission. . . . I aim, therefore, to move swiftly as possible towards a reduction of this figure to the true hard core, which might number perhaps 50.[35]

In January 1960, the prime minister visited Nyasaland, where he saw for himself the level of police brutality. This followed a scuffle that occurred on January 26, as he addressed delegates to a state-sponsored luncheon, at Ryall's Hotel, in Blantyre. The police mercilessly whipped African protestors (over 800 of them), while others were thrown into police vehicles and taken to police cells. In the aftermath of the protests, the Nyasaland Governor, Sir Glyn Jones, in February 1960 set up a commission of enquiry to investigate the causes. Judge Frederick Southworth (hence "The Southworth Commission") of the High Court of Nyasaland chaired the commission. In the end, the commission absolved the police of any wrongdoing, and even went as far as mocking the protestors for only sustaining "minor injuries."[36]

The Nyasaland Emergency stayed put until April 1960, when Dr. Banda and other leaders of the NAC were released from their year-long detention, after measures had been out in place to strengthen the Nyasaland Police Force to deal with any perceived "lawlessness."[37] Following their release, a constitutional conference was held at Lancaster House in London, in July and August 1960. The Rt. Hon. Iain Macleod convened the conference, where concerns about extending the Bill of Rights to the protectorate were discussed. The delegates agreed that while such a provision would be neces-sary, there was a need to carefully study the matter before it could be included in the constitution.[38] During the follow-up constitutional conference, held at Marlborough House in London, and convened by Mr. R.A. Butler, the Home Secretary, the subject of extending the Bill of Rights was also deliberated upon. The issue was brought up by the leadership of Nyasaland's minority political parties, especially the United Federal Party (UFP), dominated by Europeans and Asians, who wanted an assurance of state protection once the African majority was in power. Both the British authorities and leaders of the majority Malawi Congress Party (MCP), led by Dr. H.K. Banda, agreed on the necessity of such a Bill (of Rights) in the next constitutional document, and that the courts be given powers to enforce the rights. Section 25 of the agreements at the Marlborough House Conference read as follows: "The Conference agreed that the new constitution should contain a Bill of Rights guaranteeing protection of the right to life and the right to personal liberty; protection from slavery and forced labor, inhuman treatment and deprivation of property without compensation; protection of privacy of the home; protec-tion of the law; protection of freedom of conscience, freedom of expression, freedom of assembly and association, and freedom of movement; and protec-tion against discrimination."[39]

It was against that background that the Nyasaland (Constitution) Order-in-Council, 1963, included an entire chapter (chapter one) entitled "Protection of Fundamental Rights and Freedoms of the Individual." Among the key areas emphasized under the constitution, were fundamental rights and freedoms of the individual; protection of right to life; protection of right to personal liberty; protection from slavery and forced labor; protection from inhuman treatment; protection from deprivation of property; protection of freedom of conscience; protection of freedom of assembly and association; and protection of freedom of movement, among others.[40] By then, it was official British colonial policy in Africa to ensure that there were negotiated constitutional talks, where although the newly independent states would not be compelled to take after the British system of government, they had to ensure the protection of minorities and the rights and duties of the indi-vidual in the community, which was then perceived to be the essence of democracy.[41]

## POSTCOLONIAL MALAWI: CONTINUITIES
## IN REGIME POLICING

There is scholarship, such as that of Bertrand Badie (2000), that refers to the postcolonial state in Africa, as an "imported state," referring to the continuation of practices, structures, and ideologies that were previously employed by the colonial state, and were emulated by the successor postcolonial state.[42] The end of European colonial rule, as Frederick Cooper and John Darwin have argued elsewhere, did not necessarily mean a complete departure from practices, systems, and institutions that served the colonial state in Africa.[43] I adopt such a conceptualization to illustrate the continuation of colonial-era practices in postcolonial Malawi, particularly focusing on the violation of human rights by the police force.

At independence, in July 1964, the postcolonial state, under the leadership of Dr. H.K. Banda, adopted the Bill of Rights introduced in the 1963 Constitutional Order-in-Council. However, while previously the Bill (of Rights) was in chapter one of the constitution, under the Independence Order-in-Council of July 1964, also prepared by the British Parliament, it was pushed to chapter two.[44] The newly independent country of Malawi was soon hampered by political bickering. Chief among the disagreements by the political elite was the so-called "cabinet crisis"[45] of August to September 1964, barely two months after independence. Dr. Banda disagreed with his fellow cabinet ministers on matters of both foreign and domestic policies, leading to the dismissal of three cabinet ministers and the resignation of three others. One major bone of contention on foreign policy revolved around Malawi's relations with Communist China. As a pro-Western leader, Dr. Banda was against opening diplomatic relations with Communist China, while some of his cabinet ministers favored it. The goodwill and the cordial relations that were expected for the then newly independent country were completely replaced by more repressive measures. Dr. Banda sought to consolidate his own grip on the country's political and economic sectors,[46] in what Botero would describe as "the reason of state."[47]

The same leadership of the MCP, led by Dr. Banda, that championed the inclusion of the Bill of Rights in the constitution, did not hesitate to remove it from the constitution, as the leadership saw it as a threat to their goals of holding on to political power. In the Constitution of the Republic of Malawi, July 1966, the chapter on the Bill of Rights was completely removed. There were only two sentences, under "Chapter One: The Republic," where the government committed itself to abide by the UDHR, and adherence to the Law of Nations; another where it assured the citizens of the country access to equal rights and freedoms, without necessarily elaborating which specific rights would be upheld.[48] The situation would remain like that until the political changes of the early 1990s. During that time, Dr. Banda and his "inner circle" had a significant grip on the country's economic and political sectors.

In the post-1966 era, one of the main organs of the state that was utilized to infringe upon people's rights, like its colonial predecessor, would be the MPF. In the 1966 republican constitution, the president had powers to appoint the commissioner of police without the approval of any constitutional body or branch of government.[49] This often meant that the police officers served at the mercy of the president. Although the Police Service Commission (PSC) had powers to discipline and remove from office members of the MPF, that would not have been done if the "indiscipline" related to the safeguarding of the political position of the incumbent.

Just like its colonial-era predecessor, the MPF was a centralized institution with one of the commissioner of police or inspector general, aided by regional police commissioners and officers-in-charge of the district police offices.[50] While this kind of police organization is not a unique or bad practice, the major question that must be raised is that which Christian Potholm (1969) posed, regarding the social orientation of the police personnel. Potholm argued that in most cases, African police personnel, right from their screening, training, and supervision, were often less dedicated to the law, but rather were servants of the leader or of the regime. This led to a tendency where police personnel were inculcated with the sociopolitical values of the political system, rather than serving the interests of the society.[51] Elsewhere, Wycliffe N. Otiso and Ruth J. Kaguta argued that in most African countries, including their case study of Kenya, there were elements of "regime policing," where the police were/are accountable to the regime rather than to the law and the community. The police represent interests of the dominant group and have no connection with the community, nor do they have regard for protection of human rights.[52]

While the Banda regime had removed the Bill of Rights in the country's constitution, it was perhaps surprising that as a member of the UN, the Malawian leadership were signatories to the International Covenant on Civil and Political Rights (ICCPR), December 1966, which was an extension of the UDHR. The 1966 covenant called on all member states of the UN to take necessary steps, including constitutional provisions, to protect the human rights (civil, political, economic) of their citizens.[53] As a member of the Organization of African Unity (OAU), the Malawi government was a signatory to the OAU's African Charter on Human and People's Rights (ACHPR), 1981. The charter itself was but an extension of the UDHR, but the African leaders also added concerns that were specific to African contexts (such as the elimination of colonialism, neocolonialism, apartheid, and all forms of discrimination). Among the charter's main concerns were issues to deal with "freedom, equality, justice and dignity, essential for the achievement of the legitimate aspirations of African peoples." There were also guarantees for equality before the law for all; respect for the right to life, liberty, security, against arbitrary arrest and/or detention, fair trial, freedom of association and expression, freedom of movement, among the many guarantees.[54] Although the ACHPR, under Article Thirty-One, provided for the formation of a body, named the African Commission on Human and People's Rights, to oversee the implementation of the terms of the charter, it remained so at the ideological level, as most African regimes, including Malawi, continued to violate their people's human rights, without any sanctions placed on the leadership. Unfortunately, many of these international agreements lack enforcement mechanisms.

The Malawi leader developed a "slow Africanization policy," in the first decade of his administration. It represented a condition where he would not rush to immediately replace the British colonial officials with African personnel, until after he was satisfied with the qualification and quality of work that the Africans would do. It was through that policy that he retained some British policemen in his government. For instance, the Police Commissioner, Mr. P. Long, who was appointed in that position in 1964, retained his post until July 1971, when he was replaced by a Malawian, Mc. J. Kamwana. Kamwana underwent various police training courses at the Hendon Police Training School in England (1968), and at the Scottish Police College, Tulliallan, Scotland (1969).[55] Furthermore, Banda himself also retained the position of Commander-in-Chief of the armed forces and the police force. The police force itself also retained such colonial-era branches, which included General Administration; the Criminal Investigation Department (CID); the Special Branch; Police Mobile Force (PMF); Finance Branch; Radio Communication; Traffic and Transport; Immigration; the Training School; and the Depot.[56]

The period between 1964 and 1994 has a lot of case studies replete with the repression of anti-government critics, most of which involved the actions of the MPF. The local media did not produce reports of many of these due to a "culture of silence" that existed in the country. As such, international organizations, including Amnesty International and Africa Watch, produced the reports. Space not permitting, I refer to the September 1989, publication by Amnesty International, commemorating Malawi's 25 years of independence, which highlighted various human rights abuses in the country, particularly focusing on the plight of political detainees. The introduction paragraph of the 25th-anniversary edition perhaps best summarized the atmosphere that had existed in the country since independence as follows: "political imprisonment has been a feature in Malawi throughout the 25 years since the country became independent in July 1964. Under the government of Life President Dr. Hastings Kamuzu Banda, hundreds—possibly thousands—of people have been imprisoned for peacefully exercising their basic human rights to freedom of expression, association and religion. Most have been detained without ever being tried and many have been tortured. Some have been deliberately killed or have died as a direct result of their harsh conditions of imprisonment." The subsequent sections of the report included details of numerous case studies of Malawians who faced such harsh conditions, mostly through police brutality, who ranged from businessmen, politicians, academicians, religious leaders, and other ordinary peoples.[57] It seemed convenient for the Malawian leaders to infringe upon their people's human rights. This ensured their longevity in the political positions they held, and continued access to state resources. For instance, Banda remained as Malawi's leader for three decades, 1964–1994.

## POST–COLD WAR ERA REFORMS: SUCCESSES AND CHALLENGES

Following the end of the Cold War in 1991, the international community (from the West) that provided support to the Banda regime saw no need of supporting a government responsible for a wide range of human rights abuses.[58] The international community pressured the regime to liberalize the country's economic and political systems. The British government aired its concerns during the Commonwealth Conference held in Harare, Zimbabwe, in October 1991. All member states, including Malawi, were called upon to extend the Bill of Rights to their citizens.[59] In September 1991, U.S. vice president Dan Quayle also visited Malawi, where he delivered the human rights message to Dr. Banda. In June 1992, the U.S. Congress' Subcommittee on Africa also urged the Banda regime to extend human rights to Malawians by liberalizing the political and economic spaces.[60] Amid the pressure, the Banda government issued a statement defending the country's human rights record. It denied the involvement of the Malawi police and other security organs in human rights violations. It also reiterated that as a member of the UN and a signatory of international human rights covenants, the government would not tolerate any forms of human rights violations.[61]

There was also internal pressure for change within Malawi, mainly from members of the clergy, politicians, and ordinary people, encouraged by events in the international community to call for regime change. During the initial phases of the post–Cold War agitation against the Banda regime, the police also acted swiftly to nip the agitation in the bud. This included arbitrary arrests, intimidation, and killing of demonstrators.[62] In the end, the pressure was unbearable, compelling Banda to liberalize the political system. In the general elections that followed, in May 1994, Banda was defeated, marking the end of his 30-year reign.[63]

In 1995, a new constitution was enacted to go along with the democratic dispensation, bringing back the Bill of Rights. There were also other human rights-related amendments, including the creation of the Human Rights Commission, and the clarification of the role that the police force would play in democratic era Malawi. For instance, the police were now compelled not to take orders from politicians, not become members of a political party, and that they had to discharge their duties with impartiality.[64] Under the 2010 republican constitution, as amended, the name of the police was also changed from a police force to a police service, hence the name MPS.[65]

Further reforms also led to the inclusion of the component of human rights in the police training school curriculum. It followed Malawi's becoming a member of the International Human Rights Manual Drafting project, which begun in 1999, implemented in Malawi in 2005. Chapter two of the police training manual also includes an overview of the meaning of human rights; classification of human rights (civil, political, economic, social, cultural, and solidarity rights); and the various documents that have been issued internationally (such as the UDHR, 1948; and the ACHPR, 1981) to promote the human rights agenda. It also includes a brief overview of the historical trajectory of the human rights agenda in Malawi, starting from the colonial era, through the post–colonial era, and the post–Cold War era. It also highlights the roles that the police played when they were used as instruments of oppression, in such a way that the police had wide powers to deny people their rights through vicious interrogations, detentions without trial, and other cruel interrogation methods.[66]

While such reforms are commendable, over the years, practice has shown that elements of "regime policing" still linger on, especially in a system where the top police positions, including that of inspector general, are filled following "presidential appointments." That is not to state that there have not been changes in police conduct, the argument is that such changes are often minimal or that the enforcement of human rights by the police has remained relatively weak. Changes such as the establishment of "community policing" programs, where there are efforts to increase the interdependence and shared responsibility of the police and the community, can only be appreciated if they go along with the protection of human rights.[67]

There have also been various efforts by the international community, especially the U.K. government's Development Fund for International Development (DFID), which has been providing funds to the MPS to improve its operations. The most recent funding covered the period July 2013 to July 2015, where £3m was set aside to assist the MPS to improve public satisfaction with police responsiveness and accountability. This was after the DFID noted key gaps in the MPS that affect its operations, including an accountability gap, a capability gap, and an evidence gap created by a general atmosphere of insecurity. The DFID has through its plans for Malawi noted that matters of insecurity and human rights violations in the country could in the long run inhibit socioeconomic development. There are fears that the violations would lead to the withdrawal of both local and foreign investments, and the destruction of the limited developmental gains already made.[68]

Over the recent past, there have been cases of human rights violations perpetrated by the police. As posited by Diana Cammack, one would argue that Malawi's democratic transition has brought in very limited transformation in the country's political and socioeconomic systems. The behavior of the ruling elite and the state institutions they control has shown limited change.[69] This study only highlights a selected few. For instance, in November 2001, a popular Malawian reggae musician, Evison Matafale, died in police custody after the police had arrested him three days after writing an allegedly "seditious letter" to then president Bakili Muluzi. Following widespread protests, commissions of enquiry were set up by both the government and the Human Rights Commission, in 2002, and both concluded that Matafale's arrest was unlawful. They also condemned the police for transporting Matafale over a long distance (over 200 miles) while he was ill.[70] To date, no police officer has accounted for Matafale's death in custody. In December 2001, police also fired live bullets at demonstrating students (of the University of Malawi), where one student was killed. Efforts by the Human Rights Commission (HRC) to get the shooters prosecuted were not entertained by the police inspector general.[71] There were also other high-profile cases where the police were accused of doing shoddy investigations or producing inconsistent reports. For instance, the April 1995 murder of the Army Commander, Mancken Chigawa, a case that was never properly investigated.[72] It was also common for police to violate the people's freedom of assembly, where they used unspecified reasons to block opposition political parties to organize mass rallies or peaceful demonstrations, while the same was not denied to the ruling party.[73]

Similar instances of human rights violations were replicated during the Bingu wa Mutharika administration (2004–2012). Among these cases, in February 2011, a political science professor at the University of Malawi was also threatened by the inspector general of police. The professor was accused of "inciting revolution" by among other things comparing Malawi's socioeconomic challenges to those behind the "Arab spring." There were accusations and counteraccusations that led to the closure of constituent colleges of the university, police firing tear gas at protestors, and some of the professors were also suspended. In April 2011, a leaked email from the British High Commissioner to Malawi to his superiors in London perhaps best summed up the deteriorating human rights conditions in the country. The high commissioner reiterated that Mutharika had become more autocratic and intolerant to criticism by his own citizens and the international community. The high commissioner was subsequently declared "persona non grata," and was forced to immediately leave the country. Britain responded by withdrawing financial aid to the Malawi government.[74]

The most astonishing human rights violations by the police under the Mutharika regime occurred on July 20, 2011, when the police killed 20 people, who were demonstrating against the government's inaction to sort out socioeconomic challenges and also the general atmosphere of undemocratic tendencies perpetrated by the ruling Democratic Progressive Party (DPP).[75] The shootings were contrary to regulations of the MPS Act, 2003, as amended, where there are specific cases where a police officer is allowed to use firearms, including such incidences as shooting a person escaping from custody; and against a person who tries to rescue another person from custody.[76] Following public pressure and the findings of a commission of enquiry, the police reluctantly presented the names of the officers who were involved in the shootings, and as of December 2016, only one of the police officers charged, Mr. Stewart Lobo, was convicted and sentenced to 12 years imprisonment.[77] The MPS and other top politicians were also implicated in the murder of a university student and political activist, Robert Chasowa, whose corpse was found lying on campus under controversial circumstances.[78] Due to the frequency of such cases, the Mutharika regime, especially the period between 2010 and 2012, was referred to as being a "police state," where political interference and police brutality had become widely spread.[79]

The use of police brutality and politically motivated killings have sadly continued in the post-Bingu wa Mutharika era. The local and international media, as well as diplomatic cables, have documented these.[80] The most recent cases occurred before and after the May 2019 general elections. Opposition political parties and other civil society organizations challenged the credibility of the elections both in the courts and through nationwide demonstrations. The demonstrators found themselves being killed, beaten, chased, or "tear-gassed" by police officers.[81] Due to these hostilities, the Malawi army "took over" the role of protecting the protestors.[82] The judiciary also rescued the protestors by granting an unprecedented number of court injunctions each time the police and government authorities attempted to block the demonstrations.[83]

## CONCLUSION

This chapter adopted the institutional approach to analyze the role of the Malawi police in the violation of human rights in the country. Located within the frameworks of decolonization and the global Cold War, it has highlighted various cases where the police suppressed anti-government critics from the late 1940s to the post–Cold War era. The main argument is that despite the various governments being signatories of international human rights covenants and adopting the Bill of Rights in the national constitution, they have over the years been associated with various human rights violations. This has ensured the survival of the state at the expense of the citizens' human rights. This chapter has focused on civil and political rights. Although significant steps have been taken in as far as police reforms are concerned, especially under the democratic dispensation of the early 1990s to the present, enforcement of protection of human rights remains relatively weak. The police could do better if they remain neutral or independent of any political interference. It is certainly not enough, as the Malawi case has shown, to have a Bill of Rights enshrined in the constitution if it cannot be fully enforced. While the country needs the police to ensure the safety and security of the citizens, it is intolerable for the same police to be infringing upon the rights of individuals and the society.

## NOTES

1. For a history of the origins of the Malawi police, see John McCracken, "Coercion and Control in Nyasaland: Aspects of the History of a Colonial Police Force," *Journal of African History* vol. 27 (1986): 127–147.

2. Micheline Ishay, *The History of Human Rights: From Ancient Times to the Globalization Era* (Berkley: University of California Press, 2004), 3.

3. Lone Lindholt, *Questioning the Universality of Human Rights: The African Charter on Human and People's Rights in Botswana, Malawi, and Mozambique* (Aldershot, England: Dartmouth Publishers, 1997). The UN Declaration drew its inspiration from other earlier documents, including religious documents, the Era of Enlightenment, the French Revolution (1789-1799), and indeed the American Revolution.

4. *Universal Declaration of Human Rights* (Place of publication not identified: Great Neck Pub., 2009).

5. The country, now known as Malawi, was a British protectorate from 1891 to 1964. Initially, the protectorate was known as British Central Africa (BCA), from 1893 to 1907 the name became British Central Africa Protectorate (BCAP), and from 1907 to 1964 the name used was the Nyasaland Protectorate. See Annual Report, *Nyasaland Report for 1921* (London: HMSO, 1922), 2–4.

6. Daniel Nsereko, "The Police, Human Rights, and the Constitution: An African Perspective," *Human Rights Quarterly* vol. 15 (1993): 465–467.

7. The concept of "institution" has been defined in several ways. It can refer to both physical and nonphysical aspects, and it can also refer to the norms, values, and practices of the individuals operating under some form of authority structure or system. See these works: Douglas C. North, "Institutions," *The Journal of Economic*

*Perspectives* vol. 5, no. 1 (Winter 1991): 97–98; Geoffrey M. Hodgson, "What are Institutions?" *Journal of Economic Issues* vol. 40, no. 1 (March 2006): 1–8.

8. Daniel Nsereko (1993), 468–469.

9. Christian P. Potholm, "The Multiple Roles of the Police as Seen in the African Context," *Journal of Developing Areas* vol. 3, no. 2 (1968): 142–150; Wycliffe Nyachoti Otiso and Ruth Kaguta, "Kenya at Fifty: State Policing Reforms, Politics, and Law, 1963-2013," in Michael M. Kithinji, et al., eds., *Kenya after 50: Reconfiguring Historical, Political, and Policy Milestones* (New York: Palgrave Macmillan, 2016), 221–244.

10. Josiah A.M. Cobbah, "African Values and the Human Rights Debate: An African Perspective," *Human Rights Quarterly* vol. 9, no. 3 (1987): 309–331; Raimon Pannikar, "Is the Notion of Human Rights a Western Concept?" in Richard Falk, et al., eds., *Human Rights: Critical Concepts in Political Science* (New York: Routledge, 2007), 75–102; Adamantia Pollis and Peter Schwab, *Human Rights: Cultural and Ideological Perspectives* (New York: Praeger, 1980).

11. Rhoda E. Howard-Hassmann, *Human Rights in Commonwealth Africa* (Totowa, NJ: Rowman and Littlefield, 1986), 2–4.

12. Roland Burke, *Decolonization and the Evolution of International Human Rights* (Philadelphia: University of Pennsylvania Press, 2013), 1–6 and 35–58. Bonny Ibhawoh, *Human Rights in Africa* (Cambridge: CUP, 2018), 2–3.

13. Rhoda E. Howard, "Group versus Individual Identity in the African Debate on Human Rights," in Abdullahi Ahmed, *Human Rights in Africa: Cross-Cultural Perspectives* (Washington, DC: The Brookings Institution, 1990), 164–166; Bonny Ibhawo, "Cultural Relativism and Human Rights: Reconsidering the Africanist Discourse," *Netherlands Quarterly of Human Rights* vol. 91, no. 1 (2001): 56–57.

14. See for instance, John Darwin, *Britain and Decolonization: The Retreat from Empire in the Post-War World* (New York: Macmillan, 1988).

15. On the global Cold War, see Odd Arne Westad, *The Global Cold War: Third World Interventions and the Making of Our Times* (Cambridge: Cambridge University Press, 2005).

16. For U.S. and Soviet foreign policy directions during the early Cold War era, see Frank Costigliola, "US Foreign Policy from Kennedy to Johnson," in Melvyn P. Leffler and Odd Arne Westad, eds., *The Cambridge History of the Cold War, vol.2: crises and détente* (Cambridge: Cambridge University Press, 2010), 112–133; Svetlana Savranskaya and William Taubman, "Soviet Foreign Policy, 1962-1975," in *The Cambridge History of the Cold War, vol.2: crises and détente*, 134–157. On the Cold War in the "Third World," see Michael Latham, "The Cold War in the Third World," in *The Cambridge History of the Cold War, vol.2: crises and détente*, 258–267.

17. Daniel Sargent, "The Cold War," in J.R. McNeill and Kennedy Pomeranz, eds., *The Cambridge World History, vol. 7, part 2* (Cambridge: Cambridge University Press, 2015), 321–346.

18. Roland Burke, *Decolonization and the Evolution of International Human Rights*, 1–3.

19. Charles Parkinson, *Bills of Rights and Decolonization: The Emergence of Domestic Human Rights Instruments in Britain's Overseas Territories* (Oxford:

Oxford University Press, 2007), 1–11. See also "CO 936/237, no. 1 (The problem of nationalism): letter from Sir W. Strang to Sir T. Lloyd. Enclosure: FO Permanent Under-Secretary's Committee paper," June 21, 1952, in David Goldsworthy, ed., *The Conservative Government and the End of Empire, 1951-1957, part 1: International Relations* (London: HMSO, 1994), 13–19. See also "FO 371/107142, no. 13: 'Human rights covenants': letter from S. Hoare (Home Affairs) to E.R. Warner (Foreign Office),' 19 June 1953, in David Goldsworthy, Ibid., 396–398.

20. Charles Parkinson, *Bills of Rights and Decolonization*, 26.

21. A.W. Brian Simpson, *Human Rights and the End of Empire: Britain and the Genesis of European Convention* (Oxford: Oxford University Press, 2001), 340–342.

22. John McCracken, *A History of Malawi, 1856-1966* (United Kingdom: James Currey, 2012), 271.

23. For a thorough history of the CAF, see J.R.T. Woods, *The Welesnky Papers: A History of the Federation of Rhodesia and Nyasaland* (Durban: Graham Publishers, 1983).

24. Roy Welensky, *Welensky's 4000 Days: The Life and Death of the Federation of Rhodesia and Nyasaland* (London: Collins Publishers, 1964), 46–47.

25. Ibid., 47. See also Speech by the Right Hon. Clement Attlee, the British PM in the House of Commons, *Parliamentary Debates, House of Commons Official Report, 5th Series, Vol.478.* July 24 to October 26, 1950, 951–954.

26. British National Archives, hereafter, BNA: CO 537/5263: A Survey of Communism in Africa, Extract from a Paper by the Research Department, Foreign Office. See also BNA: CO 1035/126: Official Committee on Countersubversion in Colonial Territories—Communism in Africa, 1956 Report. See also "FO 371/118676, no.9: 'Soviet penetration of Africa': report by Information Research Department, FO; (Extract), February 1956, in David Goldsworthy, ed., *The Conservative Government and the End of Empire, 1951-1957, part 1: International Relations*, 226–228.

27. A.N. Porter and A.J. Stockwell, *British Imperial Policy and Decolonization, 1938-1954, Vol.1: 1938-1951* (London: Macmillan Press, 1987), 357–359; Philip Murphy, "Intelligence and Decolonization: The Life and Death of the Federal Intelligence and Security Bureau, 1954-63," *Journal of Imperial and Commonwealth History* vol. 29, no. 2 (2008): 106–112.

28. BNA: Colonial Office, hereafter CO 1015/465: Monthly Political Intelligence Reports for Nyasaland, August and September 1953. See also "Negroes renew Nyasaland riots: tear gas and batons used by police to curb crowd of demonstrating natives," *The New York Times*, August 30, 1953.

29. BNA: CO 537/6960, No.4. April 22, 1953: Position of police in later stages of colonial constitutional development: a report of a CO working party. In David Goldsworthy, ed., *The Conservative Government and the End of Empire, 1951-1957, Part II: Politics and Administration* (London: HMSO, 1994), 150–151. Note that there were two key conferences of colonial police commissioners in the early 1950s, in 1951 and 1954, where various issues were raised, including the security of tenure of the police, and the deliberate need to place the police as a constitutionally created state organ.

30. Note that states of emergency were also declared in the other territories in the federation between February and March 1959. For a study of the intelligence and violence that characterized these three emergencies, see Philip Murphy, "Acceptable Levels? The Use and Threat of Violence in Central Africa, 1953-1964," in Miguel B. Jeronimo and Antonio C. Pinto, eds., *The Ends of European Colonial Empires: Cases and Comparisons* (New York: Palgrave Macmillan, 2015), 178–196.

31. Great Britain, *Report of the Nyasaland Commission of Inquiry* (London: H.M. Stationery Office, July 1959), 94–125; "Nyasaland strife widens as 23 die: nationalist held," *The New York Times,* April 4th, 1959. See also "Nyasaland toll rises in fighting: five Africans are killed by troopers attacked while clearing a roadblock," *The New York Times*, March 6, 1959.

32. Great Britain, *Report of the Nyasaland Commission of Inquiry*, 94–125.

33. Philip Murphy, "A Police State? The Nyasaland Emergency and Colonial Intelligence," *Journal of Southern African Studies* vol. 36, no. 4 (2010): 775–778.

34. BNA: CO 1015/1519: Nyasaland Emergency: minutes by N.D. Watson (Assistant Secretary, Central Africa Office) and Sir J. Macpherson (Permanent Under Secretary of State, at the CO), March 5 to 9, 1959, in Philip Murphy, ed., *British Documents on the End of Empire: Central Africa, Part II: Crisis and Dissolution* (London: The Stationery Office, 2005), 25. See also European Convention on Human Rights, Article 15: Derogation in time of emergency.

35. BNA: Dominion Office, hereafter DO 35/7564, No. 264A: Release of Nyasaland Detainees: minute (PM 59/60) by Mr. Macleod to Mr. Macmillan, December 3, 1959. In Philip Murphy, ed., *British Documents on the End of Empire: Central Africa, Part II: Crisis and Dissolution* (London: The Stationery Office, 2005), 25.

36. Nyasaland Government, *The Southworth Commission Report* (May 1960), 112–126.

37. "Banda released from detention: Nyasaland African leaders confers with Macleod," *The New York Times,* April 2, 1960.

38. British Government, *Report of the Nyasaland Constitutional Conference* (London, July and August 1960). Note that the 1960 Constitutional Conference marked the first time when the British authorities had invited Nyasaland nationalist leaders and other political leaders to deliberate the future of the Protectorate.

39. British Government, *Report of the Nyasaland Constitutional Conference* (London, November 1962).

40. Rhodesia and Nyasaland Federation, *The Nyasaland (Constitution) Order-in-Council, 1963*, Chapter 1. Statutory Instruments, 1963, no. 883.

41. BNA: DO 35/8039, No.5: Constitutional Development in Africa: memorandum by Lord Home, in Ronald Hyam, et al., eds., *The Conservative Government and the End of Empire, 1957-1964, Part 1: High Policy, Political and Constitutional Change* (London: The Stationery Office, 2000), 161–164; Robert M. Maxon, *Britain and Kenya's Constitutions, 1950-1960* (New York: Cambria Press, 2011).

42. Bertrand Badie, *The Imported State: The Westernization of the Political Order* (California: Stanford University Press, 2000).

43. See these works: Frederick Cooper, "Decolonization in Africa: An Interpretation," in Kwame A. Appiah and Henry Louis Gates, eds., *Africana: The*

*Encyclopedia of the African American Experience* (New York: Basic Books, 1999), 571–682; John Darwin, *Britain and Decolonization*, 6–7.

44. Malawi Government, *The Constitution of Malawi* (July 1964: Chapter Two).

45. For a comprehensive study of the cabinet crisis, see Colin Baker, *Revolt of the Ministers: The Malawi Cabinet Crisis, 1964-1965* (London: I.B. Tauris, 2001).

46. See, for instance, Paul Chiudza Banda and Gift Wasambo Kayira, "The 1959 State of Emergency in Nyasaland: Process and Political Implications," *Society of Malawi Journal* vol. 65, no. 2 (2012): 5–10.

47. According to Botero, under the concept of "the reason of state," the state is preoccupied with three main objectives, namely founding, conserving, and expansion of dominion. The main objective out of the three was the "conservation" of its power, which includes securing itself from both internal and external attacks. See Robert Bireley, ed., *Botero: The Reason of State* (Cambridge: Cambridge University Press, 2017), 4–15.

48. Malawi Government, *The Constitution of the Republic of Malawi* (July 1966. Chapter One: The Republic).

49. Malawi Government, *The Constitution of the Republic of Malawi* (July 1966. Chapter Three: The Public Service).

50. Malawi Government, *The Constitution of the Republic of Malawi* (July 1966. Chapter Three: The Public Service).

51. Potholm, "The Multiple Roles of the Police as Seen in the African Context," 155–157.

52. Wycliffe Nyachoti Otiso and Ruth Kaguta, "Kenya at Fifty: State Policing Reforms, Politics, and Law, 1963-2013," in Michael M. Kithinji, et al., eds., *Kenya after 50,* 221–244.

53. The International Covenant on Civil and Political Rights. Adopted by the General Assembly of the United Nations, December 19, 1966.

54. African (Banjul) Charter on Human and People's Rights. Adopted June 27, 1981, entered into force on October 21, 1986.

55. Cyril Marlow, *A History of the Malawi Police Force,* 1971, 29–37. See also *Malawi News,* "Kamwana takes over as Commissioner of Police," July 22, 1971.

56. *Annual Report of the Malawi Police Force for the year ended 31st December 1966* (Zomba, Malawi: Government Printer, 1967).

57. Amnesty International, "Malawi: Human Rights Violations 25 Years after Independence," September 1989. In the same vein, see also Amnesty International, "Malawi: Prison Conditions, Cruel Punishment, and Detention without Trial," February 1992. See also "Malawi: Deaths in Custody, Detentions, and Discrimination," *News from Africa Watch,* April 24, 1989.

58. Note that the atrocities and human rights violations committed by the Banda regime were well known to the international community, including the UN and the country's major bilateral donors. However, many of them did not act because of the ongoing Cold War and fears that the Malawi leader would have turned toward the East for support. See for instance, BNA: Foreign and Commonwealth Office, hereafter, FCO 45/2205: "Human Rights in B.L.S.M.": Dispatch from the British High Commission, Lilongwe, Malawi, to the FCO, April 27, 1978. Appendage

from the UN High Commission on Human Rights, Geneva, sitting fromFebruary 6 to March 10, 1978. See also FCO 45/2205: "Dispatch from Mr. Quayle, FCO, Central and Southern Africa Department, to the British High Commission, Lilongwe, Malawi, titled 'Human Rights in Malawi,' 16th February 1978."

59. The Harare Commonwealth Declaration, October 1991.

60. *SA Review of U.S. Policy and Current Events in Kenya, Malawi, and Somalia.* Hearing before the Subcommittee on Africa of the Committee on Foreign Affairs, House of Representatives. 102nd Congress, 2nd Session. June 23, 1992, 7–8.

61. Malawi Government, "The Realities about the Human Rights Situation in Malawi," February 1992.

62. "Mobs challenge Malawi President: dozens are killed in protests against an idiosyncratic and durable dictator," *The New York Times,* May 10, 1992. See also Paul Chiudza Banda, "Hastings Kamuzu Banda: how the Cold War sustained bad leadership in Malawi," in Baba G. Jallow, ed., *Leadership in Postcolonial Africa: Trends Transformed by Independence* (New York: Palgrave Macmillan, 2014), 39–40.

63. H. Meinhardt, *Free at Last! Malawi's Democratic Transition* (Lilongwe: NICE, 2004), 316. See also "Malawi freed from its liberator," *The New York Times,* May 21, 1994.

64. Malawi Government, *The Constitution of the Republic of Malawi* (1995: Chapter X, XI, XII and XV).

65. Malawi Government, *The Constitution of the Republic of Malawi* (2010: Chapter xv: The Police).

66. Malawi Police, *Police Training Manual on Human Rights*, 2nd Edition. Chapter Two: Police Work and Human Rights.

67. Ibid., Chapter Ten: Community Policing.

68. UK Aid, Department for International Development, *Malawi Policing Improvement Program* (June 2013).

69. Diana Cammack, "Malawi's Political Settlement Crisis," in *Africa: Power and Politics,* Background Paper (Nov. 2011), 2.

70. Amnesty International, "Policing to Protect Human Rights: A survey of police practice in countries of the Southern African Development Community," 2002.

71. U.S. Department of State: Human Rights Report for Malawi (2002), 2.

72. U.S. Department of State: Human Rights Report for Malawi (1996), 2–3.

73. U.S. Department of State: Human Rights Report for Malawi (2002), 5–6. Note that by 2002, most of the demonstrations were against President Muluzi's wishes to extend his own term of office, from the Constitutional two terms, to either a third-term or an open-term amendment.

74. Diana Cammack, "Malawi's Political Settlement Crisis," in *Africa: Power and Politics,* Background paper (Nov. 2011), 8–9.

75. U.S. Department of State: Human Rights Report for Malawi (2011), 1–2.

76. Malawi Law Commission, Report No.9. "Police Bill, 2003: Section 44: Powers to use firearms," in Report of the Law Commission on the Review of the Police Act, July 2003.

77. *Nyasa Times,* "Malawi Police Officer jailed for 12 years for July 20 Murder," December 21, 2016.

78. U.S. Department of State: Human Rights Report for Malawi (2011 and 2012), 2 and 2, respectively. Chasowa was allegedly murdered on the night of September 24, 2011. See also Malawi Government, *Robert Chasowa Commission of Inquiry Report*, September 2012.

79. Amanda Dissel and Cheryl Frank, eds., *Policing and Human Rights: Assessing Southern African Countries' Compliance with the SARPCCO Code of Conduct for Police Officials* (Cape Town: African Policing Civilian Oversight Forum, 2012), 56–62.

80. U.S. Department of State: Malawi 2018 Human Rights Report.

81. *Reuters*, "Malawi police use teargas as opposition protests grow," June 6, 2019. See also *The Globe Post,* UN calls on Malawi to free protest organizers," July 11, 2019. See also "MHRC probes police on arbitrary arrests," *The Nation Newspaper,* October 11, 2019.

82. *VOA News*, "Malawi military blocks protestors from marching to state residencies," July 26, 2019. See also *Nyasa Times,* "Anti-Ansah protestors, police clash as Malawi army soldiers now protect demonstrators," October 1, 2019.

83. *Africa News,* "Malawi court defends right to protest: dismisses government petition," August 6, 2019. See also *Nyasa Times,* "Supreme Court refuses to suspend anti-Ansah protests," October 1, 2019.


# BIBLIOGRAPHY

Ahmed, Abdullahi. *Human Rights in Africa: Cross-Cultural Perspectives.* Washington, DC: The Brookings Institution, 1990.

Appiah, Kwame A. and Henry Louis Gates, eds., *Africana: The Encyclopedia of the African American Experience.* New York: Basic Books, 1999.

Badie, Bertrand. *The Imported State: The Westernization of the Political Order.* California: Stanford University Press, 2000.

Baker, Colin. *Revolt of the Ministers: The Malawi Cabinet Crisis, 1964-1965.* London: I.B. Tauris, 2001.

Bireley, Robert, ed., *Botero: The Reason of State.* Cambridge: Cambridge University Press, 2017.

British Government. *Report of the Nyasaland Constitutional Conference.* London, July and August 1960.

———. *Report of the Nyasaland Constitutional Conference.* London, Nov. 1962.

Burke, Roland. *Decolonization and the Evolution of International Human Rights.* Philadelphia: University of Pennsylvania Press, 2013.

Cammack, Diana. "Malawi's Political Settlement Crisis," in *Africa: Power and Politics,* Background Paper (Nov. 2011): 1–20.

Chiudza Banda, Paul and Gift Wasambo Kayira. "The 1959 State of Emergency in Nyasaland: Process and Political Implications," *Society of Malawi Journal* vol. 65, no. 2 (2012): 1–19.

Cobbah, Josiah A.M. "African Values and the Human Rights Debate: An African Perspective," *Human Rights Quarterly* vol. 9, no. 3 (1987): 309–31.

Darwin, John. *Britain and Decolonization: The Retreat from Empire in the Post-War World.* New York: Macmillan, 1988.

Dissel, Amanda and Cheryl Frank, eds., *Policing and Human Rights: Assessing Southern African Countries' Compliance with the SARPCCO Code of Conduct for Police Officials.* Cape Town: African Policing Civilian Oversight Forum, 2012.

Falk, Richard, et al., eds., *Human Rights: Critical Concepts in Political Science.* New York: Routledge, 2007.

Goldsworthy, David, ed., *The Conservative Government and the End of Empire, 1951-1957, part 1: International Relations.* London: HMSO, 1994.

Great Britain. *Report of the Nyasaland Commission of Inquiry.* London: H.M. Stationery Office, July 1959.

Hodgson, Geoffrey M. "What are Institutions?" *Journal of Economic Issues* vol. 40, no. 1 (March 2006): 1–25.

Howard-Hassmann, Rhoda E. *Human Rights in Commonwealth Africa.* Totowa, NJ: Rowman and Littlefield, 1986.

Hyam, Ronald, et al., eds., *The Conservative Government and the End of Empire, 1957-1964, Part 1: High Policy, Political and Constitutional Change.* London: The Stationery Office, 2000.

Ibhawo, Bonny "Cultural Relativism and Human Rights: Reconsidering the Africanist Discourse," *Netherlands Quarterly of Human Rights,* vol. 91, no. 1 (2001): 43–62.

Ibhawoh, Bonny, *Human Rights in Africa.* Cambridge: CUP, 2018.

Ishay, Micheline. *The History of Human Rights: From Ancient Times to the Globalization Era.* Berkley: University of California Press, 2004.

Jallow, Baba G., ed., *Leadership in Postcolonial Africa: Trends Transformed by Independence.* New York: Palgrave Macmillan, 2014.

Jeronimo, Miguel B. and Antonio C. Pinto, eds., *The Ends of European Colonial Empires: Cases and Comparisons.* New York: Palgrave Macmillan, 2015.

Kithinji, Michael M., et al., eds., *Kenya after 50: Reconfiguring Historical, Political, and Policy Milestones.* New York: Palgrave Macmillan, 2016.

Leffler Melvyn P. and Odd Arne Westad, eds., *The Cambridge History of the Cold War, vol.2: crises and détente.* Cambridge: Cambridge University Press, 2010.

Lindholt, Lone. *Questioning the Universality of Human Rights: The African Charter on Human and People's Rights in Botswana, Malawi, and Mozambique.* Aldershot, England: Dartmouth Publishers, 1997.

Malawi Government. *Constitution of the Republic of Malawi* (1966, 1995, and 2010).

Marlow, Cyril. *A History of the Malawi Police Force.* Zomba, Malawi: Pamphlet, 1971.

Maxon, Robert, M. *Britain and Kenya's Constitutions, 1950-1960.* New York: Cambria Press, 2011.

McCracken, John. "Coercion and Control in Nyasaland: Aspects of the History of a Colonial Police Force," *Journal of African History* vol. 27 (1986): 127–47.

———. *A History of Malawi, 1856-1966.* United Kingdom: James Currey, 2012.

McNeil, J.R. and K. Pomeranz, eds., *The Cambridge World History, Vol.7.1: Production, Destruction, and Connection, 1750-present.* Cambridge: Cambridge University Press, 2015.

Meinhardt, H., *Free at Last! Malawi's Democratic Transition.* Lilongwe: NICE, 2004.

Murphy, Philip. *British Documents on the End of Empire: Central Africa, Part II: Crisis and Dissolution.* London: The Stationery Office, 2005.

Murphy, Philip. "Intelligence and Decolonization: The Life and Death of the Federal Intelligence and Security Bureau, 1954-63," *Journal of Imperial and Commonwealth History* vol. 29, no. 2 (2008): 101–30.

————. "A Police State? The Nyasaland Emergency and Colonial Intelligence," *Journal of Southern African Studies* vol. 36, no. 4 (2010): 765–80.

North, Douglas C. "Institutions," *The Journal of Economic Perspectives* vol. 5, no. 1 (Winter 1991): 97–112.

Nsereko, Daniel. "The Police, Human Rights, and the Constitution: An African Perspective," *Human Rights Quarterly,* 15 (1993): 465–84.

Nyasaland Government. *The Southworth Commission Report.* May 1960.

Parkinson, Charles. *Bills of Rights and Decolonization: The Emergence of Domestic Human Rights Instruments in Britain's Overseas Territories.* Oxford: Oxford University Press, 2007.

Pollis, Adamantia and Peter Schwab. *Human Rights: Cultural and Ideological Perspectives.* New York: Praeger, 1980.

Porter, A.N. and A.J. Stockwell. *British Imperial Policy and Decolonization, 1938-1954, Vol.1: 1938-1951.* London: Macmillan Press, 1987.

Potholm, Christian P. "The Multiple Roles of the Police as Seen in the African Context," *Journal of Developing Areas* vol. 3, no. 2 (1968): 142–50.

Simpson, A.W. Brian. *Human Rights and the End of Empire: Britain and the Genesis of European Convention.* Oxford: Oxford University Press, 2001.

Welensky, Roy. *Welensky's 4000 Days: The life and death of the Federation of Rhodesia and Nyasaland.* London: Collins Publishers, 1964.

Westad, Odd Arne. *The Global Cold War: Third World Interventions and the Making of Our Times.* Cambridge: Cambridge University Press, 2005.

Woods, J.R.T. *The Welesnky Papers: A History of the Federation of Rhodesia and Nyasaland.* Durban: Graham Publishers, 1983.

*Chapter 13*

# The Constitution and Change-the-Constitution Debate in Independent Kenya, 1963–2002

Anne Kisaka Nangulu

Kenya became independent from British colonial rule on December 12, 1963, and the following year, same date and month, became a Republic. Jomo Kenyatta, head of the Kenya African National Union (KANU), the ruling political party, became Kenya's first President in 1964.[1] At Kenyatta's death, on August 22, 1978, Vice President Daniel Toroitich arap Moi became interim president. On October 14, 1978, Moi formally became president after he was elected the head of KANU and designated as its sole nominee for the presidency.[2] Moi retired from the presidency in December 2002, after amendments to the Constitution barred him from seeking reelection having ruled Kenya for 24 years.[3] In particular, amendments to the Constitution spelt out clearly that one could only be elected and hold office as president for a term of 5 years, and be reelected to serve one more term, a maximum of 2 terms, translating into 10 years.[4]

Through the general election held on December 29, 2002, KANU the dominant ruling party since independence was also voted out of power. On January 3, 2003, Emilio Mwai Kibaki, became Kenya's third president and formed a coalition government of several political parties under the umbrella of the National Rainbow Coalition (NARC). Of importance is the period under review and beyond (as from August 27, 2010, the time when the new Constitution of Kenya (2010) was promulgated)[5]; before then, Kenya was governed under one Constitution, the Independence Constitution (1963). Yet, the Independence Constitution had been considerably amended, due to various reasons, and its character by the end of 2002 was quite different from what it was originally. Most Kenyans strongly felt that the Independence Constitution (in spite of amendments) had shortcomings and had not adequately served the needs of the population. Thus, it is against this background that this study analyzes constitution-making and change-the-Constitution debate during the Kenyatta and Moi eras.

## BRIEF UNDERSTANDING OF THE CONCEPT OF THE CONSTITUTION AND CONSTITUTIONALISM

Before we delve into Constitution and change-the-Constitution debate, it is imperative that we briefly understand the concept of constitution and constitutionalism. Onalo in his book, *Constitution Making in Kenya*, considers the Constitution as the basic law in a social contract between the governing and the governed, in which adherence to the rule of law is paramount.[6] In the case of Kenya, since the country is governed and all citizens are bound by the Constitution, it is easy to note that the Constitution is the basic law of the land. It defines and lays down the socioeconomic and political structure of the country. Like other laws, it responds to the social dynamics of the society and may have to be amended from time to time. However, a good/solid Constitution has to be one that transcends time and space. While as it is influenced by the past to serve the present, it must, as reasonably as practicable in the eyes of its framers, be hawk-eyed as it projects into the future.[7]

As noted by the late Wamalwa Kijana, legislator and former vice president of the Republic of Kenya, "the Constitution is the defender of the weak, the protector of the mighty and not so mighty, and the modern defender of faiths."[8] Besides, Agbese and Kieh, Jr., state that, based on the Constitutional Politics Model, if the Constitution is not structured to defend the people's material and other interests, it simply becomes a pious document that nobody takes very seriously.[9] Therefore, the Constitution must empower the people in their daily lives.

Moreover, as noted by Macharia Munene on the concept of constitutionalism, a Constitution by its very nature is an agreement on how people in a given place would like to live together, promote and advance their interests, and protect those interests from all types of threats. That agreement is often based on a realization that people of diverse characteristics and temperaments that are often volatile and result in violence and have no choice but to live together in a particular territory. In an effort to create harmony, they are forced to make a Constitution or enter into a formal social contract.[10] Likewise, Robert Maxon notes that any Constitution represents a form of social contract in which a system of government is put in place that can maintain law and order, and provide access to national resources on an equitable basis.[11] Indeed, at Kenya's independence, all interested parties envisioned developing a Constitution that would provide a satisfactory system of government for an independent nation.[12]

Generally, from a constitutional perspective, the most significant feature of the Constitution is that it is the supreme law of a country.[13] As the supreme law of the land, all citizens, prime ministers, presidents, workers, and peasants alike, are subject to its provisions.[14] At a minimum, the Constitution, which is usually codified in a single written document, establishes the authority of the national government, provides guarantee for fundamental human rights, and sets forth the government's basic operating procedures.[15] Furthermore, the use of concepts of government as a yardstick of constitutional legitimacy gives the subject the universality and the permanency it deserves, notwithstanding a change in the constitutional regime. Jurists, historians, political thinkers, and philosophers have enunciated the concepts of government in the past for the common good. Some aspects thereof are contained in the Independence Constitution of Kenya, on the grounds that they were of universal acceptance of humanity.[16]

Worth noting, the United Nations was mandated to come up with the Universal Declaration of Human Rights, which also encompasses the internationalization of human rights. As noted by Maxwell, Friedberg, and Degolia, this is especially after the end of the Second World War in 1945, when internationalization of human rights occurred, and precedents were established into the limited rights of national states.[17] The outcome was the Charter of the United Nations—a blueprint of a new world that was drafted in 1945. In it, one of the United Nations' primary purposes is the promotion of human rights through international law and institutions. Therefore, the makers of any Constitution must be guided by legal concepts which can be seen to be of universal application to humanity. Moreover, the Constitution must be used to build the infrastructure of a government, based on legal concepts which have been developed through research into jurisprudence of the nation concerned and its proposed relationship with the global community.[18]

As stated by Maloka, it should be noted that constitutionalism is not merely the establishment of the institutions, processes, and structures the Constitution envisages, or the drafting and promulgation of legislation and the execution of duties and tasks that are laid down in the Constitution.[19] In reality, it is the manner, and decisiveness in which the Constitution is given content to determine whether or not it is in fact a living document that makes a contribution to the development of the society.[20] As further noted by Agbese and Kieh, Jr., constitutionalism enables ordinary people to assert ownership over the state and other political institutions, and it tears down the notion that government is the exclusive preserve of a few people.[21] Furthermore, the final objective of adhering to the principles of constitutionalism is to achieve good governance, stability, and the securing of individual liberties, and this adherence also breeds confidence and respect for a country's institutions and promotes their legitimacy in the eyes of the public.[22] Substantially, within a democratic framework, the Constitution must address several critical issues such as citizenship, the obligations of the state to its citizens, the obligations of citizens to the state, the obligations of citizens to citizens, cultural, economic, security, political, religious, social rights and responsibilities, the system of the state, the system of government, the form of government, the distribution of power at the broader systematic and governmental levels, minority rights, and gender equality.[23] In essence, while it is true that a Constitution cannot possibly address all the issues confronting a polity; nevertheless, it contains issues that are at the basis of every democratic compact.[24]

Generally, the rock upon which democratic government rests is its Constitution—the formal statement of its fundamental obligations, limitations, procedures, and institutions.[25] Addressing these issues is pivotal to the stability of the polity.[26] Indeed, despite their enduring, monumental qualities, Constitutions must be capable of change and adaptation if they are to be made more than admirable fossils.[27] In the words of Agbese and Kieh, Jr., more critical is the need to make the Constitution a living document.[28] Thus, understanding constitution and constitutionalism lays a foundation for us to grasp the schist of this chapter; Constitution and change-the-Constitution debate in Independent Kenya (1963–2002).

## THE KENYAN CONSTITUTION: THE KENYATTA ERA, 1963–1978

Indeed, Kenya's Independence Constitution originated in constitutional conferences held in London from early 1960 to 1963, when Kenya was still a British colony administered by a governor general. These constitutional conferences are popularly known as the Lancaster Conferences. As stated by Robert Maxon, delegates from Kenya converged in London for the start of the First Lancaster House Conference on January 18, 1960, and the Colonial Office had to make extensive and detailed preparations.[29] The First Lancaster House Conferences did prove an important step toward constitution-making in Kenya. Not only had a sizeable African majority been provided for in the reconstituted Legislative Council (Legco), but Africans were now the group so far as constitutional-making was concerned.[30] The settlement at Lancaster House was far different than that projected by the Colonial Office prior to the London Conference.[31] Nevertheless, the settlement was clearly imposed by Britain because the Kenyan political elite was unable to reach a comprehensive agreement on constitutional change.[32] Roles were now reversed with Europeans on the defensive. In this sense, Lancaster House marked an important turning point in constitution-making[33] and mapping the path toward attaining Kenya's independence. As further documented by Maxon, yet a little less than two years, a memo prepared for Colonial Policy Committee (CPC), prior to the start of the Second Lancaster House Conference, asserted that "the continuation of Europeans political power" had "passed away at the last Lancaster House Conference," as a result of "logic of arithmetic" and the tide of African nationalism.[34]

Furthermore, the goal of the 1962 Second Lancaster House Conference was to reach an agreement on constitutional principles under which Kenya would be granted its independence. The major issue before the Conference was that of *majimboism* (federalism). Pro-federalists supported the Kenya African Democratic Union (KADU), a minority party that appealed to coastal peoples, the Kalenjin, part of the Luhya, and half of the Kamba. Their support of federalism stemmed from fear that minority groups would be dominated by the larger ethnic groups. The KANU majority, composed of Kikuyu, Luo, Meru, Embu, and other ethnic groups, advocated for a centralized form of government. The British government tended to support KANU in this matter. Amid controversy, the conference drew up a document entitled "Framework (of Kenya) Constitution," which was incorporated into the later Constitution of Kenya of 1963, later known as the Independence Constitution (for details on binding nature of the Constitution see endnote as quoted from Macharia Munene, 2003).[35] This 1962 Constitution called for a parliamentary system that mandated a government responsible to parliament, a bicameral legislature, an independent judiciary, and a strong bill of rights. KANU's victory in the general election of May 1963 greatly restricted any hope of a more federalist form of government.[36]

Thereafter, a conference convened to settle the details of Kenya's Independence Constitution met in London under the Chairmanship of the Secretary of State for Colonies, Mr. Duncan Sandy's, between September 25 and October 19, 1963.[37] It was attended by Ministers of the Kenya government (KANU) and by delegations representing the opposition (KADU) and the European Community. At the plenary sessions, during the early stages of the Conference, an agreement was reached on most of the amendments and additions to the Constitution which were required to affect Kenya's change of status from self-government (*madaraka* in Kiswahili attained on June 1, 1963) to independence.[38] Thus, during the latter part of the conference, plenary sessions had to give way to separate discussions between the Secretary of State and delegations in an endeavor to secure agreement.[39] Eventually, after more than two weeks of these separate discussions, the Secretary of State reached a conclusion that a certain number of changes in the Constitution were essential. These changes were accepted by the Kenya government, as recorded in by Mr. Kenyatta's letter to the conference on October 19, 1963.[40] The changes were, however, accepted by the opposition who declined to attend the final plenary session.[41] The most important aspect of the constitutional changes concerned the police, the public service, and the procedure for amending the Constitution.[42]

Further, provision relating to Kenya citizenship after independence was agreed during the earlier plenary sessions of the conference, at which all the delegates were present. They provided various ways in which citizenship may be acquired by operation of the law (applying mainly to the person born in Kenya; one whose parents were born in Kenya); who are at independence citizens of the United Kingdom and colonies or British protected persons; and also to all those born in Kenya after independence; by registration (applying to a wider range of other persons having particular connections with Kenya); and by neutralization. Citizens of the United Kingdom and colonies or of the Republic of Ireland who were resident in Kenya at the time of independence were given the option to apply for registration as Kenya citizens at any time within the first two years after independence; during the time they did not have the right to be registered as voters or to be elected as members of Parliament (MPs) or of Regional Assemblies.[43] The Constitution did not permit dual citizenship, but persons who possessed Kenya citizenship by operation of law and also possessed another citizenship were given two years to decide which citizenship they want to retain.[44]

At the final plenary session, the Secretary of State reviewed the course of the discussion, described the differences in the altitude of the Kenya government and opposition toward changes in the "Framework" agreed by both parties in 1962, and outlined the principal changes which he had come to the conclusion were necessary in order to make Constitution workable.[45] He informed the conference that he had received a letter from the prime minister, Mr. Jomo Kenyatta (he had risen to the position on *madaraka* day June 1, 1963), stating that the Kenya government accepted the amendments as settlement of the issues raised at the conference and did not indent to seek to make more amendments except insofar as subsequent experience showed that these to be absolutely necessary.[46] A further letter from Kenyatta, laid before the conference, reaffirmed the Kenya government's intention of transforming to the Regions, with possible speed, the departments and services still remaining to be handed over in accordance with the requirements of the "Framework Constitutions."[47] The greater part of these transfers would be affected on December 1, 1963, and the remainder would be completed by January 1, 1964.[48]

Of importance, the Kenya government also declared their desire that Queen Elizabeth should become Queen of Independent Kenya.[49] Both government and opposition expressed the wish that, on attaining independence, Kenya should become a member of the Commonwealth. The Secretary of State assured them that if this were confirmed to be a resolution of the National Assembly, the British government would be pleased to convey the request to be governments of other Commonwealth member states.[50] Consequently, the date of December 12, 1963, was confirmed as Kenya's Independence Day.[51] On the same month and date, December 12, 1964, Kenya became a Republic. The Constitution inaugurated by political independence in 1963 was a detailed document of over 200 pages. It called for the retention of the monarchy, a parliamentary system, and strong regional governments. The Republican Constitution that went into effect on December 12, 1964, was named the Amended Independence Constitution [1]. Kenya's Constitution in the period under review dates from the formation of the Republic. It drew heavily from the English law and by the end of 2002 had been amended over 30 times.[52] Amendments required a two-thirds majority in Kenya's unicameral National Assembly.[53]

Indeed, the decade running from the date of independence was marked by several changes to the Constitution, with the result that, by 1970, Kenya was a one-party state. Whereas Kenya had emerged into independence with a very lively multiparty system, a clamorous parliament, and independent press, by 1970 freedom of speech was virtually a thing of the past and government critics were in detention. Thus, 1963–1970 may be regarded as the watershed period in the flowering of power concentration in the hands of the executive that would be full-blown during the Moi era.[54]

## CHANGE-THE-CONSTITUTION MOVEMENT

In early 1970, rumors were rife that a group of politicians close to Kenyatta were already making a bid to change-the-Constitution to allow for the position of the prime minister instead of an executive president. According to the stories, Kenyatta had already agreed to remain a nominal head of state. As these rumors became common, the government was forced to clear the air. On May 1, 1970, the attorney general, Charles Njonjo, issued a statement and categorically denied that the Constitution was about to be amended.[55] The attorney general's assurance notwithstanding, the rumors persisted until 1976, when those bidding the rumors to change-the-Constitution came out in the open. They included Njoroge Mungai, Kihika Kimani, James Gichuru, Paul Ngei, Jackson Angaine, and Njenga Karume all MPs. Most of these people were members of the Kikuyu, Embu, and Meru Association (GEMA)—a purported "welfare association," which was founded in 1971 to consolidate the economic, social, and cultural fortunes of its members.[56] The background for change-the-Constitution group was simple: Kenyatta's health was failing by mid-1970s, and hence the succession question could no longer be postponed. Chapter II, Part I of the then Kenya Constitution provided that on the event of the president's death, resignation, or incapacitation, the vice president would act as president for a maximum period of 90 days, during which a national election to elect a new president would be held.[57] Those who were opposed to Moi's candidature for succession wanted to amend the Constitution to prevent such a possibility.[58]

Therefore, the change-the-Constitution group held their first public meeting in Nakuru on September 26, 1976, at which they described the existing Constitution as "all wrong."[59] In October, they once again exhorted Kenyans to amend the Constitution to prevent Moi who had served as vice president since 1967 from automatically succeeding Kenyatta in the event of death. In the same way as in 1970, the Attorney General, Njonjo (a Kikuyu and supporter of Moi succession), under Kenyatta's orders, issued a stern warning that "it is a criminal offence punishable by death/life imprisonment, for any person to compass, imagine, devise or intend the death or deposition of the President."[60] The government statement ended the question as to whether there was going to be any amendment to constitutional provisions dealing with presidential succession.


## THE MOI ERA, 1978–2002

Undoubtedly, the change-the-Constitution group, under Kenyatta had benefited from major constitutional changes that helped them to consolidate political and economic power and had imposed their dominance on the state. This group mainly of Kikuyu ethnic group and their ethnic alliances (mainly Mount Kenya groups) felt threatened by the prospect of having a president who might not protect their economic gains. Even though, upon Kenyatta's death on August 22, 1978, Moi succeeded him in accordance with the Constitution, power had not been allowed to slip quietly into his hands. Upon ascending to power, Moi announced that he would follow Kenyatta's "footsteps" (in Kiswahili *Nyayo*). In other words, he told Kenyans not to expect a major transformation for he was to continue with Kenyatta's policies.[61] But, this was not to include protecting Kikuyu hegemony instead their power base was quickly dismantled.

Between 1969 and 1982, Kenya remained under *de facto* one-party rule. In May 1982, George Anyona was detained without trial and Oginga Odinga was put under house arrest when they tried to register the opposition party, the Kenya African Socialist Alliance. A Constitution amendment was rushed through Parliament making KANU the only political party. Kenya had thus become a *de jure* one-party state.[62] Moi was strengthening his position and silencing dissent. A number of politicians and academics regarded as dissents were detained without trial. In this atmosphere of rising political tension, Air Force personnel attempted to stage a coup d'etat on August 1, 1982.

Corruption and restrictions on freedom were given as reasons for seeking the overthrow of the government, but the Kenya army soon crushed the attempted coup. President Moi thus resolutely restored order and sought to buttress his authority by isolating those whose loyalty he felt doubtful. One prominent figure that fell in this category was the Minister of Constitutional Affairs, Charles Njonjo.[63] Specifically, in 1983, Njonjo, a former Attorney General in the Kenyatta regime and a strong supporter of the Moi succession was designated a traitor. Politics being unpredictable as it usually is, Njonjo was to fall out with Moi perhaps due to his growing political clout. A series of moves including public rallies at which Moi condemned his former right-hand man as the traitor plotting to remove him from office, soon followed. KANU in its characteristic style played its part in shunting "the traitor" out of its ranks. Njonjo was suspended from office, subjected to the stage-managed Judicial Commission, and "convicted" of most of the "charges." However, there was no jail sentence passed on Njonjo, for that was not within the Commission's terms of reference. In 1984, Njonjo was unceremoniously dumped into political oblivion, and the Ministry of Constitutional Affairs was done away with.[64]

Shaken by the abortive coup d'etat, the Moi government politically made amendments to the Constitution that concentrated power in the executive and substantially weakened other state organs. For example, the judiciary was reduced into a subdepartment of the executive and became the legislature's rubber stamp. It was not until 1991, after intense pressure from various sections of the Kenyan society that *de jure* one-party system was abolished and multiparty politics introduced, allowing for freedom to organize and voice dissent.[65] However, a host of oppressive laws remained on the books and provided a legal basis for President Moi to frustrate opposition parties.[66]

## STRUGGLE FOR MULTIPARTYISM AND CONSTITUTIONAL REFORM

During the initial struggle for multipartyism in 1991, fronted by the then united Forum for the Restoration of Democracy (FORD), constitutional reform was a major issue. At the time, FORD was a nonpartisan group that brought together churches, politicians, academics, lawyers, the civil society, and citizens, among other groups that insisted that the government should legalize opposition parties and restructure governance in Kenya. After bilateral donors agreed to suspend development assistance to Kenya, KANU unexpectedly bowed to some of the demands for reform, catching FORD flat-footed. FORD reacted to KANU's unanticipated victory by transforming itself from a nonpartisan group to a political party to contest the 1992 elections.[67] In the meantime, FORD rallies were heavily attended, both in urban and rural areas, many believed in 1991 that winning the presidency was within the opposition's reach. However, FORD's evolution into a political party exposed internal rivalries and ethnic tensions that previously had been less pronounced. In-fighting broke out over who was to be FORD's presidential candidate.[68] As a result, FORD split into FORD-Asili (FORD-A), a predominantly Kikuyu party supported by sections of the Luyia community; FORD People, mainly supported by the Kisii; and FORD-K mainly a Luo, Bukusu (a Luyia sub-group) party.[69] KANU's political base became the same smaller ethnic communities that had previously made up the core of KADU in 1963. Thus, power politics even within the opposition and personal and ethnic rivalries took center stage, making the discourse on the Constitution reform impossible until after the 1992 elections.

However, the resulting multiparty national elections in 1992 dramatized both the Moi regime's democratic weakness and its ability, nonetheless, to maintain power. Moi's KANU gained only 36.4 percent of the popular vote in the initial multiparty elections.[70] Yet, it prevailed because the only constitutional change effected was due to internal and donor pressure that had been to remove the barriers to multiparty elections. Parliamentary seats were disproportionately distributed leading to under-representation in opposition strongholds, including Nairobi. There were no provisions for runoff elections when parliamentary or presidential candidates failed to obtain majority votes; there were barriers to coalition government, and there was no Electoral Commission reform to provide for free and fair elections. Worse still, the Moi government employed a vote-rigging strategy of permitting a winning party to form a new government, provided it won a mere 25 percent of the vote in at least 5 of the country's 8 provinces.[71] All these factors helped KANU to secure a majority of seats in parliament. KANU majority was also augmented by the president's power to nominate 12 MPs. Seemingly, irreconcilable divisions among opposition parties prevented them from capitalizing politically on the strong majority of popular vote they won collectively.[72]

Demands for constitutional reform were voiced again in 1993 by the opposition, frustrated with the outcome of the December 1992 elections. Besides, the opposition's call for constitutional reform and the regime's response are best understood in this context. Unable to unite behind a single slate of presidential and parliamentary candidates in 1992, the opposition continued to fragment. Whereas in 1992, the opposition was divided among three major parties and minor ones, by late 1997 (election year) it had divided into at least six significant factions.[73] Although unity at the time was more elusive than ever, there was one thing that all opposition parties agreed on—the need for constitutional reform.[74]

Concluding the constitutional reform was viewed as a crucial first step in transforming the country from autocratic to democratic rule. Consequently, some members of the opposition and civil society spearheaded the quest for change in Kenya. Specifically, in November 1994, the Kenya Human Rights Commission, the Law Society of Kenya, and the Kenya Section of the International Commission of Jurists collaborated to produce a "Proposal for a Model Constitution" to stimulate widespread discussion about constructing a vision for a democratic Kenyan society. The collaborators launched large-scale civic education campaigns via the Citizen's Coalition for Constitutional Change (CCCC) to explain the model to the public and to compare it to the existing Constitution.[75]

As the 1997 elections approached, the debate on constitutional reform took a new urgency. The CCCC organized a National Convention Assembly (NCA) led by the self-styled National Convention Executive Council (NCEC), which included leading Church figures, academicians, lawyers, and nongovernmental organization (NGO) leaders. This crystallized in April 1997 in the organization of a Public Conference at Limuru on the outskirts of Nairobi. Resolutions passed at Limuru became constitutional reform demands that were supposedly to be sought prior to any national elections. Indeed, a public response reiterated this theme in placards and graffiti—"no reforms no elections."[76]

Between May and July 1997, the NCEC, civil society and the Kenyan public challenged the Moi regime at every turn for dialogue on constitutional reforms. Consistent with its long-standing approach to the opposition, the KANU government refused any dialogue with the NCEC and sought to repress the reformers. This stubborn strategy played into the hands of the opposition by setting the stage for *Saba Saba* demonstrations on July 7, 1997 (in this case, *Saba Saba* in Kiswahili meaning the seventh day of the seventh month) across the country, in support of constitutional reforms before the next election. While opposition leaders were organizing *Saba Saba* demonstrations in the countryside, the NCEC leaders also went ahead with a pro-reform rally at Uhuru Park downtown Nairobi, despite being denied a permit to do so. Participants of *Saba Saba* rallies who had come out in large numbers including their leaders were ruthlessly assaulted by the police. The clashes resulted in several arrests, injuries, and even death. About 25 people died in Nairobi and in other rallies around the country.[77] The state's *Saba Saba* repression led to international alarm, internal and donor protests and a further mobilization of civil society.[78]

In addition to civil society organizations and countryside demonstrations, another social force emerged in the wake of the reform movement—the "urban crowd." Periodically appearing on Kenya's political stage, only to dissolve after a spell, it has often left a significant residue. The urban crowd was present during the struggle for independence and became a problem for the postindependence Kenyatta regime, as the latter tried to eliminate dissent against the nascent power structure and its unequal distribution of the country's resources. The urban crowd reemerged in the early 1990s and was a significant part of the growing pressure for multiparty politics. It resurged again in conjunction with the 1997 mass meetings for constitutional reform.[79] Significantly, the vigilant and potent urban crowd is a voice for most Kenyans, as it transcends ethnic boundaries in its demands from the government for the common good.

Reacting to intense pressure, principally from rallies and demonstrations organized by opposition MPs and the NCEC, religious groups and diplomatic community, President Moi tactically agreed to negotiate a reform package on condition that negotiations involve only MPs, "the elected representatives of the Kenyan people," and not a "national constitutional assembly" involving MPs and representatives of civil society/citizens. Although the NCEC leadership had guided the reform movement and seized the moment to organize public protests, Moi and "KANU hawks" refused to countenance dealing with the NCEC. Instead, Moi and KANU, with opposition political acquiescence, shifted ground for talks under the umbrella of parliament. An Inter-Party Parliamentary Group (IPPG) was formed which was meant to bridge party divisions and was given the task of undertaking initial reforms to clear the way for national elections. Some boycotted the talks, notably Kenneth Matiba and his FORD-A party. Matiba had already adopted a belligerent posture, having declared the forthcoming elections as fraudulent and rigged, without fundamental constitutional reform involving all Kenyans, not just the politicians sitting in parliament.[80]

President Moi supported the IPPG because 70 percent of the 100 to 125 MPs who participated in the group belonged to KANU.[81] Moreover, there were some rumors that some opposition MPs were offered financial inducements by the regime to participate in the IPPG talks. Perhaps most significant, by supporting the IPPG, which ended up negotiating a reform package by early September 1997, Moi again took the proverbial wind out of the opposition sails. This sudden shift of fortunes also illustrated a fundamental problem of the opposition leaders, namely that, they invariably underestimated the political maneuver of Moi and his cohorts.[82] Details of political party results and representation in the National Assembly after the 1997 elections are tabulated in table 13.1

However, the IPPG did not have time or the mandate to consider and implement major constitutional reforms before the December 1997 national elections. Thus, as enacted into the law in October and early November 1997, the reforms negotiated by IPPG consisted of the following minimum changes to the existing Constitution: the repeal or amendment of the Chief's Authority Act, the Public Order Act, the Preservation of Public Security Act, and the Police Act—all of which the provincial administration and the police had

Table 13.1    Political Party Results in 1997 Elections

| Party | Seats |
|-------|-------|
| KANU | 107 |
| DP | 39 |
| NDPK | 21 |
| FORD-K | 17 |
| SDP | 15 |
| SAFINA | 5 |
| FORD-P | 3 |
| KSC | 1 |
| FORD-A | 1 |
| SPK | 1 |

*Source*: Republic of Kenya (1997/1998). *The Electoral Commission of Kenya: Official Results*. Nairobi: The Kenya Gazette. Quoted from Steeves, Jeffrey S. (1999). "The Political Evolution of Kenya: The 1997 Elections and Succession Politics," *Commonwealth Comparative Politics* Vol. 37, No. 2, p. 78.

used to bar opposition candidates from moving freely about in the country and from addressing public meetings. Besides, there was repeal or amendment of the sedition laws, the main mechanism by which the government had used to harass the press, academicians, and civil society among other citizens. In addition, there was an agreement to establish a Constitutional Review Commission after the December 1997 elections, to take charge of fundamental constitutional reforms.[83]

As it turned out, the minimum constitutional reforms proved to be on the whole a "time-buying gimmick." They were never meant to tamper with KANU's electoral fortunes. As a matter of fact, most of these changes were inconsequential, for little changed on the ground. The only issue of substance in the reform package was the imposition of a five-year two-term limit for the presidency,[84] a provision that some strategists in the Moi government were increasingly eager to get rid of and the Constitution of Kenya Review Act, which eventually gave birth to the Constitution of Kenya Review Commission. However, the components of the same Act proved to be a bone of contention between legislators and civil society.[85]

## CONSTITUTION OF KENYA REVIEW ACT AND OBSTACLES TO CONSTITUTION-MAKING

Specifically, the Constitution of Kenya Review Act provided for the nomination of 25 commissioners, 12 of them from civil society, the clergy and other stakeholders like the women's caucus and the disabled; and 13 from parliamentary political parties.[86] This is where the political parties parted ways, because KANU insisted on seven nominees (contrary to what had been agreed on at one of the Safari Park Hotel meetings), stating that, the numbers should reflect the party's strength in Parliament, while the Democratic Party (DP) and other parties argued that, nominations should reflect the number of votes garnered during the 1997 General Elections (see table 14.1). The whole argument essentially scuttled the constitutional talks, for neither KANU nor the opposition was willing to strike a compromise.[87] These are some of the reasons that the Act was deemed to be irreparably flawed. Yet, the need to control the review process by KANU had become an end in itself. The countless meetings at Bomas of Kenya, Safari Park Hotel, and County Hall (all in Nairobi) had been rendered worthless and would become even more so in mid-1999. When President Moi dropped a bombshell by essentially rolling back the little that had been achieved by first noting that there was no need for Constitution review, and then insisting that the review process be undertaken by Parliament, which in the president's view was the only body mandated to do so. He argued that Wanjiku (a female name of Kikuyu origin) in reference to the ordinary *mwananchi* (citizen) had no idea of what was required in the review, and there would be no use to try to co-opt him/her in the process. But the counterargument from members of the public was that it was the legislators who had passed the flawed legislation and could not, therefore, be trusted to revise the Constitution without such blunders, however, cut no ice.[88]

As a result, in late 1999, KANU marshaled its coalition with the National Development Party (NDP) representatives, Raila Odinga (Chairman of the Party) and Mbita Member of Parliament, Otieno Kajwang; Shirikisho Party's Rashid Shakombo (Party leader); and the Kenya Social Congress' (KSC) George Anyona (Party leader); and pushed for a Parliamentary Select Committee (PSC) to review the Constitution of Kenya Review Act and take amendments to parliament. The Committee was also mandated to facilitate the formation of a Commission that would collect and collate views from the public. As a matter of fact, the move for a PSC followed President Moi's 2 failed attempts at Parliament building to reach a consensus with MPs representing 10 opposition parties, who categorically stated to him that, Constitution review should be people-driven as opposed to Parliament.[89]

All the same, just as the PSC was busy setting up a 27-member Committee, about a kilometer away from Parliament building, a section of the opposition and religious groups were setting up a parallel Committee at Ufungamano Guest House near the University of Nairobi. The opposition insisted that all interested parties including churches, civil society, and members of the public should be called upon to participate in the constitutional review process. To the opposition parties, constitution-making should be people-driven as opposed to KANU-dominated PSC.[90]

Despite one looming opposition to the PSC, in January 2000, stationed at City Hall in Nairobi, it started the constitutional review process under the chairmanship of Raila Odinga, the current prime minister in the ruling coalition government under the watchful eye of President Moi and his "KANU hawks." However, a gaping loophole in the mandate of the PSC was that it lacked the time frame in which it had to report back to the National Assembly. Expectedly, the PSC in absolute interest of KANU was deliberately extended to frustrate the wishes of the people, of having a reformed Constitution in place before the next General Elections in 2002. Thanks to KANU's manipulations that it succeeded in infusing fissures in opposition to their detriment, and the stage was set for a review process in which KANU was the referee and the player alike. Thus, Moi perpetuated authoritarian rule by making piecemeal reforms. Put differently, Moi and his cohorts played for time, recognizing that even though full reform may have to be inevitable, they still had the opportunity to shape the outcome of the reform process to protect their vital vested interests.[91]

As a matter of fact, time-buying techniques as an obstruction to the constitutional reform process were publicly played by "KANU hawks." For instance, KANU politicians were at the forefront in pushing for renewed calls for *majimbo* (federal) system of government as a counterweight to the opposition demands for constitutional reform. This goes back to 1991 when Rift Valley and Coast province KANU politicians launched the *majimbo* campaign, which to them was not just a system of government, but an excuse for violent eviction of pro-opposition migrant communities in their regions. One of the most outspoken coastal politicians in that vein before the 1997 elections was Emmanuel Karissa Maitha, who made threatening remarks against different communities, starting with coastals of Arab descent before turning his attention to African migrants from upcountry. Besides, Shariff Nassir, a coast politician and Minister in the Moi cabinet also is on record for calling for *majimbo* and strongly believed that Coast province was a KANU zone—with no room for opposition parties.[92]

In addition, other senior KANU politicians and Cabinet Ministers from the Rift Valley, William ole Ntimama and Francis Lotodo made their contribution to the constitutional reform debate by threatening to push a *majimbo* initiative and expel "outsiders" from their domains, Narok and West Pokot Districts, respectively. As a matter of fact, Lotodo vocally issued threats to migrants in West Pokot, mostly Luyia, Kikuyu, and Marakwet, where he also threatened to kick out members of the Asian community.[93]

Capitalizing on ethnicity, KANU operatives busied themselves in selling the *majimbo* dogma among the country's "small ethnic groups." This backed up by the carving of the country into ethnopolitical districts that ominously pointed to the enhancement of the divide and rule policy, one that served the Moi regime effectively. The creation of such districts as Kuria, Mount Elgon, Teso, Suba—all from constituencies that were inhabited by single ethnic communities, and several others in the former Meru district—this time based on subethnic groups of the Meru community, is proof enough. More disturbing, one wonders whether proponents of *majimbo* in the Moi government—who had been sworn into office and taken an oath to uphold national unity and the Constitution—cared or knew what it actually entailed. Worse still, in the period under review, the Kenya government did not seriously take the initiative to educate the public on the Constitution and its implications on citizens' rights and responsibilities in upholding national unity. It is not surprising that the Constitution was then (particularly during the Kenyatta and Moi era) an abstract document to most Kenyans including government officials.

In sum, the deadly *majimbo* campaign was a purely home-grown initiative, part of a wider ploy by KANU hardliners aimed at subverting the Constitution reform and democratization process. Nonetheless, as illustrated within the context of multipartyism and democratization, during the 1992 multiparty General Elections, KANU claimed victory in 100 constituencies, which was more than half of the available 188 seats in Parliament. Five years later in 1997, parliamentary seats had been increased as illustrated in table 14.1. Moi's KANU carried the day again but with a relatively lesser margin of 107 seats out of 210. In fact, KANU's fortunes dipped further in 2002 elections with just 64 seats.[94] The fortunes of the domineering independence party had dwindled, and it is not surprising as noted earlier on in this chapter that KANU was voted out in the December 29, 2002, General Elections; and managed a paltry 14 parliamentary seats in the General Elections of December 2007.[95]

Indeed, Kenyans went to the polls in the December 2002 General Elections without a new Constitution or the long-awaited Constitution reforms. Thus, the change-the-Constitution debate was prolonged and pushed on by the pro-reformists to be handled by the new regime, in the Kibaki era.

## CONCLUSION

Kenya's experience with the Constitution and change-the-Constitution debate, whether due to internal and external pressure in the period under review, illustrates a complex and politicized exercise. As a matter of fact, the change-the-Constitution debate was dictated partly by ethnicity, political party affiliations, and individual ambitions to cling to power by a number of politicians and their cohorts, especially staunch KANU supporters during the Kenyatta and Moi eras. As illustrated in this chapter, Kenyatta started the process of amending as well as manipulating the Constitution that Moi would intensify the same, mainly for political and personal interests to amass power and wealth,[96] at the expense of national unity, development, and the welfare of citizens. This boomeranged and led to the call by members of the public for an overhaul of the independence Constitution partly, to clip the power of the executive, corruption in high offices and contempt for human rights. As noted by Munene, Kenyatta organized for manipulation of the Independence Constitution to be amended for reasons that were politically motivated and narrow in scope and set the example that Moi followed after 1978.[97] Indeed, in the words of Lumumba, a renowned Kenyan lawyer, educator, and public speaker, and in 2010 served as the Director of the watchdog Kenya Anti-corruption Commission, asserted that Kenya's Independence Constitution, like many independence Constitutions, suffered the fate of numerous amendments, the effect of which was to emasculate other organs of the government and to confer excessive powers in the hands of the executive.[98]

Of importance, executive manipulation, however, backfired during the Moi era, especially in the late 1980s and early 1990s, as citizens demanded that constitutional changes be in the interests of the country instead of the executive. Since then to until August 2010 when the new Constitution was voted for and endorsed by Kenyans, the constitutional debate in Kenya hinged on whether the final agreement on how Kenyans should live, run their affairs, and protect their rights should be determined by the ruling elite within the political class or whether it should be people (read citizen) driven.[99]

Indeed, in the period under review, especially with the reintroduction of multiparty politics in the early 1990s, the political system in Kenya was in a state of flux as contentious debates on the review of the Constitution continued. As noted earlier in this chapter, the Constitution to be replaced was drawn up at independence. The Constitution heavily indebted to the English law had already been heavily amended and it was widely agreed by Kenyans that it required a major overhaul that would give birth to a new Constitution. In fact, politicians, academicians, religious groups, civil society, and citizens (including the urban crowd) had continuously fuelled the struggle for constitutional change during the Kenyatta era and more vigorously during the Moi era; and prolonged the struggle and entered into a new political landscape of coalition government, the Kibaki era.

In sum, it has been necessary to trace this historical perspective in order to reveal the complex nature of constitution-making and related amendments; change-the-Constitution debate; and public demands for constitutional reforms as well as clamor for a new Constitution in Kenya. As noted by the late Wamalwa Kijana, legislator and former vice president of Kenya, "constitution-making in Kenya has been a long and rocky process."[100] Besides, as noted by Maxon, for contemporary Kenya, the lessons of the past are abundantly clear.[101]There can be no democratic constitutional order without negotiations and compromise. Most significant, ultimate power rests with the people. Just as important, it remains for the Kenyan populace to exercise that power where constitutional-making is concerned.[102] Significantly, constitution-making is and should be a continuous exercise.[103] Thus, it is a challenge to the Kenyan leadership and citizens alike, to uphold the new Constitution (voted for through the August 4, 2010, referendum) that is people-driven and see to it that it can withstand political manipulations; to address the political, economic, social, and cultural aspirations of all Kenyans regardless of gender, religion, political affiliation, ethnicity, or race in the twenty-first century and beyond.

## NOTES

1. Anne Nangulu, "Ethnic Conflicts and Cattle Raids Between the Pokot and their Neighbours Northwest Kenya, 1963-2000," *Maarifa: A Journal of Humanities and Social Sciences,* School of Arts and Social Sciences, Moi University, Vol. 2, No. 1 (2007a), 226–35; and Anne Nangulu, "The State, Ethnicity, and Resource Allocation for Socio-Economic Development in Kenya," *Maarifa: A Journal of Humanities and Social Sciences,* School of Arts and Social Sciences, Moi University, Vol. 2, No. 2 (2007b), 243–54.

2. Ibid.

3. Anne Nangulu, "The Infectiveness of the State in Handling Internal Security in Independent Kenya," *Maarifa: A Journal of Humanities and Social Sciences,* School of Arts and Social Sciences, Moi University, Vol. 3, No. 1 (2009), 1–10.

4. Ibid., 2.

5. Republic of Kenya, *The Proposed Constitution of Kenya* (Nairobi: The Government Printer, 2010). The new Constitution voted for by Kenyans on Wednesday, August 4, 2010, was entitled: Republic of Kenya, *The Proposed Constitution of Kenya,* May 6, 2010 (Published by the Attorney-General in accordance with Section 34 of the Constitution of Kenya Review Act, 2008 (No. 9 of 2008), as printed by the Government Printer, Nairobi. Wednesday, August 4, 2010, was "Referendum Day" for Kenyans to vote for a new Constitution or retain the old/ independence Constitution. Overwhelmingly, 67 percent of Kenyans who endorsed a new Constitution. The new Constitution was mainly driven by the wishes of the majority of Kenyans. Voting for the new Constitution was indeed a logical progression from the Lancaster House Constitution that ushered in independence in 1963; and the first Republic from British colonialism in 1964 (*The Standard,* The Standard Group Limited, Nairobi, Friday, August 6, 2010; published in hard copy and online—www.standardmedia.co.ke). The poll outcome was as follows: registered voters: 12,656,451; and the final count showed 6,092,593 voted "YES" for the new Constitution; while 2,795,059 voted "NO" that is against the new Constitution (these are the final figures as officially released by the Interim Independent Electoral Commission (IIEC) that was set up by the Kenya government and mandated to oversee the referendum on the new Constitution (for details on the voting patterns—by regions/provinces and constituency—for the new Constitution see *The Standard,* The

Standard Group, Nairobi, Friday, August 6, 2010; *Daily Nation*, Friday, August 6, 2010; and *Saturday Nation*, August 7, 2010 (*Daily Nation* and *Saturday Nation* are published by the Nation Media Group Limited, Nairobi, in hard copy and online—www.nation.co.ke). Indeed, a new dawn had unfolded in Kenya—the endorsing and implementing of the new Constitution was the new face of Kenya since independence.

6. P.L. Agwel Onalo, *An African Appraisal: Constitutional Making in Kenya* (Nairobi: Transnational Press, 2004), x. This quote is from P.L.O. Lumumba, a renowned lawmaker in Kenya, which was part of a "Forward" to Onalo's book.

7. Ibid., 2–5.

8. Quoted from Onalo, *An African Appraisal*. Michael Christopher Wamalwa Kijana (1944–2003), served as legislator during the Kenyatta, Moi and Kibaki era. He served as a vice president of the Republic of Kenya during the first term, specifically in the first year of the Kibaki presidency; and passed away in office on August 23, 2003.

9. Pita Ogaba Agbese and George Klay Kieh, Jr., "Introduction: Democratizing States and State Reconstruction in Africa," in Pita Ogaba Agbese and George Klay Kieh, Jr., eds., *Reconstituting the State in Africa* (New York: Palgrave Macmillan, 2007), 3–29.

10. Macharia Munene, "The Manipulation of the Constitution of Kenya, 1963-1996: A Reflective Essay," *Hekima: Journal of the Humanities and Social Sciences*, Faculty of Arts, University of Nairobi, Vol. II, No. 1 (2003), 41–56.

11. Robert M. Maxon, *Kenya's Independence Constitution: Constitutional Making and End of Empire* (Lanham, MD: Fairleigh Dickinson University Press, Co-published with Rowman & Littlefield Publishing Group Inc. 2011), 20.

12. Ibid.

13. Victoria Maloka, "The Postapartheid State in South Africa," in Pita Ogaba Agbese and George Klay Kieh, Jr., eds., *Reconstituting the State in Africa* (New York: Palgrave Macmillan, 2007), 233–75.

14. Onalo, *An African Appraisal*, 21.

15. Ibid.

16. Ibid., x.

17. John A. Maxwell, James J. Friedberg (eds) and Deirdre A. Degolia (Associate Editor), *Human Rights in Western Civilization 1600—Present*, Second Edition (Dubuque, Iowa: Kendall/Hunt Publishing Company, 1991), ix and 165.

18. Onalo, *An African Appraisal*, 5.

19. Maloka, "The Postapartheid State," 244.

20. Ibid.

21. Agbese and Kieh, Jr., "Introduction: Democratizing States," 19.

22. Onalo, *An African Appraisal*, x.

23. Pita Ogaba Agbese and George Klay Kieh, Jr, "State Renewal in Africa: The Lessons," in Pita Ogaba Agbese and George Klay Kieh, Jr., eds., *Reconstituting the State in Africa* (New York: Palgrave Macmillan, 2007), 279–94.

24. Ibid., 283.

25. Onalo, *An African Appraisal*, 20–21.

26. Agbese and Kieh, Jr., "State Renewal in Africa," 282–83.

27. Onalo, *An African Appraisal*, 2.
28. Agbese and Kieh, Jr., "State Renewal in Africa," 2007, 283.
29. Maxon, *Kenya's Independence Constitution*, 338.
30. Ibid.
31. Ibid.
32. Ibid.
33. Ibid.
34. Ibid., 338.
35. Munene, "The Manipulation of the Constitution of Kenya," 41.
36. Irving Kaplan, *Area Handbook for Kenya* (Washington, DC: United States Government Printing Offices, 1976), 189–91; and The Economic Intelligence Unit, *Country Profile: Kenya* (London: The Unit, 1998), 6–7.
37. Kenya National Archives (KNA) MAC/KEN/49/1: Kenya Independence Conference 1963, prepared for British Information Services, by Reference Division Central Office of Information, London, RF.P. 5611/1, Classification, IV.2, October 1963, 1–4 and 32).
38. Ibid., 2.
39. Ibid.
40. Ibid.
41. Ibid.
42. Ibid., 2–3.
43. Ibid., 4.
44. Ibid., 4.
45. Ibid.
46. Ibid.
47. Ibid.
48. Ibid.
49. Ibid.
50. Ibid.
51. Ibid.
52. Kaplan, *Area Handbook for Kenya*, 6–7.
53. Ibid.
54. William R Ochieng', "Structural and Political Changes," in B.A. Ogot and W.R. Ochieng', eds., *Decolonization and Independence in Kenya, 1940-93* (Nairobi: East African Educational Publishers, 1996), 83–109.
55. Ibid., 105.
56. Ibid.
57. B.A. Ogot, "The Politics of Populism," in B.A. Ogot and W.R. Ochieng', eds., *Decolonization and Independence in Kenya, 1940-93* (Nairobi: East African Educational Publishers, 1996), 187–213; and Rok Ajulu, "Politicised Ethnicity, Competitive Politics and Conflict in Kenya: A Historical Perspective," *African Studies*, Vol. 61, No. 2 (2002), 252–68.
58. Ibid.
59. Ochieng', "Structural and Political Changes," 105.

60. Ibid. Robert M. Maxon, *East Africa: An Introductory History* (Morgantown: West Virginia University Press, 1994), 272–73; and *Daily Nation*, Nation Media Group Limited (Nairobi: February 11, 1998).

61. Ochieng', "Structural and Political Changes," 106; Ogot, "The Politics of Populism," 188, 192–93.

62. Ogot, "The Politics of Populism," 202.

63. Maxon, *East Africa: An Introductory History*, 276–77.

64. Ibid.; also see *Daily Nation*, Nation Media Group Limited, February 11, 1998.

65. Introduction of multiparty politics was ushered into Kenya's political arena with the scrapping of Section 2A of the Constitution that had made Kenya a *de jure* one party state.

66. *Daily Nation*, Nation Media Group, Nairobi, September 13, 1999; and Anne Nangulu-Ayuku, "Reflections on the Postcolonial State in Kenya," in Pita Ogaba Agbese and George Klay Kieh, Jr., eds., *Reconstituting the State in Africa* (New York: Plagrave Macmillan, 2007), 127–79.

67. Maina Kiai, "Commentary: A Last Chance for Peaceful Change in Kenya?" *Africa Today*, Vol. 45, No. 2 (1998), 185–92.

68. Ibid.

69. Forum for the Restoration of Democracy as a political party later on split into three legally registered parties, namely, Ford-Kenya, FORD-Asili and Ford-People.

70. John W. Harbeson, "Political Crisis and Renewal in Kenya—Prospects for Democratic Consolidation," Africa *Today*, Vol. 45, No. 2 (1998), 161–83.

71. Ibid.; Republic of Kenya, *Constitution of Kenya*, Revised Edition (Nairobi: The Government Printer, 1998), 9; and Peter O. Ndege, James K. Chelanga and Stephen M. Singo, *The Crises of Governance: Politics and Ethnic Conflicts in Kenya*. Research Paper Series Vol. 1, No. 1 (Eldoret: Moi University Press, 2009), 23.

72. Harbeson, "Political Crisis and Renewal in Kenya," 161–83.

73. Joel D. Barkan, "Toward a Constitutional Framework in Kenya," *Africa Today*, Vol. 45, No. 2 (1998), 213–26.

74. Ibid.

75. Ibid., 213; and Kiai, "Commentary," 189.

76. Jeffrey S. Steeves, "The Political Evolution of Kenya: The 1997 Elections and Succession Politics," in *Commonwealth Comparative Politics*, Vol. 37, No. 2 (1999),71–94; and Kiai, "Commentary," 1998, 90.

77. Ibid.; Barkan, "Toward a Constitutional Framework," 217; and Harbeson, "Political Crisis and Renewal in Kenya," 171.

78. Ibid.

79. Frank Holmquist, and Michael Ford, "Kenya Politics: Toward a Second Transition?" *Africa Today*, Vol. 45, No. 2 (1998), 227–58.

80. Steeves, "The Political Evolution of Kenya," 73; Barkan, "Toward a Constitutional Framework," 219; and Harbeson, "Political Crisis and Renewal in Kenya," 171–73.

81. *The Standard,* The Standard Group Limited (Nairobi: December 29, 2009).

82. Barkan, "Toward a Constitutional Framework," 219–20.
83. Barkan, "Toward a Constitutional Framework," 220–21; Holmquist and Ford, "Kenya Politics," 236; and Stephen N. Ndegwa, "The Incomplete Transition: The Constitutional and Electoral Context in Kenya," *Africa Today*, Vol. 45, No. 2 (1998), 193–212.
84. Nangulu, The Infectiveness of the State in Handling Internal Security in Independent Kenya,'' 2.
85. *Daily Nation*, December 15, 1999.
86. Ibid.
87. Ibid.
88. Ibid.
89. *Daily Nation*, December 15, 1999; and *Daily Nation*, Nation Media Group (Nairobi: December 16, 1999).
90. Ibid.
91. Barkan, "Toward a Constitutional Framework," 223; *Daily Nation*, December 16, 1999.
92. *The Economic Review* (Nairobi: August 18–24, 1997).
93. Ibid.
94. Quoted from *The Standard*, The Standard Group Limited (Nairobi: December 29, 2009).
95. Ibid.
96. Munene, "The Manipulation of the Constitution of Kenya, 45.
97. Ibid.
98. Quoted from Onalo, *An African Appraisal*.
99. Munene, "The Manipulation of the Constitution of Kenya, 45.
100. Quoted from Onalo, *An African Appraisal*.
101. Maxon, *Kenya's Independence Constitution*, 276.
102. Ibid.
103. Ibid., Onalo, *An African Appraisal*, xv.

# BIBLIOGRAPHY

Agbese, Pita Ogaba and George Klay Kieh, Jr. "Introduction: Democratizing States and State Reconstruction in Africa." In Pita Ogaba Agbese and George Klay Kieh, Jr. eds. *Reconstituting the State in Africa*. New York: Palgrave Macmillan, 2007, 3–29.

———. "State Renewal in Africa: The Lessons." In Pita Ogaba Agbese and George Klay Kieh, Jr. eds., *Reconstituting the State in Africa*. New York: Palgrave Macmillan, 2007, 279–94.

Ajulu, Rok. "Politicised Ethnicity, Competitive Politics and Conflict in Kenya: A Historical Perspective." *African Studies*, Vol. 61, No. 2 (2002), 252–68.

Barkan, Joel D. "Toward a Constitutional Framework in Kenya." *Africa Today*, Vol. 45, No. 2 (1998), 213–26.

*Daily Nation.* Nairobi: Nation Media Group Limited, February 11, 1998.

*Daily Nation.* Nairobi: Published by the Nation Media Group Limited, Friday, August 6, 2010, in hard copy and online— www.nation.co.ke.

*Daily Nation.* Nairobi: Nation Media Group Limited, December 15, 1999.

*Daily Nation.* Nairobi: Nation Media Group, December 16, 1999.

Harbeson, John W. "Political Crisis and Renewal in Kenya—Prospects for Democratic Consolidation." *Africa Today*, Vol. 45, No. 2 (1998), 161–83.

Holmquist, Frank and Michael Ford. "Kenya Politics: Toward a Second Transition?" *Africa Today*, Vol. 45, No. 2 (1998), 227–58.

Kaplan, Irving. *Area Handbook for Kenya.* Washington, DC: United States Government Printing Offices, 1976, 189–91.

Kenya National Archives. (KNA) MAC/KEN/49/1: Kenya Independence Conference 1963, prepared for British Information Services, by Reference Division Central Office of Information, London, RF.P. 5611/1, Classification, IV.2, October 1963, 1–4 and 32.

Kiai, Maina. "Commentary: A Last Chance for Peaceful Change in Kenya?" *Africa Today*, Vol. 45, No. 2 (1998), 185–92.

Maloka, Victoria. "The Postapartheid State in South Africa." In Pita Ogaba Agbese and George Klay Kieh, Jr. eds. *Reconstituting the State in Africa.* New York: Palgrave Macmillan, 2007, 233–75.

Maxon, Robert M. *East Africa: An Introductory History.* Morgantown: West Virginia University Press, 1994.

———. *Kenya's Independence Constitution: Constitutional Making and End of Empire.* Lanham, Maryland: Fairleigh Dickinson University Press, Co-published with Rowman & Littlefield Publishing Group Inc. 2011.

Maxwell, John A., James J. Friedberg (eds) and Deirdre A. Degolia (Associate Editor). *Human Rights in Western Civilization 1600—Present*, Second Edition. Dubuque, Iowa: Kendall/Hunt Publishing Company, 1991.

Munene, Macharia. "The Manipulation of the Constitution of Kenya, 1963-1996: A Reflective Essay." *Hekima: Journal of the Humanities and Social Sciences*, Faculty of Arts, University of Nairobi, Vol. II, No. 1 (2003), 41–56.

Nangulu, Anne. "Ethnic Conflicts and Cattle Raids Between the Pokot and their Neighbours Northwest Kenya, 1963-2000." *Maarifa: A Journal of Humanities and Social Sciences,* School of Arts and Social Sciences, Moi University, Vol. 2, No. 1 (2007a), 226–35.

———. "The State, Ethnicity, and Resource Allocation for Socio-Economic Development in Kenya." *Maarifa: A Journal of Humanities and Social Sciences,* School of Arts and Social Sciences, Moi University, Vol. 2, No. 2 (2007b), 243–54.

———. "The Infectiveness of the State in Handling Internal Security in Independent Kenya." *Maarifa: A Journal of Humanities and Social Sciences,* School of Arts and Social Sciences, Moi University, Vol. 3, No. 1 (2009), 1–10.

Nangulu-Ayuku, Anne. "Reflections on the Postcolonial State in Kenya." In Pita Ogaba Agbes and George Klay Kieh, Jr. eds. *Reconstituting the State in Africa.* New York: Plagrave Macmillan, 2007, 127–79.

Ndege, Peter O., James K. Chelanga and Stephen M. Singo. *The Crises of Governance: Politics and Ethnic Conflicts in Kenya.* Research Paper Series Vol. 1, No. 1, Eldoret: Moi University Press, 2009.

Ndegwa, Stephen N. "The Incomplete Transition: The Constitutional and Electoral Context in Kenya." *Africa Today,* Vol. 45, No. 2 (1998), 193–212.

Ochieng', William R. "Structural and Political Changes." In B.A. Ogot and W.R. Ochieng', eds. *Decolonization and Independence in Kenya, 1940-93.* Nairobi: East African Educational Publishers, 1996, 83–109.

Ogot, B.A. "The Politics of Populism." In B.A. Ogot and W.R. Ochieng', eds. *Decolonization and Independence in Kenya, 1940-93.* Nairobi: East African Educational Publishers, 1996, 187–213.

Onalo, P. L. Agwel. *An African Appraisal: Constitutional Making in Kenya.* Nairobi: Transnational Press, 2004.

Republic of Kenya. *Constitution of Kenya,* Revised Edition. Nairobi: The Government Printer, 1998.

Republic of Kenya. *The Proposed Constitution of Kenya.* Nairobi: The Government Printer, 2010.

*Saturday Nation.* Nairobi: published by the Nation Media Group Limited, Saturday, August 7, 2010, In hard copy and online—www.nation.co.ke.

Steeves, Jeffrey S. "The Political Evolution of Kenya: The 1997 Elections and Succession Politics." *Commonwealth Comparative Politics,* Vol. 37, No. 2 (1999), 71–94.

The Economic Intelligence Unit. *Country Profile: Kenya.* London: The Unit, 1998, 6–7.

*The Economic Review.* Nairobi: August 18–24, 1997.

*The Standard.* The Standard Group Limited. Nairobi: Friday, August 6, 2010, published in hard copy and online—www.standardmedia.co.ke.

*The Standard.* The Standard Group Limited. Nairobi: December 29, 2009.

*Chapter 14*

# The Building Bridges Initiative Déjà Vu

## *"A Whitewash Process Taking Us Forward by Taking Us Backwards"*

Nicholas K. Githuku and Robert M. Maxon

Amid the buzz of activity and elite glitz that is not strange in the humdrum of Kenya's political theater, the national coordinator for The Institute for Social Accountability (TISA), Wanjiru Gikonyo, no doubt informed by historical context and insight, pointed out that the Building Bridges Initiative (BBI)—the signal political event of 2019 and succession politics ahead of 2022 elections—was "a whitewash process but," one that "is . . . trying to take us forward by taking us backwards."[1] This profound axiomatic statement captured an unacknowledged fact that in Kenya's relatively short political history, if one were to speak of the BBI report and launch as a moment, the people of Kenya have been here before. From the outset, it is quite clear that as a nation-state, the country is yet to merge and emerge. It is, indeed, a nation-state caught, as it were, in the pangs and throes of *Coming to Birth*[2] that have, unfortunately, occasioned needless bloodshed. This is evidenced by the bloody 1950s, quinquennial electoral violence since 1992 with a rare hiatus in 2002, and a shocking, if not worrying and concerning, tipping point in the intense and hotly contested presidential election in 2007. The buildup and run-up to the 2013 presidential race was characterized by weekly street protests dubbed by the political opposition as "teargas Thursdays," signaling a fiery and fierce 2017 contest between the incumbent, President Uhuru Muigai Kenyatta and the former prime minister, Raila Amolo Odinga. And, true to form, the political temperatures heated up following allegations of electoral malpractice and rigging by both sides; the annulment of the results by the Supreme Court of Kenya; restaging of the presidential elections under dubious circumstances; and the subsequent swearing-in of Kenyatta the Younger as the (un)duly elected president, and of Raila at

Nairobi's Uhuru Park, as the so-called "peoples' president." Matters came to a head in Kenya. There was unbearable palpable political ethnic tension that only eased when the two politicians proffered a mutual olive branch.

The rapprochement of March 2018 between Kenyatta and Raila, now famously referred to as "the handshake," which kicked up the BBI consultation process and the two reports (2019 and 2020), is emblematic of the rough-and-tumble that is the country's tumultuous political history. One of the main aims of this chapter is to put this latest political milestone in historical context while assessing the significance of the reports going forward. In this regard, this chapter argues the "the report,"[3] like other momentous occasions, is a whitecap in the undulating political evolution of the state and, as such, counsel Kenyans to, perhaps, curb their cyclic enthusiasm and euphoria. They have been here many times before and, after all, the nation-state is still coming to birth. Indeed, this chapter suggests that this bridge-building process is but a building block in a continuous state-building project and should not be expected, therefore, to be the be-all and end-all silver bullet that will solve all the country's various problems (and especially not the two twin tyrannies of ethnic expectation and institutionalized corruption that feed off each other, and are inextricably connected).[4] Another object of this chapter is to assess the pros and cons of the BBI while evaluating its value especially vis-à-vis the 2010 constitution. In this respect, this chapter argues that the BBI reports accentuate the 2010 constitution. Indeed, we make the argument that as a process calculated to stave off bloodshed and political disaster, the BBI process was, by and large, an elite initiative as opposed to being people-led and -driven as the protracted constitution-writing process of the 2000s was and, therefore, not as radical and revolutionary. It is little wonder that sections of society have characterized the Report as an "apology" for the elites' failure to live up to, and to fully implement, the 2010 constitution. As part of this objective, the authors also engage with the troubling question that continues to be a constant obstacle to the implementation of the constitution—namely, what is the price of democracy, and can Kenyans afford it? Again, going full circle, it is argued that the question of affordability harks back to the first ambitious *majimbo* or independence constitution written after Lancaster House II, which Kenyatta the Elder, quickly scuttled after independence, hence our view that the country has been here before.

## DÉJÀ VU: THE BBI MOMENT IN HISTORICAL PERSPECTIVE

Key issues in the two task-force reports (2019 and 2020) were identified as the need for greater political, economic, and religious inclusivity.[5] These are indeed key issues confronting Kenya. The roots of political, economic, and social exclusion are embedded in Kenyan history, and they must be recognized and confronted for any attempt to promote inclusion to be successful. This commentary will focus on the colonial and independence periods as these were characterized by exclusion and marginalization through legal and other means.[6]

This means that Kenya's politics, economy, and society have been polarized by divisions based on race, ethnicity, class, and religion, to name the most historically prominent, since the start of the colonial conquest in 1895. The rulers of Kenya during the colonial era and beyond put such divisions into place by legal measures and political and social usage both before and after independence. This produced a colonial society marked by rigid racial segregation in all aspects of life, including access to political inclusion and economic resources (e.g., the so-called white highlands). Social amenities were also segregated, and employment and leisure activities limited according to race, religion, and economic status. While legally supported racial discrimination disappeared after independence, other forms of exclusion, grounded in ethnicity, class, and religion, continued to thrive after December 1963. The legal and constitutional framework that concretized those forms of exclusion is what the BBI initiative seeks to alter and overturn through constitutional amendments to provide a new framework for governing Kenya in the interests of all its inhabitants.

Looked at in context, it is clear that this process will only be possible if leaders of the BBI movement take account of past history. For example, Kenya's constitutional history prior to 1963 represented a patchwork of legal decrees, colonial ordinances, and imperial directives in the form of orders-in-council. There was no single constitutional document setting out rules and philosophies for governance until the publication of the self-government constitution in April 1963.[7] Like other colonial-era constitutional instruments, the self-government constitution was imposed by the imperial power. A primary reason for this was that none were marked by negotiations involving all Kenya's people or their representatives, nor were they a product of compromise and consensus.

A conspicuous example was the introduction of elected representation to the East Africa Protectorate (after June 1920 the Colony and Protectorate of Kenya) Legislative Council (LegCo) and local government bodies. The LegCo passed an ordinance in 1919, providing electoral representation only for Europeans resident in the territory. Europeans made up most of the body, and the then governor allowed official (civil servant) members a free vote. The result was strongly opposed by Asian (primarily from British India) residents, and as a result, the British government was forced to intervene and decree, in the Devonshire White Paper of 1923, that Asian residents should have five elected representatives in LegCo and Europeans 11. The African majority was left out, and when the first African member entered the council in 1944, he was a nominated member.

This lack of inclusion for the colony's majority population and the imposition by the colonial power manifested itself after the Second World War in the form of the Lyttleton Constitution of 1954 and the Lennox-Boyd Constitution of 1957–1958. In both cases, a secretary of state for the colonies imposed constitutional arrangements that were rejected by those representing the African people. Acceptance by the European settler (or white highlander) representatives on behalf of the minuscule unofficial European population was deemed most important by the colonial rulers. In these cases, as earlier, it was only a portion of the colony's elite who participated in constitutional discussions, and once the secretary of state had made up his mind, there was no discussion or changing of constitutional specifics. Consensus, compromise, and inclusivity were not part of this process.

The constitutional alterations introduced as a result of the first Lancaster House conference in early 1960, moreover, continued the practice of elite involvement at the expense of the Kenyan masses. As before, another secretary of state imposed a formula for a new LegCo and council of ministers as the delegates at the London meeting failed to reach an agreement as far as the future legislative and executive branches were concerned. A major change in 1960 was that the 14 African elected members (AEM) of LegCo were now the key group, but even they were not able to obtain changes to the new constitutional arrangements Iain Macleod laid before them.[8] They accepted his formula while not all the European elected members did. This was a significant change as at the conference the British government recognized that Kenya's future as a state was governed by majority rule with Africans in control of the state. However, the fact remained that this was an imposed constitution discussed among a political elite not truly representative of Kenya's populace, and not subjected to a referendum. It took almost a year to work out the specifics of the new constitutional arrangements with representatives of the colonial state playing a key part in the proceedings.[9]

The self-government and independence constitutions emerged through similar circumstances. The political elite, now African-led and divided into two political parties, KANU and KADU, negotiated with the British government regarding the type of successor state that would rule Kenya. Both parties had European and Asian representatives as members of their delegations. As is well known, the second (1962) and third (1963) Lancaster House conferences were deeply divided over the issue of a federal or unitary state. At Lancaster House II, KADU advocated for *majimbo*, or a federal system of governance with powers devolved to geographically defined regions while KANU stood firm behind the call for a unitary system based on the existing administrative divisions and very much resembling the British model of parliamentary democracy. Here again, a secretary of state had to impose a settlement, this time a framework rather than a detailed constitution. It was left to Kenya's political elite to work out the specifics of the constitution for self-government.[10]

The divisions in constitutional philosophy together with an inept handling of the negotiations by the leadership of the colonial state delayed the process during 1962. Following the arrival of a new governor in January 1963, the process speeded up considerably, but agreement on many critical issues was not reached. This left another secretary of state for the colonies to decide the outstanding issues in dispute in March. Not only did the Kenyan political elite fail to agree, but the whole process did not involve participation by the population in the form of public meetings to explain the issues in dispute or a referendum. The self-government constitution (June 1, 1963) provided for an extensive bill of rights and sought to institute a governmental structure based on a separation of powers between executive, legislative, and judicial branches, and thus unlike the structure of the colonial state. However, the final form of the independence constitution, introduced on December 12, 1963, was much influenced by the universal suffrage general elections of May 1963. The victory of KANU in the House of Representatives and Senate opened the way for significant changes to that constitution in the next decade that did away with federalism and established a de facto one-party state. Significantly, it began the retrenchment of the bureaucratic-executive state.[11] This meant that over time the executive branch of government dominated the legislative and judicial through an authoritarian imperial presidency.[12]

Before turning to constitutional developments in the independence period, it is important to briefly examine the political culture and trends that marked the colonial era. Until 1961, constitutional arrangements were characterized by the politics of race. Kenya's rulers conceived of the colony as a territory of several distinct racial groups. This vision was underpinned by a firm adherence to racist ideas of Social Darwinism which emphasized inequality among humans and a need for exclusion in political, economic, and social facets of colonial life. Segregation rather than integration was the mantra of colonial officials, settlers, and missionaries. As noted, the politics of race began to change in the early 1960s to be succeeded by the politics of ethnicity which also had its roots in the colonial decades.

Both the politics of race and ethnicity shared some common elements in terms of political strategies and actions. A few will be mentioned here as they had an influence on constitutional developments as well as remaining influential in independent Kenya. Divide and rule has been an enduring part of Kenyan political history. Keeping the population divided lessened opposition to ruling groups as well as privileging certain racial and ethnic groups and disadvantaging others (collectively most of the population). The setting of the elite against the masses or the big men against the little people is another enduring part of Kenya political practice. It is influential whether applied to racial or ethnic politics. In addition, a political practice that emerged in colonial Kenya burst forth again after independence. This is what some of Kenya's colonial governors viewed as an "opposition mentality." After 1923, Kenya's European politicians enjoyed considerable influence, but could never take control of state power. This led to the adoption of European obstructionist opposition in LegCo and elsewhere combined with a refusal to support reformist programs in the political, economic, and social spheres. Their politics was that of irresponsible attack on the colonial state, knowing that they could never win control of that state in any democratic election. A similar situation existed from 1969 until 1991 when the single-party KANU government led by all-powerful presidents could not be democratically influenced or changed. That situation was the product of a neo-patrimonial political system with roots in the colonial era. Patrons (with presidents as patron-in-chief) ruled by gaining clients whom they bound loyally to them using state resources. This perpetuated the divisions noted above and also the ongoing dichotomy of the elite against the masses, oligarchy vs democracy, and exclusion and inclusion.

These themes and the practices associated with them impacted postindependence history and produced many of the issues highlighted by the two reports of the BBI task force. These political factors have been, and are, closely tied to many of the critical, and most divisive, issues confronted in any study of Kenya's history since the end of 1963. Prime among those are devolution or *majimbo*, unequal access to national resources, and income inequality with access to land right at the top. Others noted in studies of that historical period include questions relating to the "ownership" of Kenya. Does it belong to all Kenyans or to a few? Can a Kenyan citizen live anywhere within the nation's boundaries? How can gender inequality be fruitfully addressed? Another unaddressed issue is the so-called "neglected north" of Kenya that has been "left behind" in many ways. All these can be directly tied to policies and practices that have produced exclusion, at least in theory, and can certainly be addressed, in some measure, by constitutional changes.

Changes by means of constitutional amendment were relatively common during the second half of the twentieth century as that period witnessed several "change the constitution" initiatives. The first of these emerged immediately after *Madaraka* Day (June 1, 1963), and a key demand and goal of Prime Minister Jomo Kenyatta's government was to alter the procedure for amending the independence constitution. Mzee Kenyatta was partially successful in achieving change at Lancaster House III, though it was not the result of negotiations and compromise with the KADU opposition leaders.

The majorities required in both houses of parliament were reduced for certain categories of amendments, and a procedure for a national referendum was inserted in the independence constitution, though it would not be used for several decades.[13]

The changes, the KANU government's failure to implement portions of the independence constitution, and the demise of KADU in November 1964 opened the way for constitutional amendments that established a republic with an imperial presidency (itself reinforced by further amendments such as the 10th of 1968) and the seeming end to devolution through the elimination of regional powers and a bicameral legislature as well as periods for Kenya as a de facto one-party state (1964–1966 and 1969–1982). All amendments prior to the end of the century were achieved by parliamentary vote rather than by a national referendum. Many amendments to the constitution were passed quickly and with minimal debate. For example, the amendment opening the way for the "little general election" of 1966 was approved by parliament in two days as was the 15th amendment of 1975 (the so-called Paul Ngei amendment). The infamous 19th constitutional amendment of 1982 (that made Kenya a de jure one-party state) was also rapidly approved with no opposition on the second and third readings. A key characteristic of this period was that constitutional change was politician-driven (in some cases by the president himself) rather than people-driven.

The history of amendments in independent Kenya is thus important to take into consideration. The return of multipartyism in 1991 was a result of, and produced additional, change the constitution initiatives, but the changes advocated were on the whole different than those of previous years as they called for democratization of the political system and an extension of civil liberties. The failure of political pluralism to bring these about or to remove the autocratic and corrupt KANU regime of President Daniel arap Moi led many to move from demands for constitutional change by amendment to calling for the introduction of a new constitutional order. Such campaigns for change became increasingly strong during Moi's last term as president (1997–2002). A key characteristic in this drive for change was the continued conflict between those who wished a people-driven process of constitution-making versus those advocating a politician-driven pathway to a new constitution.

This conflict came to the fore after 1999–2000 when a serious attempt was launched to create a new constitution with the creation of the Constitution of Kenya Review Commission and the appointment of distinguished Law Professor Yash Pal Ghai as chairman of the review commission. The commission began to collect public views on constitutional reform during 2001 and 2002 for what many Kenyans hoped would be the basis for a new, people-driven, constitution to be introduced prior to the general election expected to be held at the end of 2002. Politicians had the last word, however, as the new constitution produced by Ghai and his team was not moved forward in parliament, and Moi quickly dissolved that body leading to the 2002 election. KANU was defeated by the NARC coalition and the hopes of many Kenyans for a new constitution under now president Mwai Kibaki seemed likely to be quickly fulfilled.

As is well known, this hope did not materialize during Kibaki's first term, and by 2007 many Kenyans had reason to despair.[14] Many factors have been put forward to explain this delay. Among these were continued division over a people-driven versus politician-driven process, which in some ways reflected the elite or big men versus the larger number of small men dichotomy of the past. The influence of the neo-patrimonial politics remained a factor with wealthy individuals seeking to control the process, and the inability to adopt democratic norms proved a barrier to a new governing order. Also critical were divide and rule traditions (producing exclusion for many) as against the ideal that all Kenyans should have a stake in their government, no matter their ethnicity or place of residence (inclusion). The opposition mentality mentioned earlier also made compromise and agreement difficult.

These divisive factors played themselves out around several key constitutional issues. Those included the shape and powers of the executive branch, the nature of the franchise and of representative government, separation of powers, civil liberties, devolution, and financing a new constitutional order. These all presented bones of contention in the framing process as Kenyans struggled particularly to find consensus around the executive (a president as head of state and government versus an executive prime minister as head of government), legislature (unicameral or bicameral), system of representation, and devolution. The latter issue had become critical since *majimbo* came back into popular discourse and political contention in the 1990s and later. Calls for federalism had accompanied the ethnic clashes that disrupted western Kenya and the coast during that decade. Furthermore, as time passed, federalism was viewed by increasing numbers of Kenyans as a constitutional means to promote inclusion and as a means of diminishing the huge powers of the executive branch that had marked the presidencies of Jomo Kenyatta and Moi.[15]

As most Kenyan adults in the 2020s know, the process of reaching a new constitution order took many twists and turns between 2002 and 2010. The divisive constitutional issues noted earlier continued to burn brightly with the struggle for a people or politician-driven governing document on center stage. 2004–2005 witnessed parliament take control of the reform process through a select committee. Although politician/elite-driven, the process of constitution-making was now, and in the days and years to come, marked by deep division among the political elite and public. Despite a lack of consensus among members of parliament (usually viewed as between those supporting

Kibaki and those opposing his reelection) the select committee dropped the revised Ghai draft constitution presented to the attorney general in March 2004. Devolution was provided for in the new document as well as a single house parliament, a powerful presidency, and a nonexecutive prime minister. A divided political class and populace moved to the November 2005 referendum, the first in Kenyan history, which produced a decisive rejection of what was then termed the "Wako draft."[16] The constitution itself was not the only factor, and other issues such as the performance of the Kibaki administration were influential.[17]

In many ways, the referendum proved to be a rehearsal for the general election of December 2007. Despite political realignments, the demand for a new constitution was a central topic for discourse and many of the issues in constitutional dispute remained contentious while politicians and populace remained deeply divided into hostile parties.[18] The most controversial election in Kenya's history was a result, and the disputed outcome led to electoral violence, loss of lives, and the displacement of thousands of Kenyans from their places of residence in early 2008. As in the late colonial period described earlier, the inability of the Kenya political elite to compromise and reach consensus necessitated outside intervention, though this time not the British government. A political settlement ending the violence emerged with the assistance and pressure of the African Union and United Nations, and a key element of this was the agreement of all political leaders and parties to work expeditiously to give Kenya a new constitution which would deal with the issues of the 2002–2007 era as well as those dating from a much earlier period.

The new constitution was achieved and promulgated in August 2010 following the approval of 67 percent of those voting in a referendum early that month, but the process was hardly easy or straightforward. Differences among the political elite, regarding the executive and devolution, again characterized the process. The latter took the form of 47 county governments, while the former, after intervention by parliamentarians, provided for an executive president and a deputy president, but no prime minister. In a major departure from the past, these leaders were to work with a cabinet consisting of nonmembers of parliament which were to be cast, as in the independence constitution, as bicameral. The referendum outcome indicated a significant level of public support and, led by Raila Odinga, most politicians supported approval in the referendum. Yet there were warning signs in this outcome that created Kenya's second republic.

Among those signs was the fact that following the promulgation, much needed to be done to fill out the details through legislation (as in the creation of a new supreme court). This proved to be a slow process and had not been completed by the time of the initial general election (March 2013) under the new constitution. There also were misgivings that despite the democratic and progressive nature of the new constitution, its promise of inclusion and a better future for Kenyans might be weakened by tribalism, inexperience, and incompetence at the level of devolved units of government, and continued corruption of the type that had plagued the previous governmental order under Moi and Kibaki. Political divisions remained as was illustrated in the outcome of the referendum. Eighty-eight percent of Kalenjin voters rejected it as did 53 percent of the Maasai.[19]

The result over the past decade has been to spark yet another change in the constitution movement despite the progressive nature of the 2010 constitution. On the whole, the factors driving the movement and leading to the handshake agreement of 2018 represented few new factors in Kenyan politics and constitutional discourse. The controversial general elections of 2013 and 2017, marked by heightened ethnic animosity and violence, were illustrative of a lack of inclusion, consensus, and a common feeling of nationhood among large segments of Kenya's population. The first-past-the-post electoral system inherited from the British model, so it was argued, discouraged compromise, heightened ethnic hostility, and left some ethnic groups feeling marginalized and excluded from national decision-making, particularly through exclusion from the executive. In the views of many Kenyans, moreover, corruption at both the level of the national and the county governments has not been tamed but grown more widespread. Unequal access to national resources and economic inequality generally continued to grow. For those Kenyans who feel that the cost of governance itself is a cause for concern, these economic factors also have emerged as critical considerations for constitutional reform. While the 2010 constitution demanded gender equity, on the other hand, it has clearly not been achieved nor has affirmative action aimed at inclusion for disabled people and other underrepresented minority groups. A particularly significant issue is that of process. Right from the beginning, the self-government and independence constitutions were fatally flawed in that they were not completely implemented, and the same has been true of the 2010 constitution, notably in the case of chapter 6 on leadership and integrity for public officers. The BBI reports discuss these and other issues and make recommendations for change, but the process remains elite-driven and far from radical. We turn next to discuss some of the more significant issues.

## ASSESSMENT OF THE REPORTS: PROS AND CONS

Addressing an assessment of the BBI reports is a critical part of the chapter, but one which can only be sketched out here without great detail. As historians, we applaud the reports support for building a national ethos through a national history. This is a worthy initiative, but it must be addressed with open minds and an appreciation that no society can progress without an understanding of its past that is built on facts and reality rather than myths and a colonial mentality. The grip of the past is strong in any society, and a critical factor in shaping an inclusive future can only be obtained by an understanding of that past.

The past has indeed had a powerful impact on the current constitutional moment. The division between the "big" and "small" people remains potent in the hustlers versus dynasties narrative just as the latter illustrates the continued influence of neo-patrimonial politics. Doubt remains regarding the gap between the BBI reports and the resulting reform agenda and twenty-first-century democratic norms. Moreover, will the deep-seated ethnic divide and rule and Kenyan opposition mentality be overcome in the name of consensus and compromise? These are key issues that will weigh in any assessment of that reform agenda.

As a start, we can state that recognition of the varied and several forms that exclusion takes and possible means of confronting them are other positive contributions to the reports. Nevertheless, it is striking that the reports ignore or gloss over several critical issues that are central to any attempt to create and build a more inclusive polity, economy, and society. Particularly significant are those related to the economy. Kenya's land issues, or addressing historical land grievances, particularly from the colonial and independence eras, were largely ignored. It is certain that many in Kenya today will not experience economic inclusion without land reform being right at the top of the agenda. Extreme income disparity and the unbridled pursuit of wealth by any means are other drivers of exclusion that the BBI reports largely overlook. If redistribution of wealth (through taxation, land reform, or government assistance to the needy, for example) is not to be a part of the BBI agenda, then many may wonder how economic inclusion is to be achieved.[20]

Another huge roadblock standing in the way of economic inclusion, not addressed in the BBI reports, is a perception of capitalist history hardly unique to elite Kenyans. This recognizes that capitalism produces inequality in income distribution and that the system produces what is sometimes referred to as a fixed quantity of prosperity. The latter concept is interpreted to mean that there will always be income inequality, with only a few able to attain prosperity and even fewer to accumulate substantial wealth. Such a proposition is at odds with Kenya's economic history, and should not be used to justify government inaction to address income inequality. For example, the widespread adoption of coffee and tea planting by small farmers starting in the late 1950s did not ruin those important export industries, but rather expanded income and enabled an improved standard of living for thousands of households.

Turning to political reforms, the majority of the press coverage relating to the proposed constitutional amendments which have emerged from the two reports has focused on the projected changes in the structure and functions of the executive branch as well as increased numbers of representatives in both houses of parliament. The addition of more than one hundred of the latter as well as a prime minister, two deputy prime ministers, and the second-place finisher in a presidential election as leader of the opposition, heading a shadow cabinet, to the state payroll is projected so as to foster inclusion. So also, it is claimed, will inclusion result from altering current practice to allow members of parliament to serve as ministers. Considering Kenya's divided political landscape, it remains to be seen whether or not that will be the case. In any event, the cost to the taxpayer of these changes will surely be heavy and further enhance the strain on budgetary resources. It must also be recognized that the proposed expansion of the executive branch does not include significant restrictions on its powers.[21] Will these changes lead to more efficient governance and service delivery? If the past is any guide, that seems unlikely.

In the area of alterations to the system of representation, the key recommendations involve increasing the numbers of members of parliament, as stated above. On the face of it, this means greater inclusion as it provides scope for better representation of the Kenyan people in terms of recognizing their wishes and needs, but workability is a question still to be answered. Restructuring of the Independent Electoral and Boundaries Commission (IEBC) should, in theory, be a key prerequisite of a more inclusive and fair electoral system, but the past suggests that this will likely not be enough to bring this about. Inclusivity in representation without some move toward proportional representation will not be easy to achieve. Two member constituencies, an option utilized during the colonial period to promote a "conservative" result by handicapping those candidates perceived by those in control of the state as too radical, will hopefully not become a reality.[22]

Another area where the proposed reforms do not go far enough is devolution. The reports give strong support for continued devolution and provide evidence of popular backing for the Kenyan brand of federalism. In light of this situation, it is hard to understand why the advocates of the BBI initiative did not push hard to further entrench this federalism by proposing the immediate end to the existing vestiges of the unitary/centralized system of control dating from the colonial period. True devolution will not take effect until the people living in the devolved units of governance have a voice in making the decisions and rules that govern their everyday lives. The continued existence of the so-called county and regional commissioners together with chiefs chosen by the central government represents a lack of inclusion and representative governance that, on the one hand, is quite amazing as Kenya approaches

60 years of independence. On the other, it demonstrates how difficult it has been for Kenya to break with the nation's authoritarian and undemocratic past and a colonial mentality.

The same tendency to cling to past systems of representation remains very much alive in Kenyan political culture and not addressed in the BBI reports. Opposition to, and push-back against, populist leaders addressing a reformist agenda characterized the colonial and early independence periods. The first representative bodies created under colonial rule had nominated members, the majority of whom were civil servants. This was the case with the first LegCo and, even more influential, with the Local Native Councils established during the 1920s in the African areas. All local representatives of the latter were at first chiefs (government servants), and later queue voting made it certain that chiefs would be members. Many of these pushed for local improvements in the form of schools, cash crops, and markets, but ultimately, they took their cues from the colonial regime and did not "rock the boat." The change to fully representative local government at independence eliminated many chiefs from the then county and location councils. However, the democratic local government did not last long as representative institutions declined in significance in favor of "guided democracy" through chiefs and local civil servants rather than elected councils.

While devolution has brought some change in this pattern of governance, the traditions that accompanied it have been difficult to change and they live on in contemporary practice. For example, the tradition that civil servants, not answerable to any electorate, should represent local communities and serve as a primary path for obtaining government actions and services rather than elected representatives remains powerful in Kenya. Too powerful, it seems, for those seeking, in the BBI reports, to challenge exclusion. Contemporary press reports confirm that it is not unusual for unelected officials to be the focus of appeals for assistance with local concerns even in the era of devolved government.[23] The BBI reports make no attempt to challenge this authoritarian tradition. No wonder that some critics have claimed that the BBI initiative appears to be a quest to take "the locus of power outside the domain of our democracy."[24]

## SIGNIFICANCE OF THE REPORTS: A POLITICAL TOOL AND/OR A STATE-BUILDING OPPORTUNITY?

When the history of Kenyatta's second term at the helm of political leadership is written, it shall cast him in Machiavellian light as a wily fox—a scheming and unscrupulous prince. This history, perhaps, shall, at the same time, be magnanimous, and laudatory of Raila's repeated efforts, over the long duration of his career, to demonstrate pragmatism and build bridges in more than three or so occasions. Indeed, these two politicians, perhaps, shall be looked upon by such an objective history quite kindly for being able, somewhat, to douse the intense fire and latent political violence before and after the 2017 elections. It is undeniable that the private talks, the subsequent highly public political and symbolic "handshake," and the BBI consultation process was "created by people in the executive to stabilize the state."[25] However, as contemporary political commentators observed, this initiative has quite a few pitfalls, blindsides, and shortcomings, and this, history shall not forgive. As the constitutional lawyer, and political commentator, Kamotho Waiganjo noted, the BBI shall not "fundamentally solve our problems." Moreover, the country's fundamental problems do not lie in the law, but elsewhere.[26]

When put in historical perspective, this political initiative, and the debate around it, only opens the more important discussion of Kenyans coming to terms with their social realities. As Waiganjo stated, citizens must have "an honest national conversation about what ails" Kenya—what takes away our ethos? Why do we celebrate unethical conduct by public servants and officials? Why do we elect people we know are thugs? Why is it that we are corrupt in every sector of our society? According to Waiganjo, that is the substantive conversation that Kenyans ought to have in every sector of society, be it private or public. As such, the BBI cannot be expected to be the end-all and be-all silver bullet that will solve all the country's various problems (and especially not the two twin tyrannies of ethnic expectation and institutionalized corruption that feed off each other, and are inextricably connected).[27] As already noted above, while the initiative staved off violence and bloodshed, it largely remains an elite initiative as opposed to being people-led and -driven as the protracted constitution-writing process of the 2000s was and, therefore, cannot be as radical, and revolutionary. And, if anything were revolutionary, it was the 2010 constitution, which was the result of a people-driven process.[28] When the account of this process is written, it shall record that this process was, indeed, anything other than "a reform document," and that, while the report may contain some strains of what could pass as reform, "it is inherently inconsistent with itself."[29]

As Wanjiru Gikonyo noted, the initiative failed the litmus test of elite accountability and answerability. In Gikonyo's own words, the two political leaders, and the elite in general, ducked being accountable and answerable regarding the precipitous 2017 events by hiding behind BBI. Neither does the report mention rampant economic or financial crimes perpetrated against the people of Kenya, nor does it comprehensively address issues of economic marginalization. As such, the report did not only "fail spectacularly to be accountable to the people," but it, for the most part, descended into "political theater." In the end, it is Kenyans who were had by the political class:

"We have been snookered," as Gikonyo put it.[30] And, given the benefit of hindsight, honest, and objective *wananchi* looking back would say, "No, we needed to get out of this charade. We were snookered. The report cherry-picked this or that carrot for women; another carrot for devolution; that carrot for youth; and put together all these various carrots in an unfathomable framework."[31] In observing that BBI was akin to trying to fix fundamental and systemic governance weaknesses and failure using a Band-Aid approach, Gikonyo could not have been more apt: "It is a whitewash process, but this whitewash process is also trying to take us forward by taking us backwards. It is taking us forward from the chaos we have now, taking us back to the coalition government, because . . . without a vision, and failing to have a progressive mindset, they [pro-BBI politicians] are saying things were a bit better when we had a coalition government. Let us put some . . . band-aid on our governance system and go back there."[32]

Lastly, it is also worth observing that, while widespread, grassroot "consensus" was sought, the process was not necessarily greeted with enthusiasm. A survey conducted by Tifa, a polling firm, at the beginning of 2021 revealed that only a paltry 29 percent of registered voters said they would vote for the BBI proposal or referendum to amend the 2010 constitution. Conversely, 32 percent of Kenyans said that they would vote "No," to oppose constitutional changes suggested by the BBI.[33] Another computer-aided telephone survey conducted at the end of January 2021 by Radio Africa Group revealed that the BBI referendum appeared to be on shaky ground. This poll found that 43 percent of *wananchi* did not support the process compared to 21 percent who were pro the process. However, there was, according to this poll, "a potentially high swing vote as 25 percent say that they 'do not know much about BBI,' while 11 percent 'don't care either way.'" Furthermore, 40 percent said they would not vote although 60 percent said that they would.[34] Without a doubt, the BBI process, like the electoral process historically, is quite divisive, which in Kenya, can only forebode trouble of a terrible kind. The irony of the BBI process is that, while it was intended to stabilize the state, build bridges between perceived rival ethnic groups, and cohere the nation by healing past divisions, it appears to have succeeded in resowing seeds of old tribal hatreds across the country. As in the past, Kenya perches on delicate tenterhooks thanks to the "building bridges initiative."

## OBSTACLES ON THE WAY TO CANAAN: CAN KENYANS AFFORD THE DEMOCRACY THEY CRAVE?

This also is a key question. Indeed, it has enjoyed a lengthy history in Kenya, particularly regarding the issue of federalism or *majimbo*. A criticism raised against such schemes from the 1940s through the early 1960s was that federalism was too expensive for Kenya. The right-wing European politicians (e.g., the Federal Independence Party) who advocated devolution of powers to settler-controlled provincial or district councils sought an exclusionary political, economic, and social order that would keep political control and land in the white highlands in the hands of the European minority while maintaining racially segregated schools and hospitals. Critics pointed out that such a system of government would be very expensive.[35] For these federalists, exclusion had to be maintained no matter what the cost, especially in the case of schools.[36]

KADU's proposed *majimbo* scheme that emerged in 1961–1962 also drew criticism as to potential cost from colonial officials and members of the public in addition to the leaders of KANU. This criticism focused on the creation of regional governments and duplication of functions. Peter Habenga Okondo, one of the architects of KADU's federal proposals and a principal spokesperson for federalism, answered such criticisms bluntly. He wrote in November 1961: "If we want to preserve individual liberty what is the cost?" No cost was too high, he asserted, if Kenyans wanted to maintain a system of separation of powers and functions and "maintain the democratic process of government" that he claimed Kenyans longed for.[37] The argument that no cost is too high to pay for civil liberties and representative government has since that time been reiterated during the debates surrounding the adoption of the 2010 constitution and by some of those supporting the constitutional changes called for in the BBI reports.

Yet these supporting arguments leave unmentioned issues which in the past have proved controversial and difficult to surmount. Two economic issues that raised concerns of cost during the transition to independence have yet to be confronted and put to rest. These are the issues of land ownership and labor mobility under a devolved system of government. At about the same time, Okondo was advocating for regional governments with control over land and the government workforce in their areas, civil servants at the British Colonial Office expressed concern that if regional assemblies were given the right to allocate land to owners and tenants, this would go against British proposals for a free market in land. The officials feared that KADU's proposed systems were "a reversion to the old tribal concepts from which we have been trying to get away in the new policy of regarding land as an economic asset" open to purchase or lease by any Kenyan. Jobs might be reserved only for individuals born in the devolved unit of government.[38] These concerns were allegedly laid to rest after the demise of KADU and the scrapping of *majimbo*, but the ethnic clashes of the 1990s and the post-2007 election violence indicated that such was not the case. Do the BBI constitutional amendments promote a constitutional and legal environment that finally "solves" these issues? This is a key question yet to be definitively answered.

## CONCLUSION: GOING FULL CIRCLE, BACK TO THE FUTURE?

As noted earlier, the Report of the Steering Committee on the Implementation of the Building Bridges to a United Kenya Task Force Report provided long-awaited principles and recommendations for the construction of "a new Kenyan nation," including several changes in the current constitution. But a portion of Kenyatta's Mashujaa Day speech on October 20, 2020, suggests a need for caution. It was rather ahistorical, and unfortunately, oblivious of numerous imposed top-down attempts at constitution-making, and other general attempts to foist government declarations or policy documents on ordinary people. Hoping to, perhaps, prepare the ground for elite-led changes to the 2010 constitution, the president's speechwriters sought to arrive at this end by using a portion of the speech to remind citizens that constitutions are not static but often change. This process, the writers asserted, should be a product of "constant negotiation and renegotiation of nationhood," and *building a constitutional consensus*. The italicized end of the president's paraphrased speech is instructive, and erroneous in the light of the country's constitutional history.

Moreover, referring to Steering Committee's report, the speech sought to prepare the ground for constitutional and other changes by calling for the building of "a sense of national ethos" that will emphasize belonging and inclusion. This, as the committee rightly observed, must include "documenting our history honestly." But not so the president as per his speech, notably.

Most historians and citizens would agree that a key element in such an honest history must be factual accuracy regarding past events and interpretations solely based upon such facts. It is this latter point that the speechwriters disregarded in putting forth an account of constitution-making. While correctly emphasizing the need for a constantly moving exercise requiring, again, note, *a consensus* among political leaders and *wananchi*, the examples from which they drew during the colonial era demonstrate no such thing! Neither the Lyttleton Constitution of 1954 nor the Lennox-Boyd Constitution (announced in 1957 and implemented in 1958) was the product of *a consensus*.

First, both constitutions were imposed by the secretary of state for the colonies that bear their names, and the terms were dictated by the then governor Sir Evelyn Baring, and his advisors—does this ring a bell yet? Elitist. Moreover, the Kenyan population, and particularly Africans, had no input whatsoever in the Lyttleton Constitution which was imposed even though all six of the Africans appointed to the LegCo refused to accept the Lyttleton plan. That plan was not about inclusion at all, but its main purpose was to create a multiracial council of ministers which, in the early stages of planning, no African would hold a portfolio. Lyttleton eventually agreed for one ministry to be headed by an African, but it ought to be recalled that the constitution provided for three European settler ministers to join the already two settlers holding the important portfolios of finance and agriculture. The key group for Lyttleton and the governor in Kenya's racial politics of the time was thus the European settler politicians. The acceptance of the plan by most of them constituted Lyttleton's success and left the African population, among whom none could vote for representatives to the Legislative Council, totally excluded. While there was little inclusion, African LegCo members did gain a promise from Lyttleton that the colonial government would take steps to provide for African representation. The promise, imposed without the agreement of settler representatives, led to the first African elections of March 1957. The eight AEM immediately launched a campaign for change that would produce a more inclusive constitutional order (European voters elected 14 LegCo members and Asian voters 6).

Amazingly, the speechwriters cast this as *consensual* by the statement that if the Lyttleton Constitution "was wrong, it was made right" by the Lennox-Boyd Constitution! This interpretation has no basis in fact as all the European settler members of LegCo opposed the AEM campaign which included a refusal to accept the two ministerial positions reserved for Africans in 1957. Significantly, most Asian political leaders came to support the AEM demands. Just as in 1954, then secretary of state Alan Lennox-Boyd, in response to the AEM campaign, flew to Nairobi in late 1957 to implement constitutional changes suggested by Baring. He was prepared to increase the number of AEM in the LegCo and determined to make them accept ministerial portfolios and introduce what came to be known as specially elected members to the LegCo. AEM rejected these proposals, including the six additional LegCo seats for Africans and the creation of a council of state.

An infuriated Lennox-Boyd convinced he knew best, and that the only views that mattered were those of the European settler population, went ahead anyway, giving up his attempt to build *consensus* and ignoring the opinions of most of the Kenyan population. The result was continued political exclusion, and a period of ongoing political tension and racial hostility. The AEM boycott of the Lennox-Boyd innovations (except the six additional LegCo positions) by April 1959 forced the British government to accept that the Lennox-Boyd plan had become unworkable. The solidarity of the AEMs won the battle.

But it was a glaring distortion of history to single out Oginga Odinga, Daniel Toroitich arap Moi, and Masinde Muliro as heroes in the president's speech while at the same time seeming to say that as AEMs they consented to the changes desired by Lennox-Boyd and Baring. Nothing could be further from historical fact as the archival records of the discussions leading to the Lennox-Boyd Constitution clearly illustrate. Asian political opinion supported the need for constitutional change, but several of the European elected members of LegCo did not favor discussing constitutional changes. The years 1959 and 1960 brought an end to consensus among the settler political elite.

The first Lancaster House constitutional conference (LH1) thus brought together Kenyan LegCo members who viewed constitutional change very differently with few apparent grounds for agreement. While the settlers were divided, the 14 AEM delegates were united in a firm stand in favor of a rapid democratic transition for Kenya leading to self-government and independence within a short period of time. European delegates were, by contrast deeply divided, with the right-wing United Party favoring continued colonial rule and the New Kenya Party (NKP) delegates favoring a gradual transition to independence, and a multiracial executive and parliament with reserved seats for Europeans and fewer for Asians. The new secretary of state Iain Macleod, like his predecessors, was unable to find or facilitate *consensual* agreement on a new constitution. Contrary to the speechwriters, therefore, there was no common ground negotiated among the delegates. Macleod moved beyond this stalemate by putting a set of proposals before the by-now-weary delegates that they were required to accept in full or reject. This was a quite different approach than in 1954 and 1957. Macleod then cleverly maneuvered the African, Asian, and NKP delegates into acceptance of his terms that went some way toward meeting the demands of African delegates, but not others, for instance, universal suffrage, the appointment of a chief minister, and the release of Jomo Kenyatta. In a real sense, for that reason, the LH1 constitution was an imposed one, and indeed many living in Kenya at the time rejected it.

Nonetheless, the AEM accepted it as ending European settler political predominance in Kenya and the new plan as a step on the way to independence. Over subsequent months, however, the *consensus* that had united the AEM disappeared as bitter divisions developed regarding the type of constitution Kenya should adopt as an independent nation. The competing visions of KANU (a unitary republic) and KADU (*majimbo* or a federal republic) were difficult to reconcile. This formed the background for the second Lancaster House conference in 1962. The absence of agreement on the basic constitutional structure was clear from the first meeting, and again, a British colonial secretary was forced to impose a settlement that did not take the form of a constitution but of a framework on which a coalition government in Kenya would work out the final document. This took a year and required the British government to draft the self-government constitution and decide key provisions because the KANU and KADU ministers could, well, not agree.

This brief narrative serves to make it clear that there was no *consensus* here any more than with the three previous constitutional talks. It is thus rather puzzling, if not amusing in an odd way, that in a desire to promote negotiated and *consensual* constitutional innovation under the auspices of the BBI in the year 2020, and by the president no less, these should be the examples put before the Kenyan public in justification. Rather, an accurate account and analysis of earlier or past constitutional innovations demonstrate very clearly the need for wide consultations among the populace (unlike the episodes described above, where only a narrowly defined political elite participated) and a broad-based *consensus*. In other words, the same message can be got across to the public by relating the correct facts. As the speechwriters noted: "The more we ponder our history in its truest form, the more liberated we become." It is always best to hark the lessons of history, not to ignore it altogether, and repeat the same grievous mistakes.

## NOTES

1. NTV Live Stream, "BBI Report Launch at Bomas of Kenya," YouTube, Updated by *Daily Nation*, November 26, 2019, Accessed, November 26, 2019, https:// www.youtube.com/watch?v=MTrTH4mq_jI.

2. Marjorie Oludhe Macgoye, *Coming to Birth* (The Feminist Press at CUNY, 2000).

3. "The report," herein, will only apply to the second and final October 21, 2020, BBI report.

4. See Nicholas Kariuki Githuku's separate chapter contribution in this volume.

5. Republic of Kenya, *Report of the Steering Committee on the Implementation of the Building Bridges to a United Kenya Taskforce Report: Building Bridges to a United Kenya from a Nation of Ideals* (Nairobi: Government Printer, October 2020), 5.

6. This is not to suggest that the precolonial period was one characterized by a lack of exclusion, but rather that the problem of inclusivity Kenyans face today is much more the product of the period since 1895.

7. It was set out in an order-in-council and published in the *Official Gazette*. It came into effect on June 1, 1963. For a detailed treatment see Robert M. Maxon, *Kenya's Independence Constitution: Constitution-Making and End of Empire* (Lanham, MD: Fairleigh Dickinson University Press, 2010), 152–75.

8. Robert M. Maxon, *Britain and Kenya's Constitutions, 1950-1960* (Amherst, NY: Cambria Press, 2011), 307–31.

9. A key reason for this is that the colonial state and the British government wished to create a system of representation whereby "moderate" candidates were

returned to the new LegCo by African and European voters in what would be Kenya's last nonuniversal suffrage election.

10. A detailed treatment of the conference is found in Maxon, *Kenya's Independence Constitution*, 77–112.

11. Daniel Branch and Nicholas Cheeseman, "The Politics of Control in Kenya: Understanding the Bureaucractic-Executive State, 1952-78," *Review of African Political Economy* 33 (2006): 12–13.

12. Ngala Chome, "What Kenyans Have Always Wanted is to Limit the Powers of the Executive," *The Elephant*, January 15, 2021, theelephantinfo/op-eds/2021.

13. Maxon, *Kenya's Independence Constitution*, 243–53.

14. This is one of several examples validating the title of Daniel Branch's political history of independent Kenya. Daniel Branch, *Kenya Between Hope and Despair, 1963-2011* (London: Yale University Press, 2011).

15. Charles Hornsby, *Kenya: A History Since Independence* (London: I.B. Taurus 2012), 623 & 625. Robert M. Maxon, "The Rise and Demise of *Majimbo* in Independent Kenya," in *Kenya After 50: Reconfiguring Historical, Political, and Policy Milestones*, eds. Michael Mwenda Kithinji, Mickie Mwanzia Koster and Jerono P. Rotich (New York: Palgrave Macmillan, 2016), 38–47.

16. Then attorney general Amos Wako was responsible for drafting the final version of the constitution approved by parliament.

17. Hornsby, *Kenya*, 740.

18. Charles Hornsby correctly observed that despite the passage of time, key politicians were still playing the same game that the founding fathers had in 1960–1966 period. Ibid., 745.

19. Moreover, only a slim majority voted in favor among the Kamba. Hornsby, *Kenya*, 780. Yet if press comments and political commentaries are any kind of a guide, the Kalenjin, following the lead of Deputy President Dr. William Ruto, now strongly support the 2010 constitution and see no need for change.

20. The two most widely read histories of independent Kenya both make clear that redistribution, in particular land, have been major issues in the national story since 1963. Hornsby, *Kenya*, 7–9. Branch, *Kenya Between Hope and Despair*, 16–18. Branch correctly contends that debates about redistribution in Kenya increasingly gave way to the demand for recognition of grievances of ethnic groups.

21. Chome, "What Kenyans Have Always Wanted."

22. Several seats in the 1961 LegCo election provided a "classic" example of this.

23. Ruth Mbula, "Matiang'i eyes Gusii kingpin role ahead of 2022 election," *The Nation* (online), January 31, 2021. Bwana Matiang'I is an unelected cabinet secretary at present. Nevertheless, the article states that people in Kisii and Nyamira counties were reaching out to him "with all sorts of problems." Such words echo colonial propaganda that ordinary people could not solve their problems unless they brought them to the attention of a European administrator.

24. Eric Ng'eno, "Catastrophe looms if Judiciary does not kill this roaring cat," *The Nation* (online), February 6, 2021.

25. Kamotho Waiganjo, NTV Live Stream, "BBI Report Launch at Bomas of Kenya."

26. Ibid.
27. See Nicholas K. Githuku's separate chapter contribution in this volume.
28. Kamotho Waiganjo, NTV Live Stream, "BBI Report Launch at Bomas of Kenya."
29. Gikonyo, NTV Live Stream, "BBI Report Launch at Bomas of Kenya."
30. Ibid.
31. Ibid. Here we are paraphrasing the words of Gikonyo in the live television broadcast on NTV on November 27, 2019, during the launch of the first BBI preliminary report.
32. Gikonyo, NTV Live Stream, "BBI Report Launch at Bomas of Kenya."
33. James Mbaka, "BBI Referendum will Flop if Held Today—Tifa Poll," *The Star*, January 8, 2021, https://www.the-star.co.ke/news/2021-01-08-bbi-referendum-will-flop-if-held-today-tifa-poll/, Accessed on Tuesday, March 16, 2021.
34. Star Reporter, "BBI Vote Appears to be on Shaky Ground—Poll," *The State*, February 11, 2021, https://www.the-star.co.ke/news/2021-02-11-bbi-vote-appears-to-be-on-shaky-ground-poll/, Accessed on Tuesday, March 16, 2021.
35. Robert M. Maxon, *Majimbo in Kenya's Past: Federalism in the 1940s and 1950s* (Amherst, NY: Cambria Press, 2017), 82 & 106. M. F. Hill, influential editor of the *Kenya Weekly News,* referred to the idea of an independent white highlands in 1953 as an "economic impossibility." M. F. Hill, "Signed Print," *Kenya Weekly News*, November 20, 1953.
36. Maxon, *Majimbo in Kenya's Past*, 83.
37. P. J. H. Okondo, "Federation—Safeguard for Future Kenya," *East African Standard*, November 23, 1961.
38. K.A.D.U.'s Proposals for Regionalism, secret, British National Archives (BNA): CO 822/2242.

# BIBLIOGRAPHY

Branch, Daniel, *Kenya Between Hope and Despair, 1963-2011* (London: Yale University Press, 2011).

Branch, Daniel, and Cheeseman, Nicholas, "The Politics of Control in Kenya: Understanding the Bureaucractic-Executive State, 1952-78," *Review of African Political Economy* 33 (2006): 11–31.

Chome, Ngala, "What Kenyans Have Always Wanted is to Limit the Powers of the Executive," *The Elephant*, 15 January 2021.

Hornsby, Charles, *Kenya: A History Since Independence* (London: I.B. Taurus 2012).

Macgoye, Marjorie Oludhe, *Coming to Birth* (The Feminist Press at CUNY, 2000).

Maxon, Robert M., *Kenya's Independence Constitution: Constitution-Making and End of Empire* (Lanham, MD: Fairleigh Dickinson University Press, 2010).

———. *Britain and Kenya's Constitutions, 1950-1960* (Amherst, NY: Cambria Press, 2011).

———. *Majimbo in Kenya's Past: Federalism in the 1940s and 1950s* (Amherst, NY: Cambria Press, 2017).

———. "The Rise and Demise of *Majimbo* in Independent Kenya," in *Kenya After 50: Reconfiguring Historical, Political, and Policy Milestones*, eds. Michael Mwenda Kithinji, Mickie Mwanzia Koster and Jerono P. Rotich (New York: Palgrave Macmillan, 2016).

Republic of Kenya, *Report of the Steering Committee on the Implementation of the Building Bridges to a United Kenya Taskforce Report: Building Bridges to a United Kenya from a Nation of Ideals* (Nairobi: Government Printer, October 2020).

*Chapter 15*

# House of *Mlungula*—"Norms in the Margins and Margins of the Norm"

## *Of Computer "Glitches," Moving Human Fingers and Illicit Financial Flows*

Nicholas K. Githuku

This chapter is the third installment in a series of three chapters addressing the evolution, in Kenya, of ethnic culture/ethnic morality or the gradual transformation of people's attitudes, set of ideas, values, and beliefs, and how they conduct themselves and work for survival and reputation—their sense of purpose, and of being in the world. The first paper in this series was "From Moral Ethnicity to Moral Anarchy: The Colonial Ideology of Order and Political Disorder in Postcolonial Kenya," which examined the evolution of the ideology of order that has in the postcolonial period disintegrated into an unabated culture of impunity characterized by runaway corruption and descended to politics of disorder. The second unpublished paper, "House of *Mlungula*—'Norms in the Margins and Margins of the Norm': Liminality and Strategic Radical Rudeness in Colonial and Postcolonial Africa," is an abbreviated case study of the disorientation of East African societies as they experience the crisis of the dissolution or collapse of order precipitated by the colonial moment, and since.

This third installment in this series examines the zenith of the complete or gross disregard of African norms of kinship, mutuality, and reciprocity. Seldom is there human progress and technological advancement that does not alter society. Whether one talks about printing in the sixteenth century which rocked Europe with the spread of Protestantism; or various machines behind the Industrial Revolution; or historian John Lonsdale's *ng'ombe na mkuki* (cow and spear) and the *njembe na kalamu* (hoe and pen) revolutions in Africa,[1] technological advancement has always transformed and/or forged societies. Although this is not a phenomenon confined to Kenya and Africa, this chapter is a reflection of how the combination of "itchy" human fingers and the rapid development of digital technologies—such as mobile banking, electronic money transfer, cryptocurrencies such as Bitcoin,[2] and online banking and gambling services all of which are quite popular in Kenya—have facilitated or contributed to illicit financial flows ranging from corruption, illegally earned, or transfer of, money and cybercrime (read: fraud) among others such as tax evasion and tax avoidance, organized crime, human trafficking, and "many other forms of crime . . . associated with these illegal activities."[3] The proliferation and establishment of digital technologies in the twenty-first century as an acceptable way for transacting business and money transfer has encouraged financial chicanery ensuring that universal ethical norms such as accountability and responsibility have not only been pushed to the outer margins but also meant that the margins of the norms have been pushed to the limit and, more often than not, been ruptured with impunity.

Thankfully, by the same token of the proliferation and widespread use of digital technologies, there have been unprecedented largescale breaches of supposedly secret and confidential, or "private" information in recent times made public by WikiLeaks. What follows below is a rough outline of the new and emerging and, therefore, understudied phenomenon that is yet to be fully understood due to "the relative newness of the problem," which means "a lack of research on the issue of digital technologies as an enabler and facilitator of . . . illicit financial flows" and "the borderless nature and decentralized architecture of the internet, combined with a complex dynamic ecosystem of the digital economy."[4]

This notwithstanding, this chapter, using a selection of a few illustrations from Kenya thanks to leaked information, attempts to shine a light on a seemingly well-established pattern and, therefore, a recurring *modus operandi*, hence, an emerging preferred "formula" (so to speak) of spiriting capital from public coffers to various tax havens, using *nostro* accounts, private properties such as houses and ranches, among other obscure offshore destinations including shell companies. Digital technologies as tools of money transfer, especially when used in combination, do not only "provide . . . countless number of opportunities to distance money from illegal sources of profit or to illegally transfer money from legal sources,"[5] but also doing so in a manner that removes any restraint, and benumbs and desensitizes whatever remnant strains of primordial conscience, personal responsibility and accountability in perpetrators of the crimes while ensuring insuperable ease and near ironclad secrecy. After all, all it takes is the moving of human fingers on the screen or keyboard of a device. Nowadays, billions of dollars can be moved across international borders with a simple click.

# TAX HAVENS AS THE CULMINATION OF DOING THINGS WITH WORDS[6] AND FINGERS, MAYBE: OF COMPUTATIONAL "GLITCHES" AND CLICKS

It took at least 400 years to acknowledge the truism regarding the influence of the pen (Lonsdale's *Kalamu*, in Swahili) in the metonymic adage attributed to Edward Bulwer-Lytton about the administrative power of communication as attested by the combined global spending in marketing service and public relations revenue worldwide that is no less than US$470 billion.[7] More often than not, people grapple, tackle, confront, and engage with social reality through its representation in language. Behind putting things into words, or giving verbal expression to anything, lies the inner promptings of action. Put differently, language can be, and is constantly being, used to represent possibilities, and to position possibilities in relation to each other. This same power of doing things with words was inherent in the British imperial enactments of power, especially the legal kind.

Such is the legal global financial system and fiscal architecture that is made of a combination of preferential tax regimes, monetary subsidies, and sweeteners including reductions in taxation—that is, the creation of tax havens.[8] According to Paul Beckett (2018), there are two principal geopolitical poles around which tax havens have originated and developed, and of the two, it is the financial Courts in London, and, specifically, the City of London, that stands to be credited for the creation "of 'virtual' residencies, allowing companies to incorporate in Britain without paying tax—a development that at least one commentator believes is the foundation of the entire tax haven phenomenon"[9] that is at the heart of illicit financial flows. But unlike Beckett, who only recognizes the U.K.-based or British Empire-based and European-based tax havens, according to Palan, the totality of modern tax havens can be categorized into three groups, including its third component—that is, the new tax havens from the transitional economies in South America and Africa. This phenomenon has its genesis in the late nineteenth century—a surprising and interestingly fortuitous coincidence with the colonization of Africa by Europe at the same time—and has come to play a prominent role in the global financial system.[10] Altogether, there are 700 independent tax jurisdictions or countries of domicile of global financial flows. These tax havens of private financial wealth provide a legal home to a total of US$21 trillion, of which US$9 trillion is from developing countries, most of which are in Africa, a situation that acts as a formidable development challenge.[11]

It comes as no surprise at all, therefore, that tax havens, as an important instrument of tax evasion and tax avoidance and money laundering especially through the preferred *modus operandi* of using *nostro* accounts, today constitute the single largest drain in developing countries' economies.[12] As it exists, a considerably vast and significant portion of the global financial system consists of a rigged and an unjust system, a murky-black shark-infested liquid mass of dynastic fiscal networks gnarled by corruption with its poisoned headwaters of British imperialism, specifically, and European colonization of Africa and elsewhere, generally. Indeed, as John Christensen (2011) has observed, tax havens are representative of "the new international order of disorder."[13] Furthermore, not only do these abusive international fiscal networks go against established rules and norms, including legal obligations to pay tax but they also—and especially, inasfar as they affect African countries—constitute the near absolute negation of African norms of kinship, mutuality, and reciprocity and are, moreover, an incredible contravention of the Universal Declaration of Human Rights; a serious barrier to the global quest for inclusive economies, and economic equity and equality, and sustainable development, and represent, therefore, a seemingly unassailable continuation of colonialism on a global scale. According to Countess (2019), illicit financial flows rob African nations of a whopping US$60–US$100 billion each year—"funds that could be used to secure basic economic and social rights," such as "rights to social security, decent work, and human dignity," but "are instead held in secret tax havens for the benefit of corporate elites."[14]

According to one of the leading financial integrity and accountability organizations, the Washington, DC-based Global Financial Integrity, whose work is dedicated to analyzing and curtailing illicit financial flows, for every dollar that illicitly crosses borders, approximately 20 percent "could have been realized as tax revenues on imports or exports and related corporate income taxes." Subsequently, what this means for developing countries is that, collectively, this lost potential revenue "represents hundreds of millions of dollars in . . . foregone . . . revenues that could have been otherwise collected and used for supporting sustainable economic growth, creating jobs, reducing inequality, poverty, and addressing climate change, among other things. With billions of dollars estimated to be illicitly leaving developing countries every year, this drain of public resources undermines the efforts of countries to mobilize more domestic resources in order to meet the internationally-agreed Sustainable Development Goals by the target date of 2030."[15] The impact of these illicit financial flows or its global implications and ramifications underscore the blatant and rife financial exploitation of developing nations and the resultant economic inequality that exists in the world today. This is too broad a subject that is beyond the purview of this present work but one that is best illustrated by figure 15.1, a cartogram that is a virtual representation of the state of global health based on data mining of global epidemics and death between 2001 and 2017.[16] Before delving into how this global underground economy and financial architecture "of tax havens, banks and legal and accounting business, and related financial intermediaries" has encouraged,

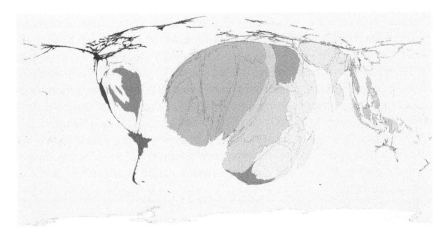

**Figure 15.1   The cartogram above illustrates the state of global health based on statis-tics of Epidemics/Deaths, 2001–2017.** According to World Mapper, the map shows the proportion of all people killed by epidemics between 2001 and 2017 by continent—most of them were in Africa. This map was generated using data by EM-DAT: The Emergency Events Database last accessed in March 2018. World Mapper aims to "map as complete data as possible and therefore estimate data for missing values. In some cases, missing data for very small territories is not used in the cartogram and that area is therefore omit-ted in the map." Indeed, this illustration eloquently and graphically encapsulates and captures the profound statement that, "the ultimate expression of sovereignty resides, to a large degree, in the power and the capacity to dictate who may live and who may die." *Source*: HEALTH—WorldMapper, Accessed on 7 January 2020.

manifested, and turned a blind eye to runaway and skyrocketing corruption in Kenya, it is worth pausing to note that the latter would, more or less, not be possible without the former, as Jeffrey Sachs and Christensen (2011) have noted with great aptness.

Jeffrey Sachs, a leading international economics professor who special-izes in how to combat extreme poverty, especially in developing countries, captures the essential nature and character of this murky-black shark-infested liquid mass of dynastic fiscal networks or what Christensen refers to as "the new international order of disorder"—that is, tax havens, and the rest of the attendant elements of this financial structure, do not just happen. Rather, they "are creations of the wealthiest and most powerful in our society. Advanced countries' governments are . . . dominated by giant multinational oligopo-lies, and bringing to end [*sic*] this abusive global system is by no means an easy task."[17] Christensen's analysis of the continuing global financial loot-ing through tax havens marred by corruption is remarkable because of the way it puts paid to "the geography of corruption." Christensen calls out the purported corruption of African countries by Transparency International's

Corruption Perception Index (CPI) that has, since 1995, "identified Africa as the most corrupt region of the world, accounting for over half of the 'most corrupt' quintile of countries." Christensen argues that, as presented by Transparency International (TI), CPI statistics "provide a very partial and biased perspective" since it never includes what he refers to the "supply-side" of developed countries in Europe and elsewhere that are tax havens such as Hong Kong, Singapore, Switzerland, the United Kingdom, and Luxembourg. Thus, seldom is it appreciated that the prevalence of corruption in African countries is incentivized by the two core geopolitical poles of tax havens earlier mentioned. And "not a single African nation is ranked in the 'least corrupt' quintile."[18]

Further, argues Christensen:

What do these rankings tell us about the current politics of corruption? And who would disagree with the prominent Nigerian politician who, during protracted negotiations to secure the repatriation of assets stolen by former Nigerian President Sani Abacha, commented that:

It is rather ironical that the European based Transparency International does not think it proper to list Switzerland as the first or second most corrupt nation in the world for harbouring, encouraging and enticing all robbers of public treasuries around the world to bring their loot for safe-keeping in their dirty vaults (Education Minister Professor Aliya Babs Fafunwa quoted in *This Day*, 2005).

The perversity of the CPI's rankings reflects the general confusion and inadequacy of the current corruption discourse. In focusing on the activities of players employed in the public sector, and in largely basing its index on the perceptions of actors with conflicting interests, TI has highlighted only part of the corruption issue and has evaded the wider issue of how the "supply side" incentivises and protects high level corruption. This proclivity to point fingers at petty officials and ruling kleptomaniacs has resulted in insufficient attention being paid to the (largely) Western financial intermediaries who facilitate the laundering of the proceeds of corruption through offshore companies, trusts, and similar subterfuges. Ditto the role of the governments of tax havens which actively collude in the process of encouraging illicit capital flight and tax evasion by providing lax regulation combined with secrecy and an absence of effective information exchange.

Indeed, according to a *New York Times* report, several U.S. firms were alleged to have helped Africa's richest woman, Isabel dos Santos, the billionaire daughter of the former president of Angola, José Eduardo dos Santos, exploit her country's wealth. According to the article—based on a trove of more than 700,000 documents obtained by the International Consortium of Investigative Journalists and shared with the *New York Times*—Ms. Dos

Santos, estimated to be worth over US$2 billion, built a vast financial empire backed by huge stakes in Angola's "diamond exports, its dominant mobile phone company, two of its banks and its biggest cement maker, and partnered with the state oil giant to buy into Portugal's largest petroleum company."[19] In addition to owning high stakes in the oil company, Galp Energia and Portuguese telecommunications firm, NOS, it was also said that she held significant shares in the Portuguese bank Eurobic.[20] This amassment of assets and wealth, the *New York Times* reported, was only made possible by a global network of consultants, lawyers, bankers, and accountants. "Some of the leading professional service firms—including the Boston Consulting Group, McKinsey & Company, and PwC—facilitated her efforts to profit from her country's wealth while lending their legitimacy. The empire she . . . built stretches from Hong Kong to the United States, comprising over 400 companies and subsidiaries. It encompasses properties around the world, including a US$55 million mansion in Monte Carlo, a US$35 million yacht and a luxury residence in Dubai on a seahorse-shaped artificial island." All this while her oil and diamond-rich country is hobbled by grand corruption accompanied by grinding poverty, widespread illiteracy, and a high infant-mortality rate.[21]

In light of the foregoing, let it suffice to say that the rise, expansion, and concentration of global finance capital in offshore financial centers and tax havens in the two core geopolitical poles of Europe in the Benelux countries—Belgium, Netherlands, and Luxembourg—Ireland, Switzerland, and Liechtenstein; and in the United Kingdom or select regions of the British Empire system (former imperial territories) and/or current British Overseas Territories is at the expense of developing countries with regard to the provision of, and access to, healthcare, job creation, and poverty alleviation (see figures 15.2 and 15.3). Considering the global mobility or flight of international capital from developing countries and elsewhere to the core tax havens, it is quite evident that the traditional accounts of sovereignty found in the discipline of political science and the subdiscipline of international relations, as Mbembe (2003) argues, are rather limited. After all, as he points out, "these accounts locate sovereignty within the boundaries of the nation-state, within institutions empowered by the state, or within supranational institutions and networks."[22] Yet, the global mobility and concentration of capital, and especially (through) dirty money flows, drains developing economies of desperately needed resources for development while developed countries, including the United States, reap the accruing benefits. Research by Global Financial Integrity suggests that about 45 percent of illicit flows end up in offshore financial centers and 55 percent in developed countries.[23] This only serves to demonstrate the perceptiveness and inherent insight of Mbembe's unique and apt understanding of the "absolute expression of sovereignty" that resides, to a large degree, in the power and the capacity to dictate who may live and who

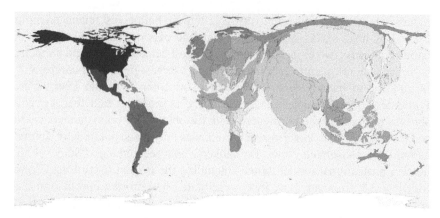

Figure 15.2 "Some Secondary Education"—territory size is proportional to the secondary school-age population (age 11 to 16) not attending secondary education in the period 2010–2015. According to WorldMapper, the data sources of this map included data from the 2016 United Nations Human Development Report and population estimates from the 2017 World Population Prospects (last accessed March 2018). The aim of this cartogram was to map as complete data as possible and, therefore, estimate data for missing values. In some cases, missing data for small territories was not used in the cartogram and that area is therefore omitted from the map. *Source*: EDUCATION—WorldMapper, Accessed on 7 January 2020.

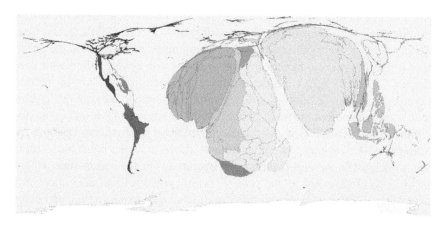

Figure 15.3 "Absolute Poverty." This cartogram illustrates the proportion of all people on less than or equal to US$1.9 in purchasing power parity a day living there in 2016. For this map, WorldMapper used data by United Nation Human Development Report (UNHDR) 2016 (last accessed March 2018). WorldMapper aims to map as complete data as possible and therefore estimate data for missing values. In some cases, missing data for very small territories is not used in the cartogram and that area is therefore omitted in the map. *Source*: POVERTY— WorldMapper, Accessed on 7 January 2020.

may die, especially in Africa, which "is a net creditor of the rest of the world in the sense that external assets, i.e., the stock of flight capital, exceed external liabilities (i.e. external debt: see Boyce and Ndikumana, 2005). The problem is that the assets are largely held in private hands, whilst the liabilities belong to the African public."[24] Indeed, as Sol Picciotto observes, the flow of capital, both legal or illegal, to offshore destinations across international borders only serves to undermine state sovereignty traditionally defined, and to also confirm the modern state, any state whatsoever, as a "legal fiction."[25] Granted, this is the face of the new international order of disorder. At home, in Sub-Saharan Africa, proportionate blame, though, must also be laid at the feet of ruling kleptomaniacs and their petty government official enablers.

## THE RACE TO GET DOWN TO THE BOTTOM WITH A "CLICK": MORAL ECONOMIES OF CORRUPTION AND THE LOOTING OF AFRICA

The adulteration of the moral economy of affection and/or the preponderance of ethnicity and nepotism among other affinities in African societies ensures that these forces are at the core of the social fabric and behind politics both local and national. Both moral ethnicity and political tribalism, as forces driving politics, have historically always been in an uneasy conflict or symbiotic tension.[26] Credited with coining the term, Lonsdale defines "moral ethnicity" as the "internal standard of civic virtue against which we measure our personal esteem."[27] Ideally, and especially in pre-European Africa, big chiefly men, that is, wealthy householders, were held in respect, but only if they paid their social debts, loaning out their assets in livestock or land, in return for the assistance of kin and clients; any failure to meet these reciprocal expectations of a redistributive civic virtue risked popular anger and a fiery death. To refuse to share the use of one's assets could be seen as sorcery, a denial of opportunity to others.[28]

For this reason, the primordial public realm (read, the ethnic realm) commanded the loyalty of African leadership. This was unadulterated moral ethnicity at work. Moral ethnicity was the reservoir of moral or mutual obligations between the authoritative bigwigs and their traditional African clients. With political consciousness and organization encouraged only within the bounds of geoethnic regions during the colonial era, however, then, and well into the postcolonial period, wealthy householders (politicians) act(ed) as guardians or custodians of their respective ethnic groups to the exclusion of others within the political context of perceived competition for public goods or state power. Perdurably present and, therefore, not simply a resource of "false consciousness" exploited by manipulative leaders,[29] ethnicity is politicized and thus becomes a crucial point of reference in the process of the authoritative allocation of value or the determination of who gets what, when, and how.

All this, in short, encapsulates the internal national dynamic of normalized corruption that seems to imbricate societies in Sub-Saharan. The same, however, cannot be said of the corruption entrenched throughout the bureaucracy and as exercised by ruling kleptomaniacs caught up, as they are, in the murky-black liquid mass of dynastic fiscal networks of tax havens, banks, insurance companies, passive investments from shell companies to shipping, frontmen, and secret trusts. This is not to suggest that capital accruing from various forms of corruption, such as the construction of mega-infrastructural projects like air trains and railway lines, airports, dams, and geothermal plants and the brazen looting of public treasuries, cannot be used for pork-barrel development that favors kith and kin of close individual supporters/enablers or cronies and ethnic clients, and/or to lubricate the political campaign machinery with the intention of the capture, accumulation, and concentration, as well as the perpetuation, of power. This, after all, is the entire internal logic driving corruption in most African countries. But, for the most part, local and national corruption is also motivated by raw greed to build financial wealth by spiriting money to tax havens. Yet, this ultimate motive is less obvious thanks to fiduciary secrecy and anonymity; lack of transparency of ownership or how difficult the traceability of assets to their ultimate owners is; and the rather deliberate opaque nature of wheeling and dealing of global finance, or how the local/national fiscal grid,[30] digitally or otherwise, interfaces with the increasingly complex international financial architecture that facilitates illicit financial flows and corruption especially money laundering.

As a result, it has not always been an easy task to try to map out the *modus operandi* or how exactly illicit financial transfers occur. Neither has it been easy to determine how extensive, as far as the dollar amount (running into billions) is concerned and, by extension, just how vast the phenomenon is. And indeed, generally, scholars, journalists, and other observers are content to paint with too broad a brush the nepotism, cronyism, and pork-barreled ethnic nature of the configuration of state patronage networks and its interface with its international finance corollary. But with the benefit of the groundswell of hope and momentum of goodwill for sweeping political and socioeconomic change that greeted the end of the Moi years at the end of 2002, there have been a few interesting developments, a sneak peek of which illumine the dark shadows of this "glocal" phenomenon and, thus, roughly allows for a more refined and closer appreciation of the gamut of, really, quite original and ingenious mechanisms, employed during the long reign of President Daniel Arap Moi, if not directly by him, by some of his highly placed lieutenants to spirit vast amounts of money to foreign accounts in tax heavens, purchase of foreign assets such as houses and ranches, dummy trusts, off-the-shelf companies, and a slew of other investments in different sectors of the economy both at home in Kenya, elsewhere in Africa and further abroad.

What follows below is an incomplete discussion of some of the preferred mechanisms used during the Moi era for illicit capital transfers and money laundering. However, this analysis is incomplete because of the paucity of the key document detailing the nature of this phenomenon, the Kroll report, which is not formally in the public domain. Further, the few details of this report that are available were anonymously leaked to WikiLeaks, which then published it—WikiLeaks *Kroll, Project KTM: Consolidated Report.* The original document, while available online, cannot be deemed authoritative because it is still under review and being proofed. In addition, and this is quite important to point out, the who's who of the so-called "Moi US dollar millionaires and billionaires" is common knowledge, as they are the staple of public knowledge of the nouveau riche Kenyans thanks not only to the contemporaneous media news coverage around major corruption scandals such as Goldenberg and Anglo-Leasing, but also a quite-in-your-face television program that ran on Citizen TV—Kenya called, *Who Owns Kenya?*[31] which hid some of the corporate wheeling and dealing; corporate gossip; and ownership of different prime companies by specific prominent individuals—in both the Moi and Kibaki governments—in plain sight. With this said, nevertheless, any reference herein to specific ownership of companies by individuals thought or suspected to have benefited financially because of being Moi's kith and kin is not an unusual imputation by or via scholarship; or an indictment or leveling of accusations, as no formal charges have been brought to a court of law in Kenya or elsewhere; or making new accusations where there have been charges preferred and no convictions determined. Rather, any such mention is merely coincidental in the process of my attempt to map out the *modus operandi* or the various mechanisms used for illicit financial transfers. To this end, whatever little information is available, especially intricate details of the Kroll report and media news of the Anglo-Leasing scandal, is used to demarcate an emergent pattern of such mechanisms. No attempt is made, however, to study the skyrocketing corruption that has rocked the administration of President Uhuru Muigai Kenyatta and Deputy President William Arap Samoei, standing, as I, and many others do, as a baffled contemporary witness to this unfolding history in the making. It is, after all, still difficult to grapple with the not-so-removed recent history of the Moi and Kibaki illicit financial transfers. But such are the vicissitudes of studying history when one is too close to it in temporal terms. All said, while people generally, not just Kenyans, have a strange, evasive and averse attitude toward truth, it is the unenviable task of historians to rise above this all too human inclination to speak the truth, especially where and when it has been gnarled and distorted by power.[32] While the Kenyatta administration is out of the scope of this chapter,[33] it is quite interesting and revealing to anecdotally preface this discussion of the *modus operandi* of illicit financial flows out of Kenya with an incident that happened during his tenure as Kibaki's finance minister.

Four months after Kenyatta was appointed to the finance docket in January 2009, and less than two months before he was scheduled to read the 2009/2010 national budget in parliament in June, Treasury was caught up in frantic efforts to have parliament approve a supplementary budget—that is, additional money on top of the 2008/2009 national budget to plug in shortfalls to cater for emergency and unforeseen expenditure to fund government projects, or to, basically, fill the national budgetary deficit. This was Kenyatta's single-most important mission after assuming office as finance minister. But when he presented supplementary budget estimates to the parliament, it was clear to the hawkeyed observers, such as the anti-graft watchdog Mars Group Kenya, that the ministry intended to withdraw a total of KES 31 billion instead of the previously approved KES 22 billion. The KES 9 billion (US$339.7 million) discrepancy affecting 200 budget line items cutting across 35 ministries was disputed in parliament by Gitobu Imanyara. In as far as Imanyara was concerned, this misrepresentation of figures was a fraudulent act on the part of Treasury. In response, an adamant and combative Kenyatta dismissed Imanyara's accusation, saying it was in bad faith. He also defended the ministry's technocrats, ruling out any mischief. A few days later, however, Kenyatta ate humble pie by returning to parliament and blaming the slightly over KES 9 billion puzzle on a mechanical "glitch" citing the complexity of computer technology or human fingers moving on the keyboard. This retraction, nonetheless, did not stop the finance minister from resubmitting a second version of the supplementary budget, this time with an extra KES 10.8 billion discrepancy that the chief executive of Mars Group, Mwalimu Mati, swiftly flagged.

Once again, Imanyara accused Kenyatta of using the systematic inflation of budget estimates to steal public funds or to pay off inexistent foreign entities à la the Anglo-Leasing corruption scandal that rocked Kibaki's first administration not so long after taking over the government. At this point, Mars Group was convinced that whatever it was, this completely new set of errors and discrepancies was not a computer glitch. It was, rather, a deliberate cooking-up of figures. This gaping variation was far from being a glitch, argued Mars Group. Claiming that it was a computer glitch was an afterthought to sneak in, and cover up for, the systematic inflation of previously approved figures. The anti-graft watchdog, for this reason, pressed for an independent forensic audit of the 2008/2009 budget and, further, advocated for a fiscal management bill (intended to reduce the monopoly enjoyed by

the Treasury over budgetary matters) which Kibaki rejected.[34] This prominent high stakes drama is foregrounded as a metaphor for the far-reaching
implications of the proliferation and establishment of digital technologies in
the twenty-first century—as an acceptable way for transacting business and
money transfer—as enablers and facilitators of grand malfeasance, fraud,
money laundering, and illicit financial flows. It is the advent of this efficient
and effective global digital infrastructure, I posit, that has facilitated quiet and
hidden, but economically lethal electronic transfers of vast amounts of taxpayers' money from Kenya to various tax havens, set up shell companies and
secret trusts, money laundering, and purchase property in the Moi, Kibaki,
and Uhuru Kenyatta eras.

## ABRACADABRA: MOI-ERA ILLICIT FINANCIAL
## FLOWS, LOST WITHOUT A TRACE

Early during his presidency in the early 1980s, Moi's government was
extremely strict with foreign currency control. So much so, although
politically motivated, that the progressive Nyeri politician, Waruru Kanja,
"became the first political prisoner of the Moi era" to be "jailed for three
years for failing to convert foreign currency back into Kenyan shillings following an overseas trip earlier in" 1981.[35] This, however, is not to say that
the political elite around the president did not hold funds in foreign banks.
On June 15, 1987, Martin Shikuku, a member of parliament, "stormed into
parliament" accusing the wealthy elite of "siphoning billions of shillings out
of the country and depositing them in foreign banks." Reporting this attack on
these illicit financial transfers, the news magazine, *New African*, stated that
Shikuku had backed his claim by dramatically waving over his head a copy of
*Finance and Development*, a publication of the International Monetary Fund
dated June 1986, which showed that funds held by Kenyans in foreign banks
amounted to KES 930 million in 1982; KES 870 million in 1983; and KES
830 million in 1984.[36]

Indeed, 30 years after the fact, in 2016, it became public knowledge for
the first time, that Samuel Gichuru, a long-serving chief executive of the
Kenya Power and Lighting Company (KPLC), a government electricity utility parastatal, was, between July 29, 1999, and October 19, 2001, laundering the proceeds of corruption using a Jersey Island incorporated company,
Windward Trading. This admission made to the Royal Court of Jersey Island
was splashed in Kenyan newspapers amid a request from the government of
Jersey for Kenya to extradite Gichuru and Chris Okemo, a former member
of parliament who was named as a beneficiary of bribes paid to the former.
Apparently, Windward Trading had been registered by Gichuru in Jersey with

company number 35512 on August 8, 1986, to receive kickbacks in exchange
for the award of lucrative tenders to foreign firms during his extensive tenure
at KPLC. Gichuru was at the helm of KPLC between November 1984 and
February 2003 when he was immediately let go after Kibaki's government
came to power. According to Beckett:

> KPLC had awarded contracts to a number of engineering and energy companies
> worldwide, who had all made payments to Winward. In his Prosecution conclu-
> sions, the Island's former Solicitor General, Howard Sharp QC said:
>     Windward Trading received and held the proceeds of criminal conduct
> perpetrated by its controlling mind and beneficial owner, Samuel Gichuru.
> The company knowingly enabled Gichuru to obtain substantial bribes paid to
> Gichuru while he held public office in Kenya. The company played a vital role
> without which corruption on a grand scale is impossible: money laundering.
> Gichuru . . . accepted bribes from foreign businesses that contracted with KPLC
> during his term of office and hid them in Jersey. . . . Winward served as a bank
> account [and] formed a barrier between the foreign contractors that paid the
> bribes and the personal accounts of Gichuru and others who benefited from the
> corrupt payments.
>     Over £3 million was repatriated from Jersey to Kenya in March 2017, and
> illustrative of the impoverishment within Kenya which results from illicit funds
> flow, and of the Kenyan people's human rights to be fully engaged as citizens,
> calls were made within the Kenyan Parliament for the funds to be paid over to
> the Kenyan Independent Electoral Boundaries Commission in order to get more
> Kenyans actively involved in choosing their leaders.[37]

It is quite clear from the foregoing that the mind-boggling Goldenberg
scandal, Moi era's biggest known corruption saga in the 1990s, involving
anything between US$600 million to US$4 billion, was not the beginning of
malfeasance during his long period in power. More likely than not, the proceeds from this rip-off of public coffers ended up in foreign bank accounts
in tax havens, properties, and trusts. Whatever it was, and much has been
written about it,[38] exactly how it was conducted is not clear. Goldenberg
"involved financial stratagems so complex even economists had difficulty
grasping all" of them.[39] But one thing is clear, though. Goldenberg "pushed
the country's inflation into double digits, caused the collapse of the Kenya
shilling and a credit squeeze so severe that it led to business closures and
mass sackings, and left the government unable to pay for oil imports and
basic healthcare and education (*Cf. with Figures I & II above, respectively*).
The resulting recession was still being felt fifteen years later."[40] But there is
precious little that is known of corruption activities in the Moi era other than
what Shikuku revealed after his discovery in *Finance and Development*, the

coming to light of the Goldenberg saga, and more recently, the Gichuru case in the second decade of the twenty-first century.

If a lot that happened in terms of illicit financial flows during the Moi era has largely remained out of public limelight, this changed with the election of Kibaki. Within a few months of being elected president, parliament passed two crucial laws aimed at cracking down on corruption, that is, the Anti-Corruption and Economic Crimes Act and the Public Officer Ethics Act. Furthermore, the Kenya Anti-Corruption Authority was reorganized and refurbished with a new name, the Kenya Anti-Corruption Commission and, as Hornsby (2012) observes, this only spelled doom for Moi-era insiders. Some of them "found themselves facing court proceedings, including Gichuru," who was "investigated for over US$2 million paid by IPP Westmont Power into the offshore bank accounts of" Windward Trading. Others charged in 2004 were ex-minister William Ruto and Sammy Mwaita, who "were charged with fraud and Gideon Moi, Joshua Kulei and ex-Commissioner Wilson Gachanja," who "were questioned over the sale of government land."[41] Moi's right-hand strongman, Nicholas Kipyator Kiprono Arap Biwott, "was barred from entering the US under new legislation that allowed the US government to ban those suspected of benefitting from corruption."[42] The writing was on the wall; Kibaki's government, even though it did not go for Moi directly, was determined to trace and seize foreign assets of his close associates, and "long-time insiders such as" Kulei and Hosea Kiplagat "tried to blend into the background, . . . to avoid indictment. Some, including Kulei, managed to obtain residency abroad, in case the situation worsened." Eventually, Moi's sons "took over their father's interests directly. In 2003, the government hired Kroll associates to investigate offshore assets held by Moi-era leaders, particularly Kulei, Gideon Moi and Biwott."[43] According to Hornsby, the Kroll report traced about US$1 billion "in assets overseas, including cash in banks, real estate and hotel investments." Not long after the Kroll report was completed, "the UK *Observer* revealed more details of Kroll's investigation, suggesting that Ksh73 billion transferred overseas by 'influential officials' was in London." These accounts were frozen, but "little if anything was actually recovered."[44] As noted, while the former president's dealings during his reign were part of the Kroll investigation, Kibaki did not go after him. This, nonetheless, had not stopped him from denying throughout the Kroll investigation that he did not have as much as a single cent abroad.[45]

But as it is now widely common knowledge after an anonymous leakage and subsequent publication of an online version of the report by WikiLeaks,[46] Kroll's investigations traced between US$2 and $US3 billion stashed by Moi and his closest associates. The very next day after the report was leaked, *The Guardian* published news of "the breathtaking extent of corruption perpetrated by the family of the former" president. The British newspaper stated that it had seen the 110-page report that alleged "that relatives and associates of Mr. Moi siphoned off more than £1bn of government money," which meant that, if true, he was "on par with Africa's other great klepto-crats, Mobutu Sese Seko of Zaire (now Democratic Republic of Congo) and Nigeria's Sani Abacha."[47] The secret report, *The Guardian* article continued, "laid bare a web of shell companies, secret trusts and frontmen" that Moi's "entourage used to funnel hundreds of millions of pounds" into nearly 30 countries, including Britain. The accumulated assets included multimillion-pound properties in London, New York, and South Africa, as well as a 10,000-hectare ranch in Australia, and bank accounts containing hundreds of millions of pounds, *The Guardian* story went on.[48]

According to the Kroll report, Moi's sons, Phillip and Gideon Moi, were reported to be worth £770m and £550m, respectively. Between them, they were said to have foreign bank accounts in far-flung places including vari-ous banks in the United Kingdom, Grand Cayman, Luxembourg, and South Africa, and different types of properties in Jersey, Liechtenstein, Australia, Belgium, Brunei, Canada, Dubai, Finland, Germany, Luxembourg, South Africa, and the United Kingdom. One of the two sons was said to have laundered US$200 million via Frankfurt.[49] Among other Moi-insiders named in the Kroll report, Biwott was said to own accounts with Credit Suisse and Citibank, and owned a bank in Belgium, whereas Kulei owned various real estate property outside London, valued at £4.5 million, and a flat in London, valued at £2 million. According to Kroll investigators, a well-known Kenyan bank was believed to be "the key to getting vast sums of money out of the country via its foreign currency accounts. The same bank had already laundered US$200m (£100m) on behalf of the late Mr. Abacha, with the assistance of a Swiss-based 'financier.'"[50] Numerous other important names in the Moi administration are mentioned in the report that notes that there was a marked flurry of activity reported within the Moi fam-ily and their close associates to preempt the possibility of losing their wealth to Kibaki's new government. Much of this activity involved securing local Kenyan assets in overseas countries. The report, however, seems to appreci-ate the fact that none of Moi's kith and kin's properties and wealth had been adjudged by a court ruling as illegal or corruptly obtained, which would be a prerequisite before the government could approach any foreign government to freeze their assets.

In the meantime, though, Kroll suspected that Moi's family and friends were expected to secure their assets in "proven trusts" known to be experi-enced enough at hiding "pursued assets" in a number of select jurisdictions with relaxed money laundering policies.[51] Whatever fears that the "Kabarnet Syndicate"[52] might have had were, nonetheless, relieved because, "soon after the investigation was launched, Mr. Kibaki's government was caught up in its own scandal, known as Anglo-Leasing, which involved awarding huge government contracts to bogus companies" based in Britain. As a result, none of Moi's relatives, close associates, and business partners was prosecuted, and no money recovered.[53] If anything, from the outset, the making of the Anglo-Leasing scandal appeared to bear all the hallmarks, especially in its setup, of having been a Moi-era brainchild. Having not set it up, Kibaki government novices, some of whom had not previously served in government, stumbled upon it, fell for it, and, in their harebrained attempt to follow through, caused the scandal dubbed "Anglo-Leasing"—the most brazen and rudimentary in terms of the mechanism involved and attempts to conceal it. According to Wrong (2009), if the financial stratagems of Goldenberg were so complex even economists had difficulty grasping them, "Anglo Leasing was so simple a child could master the technique. It was a classic procurement scam, needing only two parties although for it to work one of those parties had to be at the top of government, powerful enough to silence doubting minions and ignore institutional checks and balances." Therefore, as far as the invention of fake foreign contractors to help conceal both the *modus operandi* "and eventual beneficiaries" was concerned, this corruption scandal was, for Wrong, the "laziest of scams."[54]

## "ANGLO-LEASING": KIBAKI-ERA ILLICIT FINANCIAL FLOWS, THE LAZIEST OF SCAMS

The so-called Anglo-Leasing scandal is a testament to systemic corruption in Kenya. A kind of systemic government corruption that, for Kibaki, proved to be quite a different kind of animal to slay in one decennary fell swoop. Despite his government's commitment to the fight against corruption and for openness, there was an insatiable demand for money to feed the political machine which undermined this bid.[55] Indeed, as Branch (2011) aptly observes, for all the rhetorical boasts of change and reform, the new government was unwilling to fundamentally address corruption.[56] Hornsby makes the same observation, going further to point out that Kibaki's government had adopted the same kleptocratic attitude to state funds as its predecessors.[57] This scandal that rocked the Kibaki administration, hardly two years after it took over the government, was "a Moi-era horse" entailing an unsavory picture of bloated procurement.[58] It was the product of old corruption networks into which Kibaki's new men in government eased themselves in or adopted, although some of the malfeasances were new.[59]

In all, the scandal involved at least 18 contracts from various government departments, including finance, transport, and internal security. Most were described as "sensitive" or security-related, and included a digital multi-channel communications network for the prison service; new helicopters; a secure communications system, computer and video equipment, and security vehicles for the police; a state-of-the-art frigate built in Spain for the Kenyan navy; a data network and internet service satellite link for the Kenya Post Office; a top-secret military surveillance system dubbed "Project Nexus"; a forensic laboratory for the Criminal Investigations Department; an early warning radar system for the meteorological department; and so on.[60] Most of these contracts were based on the principle of debt financing and, therefore, did not require parliamentary approval.[61] Twelve of these contracts had been masterminded by someone in the former Moi regime but, as noted, they had found a cozy home under the Kibaki government. The other six had been signed by Kibaki's new government. As such, Kibaki's men followed the Goldenberg formula whereby the government of Kenya was set to pay tripled prices to a legal but nonexistent Liverpool-based lease finance company, Anglo-Leasing, among others. Investigations revealed a web of other fake companies which were linked to Indian business families that worked with the Moi-KANU regime.[62] The fact that this scandal straddles both the Moi and Kibaki administrations is quite telling. This scandal was unfolding since 1997 when the first "contracts" were signed, and again in 2003 with payments being made until May 2015. What this means is that high-level corruption in the country is entrenched deeply in the bureaucracy and is, therefore, insti-tutionalized. Alluding to this repugnant systemic morass of corruption, John Githongo, the former anti-corruption tsar and whistleblower who served in the first half of Kibaki's first administration as the Governance and Ethics Permanent Secretary, sadly observed in a public personal statement on May 2, 2019, that:

> The Anglo Leasing model of misappropriation of resources from the Kenyan people has continued unabated since 2001. . . . Over the past six years in par-ticular the plunder of public resources has accelerated to levels unprecedented in Kenyan history since independence. Increasingly the economic, political, social and very personal cost of this plunder by officials in positions of authority has been borne by the Kenyan people directly.[63]

All said, these contracts "were worth a gulp-inducing 56.3 billion shillings (US$751 million)."[64] In the meantime, it was ordinary Kenyans struggling to eke a living who stoically bore the brunt of grand government corruption. As Wrong observes:

> The value of the eighteen contracts amounted to 5 per cent of Kenya's gross domestic product, and over 16 per cent of the government's gross expenditure in

2003–04, the period in which the six NARC-era contracts were signed. It easily outstripped the country's total aid that year (US$521 million), and represented three quarters of the amount the hard-pressed Kenyan diaspora annually sent back home. The campaigning anti-graft organization Mars Kenya would later calculate that the funds involved were the equivalent of 68 per cent of what the finance ministry allocated to infrastructure in 2006, and thirty-seven times more than it allocated to water projects in Kenya's arid lands. The American ambassador came up with an even more depressing figure: the money would have been enough to supply every HIV-positive Kenyan with antiretrovirals for the next ten years.[65]

In terms of the mechanism for the transfer of funds, it involved mercenary merchants of death who were funneling taxpayers' money to phantom companies using several payment methods. All payments made by the Kibaki government to an opaque web of almost 20 fictitious entities abroad were, according to Wrong, "turnkey" deals "in which suppliers offered not only equipment, but the funding arrangements a cash-pressed African government needed to pay for all" the "state-of-the-art hardware." The government then signed a "credit supplier contract" through which it was loaned money while undertaking to repay "the credit via irrevocable promissory notes." This meant that these contracts were eternally binding and were as good as cash and could, as such, be bought and sold on international financial markets. Subsequent governments could, therefore, not dream of trying to disavow them.[66]

## THE MURKY-BLACK SHARK INFESTED LIQUID MASS OF LOCAL, NATIONAL, AND INTERNATIONAL FINANCIAL NETWORKS: A CONCLUSION

The inbuilt anonymity and secrecy surrounding offshore investments is probably as old as its inception at the turn of the nineteenth century. This, considering the dubious nature of international finances from developing countries, and especially from Africa, calls for a concerted effort to restructure, review, and create new laws governing the flow of global finance emphasizing greater and more comprehensive scrutiny. To the old, opaque, and anonymous nature of global financial flow has been added the revolutionization of digital technologies that have served to create unprecedented ease with which finance finds its way to offshore tax havens with little or no accountability from ruling kleptomaniacs and their petty government official enablers—or their international network of enablers, including leading professional service firms, bankers, lawyers, accountants, and consultants, for that matter.

As earlier noted, the involvement and liability, and, therefore, the complicity of legal entities, firms, and banks at the offshore end of "the vast majority of dirty money flows . . . laundered via complex multi-jurisdictional ladders operating through the global banking system,"[67] calls for more transparency, redress, and tightening of rules and regulations governing the industry in developed nations that form the bulk of countries of domicile of global financial flows.

There exists in the United States an appreciable corpus of financial rules and regulations the evolution and history of which is accessible on the website of the Financial Crimes Enforcement Network—or "FinCEN," for short. This website "contains short and accessible histories of major anti-money laundering laws." An example of commendable legislative progress in the United States was the Treasury Department's regulations updated in 2016 that required banks and other financial institutions to verify the identity of the natural persons—the "beneficial owner rule"—as basic as it sounds.[68] In Europe, growing recognition that it takes two to tango—that is, networks of local and national petty bureaucrats and their overseeing ruling kleptomaniacs and their global finance partners in crime—"culminated in the Organization for Economic Cooperation and Development (OECD)'s Convention on Combating Bribery" that was "signed by thirty-six member states." This convention "became British law in 2002," giving, for the first time, "British courts jurisdiction over crimes committed abroad by domestic companies."[69] Despite the OECD anti-bribery convention coming into force, however, Britain, by 2009, "brought only four cases against domestic companies for bribery abroad," while the United States had brought 120 and Germany 110.[70] It is quite clear, therefore, that halfhearted enactments of new legislation not backed by the political will to crack down on what is fast becoming murky-black shark infested liquid mass of local, national, and international networks that are, indeed, obliterating the sharp distinction between legal global capital and money laundering of the criminal and unethical underworld of human trafficking, narcotics trafficking, illegal arms trafficking, fraud, and embezzlement, can only serve to aggravate and encourage this vice. Furthermore, by admission, "the pace of rulemaking is not . . . commensurate with the pace of rule breaking."[71] This regrettable situation is compounded by the way the revolutionization of digital technologies has transformed the global payment system landscape.

As various illustrations above demonstrate, especially the example of alleged Moi-era international financial flows relatively laid bare by unofficial evidence in the form of the leaked Kroll, *Project KTM: Consolidated Report*, there appears to be a direct link between all the levels of local, national, and international financial networks connecting proceeds of staggering and mind-boggling corruption and the criminal underworld of money laundering, international drug and human trafficking, and illegal arms trading. Lack of regulatory and enforcement action on the part of governmental agencies, especially in the West, can only serve to fuel grand malfeasance in the developing world. And this, without saying, can only come at the expense of capitalism as a global system. The very future of "capitalism itself then runs a reputational risk"[72] unless there are real and concrete measures in place to detect, curb, and eliminate all elements of illicit financial flows including, but not limited to, cross-border tax evasion, anonymous shell companies, trade misinvoicing, and improvement of transparency of multinational corporations.[73]

## NOTES

1. John Lonsdale, "Writing Kenyan History," in this volume.

2. The New York State Attorney General's office estimates that more than 1,800 virtual currencies are exchanged around the world. See the *Virtual Markets Integrity Initiative Report,* https://ag.ny.gov/sites/default/files/vmii_report.pdf, Accessed on January 27, 2020, and as cited in a speech by Michael Held, "Michael Held: The First Line of Defense and Financial Crime," Keynote address by Mr. Michael Held, Executive Vice President of the Legal Group of the Federal Reserve Bank of New York, at the 1LoD Summit, New York City, April 2, 2019, Published on the Bank of International Settlements Website, https://www.bis.org/review/r190402g.htm#footn ote-8, Accessed on January 26, 2020.

3. Tatiana Tropina, "Do Digital Technologies Facilitate Illicit Financial Flows?" Max Planck Institute for Foreign and International Criminal Law—a paper prepared for the *World Development Report 2016 Digital Dividends* (2016). According to *Illicit Financial Flow: Report of the High-Level Panel on Illicit Financial Flows from Africa,* which was the result of work done by the African Union Economic Commission on Africa led by the former president of South Africa, Thabo Mbeki, in 2015, illicit financial flows were defined as "money illegally earned, transferred or used." This includes money laundering, tax abuse, market and regulatory abuse, along with practices that "go against established rules and norms, including legal obligations to pay tax." Also see Imani Countess, "Illicit Financial Flows Thwart Human Rights and Development in Africa," Published on the Website of the Committee for the Abolition of Illegitimate Debt, https://www.cadtm.org/Illicit-financial-flows-thwa rt-human-rights-and-development-in-Africa, Accessed on 7 January 2020.

4. Tropina, "Do Digital Technologies Facilitate Illicit Financial Flows?"

5. Ibid.

6. For more see classical work on "illocutionary force/acts" or "speech acts" by J. L. Austin, *How to Do Things with Words* (Cambridge: Harvard University Press, 1963) and John R. Searle, *Speech Acts: An Essay in the Philosophy of Language* (Cambridge: Cambridge University Press, 1969).

7. A. Guttmann, "Public relations—Statistics & Facts," Statista, https://www.sta
tista.com/topics/3521/public-relations/ , February 26, 2018, Accessed, December 12,
2019. Also see the classic by Walter Lippmann, *Public Opinion* (New York: Free
Press; Reissue edition, 1997).

8. See a comprehensive examination of the early origins and development of tax
havens by Paul Beckett, *Tax Havens and International Human Rights* (New York:
Routledge, 2018). Also see Ronen Palan, "History of Tax Havens," in *History and
Policy* Website, http://www.historyandpolicy.org/policy-papers/papers/history-of-tax-
havens, Accessed on January 7, 2020.

9. Palan, "History of Tax Havens."

10. Ibid.

11. This is according to Professor Paul Collier in an article for *Prospect Magazine*,
"In Pursuit of the $21 Trillion," penned just before the G8 Summit in June 2013, as
cited in Beckett, *Tax Havens and International Human Rights*, 115. Also see the
*Thabo Mbeki Report.*

12. See Palan, "History of Tax Havens." Even more informative is the crucial
*Thabo Mbeki Report.*

13. John Christensen, "The Looting Continues: Tax Havens and Corruption,"
*Critical Perspectives on International Business* 7 (2011): 177.

14. Also see Countess, "Illicit Financial Flows Thwart Human rights and
Development in Africa," and/or Imani Countess, "The Ugliest Chapter Since Slavery:
How Illicit Financial Flows Thwart Human Rights in Africa," Published on Foreign
Policy in Focus Website, https://fpif.org/the-ugliest-chapter-since-slavery-how-illicit-
financial-flows-thwart-human-rights-in-africa/, Accessed on November 14, 2019.

15. Global Financial Integrity, "Illicit Financial Flows," on the organization's
Website, https://gfintegrity.org/issue/illicit-financial-flows/, Accessed on November
14, 2019.

16. The author has written on this subject in a yet to be published (forthcoming)
paper, "Death Worlds: A Historical Note on the Systemic Production of Peripheral
Nether-worlds," (April 2016). But for more on this subject read Suhabrata Bobby
Banerjee, "Live and Let Die: Colonial Sovereignties and the Death Worlds of
Necrocapitalism," in *Boderlands* 5.1 (May 2006), e-Journal. Following up on the
work of Achille Mbembe, "Necropolitics" (Trans.) Libby Meintjes in *Public Culture*
15 (2003): 11–40, in which he suggests that "the ultimate expression of sovereignty
resides, to a large degree, in the power and the capacity to dictate who may live and
who may die"), Banerjee introduces and develops the insightful concept of "necrocapitalism" in discussing "contemporary forms of organizational accumulation that
involve dispossession and the subjugation of life to the power of death." Put differently, Banerjee examines "how some contemporary capitalist practices"—which
should include, I hereby suggest, as in my "Historical Note on the Systemic Production
of Peripheral Nether-worlds," illicit capital flows—that "contribute to this subjugation
of life." Also see Jean Comaroff and John L. Comaroff, *Theory from the South: Or,
How Euro-America is Evolving Toward Africa* (Boulder: Paradigm Publishers, 2012).

17. Jeffrey Sachs as referenced by Geoff Harcourt in his blurb for Oxfam Research
Reports "The Hidden Billions: How Tax Havens Impact Lives at Home and Abroad,"

Oxfam, Australia, June 2016, Published PDF version, https://www.oxfam.org.au/wp-content/uploads/2016/06/OXF003-Tax-Havens-Report-FA2-WEB.pdf, Accessed on January 7, 2020.

18. Christensen, "The Looting Continues: Tax Havens and Corruption," 185.

19. Michael Forsythe, Kyra Gurney, Scilla Alecci and Ben Hallman, "How U.S. Firms Helped Africa's Richest Woman Exploit Her Country's Wealth," *New York Times*, January 19, 2020, https://www.nytimes.com/2020/01/19/world/africa/isabel-dos-santos-angola.html, Accessed January 24, 2020.

20. *International Consortium of Investigative Journalists Impact Report*, "Isabel Dos Santos Charged With Embezzlement, Will Sell Portuguese Bank Stake," January 23, 2020, Published in the ICIJ Website, https://www.icij.org/investigations/luanda-leaks/isabel-dos-santos-charged-with-embezzlement-will-sell-portuguese-bank-stake/, Accessed January 26, 2020.

21. Forsythe, et al., "How U.S. Firms Helped Africa's Richest Woman Exploit Her Country's Wealth."

22. Mbembe, "Necropolitics," 11.

23. Global Financial Integrity, "Illicit Financial Flows."

24. Christensen, "The Looting Continues: Tax Havens and Corruption," 184.

25. Sol Picciotto, "Offshore: The State as Legal Fiction," in *Offshore Finance Centers and Tax Havens: The Rise of Global Capital*, eds. Mark P. Hampton and Jason P. Abbott (Purdue: Purdue University Press, 1999), 43–79.

26. "Moral ethnicity" refers to internal or intraethnic class dynamics which are often at the heart of debates and struggles within communities or internal deliberations over good leadership of/or within an ethnic group.

27. John M. Lonsdale, "Moral Ethnicity and Political Tribalism," in *Inventions and Boundaries: Historical and Anthropological Approaches to the Study of Ethnicity and Nationalism*, eds. P. Kaarsholm, and J. Hultin (Roskilde University, 1994), 131.

28. John M. Lonsdale, "On Writing Kenya's History," at the 55th Annual Callahan Lecture, Department of History, West Virginia University, March 28, 2019; also see the chapter by Lonsdale in this volume.

29. M. Sithole, "The Salience of Ethnicity in African Politics: The Case of Zimbabwe," *Journal of Asian and African Studies* 20 (1985): 181–92.

30. Here, as elsewhere—see work by this author entitled, "From Moral Ethnicity to Moral Anarchy: The Colonial Ideology of Order and Political Disorder in Postcolonial Kenya," in *The Omnipresent Past. Historical Anthropology of Africa and African Diaspora*, eds. Dmitri Bondarenko and Marina L. Butovskaya (Moscow: LRC Publishing House, July 2019). "National fiscal grid" refers to the configuration of state patronage and/or to the authoritative allocation of value or public goods throughout society, some select parts of it more than others. I owe this phrase to my M.A. thesis supervisor and mentor, Vincent G. Simiyu. In addition to this general meaning, Simiyu used it to specifically refer to state-based avenues of accumulation in high government among them senior cabinet and parastatal positions, credit facilities and bank loans, land and other sources of government revenue. The sum of all this is what Simiyu referred to as "state finance capital." The configuration of state patronage or the financial grid can be mapped out graphically and ethnically

for all of Kenya's government administrations—see "From Moral Ethnicity to Moral Anarchy," for a generic concentric circles graphic representation of the ethnic configuration of state patronage in the Kikuyu-centric Kenyatta (1963–1978) and Kalenjin-centric Moi state (1978–2002).

31. The program hosted by Julie Gichuru and ran roughly between 2011 and 2011. Some of the complete recordings of the program are readily available on the YouTube Website (https://www.youtube.com/).

32. The difficulty of sources in this regard is due to the fact that, while the Kroll report was commissioned by President Mwai Kibaki's government shortly after it ascended to power, it was never released to the public or followed through in terms of repatriating illicit funds outside the country nor were court cases filed against gross financial and economic crimes for the majority of those thought or suspected to be behind grand corruption in Kenya during the Moi years. Nonetheless, as noted, this information is, thanks to an anonymous high-level leak, readily available in the public domain for anyone interested, to consult. Furthermore, the verifiability and reliability of WikiLeaks' source of this key document has, to some appreciable extent, been substantiated by (i) The verifiable fact that the London-based risk consultancy group, Kroll Associates UK Limited, did confirm that it had been engaged by the government of Kenya. (ii) Cross-referencing of information or leaked public evidence gathered by Kroll via WikiLeaks can be done with Transparency International's Corruption Report on Asset Recovery available on their Website (www.transparency.org). (iii) Vital documents held and/or published on the Website of Mars Group Kenya (http://www.marskenya.org)—that monitors and documents grand malfeasance—can, moreover, corroborate leaked details of the Kroll report. (iv) In addition, widespread contemporaneous media news coverage in electronic and print news from Nairobi, London, and New York (and in between) both at the time and presently, serves as further corroborative evidence to all of the above (i–iii), and, moreover, reveals, a determination of the Kibaki government, then, to trace and seize the foreign assets of Moi's associates. (v) One could venture to argue that should any inadvertently divulged information herein be found contentious, the eventual formal release of the Kroll report to the public by the government of Kenya in the future, and further rigorous investigative follow-up, if deemed necessary, would serve to better bring even more light into these and other missing links, deals and money still sitting in tax havens and foreign assets. As it is, this, besides being a matter of historical scrutiny and examination, remains, very much, a *live* situation that continues to be a towering concern of Kenyans today, and the foreseen future. Here it is crucial to state that in the West from where most of these tax havens are managed, there is increased disquiet over the criminal and suspect nature of tainted or dirty money coming from Africa and elsewhere. There is, therefore, increasing pressure for governments there, and in tax havens, to detect cross-border tax evasion, eliminate anonymous shell companies, curtail trade misinvoicing, and further, and more importantly, to strengthen anti-money laundering laws and practices—this, most likely, will not only govern how capital crosses borders in the present, but also apply retroactively.

33. However, emergent details of some of the corruption scandals that have tainted his two-term presidency and legacy are discussed in Githuku, "From Moral Ethnicity to Moral Anarchy."

34. See James Anyanzwa, "Uhuru Blames Sh. 9.2 b Glitch on Computer," *Standard Digital*, 9 May 2009, https://www.standardmedia.co.ke/article/11440 13722/uhuru-blames-sh9-2b-glitch-on-computer, Accessed on December 1, 2019; Alex Ndegwa, "Of the Billion-shilling Error and a Deflated Ego," *Standard Digital*, May 10, 2009, https://www.standardmedia.co.ke/article/1144013778/of-the-billion-shilling-error-and-a-deflated-ego, Accessed on January 9, 2020; Wangui Kanina, "Kenya Anti-graft Body Question Budget Figures," *Reuters*, May 26, 2009, https://www.reuters.com/article/ozatp-kenya-politics-20090526-idAFJOE54P0I320090526, Accessed on January 9, 2020; and Maseme Machuka and Peter Opiyo, "Uhuru's Typing 'era,'" *Standard Digital*, May 26, 2009, https://www.standardmedia.co.ke/art icle/1144015144/uhuru-kenyatta-s-typing-era, Accessed on January 9, 2020.

35. Daniel Branch, *Kenya: Between Hope and Despair, 1963-2011* (New Haven: Yale University Press, 2011), 151.

36. George Ayittey, "The Looting of Africa—III, Kenya" Published by the Jaluo Website, April 12, 2007, http://www.jaluo.com/wangwach/200704/George_Ayittey0 41107.html, Accessed on January 10, 2020.

37. Beckett, *Tax Havens and International Human Rights*, 34. Also see Aggrey Mutambo, "Gichuru and Okemo Lose Sh. 520 Million Stashed in Jersey Island," *Daily Nation* Online edition, February 26, 2016, https://www.nation.co.ke/news/Jerse y-Island-confiscate-Gichuru-and-Okemo--stashes/1056-3092832-59m5saz/index.h tml, Accessed January 7, 2020.

38. Branch, *Between Hope and Despair*, 217–21; Charles Hornsby, *Kenya: A History Since Independence* (London: I.B. Tauris, 2012), 291–92, 302, 506; Dominic Burbidge, *The Shadow of Kenyan Democracy: Widespread Expectations of Widespread Corruption* (Burlington, VT: Ashgate, 2015), 33; Nicholas Githuku, *Mau Mau Crucible of War: Statehood, National Identity, and Politics of Postcolonial Kenya* (Lanham, MD: Lexington Books, 2016), 344, 345–47; Michela Wrong, *It's Our Turn to Eat: The Story of a Kenyan Whistle-blower* (London: HarperCollins, 2009), 62–63, 65, 86, 89, 139, 165–66.

39. Wrong, *It's Our Turn to Eat*, 168.

40. Ibid., 63. Italics in parenthesis are the present author's.

41. Hornsby, *A History Since Independence*, 705 & 706.

42. Ibid., 706.

43. Ibid.

44. Ibid.

45. Ibid.

46. WikiLeaks's typed-up version of the Kroll report, "The Looting of Kenya under President Moi," is readily available online, https://wikileaks.org/wiki/The _looting_of_Kenya_under_President_Moi, August 30, 2007, Accessed on January 8, 2020.

47. Xan Rice, "The Looting of Kenya," *The Guardian*, August 31, 2007, https://www.theguardian.com/world/2007/aug/31/kenya.topstories3, Accessed on October 10, 2019.

48. Ibid.

49. WikiLeaks, Kroll, *Project KTM: Consolidated Report*, 12 April 2004, 8, 15, 32, 33, 39, 40, 47, 53, 57, 65, 85, 86, 104 & 110; also see Rice, "The Looting of Kenya."

50. Rice, "The Looting of Kenya."

51. WikiLeaks, *Project KTM*, 12.

52. See Githuku, "From Moral Ethnicity to Moral Anarchy," 2019; and Githuku, "Ethnic Conflict and its Implications for Social and Economic Development in Kenya, 1963–2004," Unpublished M.A. Thesis (Nairobi: University of Nairobi, 2004).

53. Rice, "The Looting of Kenya."

54. Wrong, *It's Our Turn to Eat*, 168 & 169.

55. Hornsby, *A History Since Independence*, 697 and 705–07; also see Branch, *Between Hope and Despair*, 260–63.

56. Branch, *Between Hope and Despair*, 252.

57. Hornsby, *A History Since Independence*, 725.

58. Wrong, *It's Our Turn to Eat*, 200.

59. Ibid. Also see Branch, *Between Hope and Despair*, 253.

60. Wrong, *Our Turn to Eat*, 165.

61. Hornsby, *A History Since Independence*, 726.

62. Ibid.

63. John Githongo, "John Githongo Personal Statement—Statement on HCCC 466 of 2006 Chris Murungaru VS. John Githongo," Published on Twitter, May 2, 2019. Githongo was reacting to the award of KES 27 million to Murungaru, Kibaki's Internal Security and Provincial Affairs Minister of State in the Office of the President, for defamation by the High Court on Thursday, May 2, 2019. As anti-corruption tsar, Githongo, in 2005, published a revealing dossier implicating several cabinet ministers including Murungaru, in the multimillion-dollar Anglo-Leasing scam.

64. Wrong, *Our Turn to Eat*, 165.

65. Ibid., 166.

66. Ibid., 170.

67. Christensen, "The Looting Continues: Tax Havens and Corruption," 184.

68. Held, "The First Line of Defense and Financial Crime."

69. Wrong, *It's Our Turn to Eat*, 199.

70. Ibid., 328.

71. Held, "The First Line of Defense and Financial Crime."

72. Raymond W. Baker, *Capitalism's Achilles Heel: Dirty Money and How to Renew the Free-Market System* (Hoboken: John Wiley & Sons, Inc., 2005) as cited by Christensen, "The Looting Continues: Tax Havens and Corruption," 184.

73. Global Financial Integrity, "Illicit Financial Flows."

# BIBLIOGRAPHY

African Union Economic Commission on Africa, *Illicit Financial Flow: Report of the High-Level Panel on Illicit Financial Flows from Africa* (Addis Ababa: African Union, 2015).

Anyanzwa, J., "Uhuru Blames Sh. 9.2 b Glitch on Computer," *Standard Digital*, 9 May 2009.

Austin, J.L., *How to Do Things with Words* (Cambridge: Harvard University Press, 1963).

Ayittey, G., "The Looting of Africa—III, Kenya" Published by the Jaluo Website, 12 April 2007.

Baker, *Capitalism's Achilles Heel: Dirty Money and How to Renew the Free-Market System* (Hoboken: John Wiley & Sons, Inc., 2005).

Banerjee, S.B., "Live and Let Die: Colonial Sovereignties and the Death Worlds of Necrocapitalism," in *Boderlands* 5.1 (May 2006).

Beckett, P., *Tax Havens and International Human Rights* (New York: Routledge, 2018).

Branch, D., *Kenya: Between Hope and Despair, 1963-2011* (New Haven: Yale University Press, 2011).

Burbidge, D., *The Shadow of Kenyan Democracy: Widespread Expectations of Widespread Corruption* (Burlington, VT: Ashgate, 2015).

Christensen, J., "The Looting Continues: Tax Havens and Corruption," in *Critical Perspectives on International Business* 7 (2011): 177–96.

Collier, P., "In Pursuit of the $21 Trillion," in *Prospect Magazine* (2013), Unavailable Online.

Countess, I., "Illicit Financial Flows Thwart Human Rights and Development in Africa," Published on the Website of the Committee for the Abolition of Illegitimate Debt (2019).

———. "The Ugliest Chapter Since Slavery: How Illicit Financial Flows Thwart Human Rights in Africa," Published on Foreign Policy in Focus Website (2018).

Forsythe, M., Kyra Gurney, Scilla Alecci and Ben Hallman, "How U.S. Firms Helped Africa's Richest Woman Exploit Her Country's Wealth," *New York Times* (19 January 2020).

Githongo, J., "John Githongo Personal Statement—Statement on HCCC 466 of 2006 Chris Murungaru VS. John Githongo," Published on Twitter, May 2, 2019.

Githuku, N.K., "From Moral Ethnicity to Moral Anarchy: The Colonial Ideology of Order and Political Disorder in Postcolonial Kenya," in *The Omnipresent Past. Historical Anthropology of Africa and African Diaspora*, eds. Dmitri Bondarenko and Marina L. Butovskaya (Moscow: LRC Publishing House, July 2019).

———. *Mau Mau Crucible of War: Statehood, National Identity, and Politics of Postcolonial Kenya* (Lanham, MD: Lexington Books, 2016).

———. "Death Worlds: A Historical Note on the Systemic Production of Peripheral Nether-worlds," (April 2016), Unpublished.

―――. "Ethnic Conflict and Its Implications for Social and Economic Development in Kenya, 1963–2004," M.A. Thesis (Nairobi: University of Nairobi, 2004).

Global Financial Integrity, "Illicit Financial Flows," Global Financial Integrity Website (nd.).

Guttmann, "Public relations - Statistics & Facts," *Statista* (2018).

Harcourt, G., Blurb for Oxfam Research Reports "The Hidden Billions: How Tax Havens Impact Lives at Home and Abroad," Oxfam, Australia (2016).

Held, M., "Michael Held: The First Line of Defense and Financial Crime," Keynote address by Mr. Michael Held, Executive Vice President of the Legal Group of the Federal Reserve Bank of New York, 1LoD Summit, New York City, 2 April 2019, Published on the Bank of International Settlements Website.

Hornsby, C., *Kenya: A History Since Independence* (London: I.B. Tauris, 2012).

*International Consortium of Investigative Journalists Impact Report*, "Isabel Dos Santos Charged with Embezzlement, Will Sell Portuguese Bank Stake" (January 23, 2020).

Kanina, W., "Kenya Anti-graft Body Question Budget Figures, *Reuters*, 26 May 2009.

Lonsdale, J.M., "Writing Kenyan History," in *Constructing and Advancing Counter-State Narratives: Africans and the Redefinition of the Colonial and Postcolonial Worlds*, ed. N.K. Githuku (Lanham: Lexington Books, 2020).

―――. Lonsdale, "Moral Ethnicity and Political Tribalism," in *Inventions and Boundaries: Historical and Anthropological Approaches to the Study of Ethnicity and Nationalism*, eds. P. Kaarsholm and J. Hultin (Roskilde University, 1994).

Machuka, M., and Peter Opiyo, "Uhuru's Typing 'era,'" *Standard Digital*, 26 March 2009.

Mbembe, A., "Necropolitics" (Trans.) Libby Meintjes in *Public Culture* 15 (2003): 11–40.

Ndegwa, A., "Of the Billion-shilling Error and a Deflated Ego," *Standard Digital*, 10 May 2009.

Office of the New York State Attorney General, Barbara D. Underwood, *Virtual Markets Integrity Initiative Report* (Albany: Office of the New York State Attorney General, 2018).

Palan, R., "History of Tax Havens," in *History and Policy* Website (2009).

Picciotto., S., "Offshore: The State as Legal Fiction," in *Offshore Finance Centers and Tax Havens: The Rise of Global Capital*, eds. Mark P. Hampton and Jason P. Abbott (Purdue: Purdue University Press, 1999).

Rice, X., "The Looting of Kenya," *The Guardian*, 31 August 2007.

Searle, J.R., *Speech Acts: An Essay in the Philosophy of Language* (Cambridge: Cambridge University Press, 1969).

Sithole, M., "The Salience of Ethnicity in African Politics: The Case of Zimbabwe," *Journal of Asian and African Studies* 20 (1985): 181–92.

Tropina, T., "Do Digital Technologies Facilitate Illicit Financial Flows?" Max Planck Institute for Foreign and International Criminal Law, paper prepared for the *World Development Report 2016 Digital Dividends* (2016).

WikiLeaks, Kroll, *Project KTM: Consolidated Report*, 12 April 2004.

Wrong, M., *It's Our Turn to Eat: The Story of a Kenyan Whistle-blower* (London: HarperCollins, 2009).

# Index

Abacha, Sani, 322, 332
A. Bauman and Company, 216
Aden, 166
ADMARC (Agricultural Development and Marketing Corporation), 231, 236
age-sets (*laji*s), xiv, 161–62, 165; elders (*lpayiani*), 169; warriors (*murran*), xiv, 161
Agricultural Experimental Farm, 213
Ainsworth, John, xii, xiii, xv, 9–10, 33–34, 39, 87–103
Alliance High School, 11
Amnesty International, 255
Anderson, David, x, 15–17, 19, 154, 157, 172, 173, 176, 177
Angaine, Jackson, 275
Anglican, 2, 16, 18, 101
Anglo-Leasing, 327–28, 333–35
Angola, 122, 322, 323
Annales, School, viii
Anyona, George, 276, 282
Arab, 12, 52–53, 145, 186, 189, 193, 197, 258, 283
Arbore, 168
Ariaal, 169
Armitage, Robert, Sir, 250
Asembo Bay, 209, 211
Atieno-Odhiambo, E. S., 4, 32, 131, 132

Australia, 332, 339

Baberton, 213
Bahati, xiv, 136, 138, 142, 144
Baluchi, 167
Banda, Hastings Kamuzu, xviii, 250, 252–56
banking, mobile, xxii, 318
banking, online, xxii, 318
Belgium, 323, 332
Berman, Bruce, x, xxiii, 16–18, 40, 88–89, 104–6, 109, 221
Bernstein, Henry, 40, 204
Bitcoin, xxii, 318
Biwott, Nicholas Kipyator Kiprono arap, 331–32
Blantyre, 233, 251
bond partnerships, 166, 170
Boorana, 162, 165–66, 170
Boston Consulting Group, 323
Bovine pleuropneumonia (*lkipei*), 164
British Central Africa, xviii, 249
British Cotton Growers Association, 209
British Overseas Territories, 247, 323
Brunei, 332
Bukura, 205
Bulwer-Lytton, Edward, 319
Buru Buru, xiv

Butler, R.A., 48, 252
Buxton, C.E.V., 209
Byrne, Sir Joseph, 212

Canada, 129, 332
Cape Colony, 166
capitalism, ix, xiii, 8, 39, 113, 121, 129, 145, 147, 209, 216, 227, 303, 337; rural, 10–11
Carr, E. H., 1, 15
Central African Federation, 249
Chalbi Desert, 170
change the constitution movement, 1970s, xviii, 77, 270, 272, 275–76, 284–85, 298–99
Chasowa, Robert, 259
Chigawa, Mancken, 258
cholera, xiv, 14, 162
Christianity, 7, 12, 28, 109, 111, 114, 205, 206
Christie, James, 162
Citibank, 332
citizenship, 11, 54, 89, 272, 274
Citizen TV, 327
City of London, xiv, 319
class, 2, 11, 12, 90, 135, 137–39, 141–45, 148–50, 152, 208, 210, 227, 285, 295, 301, 306
climate change, ix, 320
coffee, 7–8, 31–33, 37, 99, 190, 206, 208–9, 303
Cold War, xiii, 11, 23, 245, 248, 250, 256–57, 259–60
Colonial Development and Welfare Act (CDWA), 179–80, 227
colonial occupation, second, 9
Commission, Kenya, 279
constitution, 49, 73–74, 76–79, 152, 192, 232–34, 252–54, 257, 260, 269–86, 297–302, 306, 309–12; 2010, 135–36, 143–44, 152–53, 269, 294, 302, 306–9; concept of, 270; independence, 1963, 269, 296; Lennox-Boyd, 1957–58, 47, 49–50, 52, 55, 65, 309–11; Lyttleton, 1954,

47, 49, 65, 296, 309–10; Republican, 1964, 275; self-government, 1 June 1963, 297
Constitutional Reform Movement 1990s, 277–80, 283, 299, 302
Constitutional Review Commission, Kenya, 281
Cooper, Frederick, 238, 239, 242, 243, 253, 263
corruption, xx–xxi, 13, 233, 277, 285, 294, 302, 306, 316, 320–34, 336; bakshish, xxi
Corruption Perception Index (CPI), 322
cotton, xvi, 3–4, 15, 93, 181, 185, 187–88, 190, 194–95, 202–18, 227–28; rules of, 208–10, 213, 215
cotton tax, 208
coup, attempted, 1982, 276–77
Credit Suisse, 332
crime, xxii, 117, 127, 306, 318, 331, 336; organized, xxii
cryptocurrencies, xxii, 318
cultural, approach, ix
Cunliffe-Lister, Sir Philip, 208
cybercrime, xxii, 318

Danish International Development Agency (DANIDA), 232
Dasanech, 167–70
Daua River, 165
Defoe, Daniel, 13
Delamere, Lord, 8, 11, 90, 92, 96–98
Democratic Progressive Party (DPP), 259
Democratic Republic of Congo (Zaire), 332
Department Fund for International Development (DFID), 257–58
differentiation, ethnic, 7
Director of Agriculture (DofA), 187, 205, 211, 217
Dowa, 231
drought, xv, xvi, 7, 161, 163, 167–68, 170, 210
Dubai, 323, 332

East Africa, xvi, 24–26, 28–29, 34, 39, 79, 87, 90–95, 98, 101, 114, 118, 120, 122, 124, 136, 165, 168, 216, 295
elections, Kenya, 43, 49, 70–71, 77–78, 118; 1997, 279–84; 2002, 283–84, 293; 2007, xx, 293; 2013, 293, 302; 2017, xx, 293, 302, 306; "First African elections," March, 1957, 49, 64, 310; "Independence," 1963, 121, 297; "Little," 1966, 299; "Multiparty," 1992, 277–78, 284, 293
elections, Malawi: 1961, 249; 1994, 232, 256; May 2019, 259
elite, xii, xix, xxi, 8, 11, 64, 145, 253, 258, 272, 285, 293–94, 296–98, 300–303, 306, 309, 311–12, 320, 329
Elmolo, 163, 167
Elton, Geoffrey, 2
Embe country, 167
emergency, state of, 53, 55, 66, 250
Empire, British, 2, 10, 171, 181, 196, 217, 227, 247–48, 319, 323
Empire Cotton Growing Corporation (ECGC), 212
Ethiopia, 166, 170
ethnicity, 2, 7, 12, 64, 141–45, 152, 283–84, 286, 295, 297, 300, 325; moral, 5, 14, 316, 325–29
Eurobic, 323
Europe, xiii, xvi, xxi, 23, 29, 51, 71, 163, 203, 317, 319, 322, 323, 336
Europeans, xiii, 2, 39, 54, 65, 67, 89, 92, 94–95, 97, 100, 116, 119, 125, 163, 197, 249–50, 252, 272–73, 295–96, 311
Executive Council (NCEC), 279–80

famine, 7, 161
Farm Clubs, 231
Fazan, S.H., 210
Finland, 332
First World War, x, 5, 9, 34, 93, 99, 183, 203, 211

Food and Agricultural Organization (FAO), 232
Forum for the Restoration of Democracy (FORD), 277–78; FORD Asili, 278; FORD K, 278; FORD People, 278
Foulkes and Company, 209
Frankfurt, 332
fraud, 318, 329, 331, 336

Gabbra, 165, 170
Gachanja, Wilson, 331
Gaddum, I.W., 205, 207
Galp Energia, 323
*gedech*, 169
gender, perspective, ix
Germany, 332, 336
Gethin and Dawson, 216
Gezira irrigation scheme, xv, 181–85
ghee, 216
Gichuru, James, 69, 275, 329–30
Gichuru, Samuel, 329–31
Gikuyu, Embu & Meru Association, 275
ginneries, 209–11, 215, 217
Giriama, 12
Gitari, David, 12, 16, 17
Githongo, John, 334
Githuku, Nicholas, xxiii, 40, 115, 130, 342
global, turn, vii
global finance capital, 323, 326, 335
global financial flows, 319, 335, 336
Global Financial Integrity, 323
Global South, 226
Goldenberg, 327, 330, 331, 333–34
Grand Cayman, 332
Great Depression, xvi, 21, 94, 106, 180, 182, 203–22, 227
groundnuts, 93, 206, 214

Hanler, William Astor, 167, 169
Harambee Maseno, 27
Harare, 256
Harris, Joseph E., x
Hastings, Adrian, 5, 15, 17

Hay, Jean, 9, 16, 17
Hobsbawm, Eric, 1, 15, 18
Hodge, Joseph, xxiii, 8, 16, 17, 181,
    198, 200, 202, 228, 230, 238, 240,
    241, 243, 244
Höhnel, Ludwig von, 163–64, 166–68
Homa Bay, 207, 209, 211, 214–17
Hong Kong, 322–23
Hughes, Lotte, x, xxiii, 72
human, trafficking, xxii, 318, 336, 337
Human Rights Manual, 257
Hunter, Emma, 14
Hunter, K.L., 207, 214
Hut and Poll Tax, 94

identity, xiv, xv, 2, 98, 129, 135–36,
    140–41, 143–44, 146, 148, 152, 162,
    171, 186, 197, 336
illicit financial flows, 318–20, 326–28,
    331, 333, 337
illiteracy, 323
Imanyara, Gitobu, 328
imperial, turn, ix
India, x, 10, 114–16, 118, 120, 123,
    128, 166, 295
Indians, 10–11, 114, 116, 215, 249
inequality, xiv, 121, 135, 226, 297–98,
    302–3, 320
infrastructure, xix, 92, 94–95, 186, 188,
    326, 329, 335; airports, 326; dams,
    326; geothermal plants, 326; Homa
    Bay-Marinde-Kamagambo Road,
    207, 209; Kendu Bay, 136–37, 207,
    209, 211–13, 215–17; Kisii-Kendu
    Road, 207
International Consortium of
    Investigative Journalists, 322
International Fund for Agricultural
    Development, 232
International Monetary Fund, xiii, 226,
    329
Inter-party Parliamentary Group (IPPG),
    280
Ireland, 274, 323
Irrigation Management Transfer, 232

Islam, x, 6, 14, 17, 18, 114
Italian Somaliland, 166
*ithaka na wiathi*, 10

Jeevanjee, Alibhai, 10–11
Jericho, xiv, 136, 138
Jersey Island, 329
Jinja, 211
Jubba River, 165
July, Robert, x

Kabondo, 206, 212, 214
Kadem, 205, 216
Kakamega, xi, 26–29, 205
Kakamega Black Stars, xi, 27
Kalenjin, xii, 8, 64–65, 68–71, 75–78,
    80, 273, 302
Kamba, 68, 90–91, 97, 120, 161, 273
Kampala, 25–26, 122, 136, 211
Kanja, Waruru, 329
Kanyada, 205, 214
Kanyidoto, 206
Karachuonyo, 205, 206, 212–13, 216
Karume, Njenga, 275
Karungu, 207, 214
Kasipul, 205
Kasungu, 231
Kavirondo, 12, 210, 216; Central, 205;
    North, 205; South, 208
Kavirondo Native Chambers of
    Commerce (KNCC), 205, 216
Kendu Bay, 207, 209, 211–13, 215–17
Kenya African Democratic Union
    (KADU), 51, 70–80, 273, 278, 296,
    298–99, 308, 311–12
Kenya African National Union
    (KANU), 51, 69–74, 76, 78, 118,
    120–21, 123, 127, 269, 273, 276–84,
    296–300, 308, 311–12, 334
Kenya African Union (KAU), 116–19,
    124
Kenya Cotton Ordinance and Rules of
    1937, 213
Kenya FA Cup, 27
Kenya Farmers Association, 216

Kenya Land Commission, 208
Kenya National Football League, xi, 27
Kenya Power and Lighting Company (KPLC), 329, 330
Kenyatta, Jomo, x, xviii–xxi, 3–4, 11, 13, 31, 36, 44–47, 51, 53–56, 66, 68–73, 77–80, 116–17, 119, 121, 125–29, 269–70, 272–77, 279, 284–85, 293–94, 298, 300, 305, 309, 311
Kenyatta, Uhuru Muigai, 44–45, 293–94, 327–28
Kibaki, Mwai, xix, xx, 143, 269, 284–85, 300–302, 327–34
Kibos, 213
Kijana, Wamalwa, 270, 286
Kikuyu, 9–12, 55, 69–70, 72, 78, 91–92, 102, 116–17, 119–20, 125, 144, 273, 275–76, 278, 282–83
Kimani, Kihika, 275
Kimathi, Dedan, 11, 115, 128
kinship, xxi, 5, 247, 317, 320
Kinyattti, Maina wa, 3
Kinyua, Wanjiru wa, 9
Kipkorir, Ben, 11
Kiplagat, Hosea, 331
Kisii, 30–34, 37, 39–40, 206–9, 215–16, 278
Kismaayo, xiv, 161
Kisumu, 2, 26, 31, 94, 141, 205, 207, 215–16
*kitoro*, 12
Kochia, 205, 214
Koi, David, 12
Koinange wa Mbiyu, 10, 116, 121
Korean War, 249
Koroli Desert, 170
Kroll Associates UK Limited, 331, 340
Kulei, Joshua, 331–32

Laikipia Plateau, 97, 167
Lake Baringo, 7, 163
Lake Turkana, 161–64, 167, 170
Lancaster House, constitutional conferences (Kenya), 66–68, 272–73; February 1962, xii, 73–74, 273, 294, 296; January 1960, 38, 48, 67–68, 72, 75, 120, 311; Lancaster House III, 1963, 75, 77–78, 80, 298
Lancaster House, constitutional conferences (Malawi), 252
laundering, money, 319, 322, 326, 327, 329, 332, 336
Law Society of Kenya, 279
Lbarta, 170
Legislative Council, xii, xviii, 47, 63, 114, 248, 272, 295, 310
Lembasso, 164
Liechtenstein, 323, 332
Lilongwe, 231, 233
linguistic, turn, ix
Liverpool, 216, 334
Local Native Council (LNC), 206, 305
locusts, 168
Lokerio, 163
London, xiv, 5, 11, 25, 31, 38, 48, 52–53, 55–56, 66–67, 69, 73–74, 78–79, 129, 180–81, 192, 196, 212, 250–52, 258, 272–73, 296, 319, 331–32, 340
Longue durée, viii, ix, 6
Lorian Swamp, 165
Lorroki Plateau, 167
Luo, xvi, 9, 12, 69, 72, 78, 144, 204, 206–10, 216, 218, 273, 278
Luxembourg, 322, 323, 332
Luyia, 9, 28, 30, 70, 76, 155, 278, 283
Lyttelton, Oliver, 11, 310

Maasai, xiv, 6–10, 12, 64, 70, 77, 88, 91, 97–99, 162–67, 302
Maasailand, 162–63, 166
Mackenzie, Smith, 216
Macleod, Iain, 48, 67, 251, 252, 296, 311
Macmillan, Harold, 251
Magak, Gideon, 205–6
maize, 9, 31, 93, 168, 215
*majimbo*, xxi, 8, 38, 73–75, 77, 79, 273, 283–84, 294, 296, 298, 300, 307–8, 311
Malakisi, 211

Malawi, 223–25, 228, 230–32, 234,
237, 245–50, 252–60; Criminal
Investigation Department, 255;
Devlin Commission, 250; Federal
Security and Intelligence Bureau,
249; Malawi Congress Party (MCP),
252–53; Operation Sunrise, 250;
Police Force, 250, 252, 253, 255,
257; Police Mobile Force, 255;
Police Service, 245, 254, 257;
Police Service Commission, 254;
Special Branch, 4, 50–51, 66, 69,
128, 255
Malawi Young Pioneers, 231
Manning, Patrick, x
Marakwet, 11, 76, 283
Marlborough House, 252
Massawa, Port of, 166
Matafale, Evison, 258
Mathenge, Stanley, 11
Mati, Mwalimu, 328
Matiba, Kenneth, 280
Mau Mau war, 2–3, 8–12, 53–54, 64,
66, 68, 116–17, 119, 121, 124–25,
128–29, 143
Maxon, Robert, x–xiii, xix–xx, 5, 9, 21,
43, 63, 88, 90–93, 95, 97–98, 100,
102–3, 270, 272, 285, 293
Mazrui, Ali, xi, 44, 46, 51
Mboya, Paul, 205–6
Mboya, Thomas Joseph, 11, 48, 50–51,
64–65, 67, 69, 76–78, 115, 123, 127,
129, 143, 205–6
Mchinji, 231
McKinsey & Company, 323
microstoria, ix
middle-class, xiv, 12, 135
Milligan, S., 212–13
mission schools, 114, 205
Mohuru, 207
Moi, Daniel arap, xii, xix, 36, 63–80,
128–29, 269, 275–85, 299–300, 302,
326–28, 330–33
Moi, Daniel Toroitich arap, xii, xix, 4,
13–14, 36, 63–80, 128–29, 269–70,

275–85, 299–300, 302, 310, 326–28,
330–33, 336
Moi, Gideon, 331–32
Moi, Phillip, 332
Mombasa, 91, 95, 101, 136, 141, 216
Mothers of Freedom, 14
Mount Kenya, 13, 167, 276
Mount Kilimanjaro, 167
Mount Kulal, 163, 170
Mount Marsabit, 162, 165
Muigwithania, 9
Muluzi, Bakili, 258
Mumbo, 205–6, 212
Mumboism, xvi, 210
Mungai, Njoroge, 275
Mutai, 161, 169–70
Mutharika, Bingu, 258–59
Mwaita, Sammy, 331
Mwiandi, Mary, 6, 9, 12

Nairobi, x–xi, xiii, xiv, 5, 12–13, 26,
30–32, 35, 39, 45–46, 48–49, 53,
67, 69, 71, 73, 75–76, 78–79, 91–92,
115–17, 119, 121, 123–24, 128–29,
135–45, 147, 151, 216, 278–79,
281–82, 310, 340
Naivasha, 91, 98, 162
Nakuru, 78, 98, 141, 216, 276
Nambale, 211
Nassir, Sharif, 283
National Convention Assembly (NCA),
279
National Development Party (NDP),
282
National Rainbow Coalition (NARC),
269, 300, 335
Native Affairs Department, 229
Native Authority Ordinance, 206
Native Betterment Fund, 208
Nehru, Jawarhalal, 10, 116, 118, 123
nepotism, 325, 326
Netherlands, 323
New, Charles, 162
Ngei, Paul, 117, 299
Ngome, 205

Nigeria, 2, 123–24, 195
Njama, Karari, 12
Njonjo, Charles, 275–77
Nkai (God), 165, 167
Northrup, David, x
Ntimama, William Ole, 283
Nyandoje, Aduwo, 216
Nyangweso, 209
Nyanza Commercial Company, 209
Nyanza Gulf, 26, 211
Nyanza Province, 28, 31, 91, 93–95, 97, 103, 208, 215–16
Nyasaland African Congress (NAC), 250, 252
Nyayo, 128, 276
Nyeri, 329

Obonyo, 205
Odinga, Jaramogi Oginga, xi–xii, 9, 43–56, 64–67, 69, 76, 78, 115, 121, 125, 143, 276, 310
Odinga, Raila Amolo, xx, 282–83, 293–94, 301, 305
Ogoma, Isaac, 205
Ogot, Bethwell Allan, 2–4, 11, 30, 32, 93
Ojijo, Daniel, 205, 216
Okemo, Chris, 329
Okiek ("Dorobo"), 166–67
Okullu, Henry, 12, 16, 18
Ol Doinyo Ng'iro, 163
Olola, John Paul, 9–10, 216
one-party state, 275–76, 297, 299
Organization for Economic Cooperation and Development (OECD), 336
Organization of African Unity (OAU), 254. *See also* African Union (AU)
Oromo, 165, 170
Owen, Walter & Olive, 12, 103, 104, 109
Oyugis, 209, 214

Patrons (*sotwatin*), 167
peasant, 8, 16, 37, 39–40, 97, 203, 205, 210, 214, 217, 271

Pentecostal, 12
periodization, ix, 4–8, 11
Pinto, Pio Gama, 113–30
Pokot ("Suk"), 76, 283
postcolonial, vii, ix, x, 4, 113, 115, 129–30, 189, 218, 223, 225, 238, 245, 253, 317, 325
poverty, ix, xxii, 116, 121, 149, 151, 156, 186, 226, 248, 320–21, 323
Presbyterian, Protestantism, xxi, 317
Pricewaterhousecoopers (PwC), 323
Public Works Department, 207
pyrethrum, 31, 209

Quayle, Dan, 256

Ranger, Terence, 5, 7
Rangwe, 209, 214
Renan, Ernest, 3–4, 11
Rendille, 162, 164–67, 169–70
Riddoch, John L., 216–17
Rights, Bill of, xviii, 248–49, 252–54, 256–57, 260, 273, 297
rinderpest (*lodua*), xv, 7, 165–67, 169–70
Roosevelt, Theodore, 167
Rudolf, Crown Prince of Austria, 163
Ruto, William Samoei, 331
Ryall's Hotel, 251

Saba Saba, 1997, 279
Sachs, Jeffrey, 321
Sake, 170
Samburu ("Burkeneji"), xiv, 161–71
Samburu District, Samburuland, xiv, 161, 164, 168
Samia, 211
Sandys, Duncan, 76–80
Santos, Isabel dos, 322
Santos, José Eduardo dos, 322–23
Sare, 207
secondary school, 26, 72, 77, 187, 190
Second World War, 10, 181, 183, 196, 216–18, 249–50, 271, 296
Seko, Mobutu Sese, 332

sesame, 206
settlers, 8–12, 39, 45, 51, 55, 65, 73,
    87–90, 92–93, 95–97, 99–100, 103,
    136, 204–5, 208, 249, 297, 310–11
Seya River, 167
Shikuku, Martin, 78–79, 329–30
Sio, 209
sisal, 99, 209
sleeping sickness, 168
Small, Gordon, 211
Small and Company, 209, 211–12, 214,
    216
Smallholder Floodplain Development
    Program, 232
smallpox, xv, 165, 167–69
Sobania, Neal, 162, 166, 168
soccer, xi, 22–23, 27–28, 143
social, turn, ix
social change, vii–ix
social security, rights to, 320
Soma-Gurra, 162
Somali, xiv, 74, 76–78, 161, 165–66,
    168, 171
South Africa, 118, 122–23, 164, 213, 332
South Asians (Indians), 28, 113
Southern Rhodesia, 229–30, 250–51
South Kavirondo, 204, 208
South Kavirondo Reserve, 208
South Nyanza, 67, 206
Southworth, Frederick, 251
sovereignty, 144, 191, 323, 325
Spain, 334
Spear, Tom, 6
squatters, 10, 125
Sub-Saharan Africa, 325
Sukumaland, 228
Suna, 206, 214
Sunman, W.O., 207, 215
sustainable development, 320
Swahili, xiv, 26–29, 71, 91, 161, 319
Switzerland, 322–23

Tana Rivers, 165
Tanganyika African Union (TANU),
    228

Tanzania, 14, 29, 128, 168, 236
Tax, avoidance, xxii, 318–19, 322
tax, evasion, xxii, 318–19, 322, 337, 340
tax havens, 318–28, 330, 335, 338–40,
    342
Teleki, Samuel, 163–64, 166, 168
Thiong'o, Ngugi wa, 3–5, 15, 18, 155
Third World, 248
Thomson, Joseph, 163, 165
Thuku, Harry, 10
Thyolo, 25
Tidrick, Kathryn, 2
Timothy Njoya, 12, 16, 18
transnational, perspective, vii, ix
Transparency International (TI), 321–
    22, 340
transtemporal, perspective, ix
tsetse flies, 168
Turkana, 76, 161–65, 167, 169–71

Ufungamano House, 282
Uganda, 24–26, 91, 92, 94–95, 101,
    122, 137, 168, 208, 211, 215–16
United Federal Party (UFP), 252
United Nations Organization, xiii, 136,
    153, 192, 246, 271, 301
United States of America, xvi, 25, 28,
    31–32, 34, 36, 40, 89, 129, 148,
    183–84, 203, 229, 248, 323–24, 336
Universal Declaration of Human Rights,
    xviii, 246, 271, 320
US Agency for International
    Development (USAID), 229

Valtaldas and Company, 211
Vansina, Jan, x, 28
Village Action Group, 231
Visram, Allidina, 10

Wakefield, Thomas, 162
Wakwafi, 163
Waller, Richard, x, 6
Warra Daaya, 165, 171
Washington, DC, 14
Wato, 168, 170–71

Watt, Lynn, 205
Welensky, Roy, 249
White Highlands, 8, 10, 69–70, 72, 92, 295, 308
WikiLeaks, 318, 327, 331, 340
Windward Trading, 329–30
Wolfe, H., 211–12
women, ix, 2, 4, 9, 11, 14–15, 90–91, 142, 163, 170, 281, 307
work, decent, 320
workers, 9–10, 95–97, 129, 141, 194, 197, 207, 271, 320
World Bank, xiii, 226

Wovwe, xvii, 223–26, 230–32, 235–38; rice irrigation scheme, xvii, 223–24, 232

yellow fever (*ngeyandisi*), 168
Young Kavirondo Tax Payers' Association (YKTPA), 205

Zambia, xviii, 249
Zande irrigation scheme, 1947, 181, 187–91, 193–94
Zanzibar, xv, 24, 162
Zimbabwe, xviii, 229, 249, 250, 256

# About the Contributors

**Paul Chiudza Banda** is an assistant professor of history at Tarleton State University (Department of History, Sociology, Geography/GIS). Banda received his PhD in history from West Virginia University. He has previously taught at the Catholic University of Malawi, and the University of Malawi. He has published book chapters and journal articles. Some of these have appeared in *The Journal of the Middle East and Africa*, *African Studies Quarterly*, *The Journal of Eastern African Studies*, *The Society of Malawi Journal*, and *The Journal of Public Administration and Development Alternatives*. His main research interests are in the following areas: British imperialism in Africa; the state in colonial and postcolonial Africa; the history of development in Africa; and the global Cold War.

**Nicholas K. Githuku** is an assistant professor of African history at CUNY, York College, Queens, New York, New York. He is also SUNY University at Buffalo 2020–2021 Center for Diversity Innovation Distinguished Visiting Scholar, the inaugural cohort, and summer 2018 Carnegie African Diaspora Fellowship Program (CADF) Scholar through which he was a visiting scholar and professor at St. Paul's University, Limuru, Kenya. Githuku holds a PhD from West Virginia University in African history with a focus on Eastern Africa in general, and contemporary political history in Kenya in particular; a Rotary International Mid-professional Certificate in peace, development and conflict studies, Chulalongkorn University, Bangkok-Thailand (2008); a master of arts in armed conflict and peace studies from the University of Nairobi (2004); and a bachelor of arts (1st class honors) degree in history and political science and public administration, University of Nairobi (2001). His research interests include cross-cutting themes in the making and evolution of the generic colonial and postcolonial African state such as the political economy

355

of race and ethnicity and emergent politics; gender and women history; class; and social movements. Githuku's first book was *Mau Mau Crucible of War: Statehood, National Identity and Politics in Postcolonial Kenya* (Lanham: Lexington Books, October 2015: 574) and he has also authored a number of chapter contributions, which include "From Moral Ethnicity to Moral Anarchy: The Colonial Ideology of Order and Political Disorder in Postcolonial Kenya," in *The Omnipresent Past: Historical Anthropology of Africa and African Diaspora* (Moscow: LRC Publishing House, July 2019: 25) and "The Unfolding of Britain and Kenya's Complex Tango: An Uneasy Return to a Critical Past and its Implications," in *Dedan Kimathi on Trial: Colonial Justice and Popular Memory in Kenya's Mau Mau Rebellion* (Athens: Ohio University Press, 2017: 17) to name but a few.

**Gift Wasambo Kayira** holds a doctorate degree in history from West Virginia University. He lecturers at the University of Malawi, Chancellor College, and researches on histories of development and ethnicity in twentieth- and twenty-first-century Malawi. He has published in the *Journal of Eastern African Studies*, *Journal of Public Administration and Development Alternatives*, the *African Studies Quarterly*, and the *Society of Malawi Journal*. He also has book chapters to his credit.

**John M. Lonsdale** is an emeritus professor of modern African history at the University of Cambridge. His first professional post was as a lecturer in history at the University College, Dar es Salaam, 1964–1966. He is an author/co-editor/editor of *Unhappy Valley: Conflict in Kenya and Africa* (1992); *Mau Mau & Nationhood* (2003); *Writing for Kenya: the Life and Works of Henry Muoria* (2009); *Ethnic Diversity & Economic Instability in Africa* (2012); S. H. Fazan's *Colonial Kenya Observed* (2015); and *From Divided Pasts to Cohesive Futures: Reflections from Africa* (2019).

**Robert M. Maxon** is an emeritus professor of history at West Virginia University. He served as an Education Officer in Kenya from 1961 to 1964 and has served as a visiting professor of history at Moi University in Kenya on four separate occasions. Maxon has carried out research in East Africa on numerous visits since 1968. He is the author of several important books including *Majimbo in Kenya's Past: Federalism in the 1940s and 1950s* (Cambria Press, 2017), *Kenya's Independence Constitution: Constitution-Making and the End of Empire* (Fairleigh Dickinson University Press, 2011), and *Struggle for Kenya: The Loss and Reassertion of Imperial Initiative, 1912-1923* (Fairleigh Dickinson University Press, 1993) to name but a few.

**Anne Nangulu** is an economic historian in the Department of History, Political Science and Public Administration, School of Arts and Social Sciences, Moi University, Eldoret, Kenya. She attained her bachelor of arts degree in history from the University of Nairobi, Kenya, in 1986; master of arts in history, University of Nairobi, in 1990; and an outstanding PhD in history, West Virginia University, USA, in 2001. She has taught at University Moi since March 1989 and West Virginia, August 1996–May 2001, while undertaking PhD studies. Since March 1989, she has risen through the ranks—as tutorial fellow; lecturer, senior lecturer, associate professor; and professor of history as from November 2011 to the present. She has served at Moi University in various capacities; Head, Department of History, Dean, School of Arts and Social Sciences, Director, Quality Assurance, Acting Deputy Vice Chancellor (DVC), Academic, Research & Extension and Secretary to Senate; and she is a "permanent" Member of the Moi University Senate. From July 1, 2014, she served as the Deputy Commission Secretary, Quality Audit & Standards, Commission for University Education (CUE), Kenya; and from October 1, 2019, to present as Principal Bomet University College, a Constituent of Moi University and Professor of Moi University.

**Peter Odhiambo Ndege** is a professor of African history in the Department of History, Political Science and Public Administration, Moi University, Eldoret, Kenya. He received his BA honors from Makerere University, Uganda; postgraduate diploma in education and master of arts in history, respectively, from the University of Nairobi, Kenya; and doctor of philosophy in history from West Virginia University, Morgantown, USA. He has written on different aspects of Kenya's economic and political history in books as well as journals. His other publication is in *Olonana Mbatian* in the series, *Makers of Kenyan History*. He is a former Head of Department of History and Dean, School of Arts and Social Sciences, Moi University.

**Okia Opolot** is a professor of African history at Wright State University. His research examines forced labor in colonial East Africa and the impact of changing international discourses on acceptable labor practices. He has published several articles and two books, *Communal Labor in Colonial Kenya: The Legitimization of Coercion, 1912–1930* (New York: Palgrave Macmillan, 2012) and *Labor in Colonial Kenya After the forced Labor Convention* (New York: Palgrave Macmillan, 2019). Dr. Okia has also twice served as a Fulbright scholar at Moi University in Kenya (2007–2009) and Makerere University in Uganda (2016–2017).

**George L. Simpson Jr**. is a retired professor of history at High Point University and the editor-in-chief of *The Journal of the Middle East and*

*Africa.* Simpson was a 1992 Fulbright-Hays scholar to Kenya and received his PhD in African history two years later under the direction of Professor Robert Maxon. He has especially concentrated on the colonial history of the Samburu of northern Kenya but has also published journal articles and book chapters on the history of the Somali as well as the United States Middle East policy during the 1970s.

**Joseph M. Snyder** is an assistant professor of history at Southeast Missouri State University, where he teaches graduate courses in British imperial history and world history, as well as undergraduate courses in modern Britain, African history, the classical Mediterranean world, and historiography. His research interests include British colonial development policy in Africa, identity, indigeneity, and conflict in the African Great Lakes region, and identity and ideology in the classical Mediterranean world. His recent publications include articles on the influence of the Fabian Society on postwar development policy in British East Africa, the historicity of Axial Age epic literature, and plague in seventeenth-century England. His current projects include Fabian influence on pre–World War II Labor Party policy, the impact of the British Empire on literature from the sixteenth to the twentieth centuries, an examination of U.S. foreign policy and Britain's postwar imperial policy in Africa, and historiography and heutagogy in the undergraduate classroom.

**Betty Wambui** is an associate professor in the Africana and Latinx Studies Department at the State University of New York, Oneonta. AUUP/SUNY Drescher Awardee (2014/15), she received her PhD in philosophy from Binghamton University (SUNY, New York) and her MA in philosophy from the University of Nairobi, Kenya. Her areas of specialization within social and political philosophy include African philosophies, feminist philosophies, critical race theories, and critical legal studies. She has a particular interest in social contract theory, discrimination, and morality. A member of the Women Caucus of the African Studies Association and former co-convenor; she also served as president of the New York Africana Studies Association. Executive editor of *Praxis: Journal of Gender and Cultural Studies*; her most recent publications include "Buffeted: Women, knowledge and the environment – Developing an Afro Feminist Response to Environmental Questions," in *African Philosophy and the Epistemic Marginalization of Women* (Jonathon Chimakonam, Thaddeus Metz and Louise du Toit (eds.) Routledge, 2018 and "Arrow of God: An Exploration of Psycho-Social and Political Health," in *Illuminations on Chinua Achebe: The Art of Resistance* (Eds.) Micere Githae Mugo and Herbert G. Ruffin II (Africa Press, 2017).

**Godriver Wanga-Odhiambo** is an associate professor, Department of History at Le Moyne College. She received her PhD at West Virginia University in 2010. Her area of specialty is African history, with research interests in African refugee women and economic history in colonial Kenya. She is an author of two books: *Resilience in South Sudanese Women: Hope for the Daughters of the Nile* (Lexington Publishers, 2014) and *The Political Economy of Sugar Production in Colonial Kenya: The Asian Initiative in Central Nyanza* (Lexington Publishers, 2016). Additionally, she has written and presented several papers about the geopolitics and women of South Sudan, and Afro-Asian link in Africa. Wanga-Odhiambo is an Africanist revisionist historian focusing on the rigorous and extensive use of archival sources. Her latest research projects are first, the Challenges to African Democracy, focusing on political thuggery such as assassinations and forceful eviction of people within independent Kenya, secondly, environmental refugees due to impact of global warming in Africa.

**Peter Waweru** is a senior lecturer at Laikipia University, Nyahururu, Kenya. He holds a PhD in environmental history. He has researched and written on both the precolonial and colonial environmental and economic history of nomadic pastoralism in Kenya. He is a long-serving history lecturer at the above-mentioned institution and a former Chairman of the Department of Public Affairs and Environmental Science within which the discipline of history is domiciled. He also supervises postgraduate students and is an external examiner for a number of universities in Kenya.

Milton Keynes UK
Ingram Content Group UK Ltd.
UKHW021509170823
427035UK00033B/619